"A must-read for any would-be Chanc〈
blueprint for how to end decades of
ANDREW PIERC

"A trenchant, eye-opening and controversial tour de force from one
of our foremost economic brains. Anyone who wants growth and
wonders why it has become so elusive in western social democracies
needs to pick up *Return to Growth* and take urgent note. Jon
Moynihan shows, in crystal-clear and accessible prose, that you can
either have ever greater government expenditure or you can have
decent levels of growth. Contrary to cakeism, you can't have both.
Rising public-sector expenditure brings greater debt, inflation and
ultimately, if it is not controlled, national bankruptcy. A smaller
state which does not crowd out the private sector is better able to
preside over higher economic growth, which raises standards of living
for the country as a whole. If the analysis of how we got into our
current economic predicament is sobering, Moynihan's meticulously
elucidated prescription offers a more hopeful way forward for
those brave enough to take it. *Return to Growth* is an essential and
compelling read for policymakers and general readers alike."
JUSTIN MAROZZI

"Jon Moynihan is right – it's time for a fresh look at how our economy
should work. Growth and aspiration will only return when private-
sector entrepreneurialism is allowed to thrive in a low-tax, free-market
setting. More hard work and less regulation is the way forward."
LORD BAMFORD

"If Rachel Reeves is serious about her growth agenda, she should
buy herself a copy of Jon Moynihan's book. Lucid, passionately
argued, contemptuous of the groupthink that landed our country in
debilitating stagnation; here is a manifesto to get Britain motoring."
ALLISON PEARSON

"Since the election, Conservatives have been desperately looking for
a solution to Britain's economic malaise that isn't just a retread of the
failed policies of the past twenty-five years. They need look no further.
This book is the answer. Future governments will ignore it at their peril."
TOBY YOUNG

RETURN TO GROWTH

RETURN TO GROWTH
How to Fix the Economy
JON MOYNIHAN
VOLUME ONE

Biteback Publishing

First published in Great Britain in 2024 by
Biteback Publishing Ltd, London
Copyright © Jon Moynihan 2024

Jon Moynihan has asserted his right under the Copyright, Designs and Patents Act 1988
to be identified as the author of this work.

ISBN 978-1-78590-903-0

10 9 8 7 6 5 4 3 2 1

A CIP catalogue record for this book is available from the British Library.

Set in Adobe Caslon Pro and Gill Sans MT Pro

Printed and bound in Great Britain by
CPI Group (UK) Ltd, Croydon CR0 4YY

FSC
www.fsc.org
MIX
Paper | Supporting
responsible forestry
FSC® C171272

And now referring the well set Reader *to the* History *it selfe, where satisfaction lyeth ready to receive him, and expectation desirous of deserved thankes. I come to talke with the scelerate Companion: If thou beest a* Villain, *a* Ruffian, *a* Momus, *a* Knave, *a* Carper, *a* Critick, *a* Bubo, *a* Buffon, *a stupid* Asse, *and a gnawing* Worme *with envious Lips, I bequeath thee to a Carnificiall reward, where a hempen Rope will soon dispatch thy snarling slander, and free my toylesome Travailes and now painefull Labours, from the deadly Poyson of thy sharpe edged calumnies, and so goe hang thy selfe; for I neither will respect thy Love, nor regard thy Malice: and shall ever and always remaine,*

To the Courteous still Observant:

And to the Criticall Knave as he deserveth.

W. M. LITHGOW (1640)

CONTENTS

—

Readers who connect with this QR code can access
web links to the referenced works in this book

CAVEAT TO THE READER

———

An important note about this book: I am not an economist. The book is about the UK's economy and the economic steps that governments can do, and sometimes do or don't do, to make it grow faster. On occasion, I slip into economist's language, appearing to be talking like, or even thinking I am, an economist. I'm not. Any authority I have to say the things I say in the book, I derive from my careful research into what economists have concluded and written about on the topics in this book; from my decade or more working closely in the markets with the traders who actually deal with the financial commodities – currencies, exchange rates, tax rates, surpluses and deficits, regulations – that governments try to control and impact; from the knowledge gained in my many decades of interacting (until recent times) with economists at MIT Sloan School – particularly the much-lamented Rüdiger Dornbusch – where I served for over twenty years on various advisory committees; and, above all, from having spent fifty years in business advising, starting and building firms that had to deal on a daily basis with the consequences of decisions made by governments over that time.

I hope that is enough to make my conclusions in this book sensible and acceptable. I have throughout the writing of it benefited from research work, and advice and reaction, from the economics consultancy CEBR. All mistakes and misstatements are, of course, my own fault.

Volume Two will review the importance of free markets, free trade and sound money and will sketch out an action plan for how a 'return to growth' programme could be implemented.

OVERVIEW:
THE CHALLENGE

———

Over the past half-century, a crisis in economic growth has arisen in many developed economies. Western European economies, most of which have adopted the 'social democratic' model (high government expenditure, high taxes, high regulation), are barely growing at all. For two centuries, those same countries had embraced an economic model that worked spectacularly well. The economies of advanced nations grew at an extraordinary pace, transforming their citizens' lives by creating jobs, wealth, health, longevity, scientific breakthroughs and consumer products that have made our lives far easier.

And yet, as chart A shows, western Europe, the original home of economic growth, has adopted an economic approach that is at odds with the success of previous centuries and at odds with the approach of most developing countries. As a result, it has descended into stagnation. To take the UK as an example, our economic growth is now close to zero. Had our economy continued to grow over the past twenty-three years at the same rate as it had in the 1960–2000 period, our real GDP would now be some 29 per cent higher than it is currently,[1] and average annual earnings, currently

£34,840 in 2023, would be £52,546 per year, assuming earnings had grown at the same rate over that period.[2] This means the average UK citizen would have an extra £12,430 a year in their pocket, even if tax *rates* were kept at their current level, which they wouldn't need to be because the government would be receiving more tax *revenue*.[3]

This book examines the reasons for this decline in growth, not just in the UK but across western Europe. The governments of the social democracies have adopted interlinked policies that have led to economic growth more or less grinding to a halt. We in the UK have, in the main, gone along with those policies. In particular, the size of their governments have increased too much to permit economic growth (which can, for the most part, only be created by the private sector).

As chart B shows, the relationship between government spending and growth is unignorable. As the UK government's expenditure has got bigger it has sucked up resources, imposing such a high burden of tax and regulation on the private sector that a decent rate of economic growth has become impossible. The UK's private sector can no longer provide the growth the country needs because it is carrying on its back state expenditure that is about the same size as the entire private-sector economy. The lion's share of the UK's resources are employed in non-productive and growth-hindering endeavours; entrepreneurial energy is increasingly directed towards rent-seeking activities, while the government swallows too much of the nation's income for enough to be left over to power economic growth. Our citizens are the losers.

Chart A: World 2023 GDP Growth Percentage by Country

The social democratic approach of large government and extensive welfare seems inimical to growth.

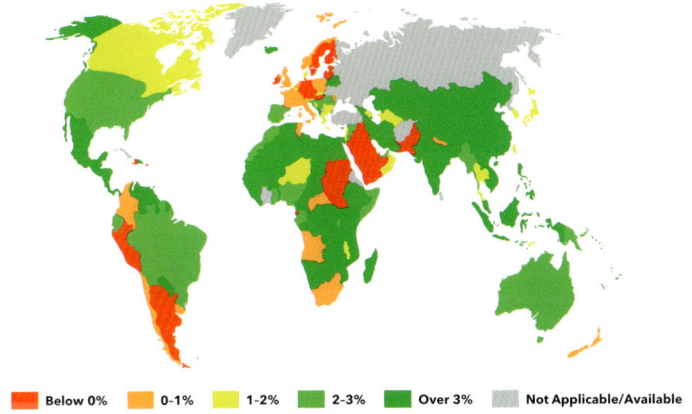

Below 0%   0-1%   1-2%   2-3%   Over 3%   Not Applicable/Available

Source: International Monetary Fund, moyniteam analysis[4] • *See Chart 2.63*

Chart B: Size of Government and the Annual Growth of Real GDP
OECD Countries, 1960–2019

It is clear that a precondition for growth is small-sized government.

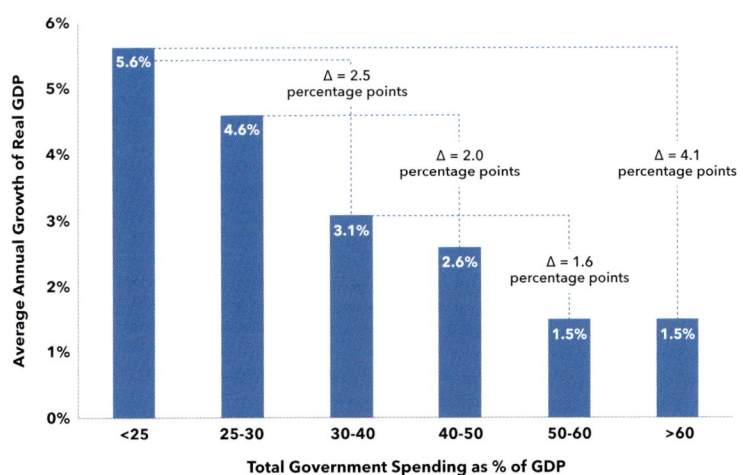

Source: International Monetary Fund, moyniteam calculations[5] • *See Chart 2.5*

This situation is not stable: most social democratic economies across western Europe are barely ticking over and cannot pay for their increasingly large governments and welfare programmes. Inexorably, their debt will become so large it precipitates financial collapse. This is likely to happen along the following lines:

- First, the larger the government, the harder it is to raise enough tax revenue to pay for it (see Chart C) – *regardless of whether high or low tax rates are imposed* – and the larger the financial deficit becomes.
- Second, and in consequence (Chart D), government debt balloons – and gets worse and worse while the size of the state stays high.

Chart C: Tax Versus Size of Government
Government revenue versus expenditure as a percentage of GDP.
OECD countries, 1990–2023

The more a government spends, the less it is able to finance spending through tax.

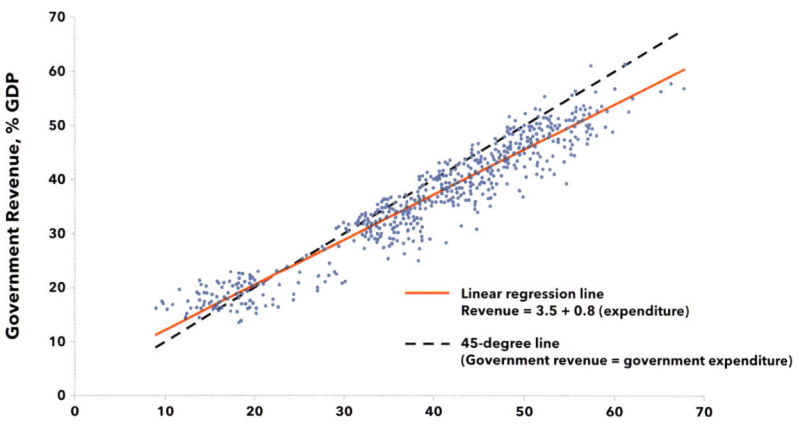

Source: International Monetary Fund, moyniteam analysis[6] • See Chart 1.20

Chart D: General Government Debt as a Percentage of GDP
Advanced economies, 2000 versus 2023

As tax revenues fall short, debt inexorably balloons.

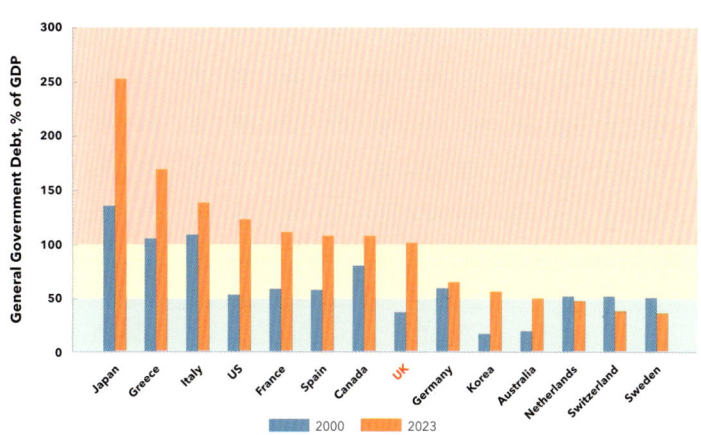

Source: International Monetary Fund, moyniteam analysis[7] • See Chart 1.26

- The end result of this chain of events (see Chart E) is that debt payments become unsustainably large and the deficit grows, since servicing that debt takes a larger and larger share of annual tax revenues.
- In the case of the UK, carrying on as we are will lead to crawlingly slow growth in GDP per capita (cutting off almost all personal opportunity for average citizens to advance themselves) and an accelerating, likely unsustainable, level of national debt (see Chart F).

The terminus of this process must eventually be national bankruptcy.

• • •

In the following pages, expanding on this list, I show *first* (Part I) that governments have not only a moral but also a practical imperative to grow their nations' economies; *second* (Part II) that there are clear aspects of the social democratic approach to managing the economy – large government, high taxes, stifling regulation – that appear to result, inevitably, in low to no growth. In the upcoming Volume Two, I will show *third* (Part III) that the foundations for a growth economy lie in free markets, free trade and financial sobriety; and *finally* (Part IV) that a programme can be initiated to return growth to the UK's economy. Such a programme can transform the UK into a successful, high-growth model, with all the commensurate, and badly needed, resultant benefits for its citizens.

Chart E: Percentage of Government Revenue Needed to Service National Debt, 2010 & 2022

The level of debt payments becomes unsustainable.

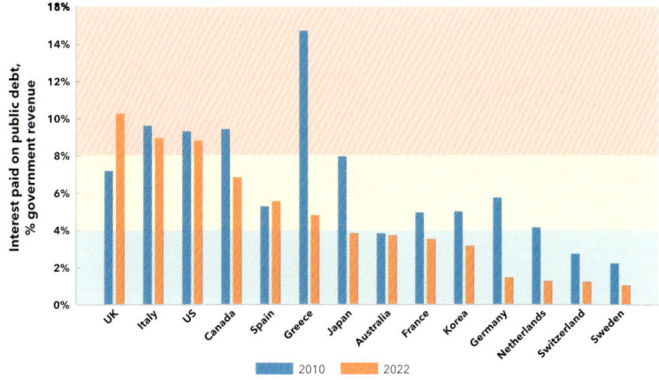

Source: International Monetary Fund[8] • *See Chart 1.21*

Chart F: Forecasted Development of the UK's Economy, 2024–39
Status Quo Scenario

On our current trajectory, our GDP per capita growth declines and debt grows to over 150 per cent of GDP.

STATUS QUO	-1 2023/24	0 2024/25	5 2029/30	10 2034/35	15 2039/40	20 2044/45
KEY INPUTS (ASSUMPTIONS)						
Government Spending as % GDP	44.5%	43.9%	43.8%	44.1%	44.6%	45.1%
Government Receipts as % GDP	40.4%	40.4%	40.4%	40.4%	40.4%	40.4%
Annual Productivity Growth	0.1%	0.1%	0.1%	0.1%	0.1%	0.1%
Gross fixed capital formation as % GDP	18.4%	16.8%	17.2%	17.4%	17.4%	17.4%
Human Capital Index annual growth rate	0.2%	0.2%	0.2%	0.2%	0.2%	0.2%
Total population, million	68.4	69.0	69.6	71.4	73.0	74.6
Working population, million	35.8	36.2	36.5	37.3	37.7	38.0
KEY OUTPUTS (RESULTS)						
GDP Growth	0.2%	0.8%	1.2%	0.9%	0.7%	0.7%
Real GDP, £trillion	2.7	2.8	2.8	2.9	3.0	3.1
GDP per capita	39,963	39,889	40,002	40,603	41,229	41,817
National Debt as % GDP	100%	103%	105%	116%	131%	149%
Budget Deficit, £billion	114	97	96	110	128	149
Budget Deficit as %GDP	4.2%	3.5%	3.4%	3.8%	4.2%	4.8%

Source: moyniteam • *See Chart 1.29*

PART I

REASONS WHY GROWTH IS CRUCIAL

———

A GOVERNMENT HAS BOTH A *MORAL* AND A *PRACTICAL* DUTY TO PROVIDE ECONOMIC GROWTH FOR ITS CITIZENS

TWO CENTURIES OF FAST GROWTH FOLLOWED BY ALMOST TWO DECADES OF BUST

———

The debate over growth in the UK, always contentious, has recently become even more heated. Wages, economic growth and economic opportunities have skidded to a halt this century, a period where the UK was mostly inside, but is now more recently outside, the EU. During the past two decades, the UK economy has joined that select group of economies around the world that have had poor to no economic growth, have increasing household distress, and, in particular, have annual increases in real wages that, over a fifteen-year period, have actually turned negative (particularly, but not only, as a result of a spurt in inflation), averaging -0.3 per cent per annum. The compounding result of that average annual drop, as shown in Chart 1.1, is that real earnings in the UK are now 4.8 per cent lower than they were in 2008.[*]

---

[*] According to the Office for National Statistics, real weekly earnings (total pay) declined from the February 2008 peak of £532 to £506 in January 2024 (in 2015 prices), which is c.4.8 per cent lower and implies an annual growth rate of c.-0.3 per cent. See Chart 1.1.

Chart 1.1: Real Average Weekly Earnings, UK Economy, Total Pay
Using consumer price inflation, seasonally adjusted, in 2015 prices

In 2023, real earnings are almost 5 per cent lower than in 2008.

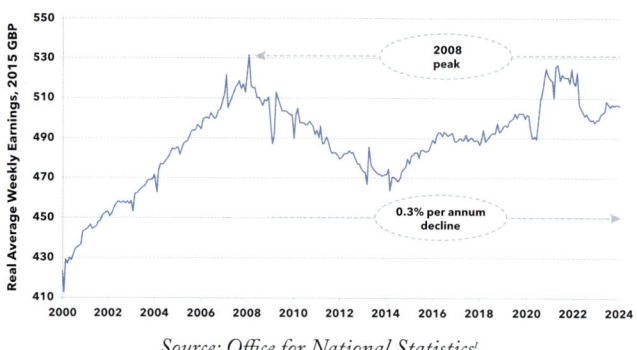

Source: Office for National Statistics[1]

Since the year 2000, government expenditure has oscillated but, in general, expanded. It is now at some 45 per cent of the economy, up from 35 per cent in 2000 (see Chart 1.2).

Chart 1.2: UK Public Spending as a Share of GDP 2000–2023

UK government expenditure has risen from around 35 per cent of GDP at the turn of the century to some 45–50 per cent, two short decades later.

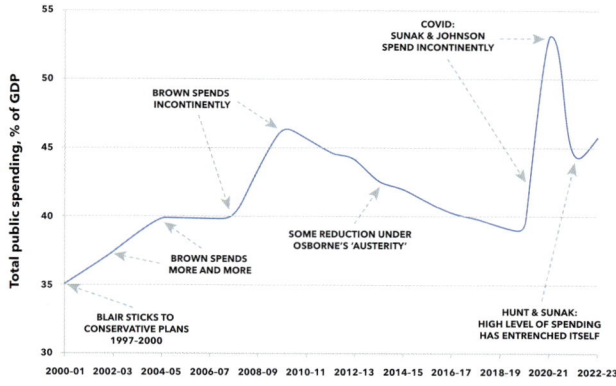

Source: Office for Budget Responsibility[2]

An article in *The Economist*, late in 2022, bemoaned that the west has fallen 'out of love with the economic growth'.[3] The article seemed confused as to whether to blame left-wing 'unsophisticated' politicians, right-wing 'reheated Reaganism', 'growth champions', NIMBYs, or overdemanding electorates. It offered various sensible pointers for restimulating growth yet sneered at those who had tried to implement those sorts of policies and implied (for no stated reason) that something like 'another financial crisis' might be necessary to put the west back on a pro-growth path. It did not contemplate the possibility that the prospects for future growth in the UK might be as poor as they have been in, say, Venezuela in recent decades – a one-way path. How did the UK and other, similar countries get into the state shown in Charts 1.1 and 1.2? Is our current economic direction – low growth and stagnating wages, accompanied by governments that are ever-increasing in size – inevitable? Are we on our way back to having to live, possibly permanently, with the 'British disease' of the 1970s: namely, stagflation, unemployment and social unrest?

To answer these questions, we have to first look at the UK's longer-term economic history and review how we got to where we are.

THE UK'S HISTORY OF GROWTH AND SUCCESS OVER THE PAST MILLENNIUM: THEN AND NOW

For many centuries after the Norman invasion of 1066, life for most Britons was a soul-destroying pattern of uniformity and conformity, bearing out Thomas Hobbes's famous description of life outside society: 'solitary, poor, nasty, brutish and short'.[4] At that time, something that many are unaware of, a majority of the population of the UK were not free: about 10 per cent of the population recorded in the Domesday book were shown as slaves and over 70 per cent as serfs (a state of semi-slavery, which encompassed unfree peasants such as villeins, bordars and cottars).[5] In the mid-1200s, serfdom was legalised and continued for some centuries thereafter (the last serf was freed in 1574).

Even after that, and regardless of whether they were free citizens or not, for most, the position they were born into was the position they held for the rest of their lives, and their children, at best, would continue to hold that same position. The best that the vast majority of citizens could hope for between 1000 and 1800 was to be free, get a job, keep that same job and remain with unchanging status, wage and standard of living for the rest of their lives. The summit of most people's aspiration was to live modestly and unchangeably, stay out of trouble and avoid falling into penury. The opportunity for self-improvement or advancement, was, for most people, zero. The average life expectancy was thirty. If you didn't work or have someone looking after you, you would starve and then die.

Chart 1.3: UK Wages 1600–2000
Real average weekly earnings, 2015 GBP

After centuries in which workers could never expect to earn more than a standard – fluctuating but not overall rising – remittance, real wages between 1800 and 2000 had risen some sixteen-fold.

Source: Bank of England[6]

And then, towards the end of the eighteenth century, there was a sudden, startling change that completely transformed possibilities and personal ambition for the average citizen. It was precipitated by the Enlightenment's scientific discoveries, the humanistic and individualistic approaches of thinkers such as Adam Smith and the bold entrepreneurial spirit of some enterprising Britons. These discoveries led to the simultaneous emergence of technological breakthroughs and individual freedom. This, in turn, resulted in an explosion of industrial entrepreneurship, which drove the creation of new jobs across the economy, with major increases in the size of the wage that employers could, and did, pay for a given job. Suddenly, growing wealth and social mobility became the norm. Between 1800 and 1950, the average wage quadrupled; it quadrupled again over the following half-century. By the year 2000, the earning power of the average Briton was, in real terms, *sixteen times* as much as it had been in 1800.

Between 1900 and 2022, the number of jobs in the UK doubled from 16.7 to 33.2 million (see Chart 1.4); the amount paid in the national wage bill was at least thirty-two times what it had been in 1800.

Chart 1.4: Employment in the Twentieth Century and Beyond
Total employment in the UK (including self-employed) 1900–2023

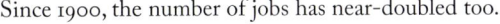

Since 1900, the number of jobs has near-doubled too.

Source: Bank of England, Office for National Statistics[7]

And the extraordinary range of novel goods and services that the modern citizen can now buy with their money gives them a standard of living and choice well beyond anything that even the very richest people of Britain in 1800 could ever have dreamed of.

These advances in jobs, wages and standards of living were, as we know, accompanied by major improvements in education, health, longevity and – with universal suffrage – democracy.

Over the past two centuries, the average Briton's conception of what they can expect to learn, experience and achieve over their lifetime has changed dramatically. In the western democracies, the generally held view over the past few decades has been that every citizen has the right, or at least a reasonable hope, to:

- Live up to eight or nine decades, mostly in good health.
- Fulfil themselves by finding ever-increasing work responsibilities, challenges and opportunities that stretch their potential and improve their life satisfaction.
- Receive annually higher real pay, whether or not their job responsibilities have increased – a function of productivity improvements, mostly brought about through investment of capital – and better working conditions.
- Have the opportunity to fulfil, over their working lives, their best possible personal potential in terms of life, health, achievement, prosperity, human relationships and happiness.

There is a general understanding in modern democracies that all who are willing to work and who want to better themselves should have the opportunity to do so and, through that, to experience personal success and happiness. As noted earlier, all this is something new; before 1800, any such attitude would have been met with astonishment. Citizens now see themselves as having the right to expect that:

- enough jobs are created to prevent more than a minimal level of unemployment
- an individual's annual wages increase steadily
- prosperity, in general, grows at a sufficient pace to pay for ever-improved schooling, ever-better healthcare, ever-better housing and ever-improving living standards

Across western Europe, however, including the UK, the larger economies have seen, over the past half-century, a steady deceleration in economic growth and, in the past two decades, its disappearance. As can be seen in Chart 1.5, growth in these countries has dropped dramatically.

Chart 1.5: Real Average Annual GDP Growth in Major Western European Economies 1960–2019

Declining growth over the past half-century can be seen right across the advanced economies of western Europe.

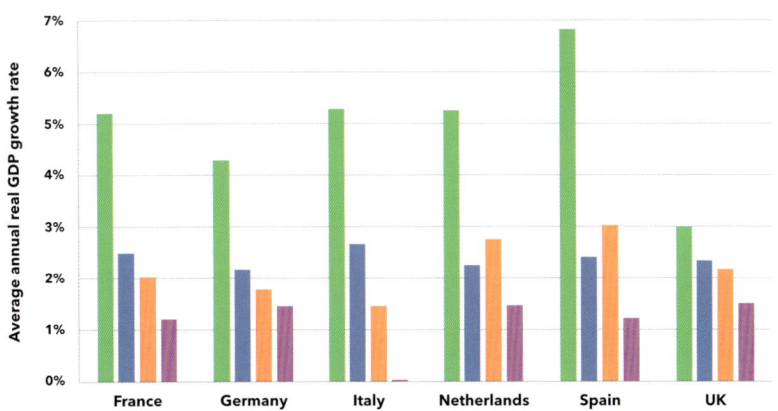

IMF advanced economies with annual GDP over $1 trillion
Source: International Monetary Fund[8]

And, of course, for any country, the key measure is not GDP, but GDP per capita. What matters most is whether additional wealth and opportunities are accruing to the individual and their family – rather than whether the country as a whole is getting wealthier.

Chart 1.6 shows how the four great twentieth-century powers – the US, UK, Germany and France – have each performed against national expectations to grow their GDP per capita. In the early 1930s, all had similar levels of GDP per capita – the first two somewhat higher than the latter two. Over the next century, that changed dramatically. In the US, GDP per capita has bounded ahead, decade after decade, so that its GDP is now massively higher than that of the other three. Within those other three, post-Second World War, Germany rebounded from military and economic catastrophe to outperform the UK and France – who have both done worse.

Chart 1.6: Real GDP Per Capita for the UK, US, Germany and France
1929–2023, in Constant 2011 Prices

Margaret Thatcher's policies improved economic growth for several decades, but now the UK economy has been falling further and further behind

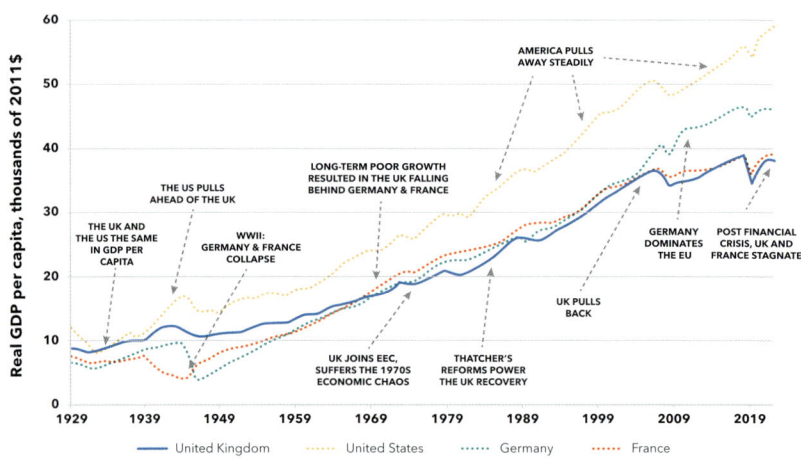

Source: Maddison Project, International Monetary Fund[9]

The 1970s was the nadir of this story for the UK. That decade saw inflation, the three-day week, the 'Winter of Discontent', and significant economic decline in the UK. The wrong prescription for the UK – namely, for it to join the European Common Market – was adopted; decline continued. What was actually needed was economic reform, which was finally provided by Margaret Thatcher in the 1980s. Her reforms reversed the decline of the post-war years, leading to economic growth through the 1990s and taking the British economy optimistically into the new millennium.

In the past decade and a half, however, growth in GDP per capita for western European economies has now slowed to a crawl. For all these countries, economic growth has declined in each decade. The slowdown expressed on a per-capita basis (Chart 1.7) is even worse than the drop in actual GDP growth.

Chart I.7: Real GDP and Real GDP Per Capita Growth in Major Western European Economies 1960–2019

Even pre-Covid, annual GDP-per-capita growth had shrunk to 1 per cent or less in major Western European economies

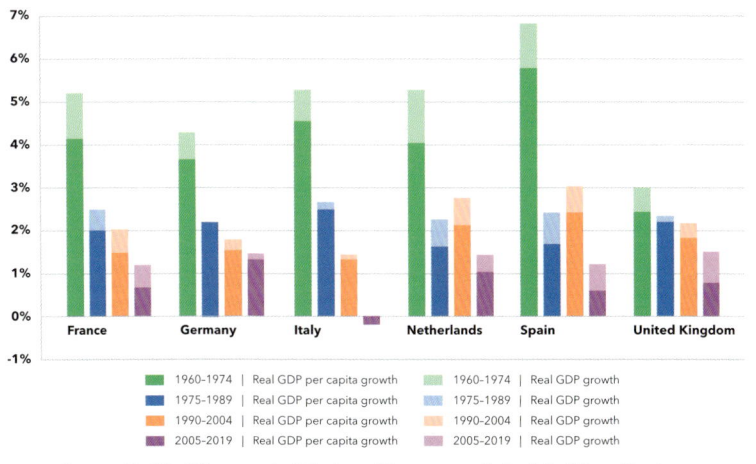

Source: Public Finances in Modern History[10] and the Maddison Project[11]

Economist Thomas Piketty focused on this point, discussing whether growth in a particular country benefited the workers or the owners of capital.[12] Piketty's results have been pretty much discredited,[13] and in particular it has been shown that there are more plausible reasons than Piketty's for the specific phenomenon he observed, but in any event, the first issue is whether the economy per capita has grown and will continue to grow in the first place.[14] Only once that has happened can we start talking sensibly about redistribution and improving the safety net.

Set against that measure, we're not doing well. Not only has GDP growth been very low in the UK in the past three decades, but we have added over 10 million to our population since 1995.[15] As a result, our GDP-per-capita growth has, as we can see in Chart 1.8, been almost non-existent in recent years.

Chart 1.8: Real GDP Per Capita Growth in the UK 1975–2024

Rapid increases in immigration this century led to major increases in population. The already anaemic level of GDP growth consequently becomes even worse when looked at as GDP-per-capita growth.

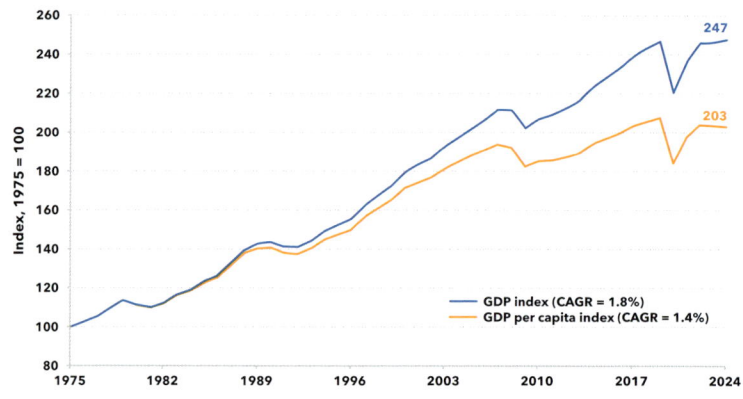

Source: *International Monetary Fund and Maddison Project*[16]

As Chart 1.9 shows, there's not only a general problem of growth among Europe's advanced economies. More specifically in the UK, growth in household income has, over the past two decades, more or less ceased.

Chart 1.9: Median Household Income Per Person
Annual $,000 at PPP, 2019 prices

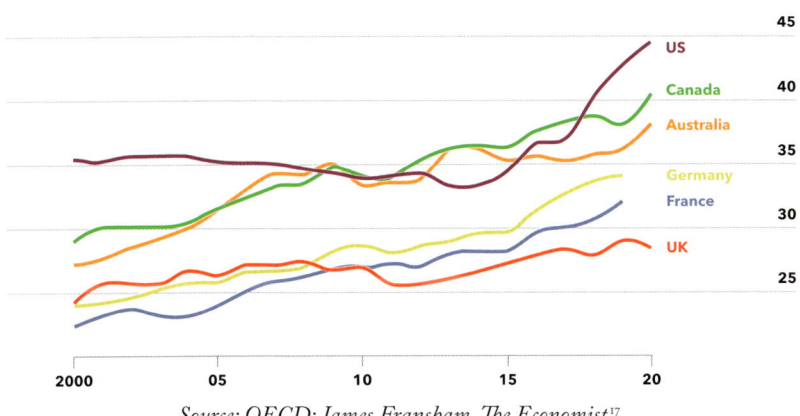

Source: OECD; James Fransham, The Economist[17]
Note: At purchasing power parity (PPP). Income per person after taxes and transfers

While GDP itself may increase as the working-age population grows, the mathematical relationship between GDP and GDP per capita is a function of population growth or shrinkage. This in turn depends on two things: the level of the indigenous birth rate and net migration.

Taking the first of these, since around the mid-1970s, birth rates in western Europe have collapsed to below the replacement rate (2.1 children per woman). See Chart 1.10.

Looking at Chart 1.11, we can see that any drop in the indigenous birth rate in the UK has been overwhelmed by the large size of net migration.

Chart 1.10: Fertility Rates Versus Replacement Level Across Major Western European Economies 1960–2022

The average number of live births per woman has declined drastically over the last decades across western Europe and dropped below the replacement level.

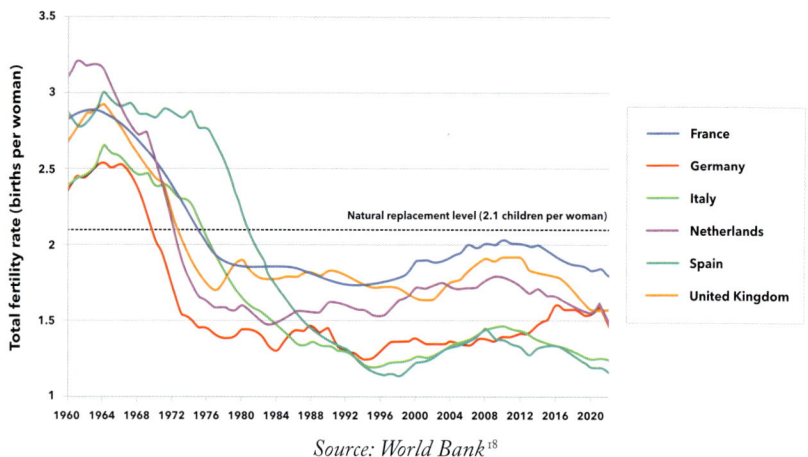

Source: World Bank[18]

Chart 1.11: Long-Term Migration in the UK 1964–2023

Both immigration and net migration in the UK have skyrocketed since the end of the last century and particularly post-Brexit.

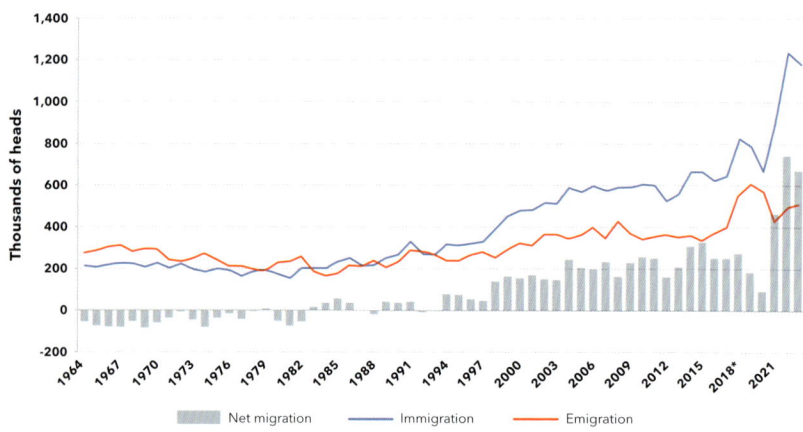

The methodology for estimating migration was changed in 2018
Source: House of Commons Library[19]

So, as Chart 1.12 shows, the UK's population (as with other European countries) has increased significantly.

Chart 1.12: Population Growth in Major Western European Economies, 1960 Versus 2023

Between 1960 and 2023, as a result of high levels of immigration, populations across the major western European economies have grown on average by 37 per cent and in the UK by 28 per cent.

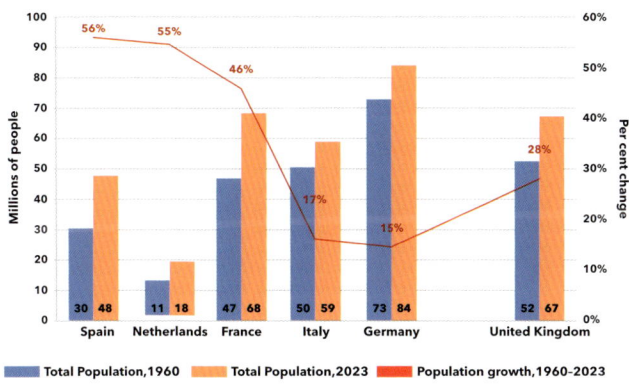

Source: World Bank[20]

Notably, the UK's Office for Budget Responsibility (OBR) uses a model that predicts that the more immigration we have, the more GDP will rise. But, of course, the rise in GDP *per capita* will not be commensurate with the rise in GDP overall. The OBR has, in the past, overstated the benefits of mass immigration.

The OBR's previous stance explains why recent governments have allowed plentiful immigration. If a Home Office minister tells the OBR they want to reduce immigration, it responds that its report to the government will predict that the economy won't grow as fast, so you won't have much future 'fiscal headroom' – and as a result, you must cut back government expenditure on, say, welfare or increase taxes. In other words, don't plan to reduce immigration. If you ignore this advice and press on, the OBR leaks your decision to the press (as is believed to have happened with Liz Truss's mini-budget) to undermine your proposed approach.[21] As a result, Chancellors keen to spend more on welfare or cut taxes could have seen themselves as having limited ability to restrict immigration. But, as even the OBR now agrees, not restricting migration is likely to result in lower, not higher, growth in GDP per capita.[22]

While our overall population has (through immigration) grown, we also face the problem, as shown in Chart 1.13, of an increasingly ageing population – even though the younger age of immigrants has managed to maintain the overall percentage of our population of working age.

Chart 1.13: UK Overall Working-Age and Retired Population 1970–2022

The UK's population is rising, but ageing.

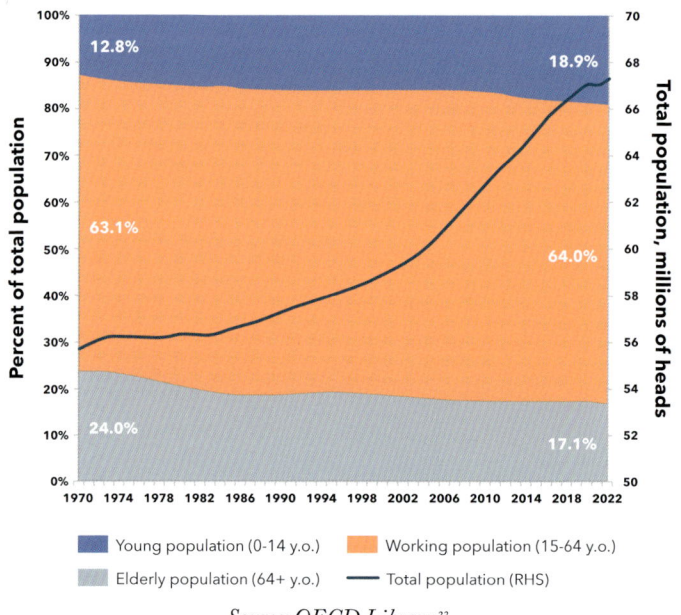

Source: OECD Library[23]

And, as shown in Chart 1.14, as a result of slower growth decade after decade, along with a growing population due to higher and higher immigration, the UK is now – shockingly – only just in the upper half of GDP per capita among OECD countries.

Chart 1.14: GDP Per Capita in the Thirty-Eight OECD Countries* 2022
In PPP Terms, Current Dollars

The UK is no longer a stellar economic powerhouse.

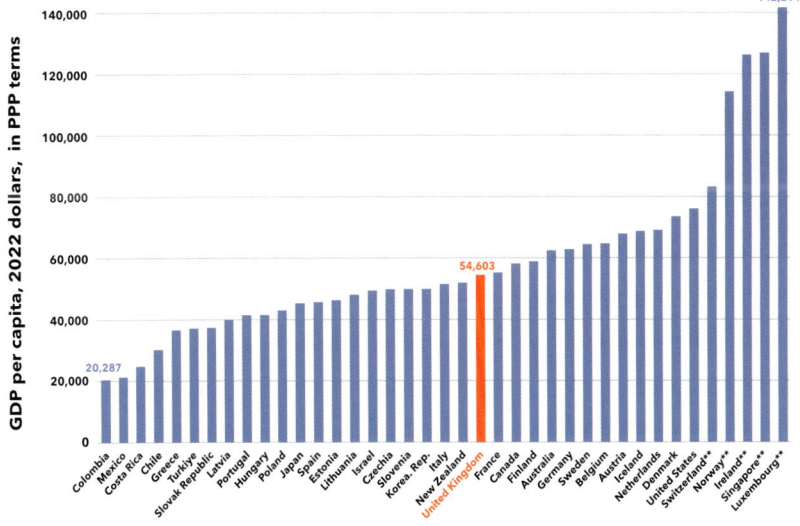

Plus Singapore (non-OECD)
*** Luxembourg and Ireland, as pass-through locations for the washing of corporate profits in their low-tax jurisdictions, have artificially high GDPs, but the money washing through benefits the citizens of those countries very little. Switzerland and Singapore have the same but to a lesser degree. • Source: World Bank[24]*

Part of the cause of that is, as we have seen, our immigration policy. Chart 1.15 shows the empirical result: higher immigration is clearly associated with lower individual wealth because, as the chart shows, even if GDP were to increase through immigration, GDP per capita doesn't.

Chart I.15: Average Population Versus GDP Per Capita Growth 2005–2019

On average, higher levels of immigration are associated with reduced growth in GDP per capita.

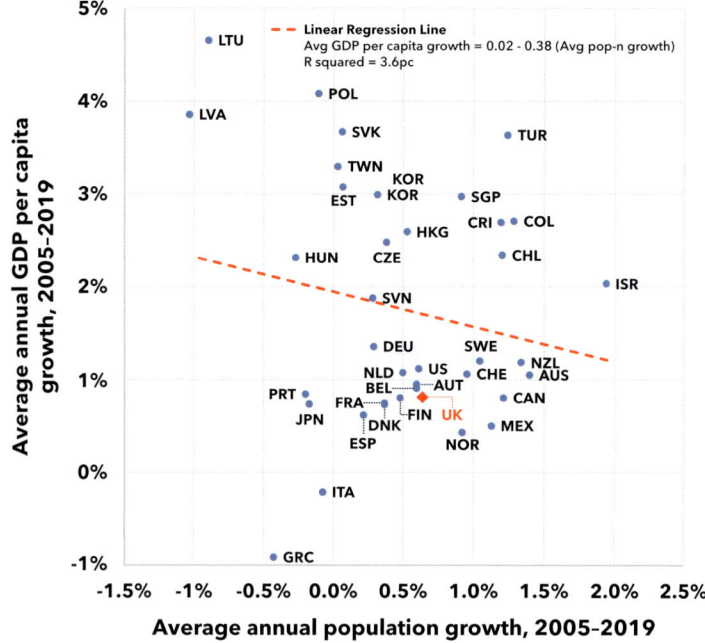

Source: *International Monetary Fund, moyniteam analysis* [25]

Obviously, the more or less productive the immigrants are that come into a country, the more or less GDP will grow, assuming not too many remain unemployed. But immigration has a negative impact on GDP per capita, and when the additional negative impacts and demands on housing, health, emergency services, schools and infrastructure are taken into account, there are significant negatives to having such a high immigration level – unless, as in the US, you can, by having a relatively light social safety net that is not offering them much in benefits, put most of the new immigrants speedily into the workforce (much of which will be in the 'informal' or 'black' economy). In the US, that proposition is being put to the test by the astonishingly high level of immigration across the Rio Grande – at least 6.3 million since Biden became President.[26]

So – after that short detour to review the additional issues raised by looking at GDP rather than GDP per capita – to summarise, since the mid-1700s, for some 200–250 years, there has been in western countries a regular trend of ever-more jobs and ever-higher wages. But for the UK, and for many of the most advanced western economies, that trend has, in the past fifteen to twenty years, vanished. In western Europe at least, growth in GDP per capita has almost disappeared. The vanishing of growth in these countries is because of a double whammy: growth is very low, while population is still, due to immigration, growing rapidly. Addressing this problem, should we wish to do so, seems to have been made more difficult by declining economic understanding among politicians, pundits and the electorate; a return to social justice-style debates; the increasing demand for 'equity' (equality of outcome) and redistribution; and eco-style arguments that condemn growth out of hand and that have led to frequent claims that our country's economy should not grow at all – or even that it should shrink.

• • •

Those arguing *for* growth believe it is not just something that is nice to have but that it's both morally desirable and essential. Growth has brought enormous contentment and prosperity to the people of our country, to the people of other developed countries and, prospectively, to almost the entire world. In the UK, we all live lives that benefit hugely from the economic growth that has taken place since the late eighteenth century. But now, our economy seems to have lost the knack of growing and a focus on economic growth no longer takes pride of place in the economic agenda.* Our main political parties, whether or not they pay lip service to growth, initiate policies that are, bemusingly, anti-growth. Political movements, some pseudo-religious in their beliefs, preach that growth is bad and must be stopped; or preach philosophies that, even if they do not overtly admit to it, effectively mean an end to any future growth.

In any event, given the general (and, it seems, prevailing) levels of either indifference or hostility to economic growth, the case for growth now has to be remade.

A recent paper by the Centre for Policy Study's Robert Colvile set forth the moral case for growth.[27] I gratefully borrow some of Colvile's ideas. Benjamin Friedman from Harvard University and Tyler Cowen from George Mason University have separately written extensively on the matter in recent decades, pointing out the many benefits that make it a moral imperative for governments to seek growth.[28]

In Part I, I present that case for growth. In the following pages, I review a series of both *moral* and *practical* arguments for economic growth.

---

* Since I originally wrote these words, growth is – at least rhetorically – coming back into fashion. Even the Labour Party, possibly surprisingly, adopted a rhetoric of growth being 'at the heart of its policies'. See 'Sir Keir Starmer: UK needs growth, growth, growth', BBC News, 25 July 2022, https://www.bbc.co.uk/news/av/uk-62292281

Growth is morally desirable because:

- Aspiration is a central feature of human existence.
- Without growth, all economic conversations necessarily become about redistribution because there is no 'extra' to go round for all.
- Growth has accomplished and continues to promise enormous benefits to the human race and the planet.

Growth is essential because:

- As the electorate demands that the state do ever more, growth is the only reliable and sustainable way of funding these increased services.
- Without growth, developed countries must eventually, in any event, go bust.

In the following chapters, which elaborate on these points, some of the arguments may seem commonplace; yet they often, particularly recently, seem to have been lost in the cut and thrust of the political debate around the desirability, or otherwise, of higher or lower taxes, bigger or smaller government, higher or lower (or no) growth in the UK. So, if you find any arguments in what follows to be obvious, bear in mind that these points are nonetheless rarely made, so to others they may be novel. Also bear in mind that experience shows that the case for growth, for whatever reason, needs to be made over and again.

CHAPTER I

ASPIRATION IS A CENTRAL FEATURE OF HUMAN EXISTENCE

———

Contemplating the issue of whether or not growth is a good thing can be challenging, when one considers the often plausible-sounding exhortations of the anti-growth campaigners. Their arguments appeal to grand, albeit challengeable, concepts, such as (alleged) global ecocide or the need to 'decolonise the atmosphere'.[1] It is not always easy to discern the truth or potential impact of such approaches, nor the claims as to likely future outcomes – or to cost these allegedly affordable approaches. The average person, quite reasonably, sometimes feels inclined to agree with these anti-growth arguments; by doing so, they imagine themselves to be on the virtuous side of what is presented as a moral dilemma. Agreeing with the anti-growth campaigners is a relatively painless approach, since agreeing with such arguments usually comes with very little personal cost, at least in the short term.

Turn the conversation around, however, and ask yourself: 'Do I personally want to achieve, to do better bit by bit, as I go through my life? Do I want to have a slightly better flat or house, a better car, a happy retirement, overseas holidays from time to time?' And if you have children, or plan to have them: 'Do I want to provide for my children, give them a better life, a better education, a better (or as good an) upbringing than I was able to have?' If your answer is 'yes' to any of that, then you implicitly believe in growth, and if you believe the average person is entitled to think the same way as you, then again you are, even more explicitly, pro-growth. And that's before you get to the 80 per cent of the world that is outside our fortunate circle of highly developed economies. For the rest of the world to catch up with us, to have a better life, major economic growth is the only feasible path.

A growth agenda is not anti-planet. It considers that increasing wealth and improving technology is the only practical way of addressing the problem of the amount of carbon dioxide we put into the air. And growth has the added benefit of giving the average human being an opportunity to fulfil their life ambitions.

All human beings are born with aspiration – the desire to use their abilities to the utmost, to achieve for themselves and for their families, to experience and enjoy success. In a successful society, a child's ambition expands and flourishes as they grow to adulthood, so that the mature citizen is able to deploy their talents to the full and into personal success that leads to the reinforcement of ambition, further success, fulfilment and satisfaction. Fulfilling the individual citizen's need to feel free, to exercise their drive to succeed in their chosen path of life, is nowadays seen by most as an essential component of a just government.

Communist ideology imposed on the citizens of communist countries (although not on its leaders) the belief that humans can be made selfless, with satisfaction and fulfilment coming from self-sacrifice and helping the commonweal. This approach has, over the past century, been tested to destruction, in a vast range of countries and economies. The outcome has *always* been an impoverished populace, an enriched ruling caste, increased totalitarian control over the individual, and repressive violence to preserve the ruling caste. The final phase of that outcome has been, at best, the ultimate collapse of the country's political and economic system.* These outcomes were inevitable because the communist approach is at odds with human nature, core components of which are the desire for personal freedom and autonomy and the need to succeed on our own terms. A major reason for the failure of the communist approach is that virtually all striving individuals – even those of a socialist bent – want and work to see a good part of their endeavour and ambition accrue to themselves and their families; such striving is what produces economic growth. Indeed, Adam Smith showed how 'selfish' self-interest – as much as moral sentiments like empathy – was necessary for the commonweal to prosper and for economic growth to take place.

> In short, economic growth is morally essential for each human individual to fulfil their aspirations as they interact with society.

---

* A few socialist/totalitarian countries have to date succeeded, through state violence, in keeping their repressive regimes in place (but only for now).

CHAPTER 2

WITHOUT GROWTH, ALL ECONOMIC CONVERSATIONS BECOME ABOUT REDISTRIBUTION

———

Without growth, the deeply embedded and unalterable human aspiration to strive and be free cannot be universally fulfilled. The average UK citizen wants, reasonably enough, a family, enough cash to meet basic needs, a house or a flat, a vehicle, a smartphone and the like, holidays abroad and other such relatively modest trappings of a successful life in a twenty-first century developed economy. To achieve this, these citizens need a job that pays well (and increasingly well over time, as their and their families' needs expand) and a job that grows, so that they can grow in turn – in wealth, in capability and in knowledge of the world and of themselves. Without growth, all this disappears because if the economic pie stays the same size, one citizen can only get a larger portion if another citizen gets a *smaller* one – successful striving would require that others be impoverished. Growth is necessary because if striving results in no reward, aspiration withers and dies.

If there is no economic growth, the pie does not expand and no new wealth is generated. In such circumstances, every citizen, often with a growing family and thus a growing financial need, can only achieve that by taking something away from other members of society – whether from richer citizens or poorer ones. Citizen is necessarily set against citizen as each strives to better themselves individually. To point out a truism: this is the case even for social-istic politicians and their civil servants; without growth to pay for their own *higher* wages and benefits, they must necessarily have to tell everyone else in the country to be condemned to a standard of living that is *lower* than what the average would otherwise have been. And the more benefits these politicians and civil servants award themselves over time (which they do), the less there will be for anyone else.

To want to better yourself is not reprehensible; it is natural and often necessary, if only to feed, clothe and house one's growing family. But few of us want to accomplish that betterment just by taking from another's plate. For all striving humans to be able to make a better life without creating a worse life for their fellow cit-izens, there has to be a growing pie, from which each can take a growing share.

In an interesting essay in the *Financial Times*, John Burn-Mur-doch discusses what growth looks like if you have a 'zero-sum' mindset.[1] If one group increases their prosperity, this thinking goes, another group will be commensurately impoverished. This pro-foundly pessimistic view flies in the face of what has actually been achieved in the past two hundred years – yet it is gaining traction. Scientific solutions to our various problems are growing at an expo-nential rate, yet the ability of these breakthroughs to create growing prosperity for all is handicapped by such thinking. The more people believe that the future is zero-sum, the crazier (and more redistrib-utive) are the policies such people embrace.

The economic growth that is needed for a non-zero-sum future has to be *real* – that is, it has to be above inflation. And as discussed, it has to be *per capita*. In countries that have a growing population, such as the UK, if there is little or no economic growth, the end result is negative growth per capita. The UK's population has grown by over 10 million (16 per cent) in the past three decades. In recent years, it has grown by half a million souls or more each year because of our (sometimes inadvertent) pro-immigration policies. This growth in population creates the need for real annual economic growth of around 1 per cent *just to keep the real GDP per capita constant* (ceteris paribus). Any increment to national wealth *per head* will only accrue when there is real economic growth *beyond* that real c. 1 per cent level. Less than that, and if GDP and wages track each other, the average real wage is going to be declining steadily – as has happened in the UK in recent years (see Chart 1.1). Real hardship, and a downward adjustment of living standards, is the result. It is hard to see any of that as a morally desirable outcome.

One key, and often underappreciated, foundational underpinning of the moral argument for growth is the magic of compounding. Even a small amount of extra growth per annum will make an enormous difference to a country's and its citizens' wealth as it compounds over the years.

The following example illustrates the point. In 1870, the real GDP per capita in the UK amounted to $5,829, which was over 21 per cent higher than the $4,803 level recorded in the US (all measured in constant 2011 prices), as shown in Chart 1.16. In the 150-year period 1870–2019, the US economy grew on average at an annual rate of slightly over 1.6 per cent, while the UK's growth rate averaged a little less at 1.3 per cent per annum. This small divergence resulted in US citizens, whose GDP per capita in 1870 was in fact 17.6 per cent *less* than that of UK citizens, drawing level with the UK by around

1930 and accelerating past the UK in subsequent decades. By 2019, US citizens were enjoying a GDP per capita of $56,469, which is 44 per cent *higher* than the $39,113 per capita GDP in the UK. This trend has not stopped: year after year, the US continues to grow its GDP per capita faster than the UK. A recent article emphasised the practical upside for the US in terms of actual salaries and the downside for the slower-growing UK.[2] In Alabama (the poorest US state) a car wash manager earns over £100,000, compared with £33,000 in the UK; a surgeon £220,700 versus £82,600 in the UK. These gaps continue to widen each year.

Chart 1.16: Real GDP Per Capita in the UK and US
1870–2019, in 2011 prices

Small differentials in growth rates, compounded over long-term periods, lead to substantial differences in the wealth levels of different nations.

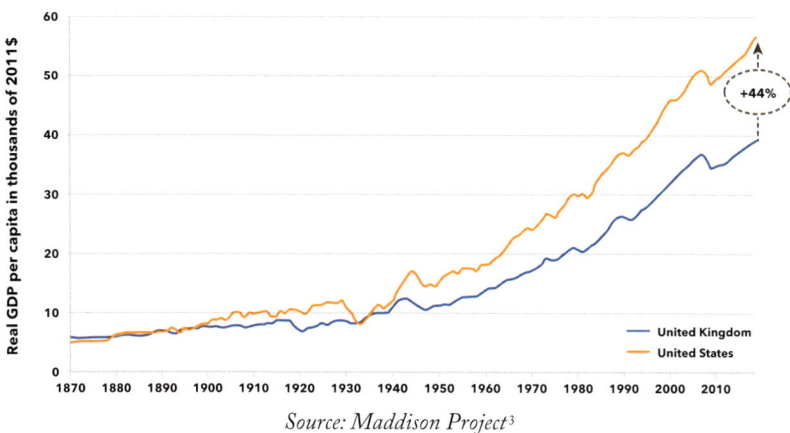

Source: Maddison Project[3]

So, as demonstrated here, the GDP-per-capita pre-pandemic gap between our two countries is $17,356. That translates into an even higher gap in wages for individual jobs, but even if it translated just one for one from GDP per capita to wages, the resulting $17,356 extra in annual wage for the average worker (and with lower taxes to boot) would not only put to bed most concerns in the UK about wage poverty for workers, it would likely, along with a concurrent increase in corporate profits, provide enough extra tax revenues to eliminate the UK's annual budget deficit. Our lost opportunity to grow even just slightly faster each year in the modern era therefore has had major economic and political repercussions for the UK. If we could have grown our economy faster, we would have been able to offer improved material and financial benefits to workers in the economy; improved state benefits in terms of health, education, housing and other 'entitlements'; and sounder, less destabilising financials for our country.

> In short, economic growth is morally essential if self-betterment is not to be accomplished at the expense of others.

CHAPTER 3

GROWTH HAS ACCOMPLISHED ENORMOUS BENEFITS FOR THE HUMAN RACE AND THE PLANET

———

Economic growth is a *sine qua non* for improved job prospects and improved personal prosperity for our country's citizens. For those who see themselves as concerned about or even involved in the job of expanding human happiness, growth has a further large moral dimension – of course, for the impoverished populations of developing countries but for the comparatively wealthy populations of advanced countries, which themselves will always have the capacity for continued growth.

As we show in the following pages, growth is the raw material for a huge range of life-enhancing improvements:

1. Standards of living: higher wages satisfy more of our needs, wants and happiness.
2. Personal and national opportunities: increased growth in the economy means new businesses, new industries and therefore new opportunities for individuals.
3. Resilience: growth gives us a better ability to adapt to global events, whether natural, political, economic or technological.

4. Public services: a larger economy can afford higher per-capita spending when providing public services to its citizens.

5. Solutions to global issues: growth and technological innovation go hand in hand. Together they can resolve the world's problems, from global poverty to war and famine to ecocide and more.

STANDARDS OF LIVING

It is easy to belittle the impact of improvements in standards of living over time, but they have transformed opportunities for humans to live productive lives – and they continue to do so, even for developed economies such as the UK. Few of our citizens would want us to go back to even just seventy years ago, with an expectation of living around fourteen fewer years or of living a far less healthy life.[1] Beyond that, even just on the materialistic side, few would be interested in no longer enjoying the enormous benefits that growth and innovation have, even just recently, created for humankind. Post-Second World War, laundry machines, dryers and dishwashers liberated housewives. Before the 1970s (see Chart 1.17), other household goods that today seem basic were either non-existent or at best, were the preserve of a lucky few. Growing national wealth has now allowed those goods to become widespread, everyday possessions; it is hard to imagine a UK today where most people don't possess them or indeed where they give them up.

Some feel that technology can replace growth: if we all become more virtual, we can enjoy the benefits of travel without travelling, of performance without visiting concert hall, even, one day – some say – sex without, um, sex. But all that is far in the future. Britain's growth should be not so much about (the probable chimera) of virtualising the UK but more about developing advanced technology and market capabilities and then bringing them, through exports, to the rest of the (currently, mostly underdeveloped) world: there are many decades, probably centuries, before the world significantly transcends its physical needs and is able to produce everything it needs without the massive needed investments that themselves power growth.

Chart 1.17: Ownership of Household Goods 1970–2022
Percentage of households with durable goods

All kinds of goods that until recently were, at best, the preserve of a fortunate minority are now treated as commonplace or essential.

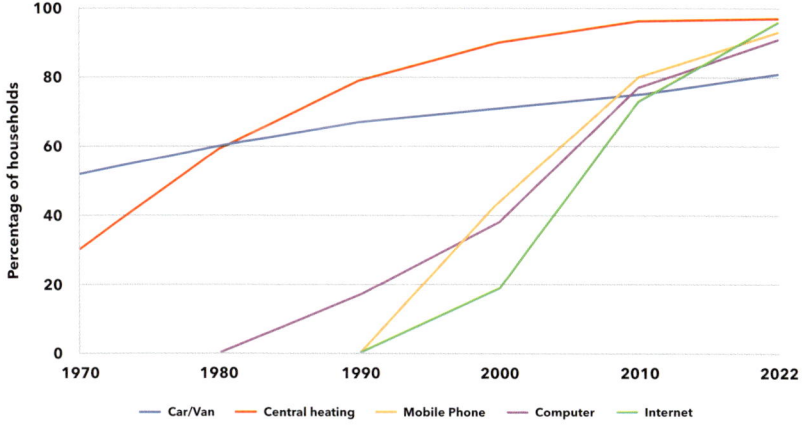

Source: Office for National Statistics[2]

The many life-enhancing improvements in our material standard of living – itself the result of investment, invention and innovation – affect enormously how we live. For example, the trauma of losing an infant has come to hit less than one third as many people in developed economies than it did forty years ago because the child mortality rate in England and Wales has declined from twelve per 1,000 live births in 1980 to 3.7 per 1,000 live births in 2021.[3] All this has come from economic growth.

Economic progress propels scientific research and advances in technology, food and agriculture: yields in wheat crops quadrupled to eight tonnes per hectare in the second half of the twentieth century, maize crops increased five-fold and still climbing, chickens grow to maturity in half of the time they used to.[4] All this provides enormous benefit to the entire world.

UK citizens are also more able to travel abroad. Fifty years ago, any foreign travel was a rarity for almost all of the population but now it's commonplace. Even in recent years, from 2001 to 2019, the number of holidays abroad by UK residents has risen from under 40 million (one trip a year only and on average, only for two out of every three citizens) to nearly 60 million (on average, one for each citizen).[5] A generation previously, the large majority of the population had never (except in war) travelled abroad. All this has come from economic growth.

Let me try to bring this point to life. You, as you read this, probably possess a smartphone – an iPhone, say. It provides more and more benefit for you the longer you have it. Being in touch with friends and family, getting better news, making your life more efficient, possibly playing games – whatever. As Chart 1.17 showed, the majority of your fellow citizens (assuming you reside in the UK) are in a similar position to you. But around the world, that's not the case. Billions of people don't have their lives enriched by possession of a smartphone.[*]

Now, how would you like to lose all use of your smartphone and return to life as it was before you had one? Likely, if you're honest

---

[*] They don't have one because their country has had, so far, insufficient economic growth – even though in some countries, more prosperous citizens have leapfrogged over the western world's use of their mobile phones to create and participate in local markets, make electronic payments and the like. But that's only a relatively small slice of those populations, and only a small part of what a full expensive smartphone can do.

with yourself, you recoil at the thought. But that is the life that the almost half of the world, the many billions without a smartphone, are condemned to – not just now but for quite a while into the future, unless their country's economy grows at quite a fast pace for quite some years. Only with economic growth can the entirety of the world's citizens hope to lead the kind of empowered life that we enjoy thanks to our smartphones.

And that's just one example. To deepen the conversation: you, dear reader – unless you already have some life-threatening disease or similar – can expect to live to your mid-eighties or beyond. For most of that, you can expect to be in robust health. Out there though, in the majority of the world, the chances are high that you would die from a simple infection that leads to sepsis, or from having undetected and untreated colon or breast or prostate or lung cancer, or maternal death in childbirth, or some other health disaster that results in your dying, say, forty years before your natural time. Imagine being one of those people seeing their premature death approaching, knowing that in other, better-developed parts of the world, the cancer would have been detected, would have been cured, their lifespan extended by decades. Again, until the economy of that person's country has grown sufficiently to provide a well-staffed and well-funded (whether privately or publicly) health service, that country's citizens will not enjoy the kind of extended lifespan that we do. Without growth, it will just not happen. Chart 1.18, phase IV, shows elements of the future that further investments in the economy can bring. Note that all the benefits to humankind that have already occurred, and most likely those that will occur in the future too, were and will be not provided by government action or interference or 'industrial strategy', nor were they invented under any socialist or communist regime; they all came about as a result of free markets and private enterprise, with government kindly getting out of the way.

Chart 1.18: Transformational Goods
Post-war to present, developed countries

Any humanity-based approach should endorse past and future global spreading of products that transform lives – escaping from drudgery, achieving personal autonomy, enhancing thinking and understanding.

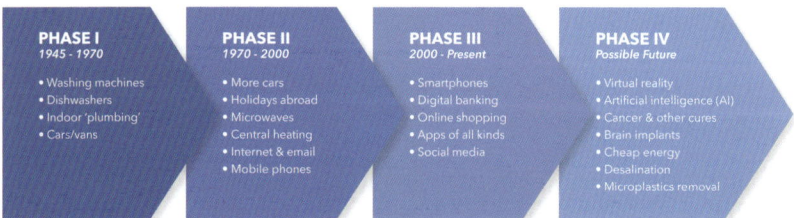

Source: moyniteam

So, all this talk of economic growth is not just some fanciful economist's theoretical meanderings. Growth is about bringing fulfilled, extended, healthy lives to all 8 billion (and growing) souls on the planet right now, not just the 1.4 billion citizens of the OECD, and growth is about continuing to enhance their lives more and more into the foreseeable future.

There are those in the enriched part of the world who, ignoring global needs, hold what the PhD student Rob Henderson has dubbed 'luxury beliefs', which he defined as beliefs about how others should restrict or damage their lives while the signaller doesn't have to – for example, stating that all growth should now cease if the world is to be 'saved'.[6] If that zero-growth demand was put into action and enforced, the direct result would be, compared to any growth scenario, much higher disease around the world, much higher death rates than would otherwise be the case, much lower lifespans, and greatly reduced human happiness across the globe – for literally billions of human beings.

It is unthinkable to accept that even more of these benefits (some hypothesised in Chart 1.18, many more unknown) should be denied to humankind, let alone some of our existing benefits being reversed, as the no-growth advocates threaten. Even more unconscionable is the idea that developed economies should continue to enjoy these current benefits, but the rest of the world should be denied them. And yet for the developing nations to be able to achieve these benefits and for the developed nations to continue along the path of providing new benefits, an enormous amount of global economic growth is needed. Without it, it will be impossible for all but a favoured few around the world to enjoy these life-enhancing benefits. It is all very well for some of the more narcissistic of that favoured few to argue (with dodgy logic) that growth damages the environment (or some other equally specious reasoning) and we should all stay as we are, but this is not something that is likely to be particularly persuasive to the over half of the world that is still striving to reach even minimal levels of economic comfort for their populations overall.

PERSONAL AND NATIONAL OPPORTUNITIES

Economic growth means more opportunities for citizens. It creates more and higher-earning jobs, and it creates a range of new sectors in which people can start and grow businesses – either way, earning an increasingly comfortable living.

Chart 1.19: Cumulative Impact on the UK's GDP Per Capita by 2040 of Different Growth Rates

Slightly higher economic growth leads to startling improvement in wealth per capita.

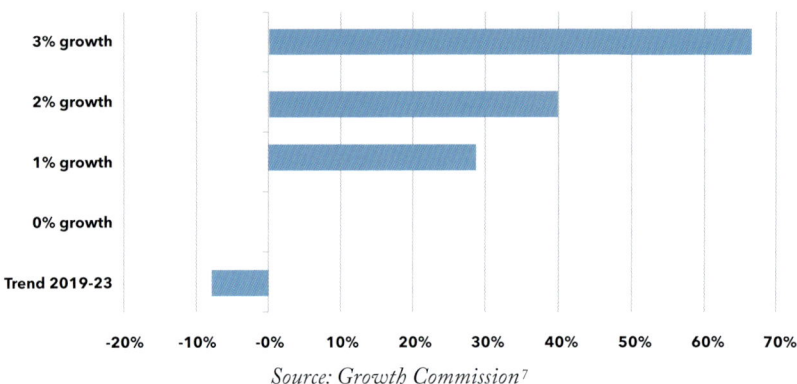

Source: Growth Commission[7]

The prospects for start-up businesses – which contain the promise of even more and better consumer goods and services, enhancing human life even more – will also be better. Starting a business is a risky exercise; most new businesses fail. To make up for that risk, there needs to be the incentive of wealth creation for the entrepreneur. Inhibiting incentives to entrepreneurship (e.g. through tax and regulation or cutting off wider job choice) has a negative impact on political and social cohesion. When people are not able to realise their aspirations through productive entrepreneurship or through finding a job that suits them, they will look to alternatives that they see as improving their own personal condition. This can lead to populist politicians threatening to seize money from convenient targets such as millionaires and billionaires – a short-term strategy, inevitably leading to a severely negative longer-term outcome. This then leads to more or less overt corruption or 'crony capitalism', aka 'rent-seeking', as clever people respond to the implicit incentive to divert their talents to the task of battening onto the expanding state.[8] Over time, high-tax, high-regulation policies create countries where the best and brightest seek better opportunities elsewhere, so that now we see Britain again facing the 'brain drain'.[9] This argument is expanded on in Part II.

With growth, however, comes room for fulfilment, better material lives and better wealth creation. As the Growth Commission has pointed out, the recent trend has been for GDP per capita to decline: if we returned to the level of the 1950s, where per-capita growth in GDP was over 2 per cent, then by 2040, GDP per capita would be some 40 per cent higher than it is now (Chart 1.19).

RESILIENCE

Higher national income enables states, businesses, families and individuals to invest more in protection against disaster and to pool more resources, over time and across society, to dilute the impact of any disaster – to respond and recover more quickly.

This can be seen in the trend over time for deaths from natural disasters. Despite a rise in the global population, and despite the alarmism of climate doomsters, average decadal deaths globally from natural disasters have fallen 92 per cent between the 1920s and the 2010s. Despite massive population growth since this time, nearly half a million fewer people each year are dying from natural disasters.[10]

It is in the developed capitalist economies that almost all the important healthcare breakthroughs have been made. For example, because the UK had a strong scientific position, it was the country that figured out relatively early on in the Covid-19 pandemic that Dexamethasone was an effective treatment in acute cases. In the US, the discovery was made that ventilators didn't help Covid patients. These discoveries saved countless lives around the world. The US and UK economies had the large and flexible resources and the scientific and academic base to make medical breakthroughs. Over time, these two countries had, because of their wealth and openness to new investments, developed research centres of excellence, benefiting from the openness to free enquiry that allows such institutions to thrive and develop medical treatments. (As will be discussed in Part II, these advantages are rapidly disappearing in the UK as taxes and regulation inexorably balloon.)

PUBLIC SERVICES

The electorates of democracies expect an ever-increasing level of public services. This is Wagner's Law, first formulated in the 1860s: public expenditure (as a share of GDP) increases as national income rises.[11]

Some politicians see high taxes as a way to fund the increase in public expenditure that the public increasingly demands; this big government, tax-and-spend approach is generally known as social democracy. As only the foolish fail to understand, higher tax *rates* are not likely to yield a one-to-one increase in tax *revenues* because of the dynamic reactions of taxpayers as they change their behaviour in response to higher taxes. But as an alternative to imposing higher tax rates to pay for the consequences of Wagner's Law, growth can reliably provide the needed additional tax revenues *without increasing the size of the state as a percentage of GDP.* Over five years, a 1 percentage point increase in the annual UK growth rate would, much more certainly than increased tax rates, increase current government revenues by some £50 billion – an addition to

the country's tax revenues of some 5 per cent.[*][12] Over longer periods, and for larger increases in the economy's growth rate, the
benefits of growth-making cash available for public expenditure
will be even greater.

The most commonly discussed trio of public services are health,
education and housing. There are, of course, many other public
services. For example, defence expenditure could, and likely would,
have been much higher if the UK had grown faster in recent years,
thus allowing us to be better prepared to defend democracy (for
example, in Ukraine).

Those opposing growth, or proposing an economic approach in
which economic growth is restricted or cut off entirely, have for
decades forecasted that either Malthus-style resource depletion
and economic collapse or climate catastrophe will occur if growth
continues, so they advocate an approach to policymaking and consumer behaviour involving either a forcible or 'nudged' reduction in
demand, as well as the 'right to idleness' and 'slowing capital down'.[†]
Evidence for the efficacy of these suggested solutions is scant to
non-existent, even if the dire environmental forecasts were to
materialise, which so far they haven't (although this does not stop
growth deniers from continuing to make renewed, equally grim
forecasts, which in turn haven't happened either).[13] The naivety and
ignorance exhibited by those in western nations who embrace these
beliefs carries massive disadvantages for their countries, for themselves and for their fellow citizens, relative to other, more sensible

---

[*]   According to the IMF (see endnote) nominal UK GDP in 2023 was £2.69 trillion. Additional growth of
1 per cent per year over five years roughly translates to 5.1 per cent of GDP or £137 billion of additional
national income. The OBR's March 2024 tax-to-GDP ratio is expected to average 36.8 per cent between
2024/25 and 2028/29, which, if true, would mean that additional national income would result in over £50
billion of additional tax revenue.

[†]   See, for example, Giorgos Kallis, *In Defense of Degrowth*.

countries – even those with far worse governance and human rights records – which makes the future of the world less stable.

Any commentator who wishes to assert that the UK economy should not grow further, or only slowly, has an obligation to tell us: where will the money come from to provide the ever-expanding services – healthcare, education, housing, defence or any other – that the electorate rightly demands for themselves and their country? And for those jobs where society believes workers are currently not paid enough – nursing, teaching, the many workers on minimum wage and so on – if we have no national economic growth, where will the money come from to increase the pay of those workers?

SOLUTIONS TO GLOBAL ISSUES

In recent years, irrational and anti-scientific claims have begun to take hold on a number of global topics. The proposed solutions to these claimed problems are mostly for the western world to denude itself of its power and wealth, embracing impoverishing approaches that are supposed to solve (but won't) these alleged problems.[14]

Without growth, the vast proportion of the world's population that lives in developing countries will remain impoverished and brutalised. As our economy grows, so we help these other economies grow by not imposing anti-growth policies on them, by trading with them and by developing technologies that will go on to be adopted there, propelling their countries out of poverty. As their economies grow, billions of citizens of the world will be – are being, have been – lifted out of poverty. In a study by Palumbo and Iacono titled *In Defense of Classical Liberalism*, that I will reference numerous times in this book, they refer to a World Bank study that showed, across 118 countries over four decades, that three quarters of the income gains accruing to the bottom 40 per cent of income earners were a result of economic growth.[15] They cite other studies including one by the National Bureau of Economic Research, which showed that global poverty had dropped by 80 per cent over thirty-six years, with poverty rates and GDP per capita behaving as inverse mirror images of one another.

Without growth, the technologies we need – for example, anti-plastic, anti-runoff, more productive farming – will not be developed to fight the ecocide of plastic in oceans, coral reefs destroyed by runoffs, disappearing rainforests.

Without growth, developed countries will be unable to defend the world against ever-more-powerful tyrannies – Russia, China and others – that torment their own citizens and brutalise those of other countries, all the while expanding their reach over the world.

Without growth, we will not be able to develop long-term solutions to any (real or asserted) need to decarbonise the world; current approaches are not only dubious, ruinously expensive and unproven but are leading to the shutting down of the UK's industrial base, thus impoverishing us and handing that part of the economy over to other countries such as China – whose energy sources are dirtier than ours, so that even apart from the impoverishment we are causing to ourselves, the net effect on the world's environment is to pollute it more, not less.

In short, economic growth is morally essential if we are to create a fairer, more effective future, one where the west's vision for humanity wins out.

CHAPTER 4

GROWTH IS ESSENTIAL BECAUSE THE ELECTORATE DEMANDS THAT THE STATE DO EVER MORE

———

Wagner's Law, described earlier, means a democratic government that can't provide healthy, regular new doses of more 'free stuff' will, in normal times, quickly be thrown out at the next general election. Middle-class dreamers, mostly well provided with material goods, can advocate luxury policies that cut off the rest of society from future increases in social benefit; or can look with complacency at a future 'net-zero' economy where, for example, air travel for all but the rich is banned, where government mandates determine what goods can or should be produced and purchased, where opportunity is shrunk. Those who promote such policies do so because they don't imagine the policies will apply to them; individuals advocating that society should immiserate itself rarely divest themselves of their own comforts. Governments that go along with an immiserating approach, however, will, assuming democracy survives – and as appears to have happened in the 2023 Uxbridge by-election, where the Conservative candidate narrowly won due to the anti-ULEZ protest vote – be indignantly voted out by the rest of the electorate once (but only once) they realise what the dire impact will be or has been.

As has been frequently observed, the problem with this is – as with, for example, Boris Johnson's acceleration of some net zero targets to 2030 – the politician in question is often long gone from the political scene by the time the policy's impact starts hitting the average person. Governments usually understand that they will be punished if they impose draconian restrictions during their own term of office. Most anti-growth laws are therefore due to come into effect some time into the future, when the politicians who initiated them have left the arena. In the present, they focus on making economic goodies – both financial and material – more freely available.* The problem that results from this is that democratic governments in low-growth economies have to offer short-term and often unaffordable consumption benefits at the expense of long-term investment. The result can be encapsulated in a single sentence: 'With universal suffrage, it becomes impossibly expensive to bribe the entire electorate.' Only with decent economic growth can the imperatives of Wagner's Law be fulfilled without running out of money.

In short, economic growth is practically necessary if the ever-expanding benefits that the electorate demands from government are to be provided. Governments that, whether inadvertently or not, go against that imperative and introduce anti-growth policies do so by destroying the future, not the current economy.

---

*   They also sign interlocking binding global treaties that make it nigh-on impossible for future governments to resile from the immiserating policies. One such example is the UN Paris Agreement.

CHAPTER 5

WITHOUT GROWTH, DEVELOPED COUNTRIES MUST EVENTUALLY GO BUST

If, due to Wagner's Law, government expenditure as a percentage of GDP is increasing, government tax policy has to trend inexorably to higher and higher levels (when expressed as a percentage of GDP), in an (almost always vain) effort to raise enough revenue to pay for its ever-rising expenditures. Chart 1.20 shows tax versus expenditure for different OECD governments in different countries over the past thirty-four years. Had those governments been able to raise, on average, enough tax revenues to pay for 100 per cent of their country's (increasing) expenditure, the dots would straddle the dotted black 45° line, where tax revenues equal expenditure. As can be seen from the chart, however, most of the dots are *below* the 45° line. As government spending as a percentage of GDP gets larger, the dots (averaging around the red regression line) fall further and further below the dotted line because these governments, as they spend more, fail to raise the needed amount of tax revenue. The higher the government expenditure as a percentage of GDP, the more impossible it is for it to raise enough tax. Countries whose governments spend no more than 20 per cent of GDP do, as we can see from the chart, raise more tax revenue than they spend.

Chart 1.20: Tax Versus Size of Government

Government revenue versus expenditure as a percentage of GDP in advanced economies 1990–2023

The more a government spends, the less it is able to finance the spend through tax.

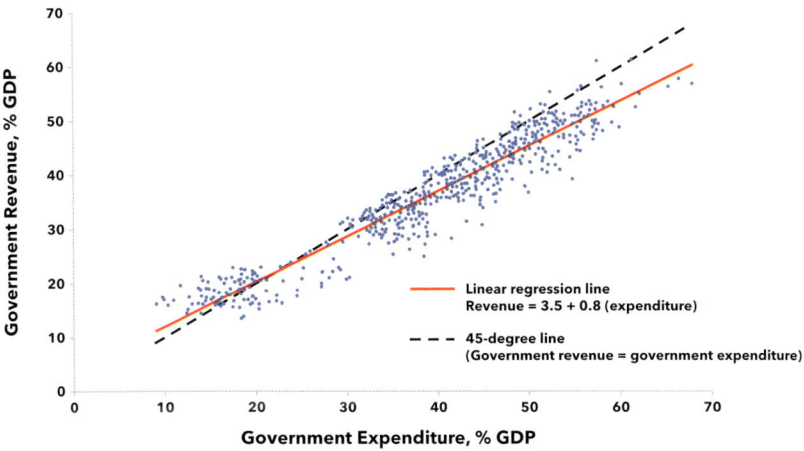

Note: *Advanced economies are defined by the IMF classification. For social democracies, a popu-lation over 10 million and an expenditure ratio over 40 per cent in 2019. For hybrid economies, population over 5 million, expenditure ratio between 35 and 40 per cent in 2019. For free-market economies, population over 10 million, expenditure ratio below 35 per cent in 2019*
Source: International Monetary Fund[1]

As can be seen from Chart 1.20, high-spending governments quite rarely raised sufficient tax revenue between 1990 and 2023 to fund their expenditure. Some high-spending governments, as the chart shows, have in some years been spending up to 25 per cent more than they were raising in taxes, in spite of their high tax rates. Such countries, if they continue on that path, will necessarily soon find it difficult to avoid going bust and/or going through a monumen-tal national debt restructuring. The regression line shows that a country with a government sized at 50 per cent of GDP raises on average revenues that are only around 45 per cent of GDP – leaving 10 per cent of their expenditure unfunded, except by adding to the national debt. This is the *average* of such countries; many are in a far worse position. A persistent 10 per cent funding deficit will inevitably pose a significant problem for a country in the medium term – or even, for some, and not too far from now, the short term. This concern is frequently expressed about such countries as France, Italy and Spain; the same concern for the UK was said to be behind volatility in the gilt markets in 2022. Greece, miraculously, seems to be working its way out of its high-spending past, as can be seen in Chart 1.21.

Looking again at Chart 1.20, developed countries with smaller levels of government spending as a percentage of GDP (often referred to as free-market economies) are not in such trouble. For example, those spending at a rate of 35 per cent of GDP raise taxes on average at 33 per cent* – a deficit of less than 6 per cent of expenditure, rather than 10 per cent. This is a gap that over time is easier to bridge. Free-market countries with small-sized government find it easier to balance their budgets: for those with even smaller governments, sized at say 20 per cent of GDP, their tax levels too are just about at the 20 per cent level (on the dotted black line). When that is so, budgets are in balance, and there are few borrowing or inflationary pressures.

Note that having small-sized government expenditure as a percentage of GDP does not inexorably mean that government services are too small. Whether or not that is so depends on the size of the economy per capita, as well as on the efficiency and effectiveness of how the government is organised. That is why economic growth is key; if an economy can grow large enough, then only a

---

* That's an average – some low-spending countries run persistent surpluses.

small percentage of GDP needs to be confiscated in taxes to pay for needed services. Later in this book, we look at examples of that.

For countries with growing levels of indebtedness, the cost of borrowing goes up over time unless the interest rates fall. However, the age of 'financial repression', with its artificially depressed rates of interest, seems for now to have come to an end. As a result, as old debt is paid off by issuing new debt, the overall cost of debt service rises. When inflation increases, the effect is more pronounced for countries with a higher proportion of index-linked bonds, such as the UK, whose stock of index-linked bonds is the highest in the G7 countries and accounts for about a quarter of the national debt portfolio. The repercussions of this are explored in more depth in Parts II and III of Volumes One and Two of this book.

In any event, for any country, as the size of its debt rises, the cost of servicing its ever-larger debt rises as soon as interest rates don't decline. The UK is now, gradually but seemingly inexorably, being swallowed up bit by bit by its debt monster. Chart 1.21 shows the proportion of government revenues consumed by debt servicing for leading countries, including the UK, for 2010 and 2022. The UK's position has deteriorated considerably, with the short- to medium-term prospect being for that deteriorated position to get even worse. As can be seen in Chart 1.21, the UK, which had a relatively sustainable level of debt service costs in 2010 (note, post the financial crisis), is now the most indebted (in terms of cost of debt as a proportion of government revenue) country in this group. That is a combination of reckless expenditure, leading to large deficits and a greater pile of national debt, and an excessive amount of index-linked bonds (which at the time appeared wonderfully cheap but became chickens coming home to roost).

Chart 1.21: Percentage of Government Revenue Needed to Be Set Aside to Service National Debt, 2010 Versus 2022

Countries such as the UK and the US have been on such a borrowing binge that their debt-servicing costs have, for now, risen into the 'red zone'.

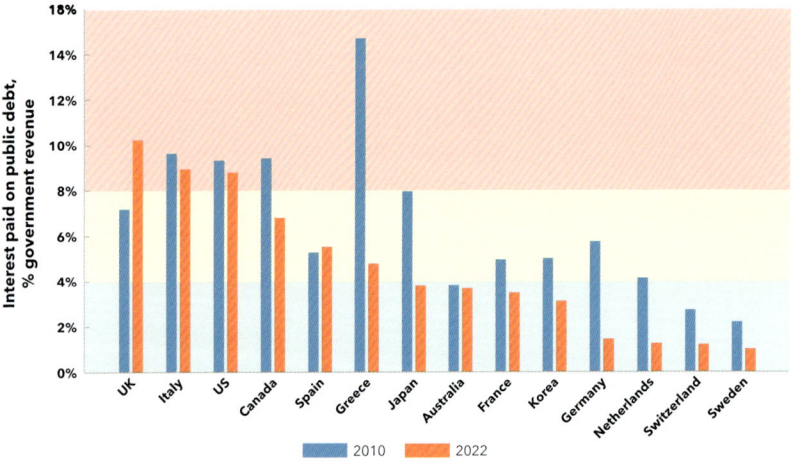

Source: International Monetary Fund,² moyniteam analysis

As Chart 1.20 showed, in most cases the bigger the size of government, the bigger the deficit. As discussed earlier in the book, we refer to countries with small-sized governments as free-market economies and those with large-sized governments as social democratic economies. Those countries that were originally in the free-market category but in obedience to Wagner's Law are expanding the size of their governments to above free-market levels we call hybrid economies; these incur substantial deficits when they spend beyond their means. Chart 1.22 depicts the general situation in the OECD for 2019 (i.e. before those distortions created by Covid-19). The chart shows that even in 2019, the UK was running high deficits and the US was even worse than the UK. It is probably right to see both the UK and the US as countries where recent governments (with leaders such as Obama and Biden in the US and Blair, Brown, Cameron, May, Johnson and Sunak in the UK) have been making efforts to transition themselves from free-market economies to social democratic economies – but without as yet having imposed social democratic levels of taxation.

Chart I.22: Tax Versus Size of Government 2019

By 2019, the UK and the US were already transitioning themselves away from the free-market paradigm.

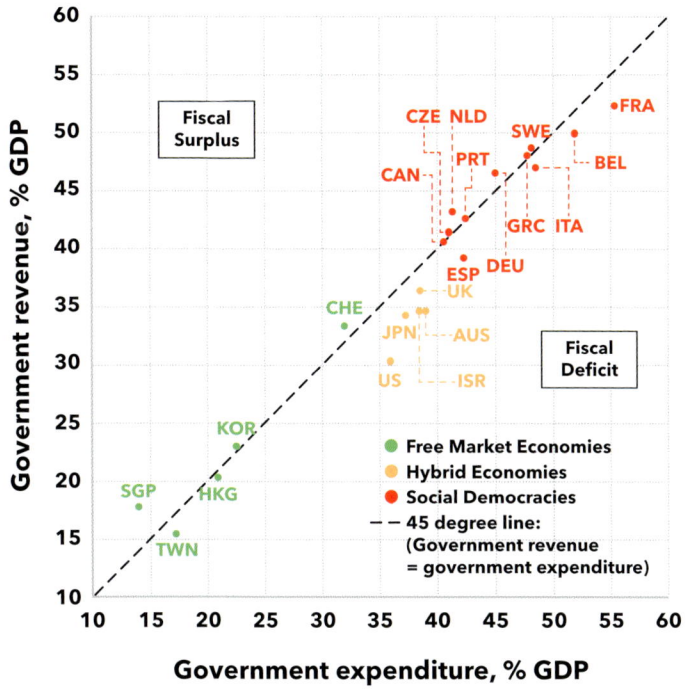

Source: *International Monetary Fund*[3]

Chart I.22 seems to be saying that there is a successful model of how to run a free-market economy (those countries in green), with low taxes and low government expenditure. As we know, those countries have high economic growth and as we can see from the chart, most have either balanced budgets or run surpluses rather than deficits.*

At the top end of Chart 1.22, however, social democracies, with high levels of government expenditure, also have high tax revenues but more often than not, these revenues are so low that a deficit occurs (the few exceptions being mostly Nordic or northern European economies).

Chart 1.23: The Battle of Ideas Between Social Democracies and Free-Market Economies 2023

The UK has barely grown since 2016. Will its high-expenditure experiment play out well?

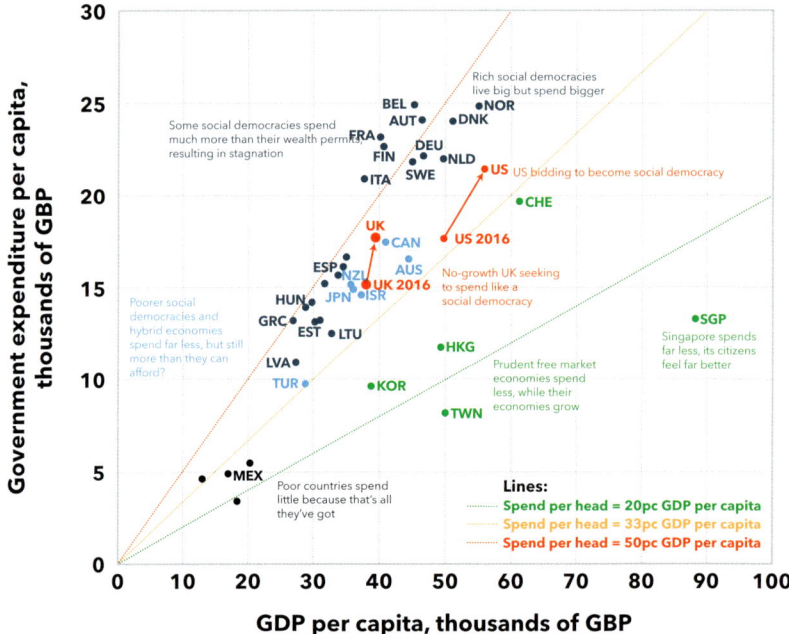

Source: International Monetary Fund, World Economic Outlook (April 2024)[4] and Fiscal Monitor (April 2024)[5]

---

* As we will see later in the book, these countries are also successful at providing for their citizens.

How much can a government spend on its citizens? Clearly, the richer the economy, the more it can spend. As can be seen in Chart 1.23, the social democratic countries currently spend up to 50 per cent of GDP per capita, a rate well above what most countries can collect in taxes. Most countries spend above 33 per cent of GDP, a level that would need more than one third of GDP to be confiscated in taxes, so have difficulty in growing. The faster growing free-market economies tend to spend much less than that.

The higher the spend, the greater the likelihood of a deficit because it becomes harder and harder to raise the taxes to finance that spend. As we will see in a later section, each country mostly seems to have an obstinately fixed level of taxes to GDP that they are able to raise; most countries seem to have difficulty in extracting more tax revenue as a percentage of GDP than the particular fixed longstanding level that each one individually has. We explore that later in Part II Chapter 7. The UK is attempting to become more like the social democracies in its level of spending: how will that work out? Will it be able to raise much more tax as a percentage of GDP than it currently does?

In the middle, we have the hybrid economies; all of those shown are in deficit, probably because they are attempting to provide social democracy-style benefits, yet to date have only succeeded in raising much lower tax revenues.

During Covid, some countries restrained themselves from overexuberant spending; others did not. As Chart 1.24 shows, the UK was, unfortunately, one of the worst offenders in terms of overexuberant spending, in particular because its furlough payments, at 80 per cent of wages, were higher than those of other countries and because those payments and a number of other stimulus measures went on for eighteen months, rather than the few months that were all the UK could truly afford. In addition, business incentive schemes such as 'Eat Out to Help Out' and the like added even more to the deficit.

Chart 1.24: Covid Continence Versus Incontinence

Using admittedly subjective judgement in labelling differing levels of Covid spend, it is nevertheless clear that some countries went massively overboard in the size and length of handouts during Covid.

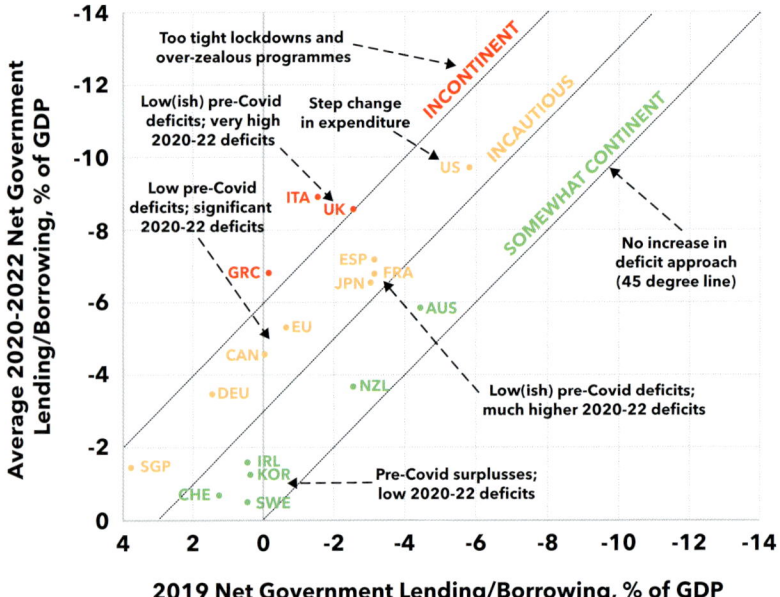

Source: International Monetary Fund[6]

As a result of its high Covid-era spend, the UK, already running a high annual deficit, increased that deficit considerably during the Covid years. And because of much larger money creation during that period, we have seen a higher and more persistent level of inflation than other countries (see Volume Two for detail).

Chart I.25: Government Deficit as a Percentage of GDP, March 2024

The high level of spend that started in the Covid era is now apparently firmly embedded in both the UK and the US; they are now having to borrow more each year than even the social democracies.

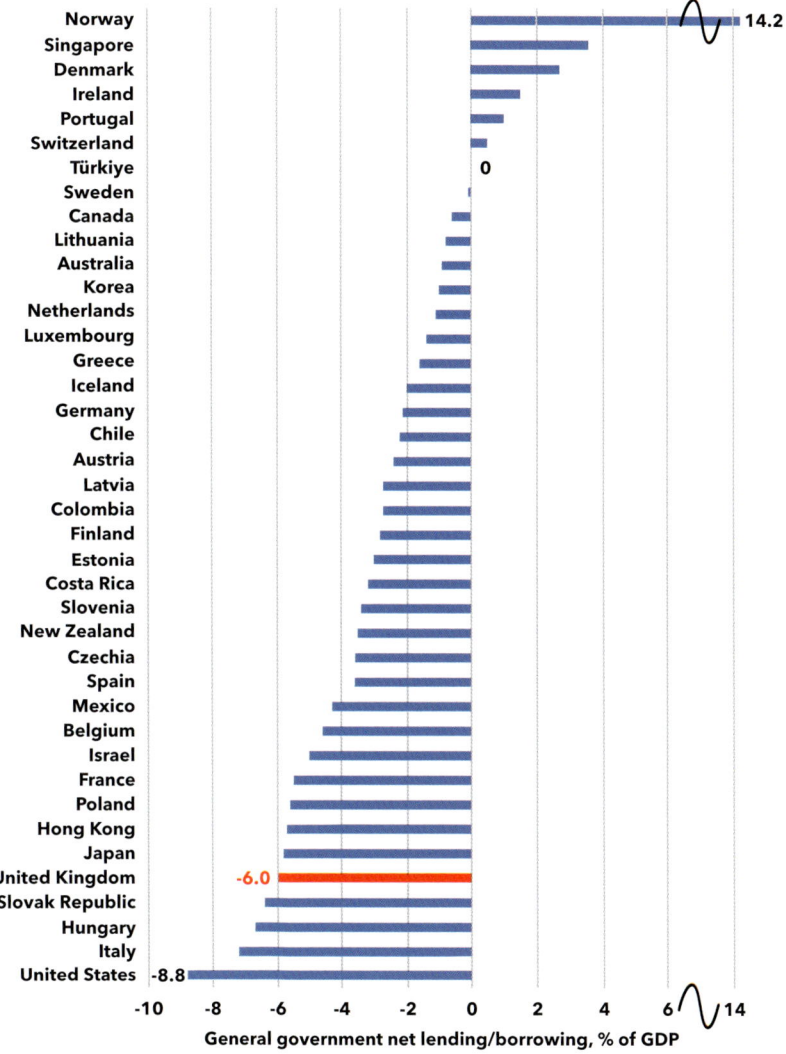

Source: International Monetary Fund, World Economic Outlook (April 2024)[7]

So, from its already poor but not disastrous 2019 position, as shown in Chart 1.24, the UK went on to overspend by significant amounts in the years 2020–22, the initial excuse being to cope with the Covid-19 crisis – with the energy crisis replacing that as a further reason to run a very large deficit. These emergencies are, at any rate, now over; yet the size of government expenditure in the UK has not been brought back to its pre-pandemic size. The UK's level of expenditure is now some 15 per cent higher than pre-Covid; tax take, already much less than expenditure, has failed to keep pace. In 2023, the high level of expenditure did not shrink. Post-2023, despite various vows made by the Conservative government in the run-up to the election, expenditure is forecast to continue to grow.[8] In a stroke, Britain's economy has been transformed, from being a country at the high end of what a free-market government spends, into the centre of the spending levels seen in western European social democracies.

The US, under President Biden, has followed suit. As Chart 1.25 shows, the US and the UK, along with Japan, now have the worst deficits.

Large governments contain the seeds of their own downfall as their deficits rise increasingly over time. As Margaret Thatcher famously put it, 'Sooner or later, you run out of other people's money.'

In recent years, as Chart 1.26 shows, total government debt as a percentage of GDP has ballooned for most social democratic countries and for the US and the UK, whose recent levels of expenditure, as discussed, will, if they remain at current levels, put them at the same level as the social democracies. The problematic outcome for the US and the UK is threefold: national debt is increasing disastrously; GDP (for the UK, anyway) is hardly increasing at all; and taxes are way below what they need to be to pay for this higher rate of expenditure.

Chart I.26: General Government Debt as a Percentage of GDP
Advanced social democracies and hybrid economies, 2000 versus 2023

In the past two decades, most social democracies have increased their level of national debt by enormous amounts. This trend is not something that can go on for ever.

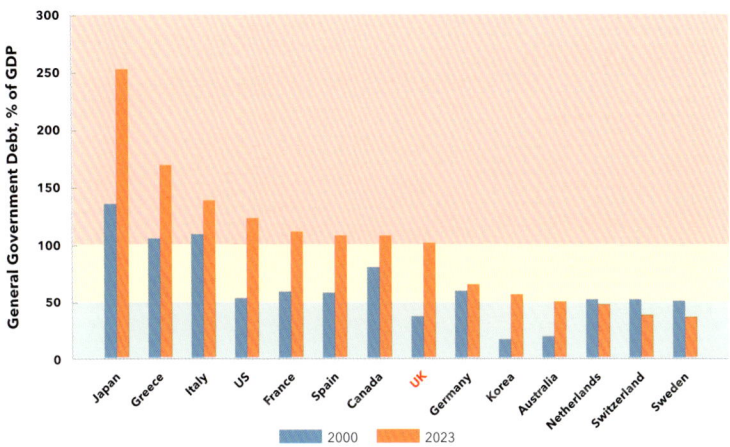

Source: International Monetary Fund[9]

In the UK, as in other western countries, the debt and deficit situation is *much worse* than the reported figures. Bad as the reported situation is, both future trends and unreported liabilities make the true situation far worse.

Future trends mean that deficits are due to get even larger as various fiscal chickens come home to roost. Our ageing population means more pensioners and less tax to support them. The public-sector pension schemes, mostly (as we discuss in Part II Chapter 6) unfunded Ponzi schemes, are just reaching the crossover stage, fatal to all Ponzi schemes, where annual outgoings (actual pension payments) start exceeding annual incomings (pension contributions by employees supposed to fund future obligations but in fact paying for past obligations to now-retired civil servants). The legislation offering lifetime disability payments such as Personal Independence Payments

(PIPs) or Disability Living Allowance (DLA) to an ever-larger pool of claimants – especially those certified as having mental health problems – has led to ballooning payments already, which are forecast to grow by some £8 billion in the coming years (Chart 1.27).

Chart I.27: Forecasts Compared to Actual Working Age PIP/DLA Expenditure
England and Wales, real terms, 2024/25 prices

The number of individuals claiming disability rises and rises; the forecasts always prove inadequate to the actuality.

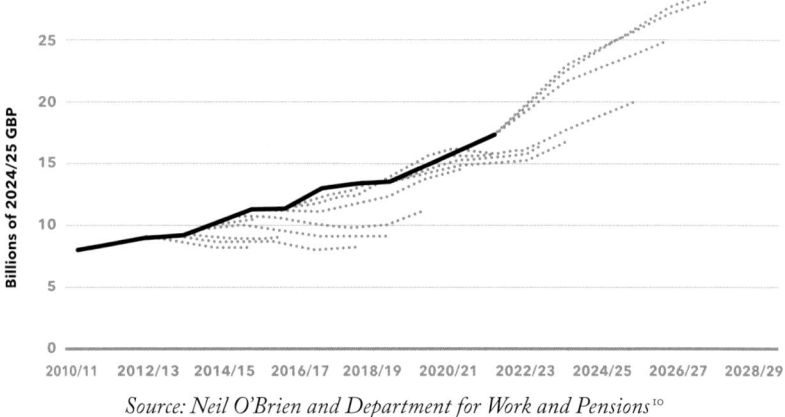

Source: Neil O'Brien and Department for Work and Pensions[10]

Unreported liabilities, on the other hand, mean that the UK's officially reported liabilities are as much a work of fiction as anything else: even a superficial analysis shows that our true liabilities are almost five times as big as what we report (Chart 1.28).

Of particular concern, but of uncertain size, is the extent of our committed, but weirdly unpublished, residual liabilities to the European Union, as part of the disastrous Withdrawal Agreement. Given our continued commitments to fund various EU institutions, what these will end up costing us depends on what happens to the EU, whose future state could involve mild recessions, much worse depressions, internal schisms, bankruptcy of individual states or, in the extreme, a breakup of the union itself.* Much of these financial institutions' holdings consist of junk bonds of zombie EU companies; we still, ludicrously, stand to lose our share when the losses come to be counted.

Chart I.28: Total UK National Debt in 2022–23 Is £11.3 Trillion

A non-comprehensive review of actual unfunded liabilities shows that the UK's true national debt is at least four and a half times the stated number.

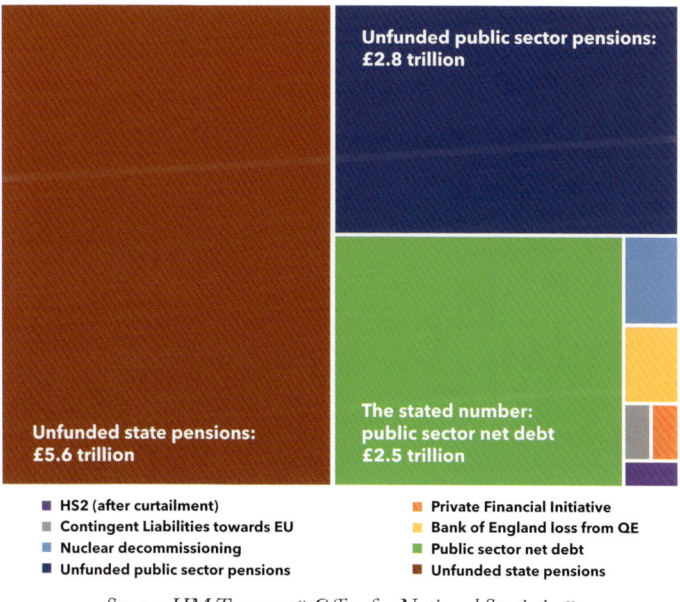

Source: HM Treasury,[11] Office for National Statistics,[12]
Office for Budget Responsibility,[13] moyniteam analysis

---

* For example, the UK is to receive (or maybe has already received – the communications are opaque) the £3.5 billion of its original paid-in capital to the European Investment Bank (EIB). However, and oddly, the agreement replaced that with a guarantee against losses of €39 billion for EIB operations undertaken before January 2020. Losses from operations under InvestEU (the European fund for strategic investments) may have no end date. Again, the OBR has given sparse detail of 'unfunded Article 143 liabilities' amounting to €91 billion. These are just some of the more identifiable obligations under the Withdrawal Agreement, and then there are Copernicus, Horizon, PESCO, Erasmus and on (all involving, inevitably, payments out by us, often for net benefits offered in the programme *by* the UK *for* the EU). One would have thought that a clear report could be produced detailing all these actual and contingent liabilities with their upper and lower bonds, but there hasn't been one.

Even on the reported figures, the future looks bleak.

We have written a simple model (specified in detail in Appendix B) that forecasts what will eventually happen to the UK's GDP growth rates, its primary deficit or surplus and its national debt as a percentage of GDP. (The status quo scenario after fifteen years is shown in Chart 1.29.) The UK, our model predicts, is in line to grow its debt-to-GDP ratio by then to around 150 per cent. It is not clear that, exposed as we are in our borrowing to international debt markets, this ever-worsening position will be sustainable.

Chart 1.29: Forecasted Development of the UK's Economy 2024–39

If we stay much as we are, our annual growth in the long run will be below 1 per cent a year. GDP per capita will grow at an even slower pace and the government debt will inexorably balloon to about 150 per cent of GDP.

STATUS QUO	-1 2023/24	0 2024/25	5 2029/30	10 2034/35	15 2039/40	20 2044/45
KEY INPUTS (ASSUMPTIONS)						
Government Spending as % GDP	44.5%	43.9%	43.8%	44.1%	44.6%	45.1%
Government Receipts as % GDP	40.4%	40.4%	40.4%	40.4%	40.4%	40.4%
Annual Productivity Growth	0.1%	0.1%	0.1%	0.1%	0.1%	0.1%
Gross fixed capital formation as % GDP	18.4%	16.8%	17.2%	17.4%	17.4%	17.4%
Human Capital Index annual growth rate	0.2%	0.2%	0.2%	0.2%	0.2%	0.2%
Total population, million	68.4	69.0	69.6	71.4	73.0	74.6
Working population, million	35.8	36.2	36.5	37.3	37.7	38.0
KEY OUTPUTS (RESULTS)						
GDP Growth	0.2%	0.8%	1.2%	0.9%	0.7%	0.7%
Real GDP, £trillion	2.7	2.8	2.8	2.9	3.0	3.1
GDP per capita	39,963	39,889	40,002	40,603	41,229	41,817
National Debt as % GDP	100%	103%	105%	116%	131%	149%
Budget Deficit, £billion	114	97	96	110	128	149
Budget Deficit as %GDP	4.2%	3.5%	3.4%	3.8%	4.2%	4.8%

Source: moyniteam modelling

The overall output of our model, when we run it on an 'as is' basis, is set out in Chart 1.29. Annual GDP growth for the next fifteen years is 0.8 per cent and GDP *per capita* growth is a tiny 0.34 per cent per year, on average – so GDP per capita is only about 5 per cent higher after a full fifteen years. The budget deficit steadily widens and consequently, government debt rises from about 100 per cent of GDP to a dangerous 150 per cent of GDP, and rising, after that fifteen years.

In our model, we assume that the economy will start to recover after the 2023 recession in line with the central IMF forecast, growing by 0.8 per cent in 2024.[14] The recovery then continues into 2025.

Thereafter, however, the combined weight of large government, high taxes, cumbersome regulations and protectionist trade policies gradually drives the growth rate of the economy down to a corridor of 0.7–0.8 per cent per annum.

Debt-servicing costs in 2023 already amounted to a massive 11 per cent of government revenues.* Although that number is dropping slightly as inflation falls, over the long term it will rise even further as debt mounts and the government refinances expiring debt at higher interest rates. Even if the UK were able to continue as is (at the current 1 per cent real GDP growth rate and the current negative 3 per cent primary balance), within fifteen years our debt-to-GDP ratio would be 150 per cent – a level that would threaten our entire economy. To even reduce the current ratio of debt to GDP down to below 50 per cent (currently 100 per cent) would require better economic growth *and* a primary surplus that was positive or better.[15] Such would require a complete transformation of the economy. (Chart 1.30.)

The UK is not alone in racking up debt; many social democracies are facing the same fate. Debt costs, in combination with

---

* They are set to be lower than 11 per cent if inflation is defeated.

high government expenditures, will lead, if we continue as we are, to financial collapse.

Chart 1.30: General Government Debt as a Percentage of GDP
Advanced social democracies and hybrid economies 2023 (actual) versus 2038 (forecast)

If the current trajectory of public debt persists over the next fifteen years, some countries, including the UK, are steadily heading in the direction of fiscal collapse.

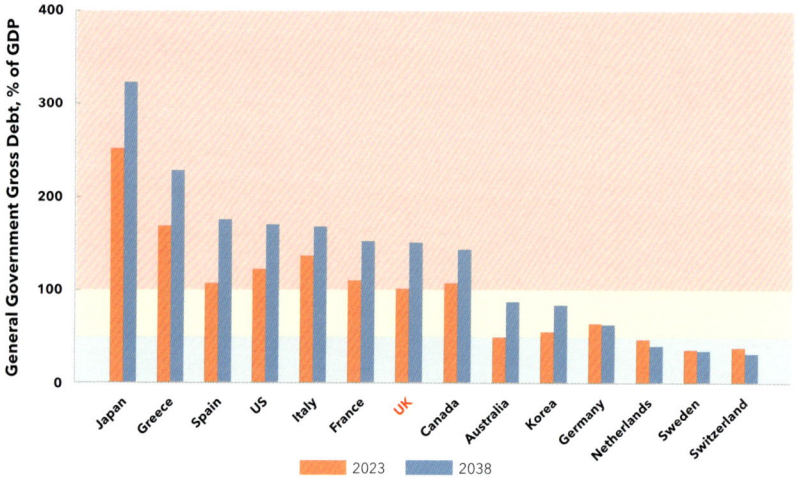

Simplistic assumptions used, based on continuation of current economic situation and practices for each country
Source: International Monetary Fund,[16] moyniteam forecasts

SUMMARY

———

In Part I, I have focused mainly on the impact of growth on the UK's position and, for comparison purposes, on the other advanced economies of the world. The case made for growth in the previous pages does, of course, have even greater relevance for the 70 to 80 per cent of the world that has not reached a 'western' level of wealth and whose citizens therefore do not yet have access to much of the goods and services we do.

I have discussed the moral case for growth – to satisfy human aspiration, avoid the penalties of redistribution and benefit the human race. For politicians in advanced economies, with the low growth we have seen, the issue is whether voters are prepared, first to live with stagnation in jobs and wages (and declining relative global importance, at a time of increasing geopolitical uncertainty); second, to give up aspiration and the potential for an improved standard of living for them and their children; third, to live an increasingly precarious life as we become less and less resilient to changes in the world; fourth, to live with no improvement in government services; and finally, to live in a country too impoverished to rise to the challenge of the world's problems.

In the final chapter, we saw that spending lots of money and increasing the debt pile, far from providing a long-term solution, instead threatens our future further. The issue is whether our politicians and electorate understand this point. In our current approach to our economy, we are implicitly agreeing to embrace a low-growth, wage-reducing, job-loss model that is not going to end well. If we don't understand that, or don't agree to it, then the national discourse needs to change rapidly, so that we can all understand this and decide how to do something about it.

> The UK's low growth risks eventual bankruptcy. Improving our level of growth is not just morally and practically essential but imperative.

Low, no or negative growth?

In the following chapters, where we explain our methodologies and review our evidence, we show that the key drivers that propel growth in a modern economy indicate future economic growth rates for the UK of less than 1 per cent per annum (and, correspondingly, growth even lower than that on a per capita basis). This is the base case shown in Chart 1.29.

This is not by any means the worst-case scenario. As the following chapters show, recent years have seen an unprecedented attack, whether by Labour or Conservative governments, on the growth-generating parts of the economy. Investors, entrepreneurs, non-doms, North Sea oil companies, pharmaceutical companies, and manufacturing companies of all kinds are investing less and less in, and a large number are leaving, the UK. It is not impossible that we are about to enter an era whereby the UK economy actually shrinks every year, potentially entering a negative downward spiral – higher taxes, more money printing, more state support of failing enterprises, further negative growth – with an unforeseeable terminus.

PART II

THREE KEY PRO-GROWTH POLICIES

———

SMALL GOVERNMENT, LOW TAXES, MINIMAL REGULATION

ECONOMIC GROWTH IN THE UK IS NOW BLOCKED BY A SOCIAL DEMOCRATIC APPROACH TO THE ECONOMY

————

In this modern era, a useful albeit rough categorisation of economies around the world is to divide countries into four types of economy:

1. The extractive economy: as characterised by Acemoglu and Robinson, with resources and wealth controlled by and channelled to elite groups.[1] Tyranny, gangsterism and corruption prevail. Russia, Venezuela, North Korea, Myanmar, Zimbabwe and numerous other African states are examples. *Such economies, unless bolstered by natural resources, tend to run at around zero, or often sharply negative, growth per annum.*

2. The dictatorial, quasi-free-market economy: these have adapted some of the features of true capitalist economies, but they are governed in an authoritarian, repressive manner. Examples range from Pinochet's Chile (which eventually returned to a democratic path) to China (whose government becomes more repressive by the day). *At the expense of freedom and civil liberties, growth rates in such economies can, at least for a while, be high.* Over time, however, the lack of freedom stultifies innovative growth.

3. The democratic free-market (small-state) economy: with salient features such as a smaller government, lower taxes, less state intervention and a smaller welfare state. *Such economies have high growth rates of 2 per cent, 3 per cent, 4 per cent, or even much higher, per annum.* Corruption is less frequent because there is more financial incentive to grow a business in the private sector and a smaller size of government pie to seek to extract 'rent' from.[2]

4. The social democracy: these typically have big government, high taxes and a big welfare state. These are fundamentally democratic but are, in practice and often to a considerable degree, controlled by disparate extractive groups such as political elites, bankers, senior (retiree) voters, large corporations, semi-monopolistic state enterprises, and civil servants. The European Union is the most prominent example globally. *Such economies have averaged, in recent decades, growth rates of, at best, 1 to 2 per cent per annum.*

Some countries, as I discussed towards the end of Part I, occupy a hybrid or transition ground between categories three and four. (Note that the indicative growth rates mentioned here, for each category, are for overall growth of GDP. Real growth *per capita* is often significantly less.)

Deciding which category any given country should be potted into is often tricky; all countries and their economies change over time. In this book, I mostly focus on free-market countries and social democracies (types three and four). A notable difference between the two categories is the size of government as a share of the economy, i.e. the ratio of government expenditure to GDP in 2019.[*] The US government, for example, has increased its expenditure from around 34 per cent of GDP

---

[*] I thereby bypass the impact of dramatic increases in public spending and sharp economic contractions in the advanced economies during the Covid-19 pandemic.

at the end of the twentieth century to 38 per cent this year.[*] Worse than the US, the UK's level of public spending rose in that same twenty-year period from some 35 per cent of GDP to some 45 per cent now.[†] I have categorised those economies with a pre-pandemic government size of less than 35 per cent of the economy as belonging to the free-market category; those with a size exceeding 40 per cent as social democratic economies. Economies falling between these thresholds, I designate as 'hybrid' or 'transition'. Chart 2.1 illustrates the economic growth outcomes for certain of these three types of economy and throws in examples of a couple of extractive economies. Free-market economies can provide higher growth rates and, as a result, better living standards for their citizens than major hybrid economies or social democracies – and, of course, far better than for the extractive economies.

Chart 2.1: GDP Per Capita Over Time
Shown by type of economic model

Free-market economies produce a better standard of living for their citizens.

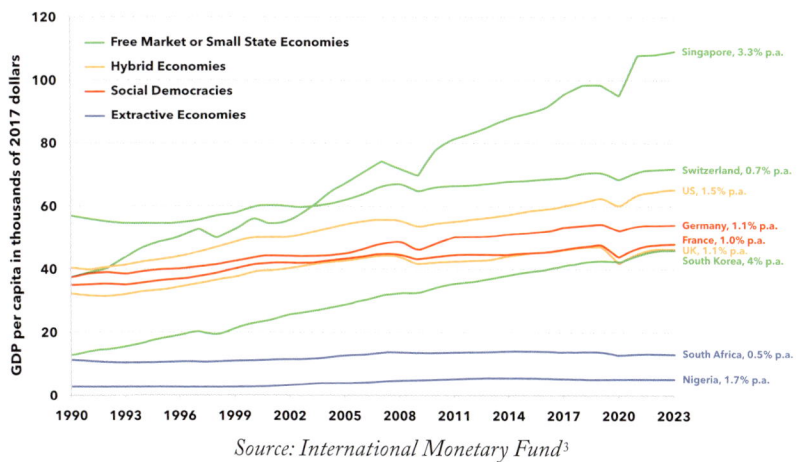

Source: International Monetary Fund[3]

69

In the UK, an intense political debate has been ongoing regarding the role of government in the economy. The argument essentially boils down to which of the two economic models (social democratic or free market) the UK should pursue:

- Advocates of the social democratic model assert that there is no alternative to the UK running a large-government, social-democrat state. Economists who believe that high rates of growth are only possible for 'catch-up' economies (poorer countries that can take advantage of richer countries' technological breakthroughs) argue that high economic growth is no long achievable for us.[4] They believe that the UK will not grow any faster if it has a smaller government and that we should not unleash allegedly dangerous market ('capitalist') forces by undertaking any attempt to seek higher growth.[*]

- Advocates of a free-market, small-government economy assert that the only possible way to escape the anaemic growth trap of redistributive, big-government social democracies is to free the country's private sector from the dead hand and high cost of large-state bureaucracy, which protects large businesses from competition and consumers from competitive prices. The significant increments to national wealth that will result from a faster-growing economy are, in fact, these advocates claim, the only route to being able to afford the ever-increasing demands of the electorate for social support.

As is no doubt obvious, I – both intuitively and on the evidence (as shown in Chart 2.1 and discussed later) – side with the free-market,

---

[*] Risible claims by the new Labour government that their 'Green Prosperity Plan' will create discernible economic growth can be safely disregarded.

small-government advocates. In the current era, countries such as South Korea, Singapore and Switzerland not only enjoy high rates of economic growth but also attain significantly and increasingly higher standards of living – in GDP per head, wages, literacy, health outcomes – than almost all 'advanced' social democratic countries. There is also the increasing gap between the general standard of living in the US versus that of the UK – the US economy could, at least pre-Covid, be characterised as maybe one third social de-mocracy, two thirds free market, the UK as one third free market and two thirds social democracy. The US is pulling away at a steady pace economically from both the UK and the European Union (the standard bearer of social democracy). Social democracies, focusing (as they have to) on redistributive measures within the context of a static or low-growth economy, fail to deliver the many superior benefits that citizens of free-market economies increasingly enjoy, such as better life expectancy (see Chart 2.2) and significantly higher wealth.

Calling for an efficient small-state approach in the UK faces the difficulty of persuading our polity – and in particular its extractive groups, such as the large public sector, major multinationals, state monopolies etc. – to acknowledge the potential benefits that could accrue for the UK were it able to break out of its increasingly low-growth, big-government mode.

· · ·

Beyond the UK-specific argument, there is a wider point. All the low-growth, big-government countries – and the UK, as it increas-ingly adopts the social democratic model – are facing a major issue: will their electorates accept a future in which well-paid jobs are increasingly scarce, real wages are not going up and the quality of public services deteriorates, while taxes continue to rise? Or, for all these countries but especially for the UK, can the case for the free-market economy be more effectively made and actually put into practice, to everyone's benefit?

Chart 2.2: Life Expectancy at Birth

Free-market economies have leapfrogged social democracies in producing better life expectancy for their citizens

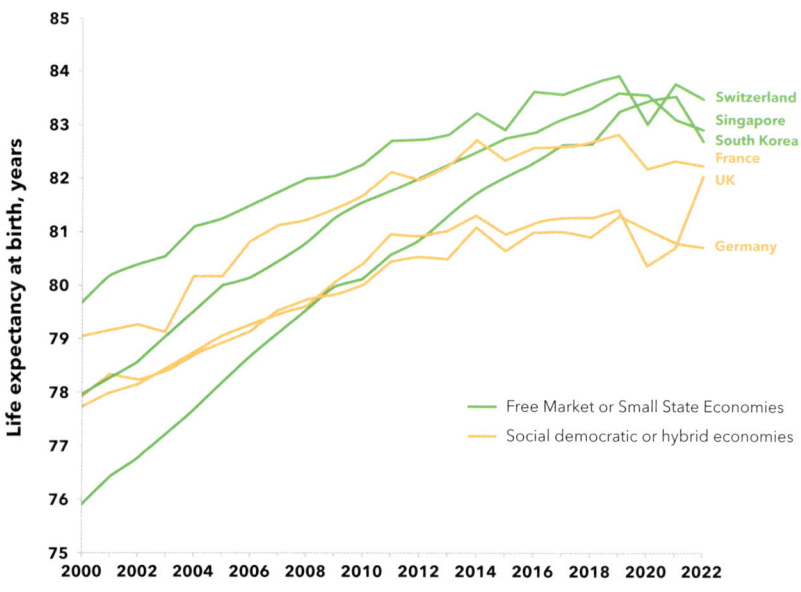

Note: Dips 2020–21 due to the Covid pandemic
Source: World Bank[5]

---

* The US has been omitted due to data discrepancy. Almost all countries apart from the US don't count 'stillborn' deaths (those within twenty-four hours of birth) in their child mortality statistics. This (and high murder rates and high levels of opioid deaths) skews the overall mortality statistics for the US.

An article in the *Sunday Telegraph* on 23 April 2023, also discussed in Part I, highlighted how decisively Britain is being outpaced in economic competition with the US.[6] Combined with much more affordable housing and lower taxes, higher wages often influence citizens' choices to leave the UK and move to the US or elsewhere.

The article also noted that the UK's GDP per capita has been consistently lower than in the US since 1880 (except during the relatively short period of the Great Depression in the 1930s). We now see, in 2023, a 67 per cent higher GDP per capita in purchasing power parity (PPP) terms in the US than in the UK.[7]

This news was old hat; what was new was the focus of a major newspaper in reporting on it. Since the article, the point was, during 2023, taken up by many commentators.

The article, well researched and documented, didn't go too much into *why* the US was so much richer, although differences in regulation were mentioned, as was the current parlous state of the London Stock Exchange (discussed later). Hopeful remarks were made by the author of the *Telegraph* piece, and by the then shadow Chancellor of the Exchequer, Rachel Reeves, along the lines of how Britain could develop a 'national strategy' to subsidise companies in chosen areas, such as the green economy, and that this would create long-term economic growth. But elsewhere, the *Financial Times*, pleasingly sagacious in this case, poured cold water on the 'green jobs' trope: 'There is an iron law of politics in the age of climate change: every time you discuss your plans to reach net zero you must also mention jobs, preferably an impressive sounding number of them, ideally with terms like "well-paid", "blue-collar" or "heart-lands" attached.'[8]

The *FT* quoted Anna Valero, a senior policy fellow at the London School of Economics, saying that however you define 'green jobs', there is no sign of large growth in them. An agency, Nesta, that analyses internet job adverts, is reported as saying the same, as does a report by the usually relatively 'progressive' think tank, the Resolution Foundation.[9] The report asserts that so far there has been 'little change in the relative size of green and brown occupations over the past decade' and the 'small net growth' in green jobs to date, driven by higher-paid rates for energy, had been largely in roles such as marketing and sales directors.

This claim that 'green jobs' (a term without any coherent definition)[10] will provide the country's future needed growth, seems unsubstantiated and has been generally discredited.[11]

Chart 2.3: Average Salary by Country*
Using purchasing power parity, 2022

Numerous countries now offer their citizens much higher average wages than the UK can. In the US, average salaries are 43 per cent above the UK's.

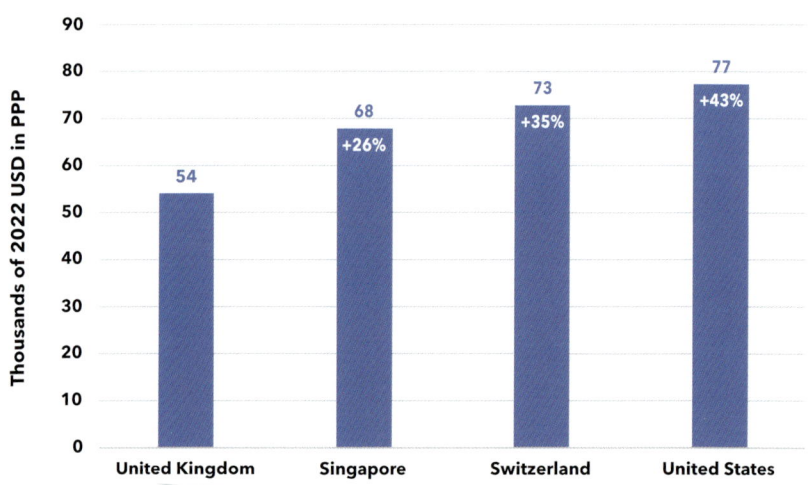

Median salary for Singapore • Source: OECD, Singapore Ministry of Manpower[12]

The *Telegraph* article did not, moreover, discuss whether a 'national strategy' of subsidising chosen industries was likely to be any more successful than previous failed attempts. Peter Mandelson spoke immortal words to the Labour Party Conference in 2009, acknowledging that in the past Labour had thought they were picking winners, but in actuality, the losers were picking them.

How does the ordinary worker fare in free-market economies versus social democracies? The statistics from various sources sometimes contradict each other through different modes of comparison and changes over time, but Chart 2.3 seems reasonably accurate and should be of great import to every Briton.

Singapore, Switzerland and the United States. Statist politicians in the UK often contort themselves to dismiss the success of these countries, implying that living in each of them would apparently involve some vital flaw that we in the UK would never tolerate. Comparing ourselves with those countries is wrong, the politicians say; we don't want to be 'Singapore on Thames' or whatever.

But let's just think about it. In the Legatum Prosperity Index 2023, Singapore (the most derided of this trio) is the *top country* (out of 167 countries) in four out of Legatum's twelve measures, including health and education.[13] (Singapore was, in the often quoted phrase, nothing much more than a 'malaria-infested swamp' not that many decades ago.[14]) The UK is thirty-fourth and fourteenth respectively on those last two measures. Somehow, these countries – Singapore, Switzerland, the US – have, over the past decades, year after year, added that extra bit of economic growth, and therefore economic wealth, that has cumulatively led each of these countries to be, overall and for the average citizen, much, much richer than us, with far better outcomes for the average citizen. As Chart 2.3 shows, average earnings in the UK are about $54,000 per annum, as of 2022. In Singapore, they are $68,000 per annum (26 per cent higher than the UK). In Switzerland, they are $73,000 (35 per cent higher). In the US, they are $77,000 per annum (43 per cent higher). What, exactly, could be so bad about these countries as to put our citizens off from wanting to enjoy the same levels of reward in the UK as the citizens of those countries enjoy? Let the reader consider: what would you do with the extra 43 per cent of wage that you would earn, from doing much the same job, if you lived in the US? Or the extra 26 per cent, if you were in Singapore? Or the extra 35 per cent, if you were in Switzerland?

And it's not as if these countries fall behind the UK in any important areas. South Korea is third best in the world on both health and education and Switzerland is fifth overall. In these countries, children stand better life chances because of their great education and adults get better treatment, have better health outcomes and can expect to live longer than Britons.[15] These free-market countries see their GDP growing at a fast rate and so they can afford better health outcomes and education because their economic growth (combined with healthcare and education systems that are most likely better structured than the NHS and the UK's education setup) give them the extra resources to build such results.

Presumably it's not controversial to say that if those particular countries have been able to grow their economies fast enough in the past couple of decades to achieve that sort of benefit to their citizens, then we in the UK should have been able to do the same and still could do so in coming decades.* Which means that it's perfectly fair to say that compared to those countries, over the past couple of

---

* The difference is both in earnings, and in better, more efficient delivery of public services.

decades we – and for that matter our companion major economies of western Europe, who have seen the same, or worse, slow growth as us – have pursued objectively inept economic policies. Had we done as well as those better-run economies have done, workers in the UK would be earning on average 30 per cent or 40 per cent more than they are earning now. Instead of our GDP being about £2.7 trillion, it could have been over £4 trillion.[16] Instead of government spending being at around £1.2 trillion, we could have had anything up to some £500 billion of extra tax revenues to spend on public services or on tax reductions – an enormous, nation-changing amount.[*]

So, what are the mechanisms that trigger and sustain economic growth? It is, of course, possible for governments to artificially stimulate GDP growth for a year or two, but in general, long-term, sustainable growth comes from:

- new products
- new jobs
- improvements in productivity

These, in turn, initially spring from and only fundamentally from:

- new technology
- product innovation
- entrepreneurial skill and risk-taking
- capital investment

---

[*] To be fair, as we have already posited and will get into the detail of shortly, a prerequisite for a faster-growing economy is to have lower taxes, so probably not as much as that. But clearly, our national finances would be in far better shape.

It is in creating growth in that way that the US has moved to a GDP per capita that is some 67 per cent* higher (in PPP) than the UK's: encouraging such activities and capabilities would allow us to achieve similar growth.[17] Growth will not come from our government 'creating jobs', green or otherwise. We must surely know by now that any claim by a government that it can create real, long-term jobs is a chimaera. All governments can do to help growth is to create the *environment* for new jobs, capital investment and entrepreneurial risk taking. I show in the following pages that the needed structure for such an environment is small government, low taxes, minimal regulation, flourishing scientific academia, incentives to encourage investment (all of which we discuss later), free markets, free trade and prudent financial management.

What kind of annual growth, over what period of time, would be needed to increase the UK's GDP by an enormous, life-changing 50 per cent? The answer is that if we could grow our economy reliably at 3 per cent each year, it would take us just fourteen years to have an economy that is 50 per cent larger than now. At a 4 per cent annual growth? A mere ten years.[†] Such is the power of growth, boosted by the magic of compounding. We are not talking about half a century. The gains are possible in a timeframe that would enable the vast majority of our current workforce to see the benefits of those gains in their working lifetime – and, of course, subsequent generations will benefit even more from such growth.

So why, over recent decades, have we failed to achieve such growth? Others have reliably done it. What is it that other countries have done but that we have failed, or are failing, to do? In view

---

* Figure for 2023.

† Of course, as discussed earlier, the key measure is GDP *per capita*. If our population continues to grow substantially during that hypothesised period, significantly greater growth than these numbers would be required to achieve these results on a per-capita basis.

of the only minimal degree of discussion of the topic in this country and the general cross-party failure in past years (at least until recently) to express concern about or even offer any theories on this point, one would assume that growth theory remains something of a black box and that the preconditions for achieving growth have not been explored. But the contrary is the case: over recent decades, there have been numerous academic studies exploring the drivers of growth, which I take a look at in the following chapters.

The primary conclusions of these studies are relatively straightforward. As just one example, Robert Barro of Harvard University did years of pioneering research, culminating in a series of defining lectures on the crucial importance of, and the apparent sources of, economic growth.[18]

The preconditions for growth that he uncovered are numerous. In Part II, I focus on the three key areas which, from both his work and that of many others, seem most central to creating growth: size of government, level of taxes and degree of regulation. The indicated impact of each of the three chief drivers on economic growth, as demonstrated by many academic analysts, is so large, it seems, that getting just these three right would transform the growth rates of any country that currently is getting them wrong. Other important factors that research has shown also drive growth are also discussed, albeit given less detailed treatment here – to avoid making the book even longer and (if possible) even more boring – but also because, and particularly in the case of the UK, their undoubted important impact on growth is seemingly less important than my three chosen determinants.

To acknowledge the key further preconditions for growth, before I then sideline them, these other factors – important yet subsidiary to the big three of small government, low taxes, light regulation and their ancillaries free markets, free trade and sound money, which I discuss in Volume Two – are:

1. rule of law
2. property rights
3. low corruption
4. suppression of 'extractive' institutions that cream off economic surpluses
5. decent education[*][19]
6. a good science base
7. transportation and infrastructure

In the following three chapters, therefore, I review how if growth is desired, changes to the government's economic approach should, at least in the first place, be focused around these three key factors:

- The larger the government, the smaller the economic growth.
- The higher the level of tax, the smaller the economic growth.
- The greater the amount of regulation, the smaller the economic growth.

---

[*] Out of these seven, the one area that is most crying out for improvement is item five, education, where almost *one in five* children in the UK left education at eighteen in 2019 without basic qualifications. This bottom 20 per cent are entirely unequipped to make their way successfully through the modern world. The topic of education, however, needs a book all to itself, so has to be left to another time (and probably another author).

CHAPTER 6

THE LARGER THE GOVERNMENT, THE SMALLER THE ECONOMIC GROWTH

———

Looking at figures from the past half-century or more, it is not difficult for the observant onlooker to understand that, in recent decades, as the large, westernised countries have grown their public sectors, so has their economic growth plummeted. Recognising this, and as I detail later, a considerable number of economists have studied that relationship and have developed data that points inexorably to the conclusion that as the size of the state increases, so it becomes increasingly impossible to have a fast-growing economy.[*] Surveying the findings of these economists, I begin this chapter by reviewing the finding that:

1. **Excessive government expenditure chokes off economic growth**

However, it's not just how much money a government spends that affects its economic growth; growth will also be impacted by *what* exactly the government spends its taxpayers' money on. Researchers have found that, within the context of smaller-sized government overall being better, some types of government expenditure are associated with positive economic growth and others

---

[*] All findings of econometric studies are bedevilled by the potential for confusion between correlation and causation. Such potential exists in any study that analyses the relationship between size of the state and growth – just as much as for any other econometric study. We explore this, and hopefully largely resolve it, in the following pages – for this, as well as (in subsequent chapters) for taxes and for regulation.

with negative growth. I therefore include in this chapter a further discussion of how:

2. **Spending money on the wrong things shrinks growth even more**

Of course, governments who spend less in a given area than others do yet achieve the same benefits for their citizens as higher-spending governments in that area, will achieve a smaller-sized government and thus, putatively, faster economic growth. I therefore also discuss the *efficiency* with which governments spend our money, in particular focusing on the UK and its ever-expanding civil service, its regulators and quangos, and their ever-decreasing productivity:

3. **Beyond being too large, a further key driver choking off growth is the inefficiency of the public sector overall**

Having done all that, I seek to conclude on what we need to do to reduce our government expenditures, so as to turn to a growth-promoting path in the UK.

EXCESSIVE GOVERNMENT EXPENDITURE CHOKES OFF ECONOMIC GROWTH

As mentioned a few pages back, a notable economist who studied the drivers of economic growth was Robert J. Barro of Harvard University; originally in a series of lectures and then expanded in 1997 into a book *Determinants of Economic Growth: A Cross-Country Empirical Study*.[1] One of Barro's important conclusions was that the larger the government, the smaller the growth and, in particular, his conclusion that the larger was the government's 'unproductive' share of GDP, the even less fast the economy would grow.

We review the issue of 'productive' versus 'unproductive' expenditure later in this chapter (and in Volume Two), but in the meantime, we focus in on the core of Barro's finding.

The estimated impact from size of government was, Barro found, considerable: smaller-sized government, compared with larger-sized, was associated with 1 per cent of additional growth per annum. The earlier discussion showing the enormous effect of compounding highlights that even just 1 per cent additional annual growth over only a decade can have a transformative effect on the wealth of a country and its citizens.

Of course, Barro's finding used data that is now thirty to fifty years old; the world has changed considerably since that 1970–90 period. So let us look at a series of most recent studies that have confirmed, and even much enlarged, Barro's conclusion.

Shortly after the publication of Barro's book, a trio of economists – James Gwartney, Randall Holcombe and Robert Lawson – explored the impact of government size on a country's pace of economic growth in their paper 'The Scope of Government and the Wealth of Nations'. This paper drew upon an earlier study of theirs that they had prepared for the US Congress Joint Economic Committee in 1998.

The key finding of their study, which used a data set of the twenty-three long-term OECD member countries[*] from 1960 to 1996, was that 'there is a persistent robust *negative* relationship between the level (and the expansion) of government expenditures, and the growth of GDP'. In other words, bigger government means smaller growth. They estimated that a 10 per cent expansion of government spending penalised annual economic growth by around 1 percentage point.[†] Given that the countries studied ranged in expenditure

---

[*] Australia, Austria, Belgium, Canada, Denmark, Finland, France, Germany, Greece, Iceland, Ireland, Italy, Japan, Luxembourg, Netherlands, New Zealand, Norway, Portugal, Spain, Sweden, Switzerland, United Kingdom, United States.

[†] They also found a negative relationship between government expenditures and investment rate of the economy: an increase in government expenditures by 10 per cent was associated with slowing of the investment rate by approximately 1.6 percentage points.

from 20 per cent or less of GDP up to 50 per cent, this appeared to be a significant advancement of Barro's result.

As can be seen in Chart 2.4, Gwartney et al.'s study confirmed a difference in annual growth rates, consistent across the board as size of government grew, for small-government versus large-government countries.* The magnitude of impact was considerably greater than Barro's 1 per cent; small-government economies had on average a 2 per cent or even higher additional growth rate than large-government ones. Indeed, countries with governments that only took up 25 per cent or less of the economy grew at an astonishing 5 percentage points faster, year by year, than those that were sized at over 60 per cent of their economy.

Chart 2.4: Size of Government and the Annual Growth of Real GDP for OECD Countries 1960–96

Large government highly correlates with low economic growth.

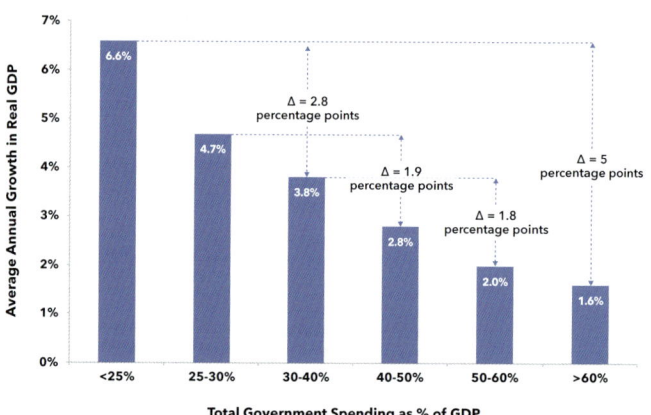

Source: Gwartney et al. 1998[2]

---

* The chart illustrates the association between a government's size measured by its spending relative to GDP and average annual growth in real GDP. Each observation includes the government size for a particular country and its real GDP growth rate in a given year. The total number of observations is 851, spanning a time period of thirty-seven years (1960–1996) and encompassing data from the twenty-three OECD countries.

In 2012, Joseph Connors and Seth Norton, in 'The Scope of Government and the Wealth of Nations Revisited', re-ran Gwartney, Holcombe and Lawson's study using more recent data.[3] Their result was almost identical to Gwartney et al.'s.

As can be seen from Chart 2.4, therefore, while big government is advocated by many as socially desirable,[*] it is associated with relative economic stagnation – and even more so when expressed on a per-capita basis, i.e. where the population is growing. Assuming (for now) causation, not just correlation, then to achieve decent growth, an optimal size of government, according to these results, would be less than 25 per cent of the economy. Gwartney et al. and Connors and Norton confirmed that during the time period up to 2010, even a government sized at 35 per cent of the economy was growing (at that time) on average at nearly 4 per cent per annum, compared with only 1 per cent to 2 per cent for the economies with the largest-sized governments (50 per cent or more of the economy). Barro's findings implied the desirability of keeping government small, yet Connors and Norton's analyses showed that since Barro, OECD governments in general had gone on to make their governments' overall share of the economy ever larger. Events since Connors and Norton have shown governments as acting either ignorant of or paying no attention to the implications of those findings; governments bound up in the electoral implications of Wagner's Law have steadily spent themselves into taking up a larger and larger share of their economies.

Still, Gwartney et al.'s results use data only up to 1996 and Connors and Norton's only up to 2010, so it was important that for this book that I confirm that their findings, as well as those of Barro,

---

[*]   But this is not proven.

still hold up. Using current data for the same twenty-three OECD countries, I have (Chart 2.5) brought the numbers up to date (stopping at 2019 to prevent the disparate economic impacts of Covid-19 policies from distorting the baseline). The results are, again, startlingly clear – and surprisingly close to the results shown earlier in Chart 2.4. All in all, the findings of Gwartney et al. hold up.

This strong evidence supports a conclusion that faster-growing economies are growing faster in large part because they have governments that are much smaller.

Governments are, therefore, well advised to target their level of expenditure to be, at the very least, significantly below 40 per cent of GDP.

Chart 2.5: Size of Government and the Annual Growth of Real GDP for OECD Countries 1960–2019

A government that is sized at 50 per cent or more of the economy can expect anaemic growth and below 30 per cent, very strong growth.

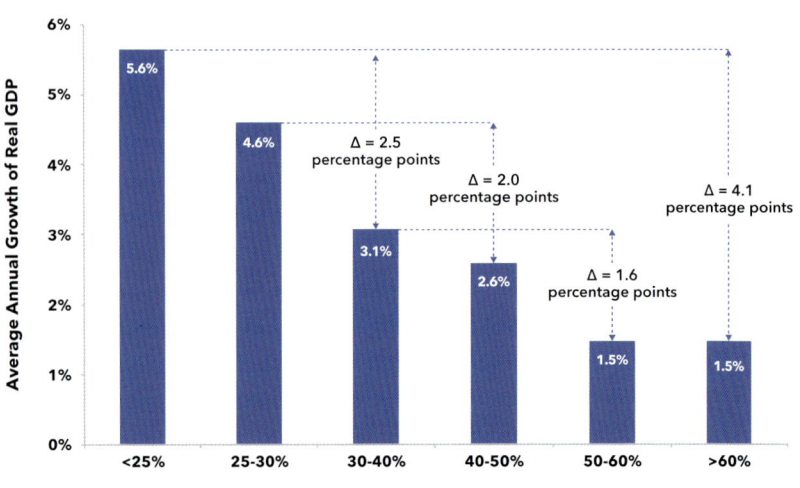

Source: International Monetary Fund, moyniteam analysis [4]

With this new data, as can be seen – and again, for now, assuming causation not just correlation – we arrive at the same conclusion as the original argument from Gwartney et al.: the growth penalty increases substantially with the size of the government. For governments sized at over 50 per cent of GDP, growth on average has been about 1.5 per cent over the period.[*]

Different studies claim that the optimal size of government as a percentage of GDP is 25 per cent or less.[5] Even if you get the size of your government down to between 25 per cent and 30 per cent of your GDP, the data indicates you can hope to grow, all else being equal and assuming a causative not just a correlative relationship, at 4.6 per cent a year.[†] If you can do that for two decades, your country's wealth, and the living standards of your citizens, will be utterly transformed.

If we look at a scatter plot of all these economies in the past three decades, tracking size versus growth (Chart 2.6), then there's a clear trend of more government equating to lower growth. Of course, the data points don't all sit neatly on the regression line – as we would expect, multiple other factors also impact growth. The regression line shown implies that a full 33 per cent of the difference in growth rates is a function of the size of the country's government. Other elements cause the rest of the variation; the chief of these are tax and regulation (the topics of Chapters 7 and 8).

All else being equal, the regression line implies that the impact, when a country's government takes up 50 per cent of the economy instead of 25 per cent, is a reduction in that economy's growth rate

---

[*]   Note that this is total GDP, not GDP per capita. If the population is growing sufficiently fast, GDP per capita for such countries would be flat or even shrinking.

[†]   The studies cited in the endnote claim that the optimal size of government for high growth is 25 per cent or less. In this book, we are not as ambitious: we aim only to get government down to 33 per cent of GDP, the level that existed at the end of the last century under the Major and early Blair governments.

of some 2 percentage points per annum. Having a large government seems (assuming causation, which we cover soon) to wreak enormous damage on the long-term economic outlook. The UK 1960–2010 shows this.

Chart 2.6: The Impact of Size of Government on Long-Term GDP Growth 1960–2019

The larger the government, the slower the growth rate.

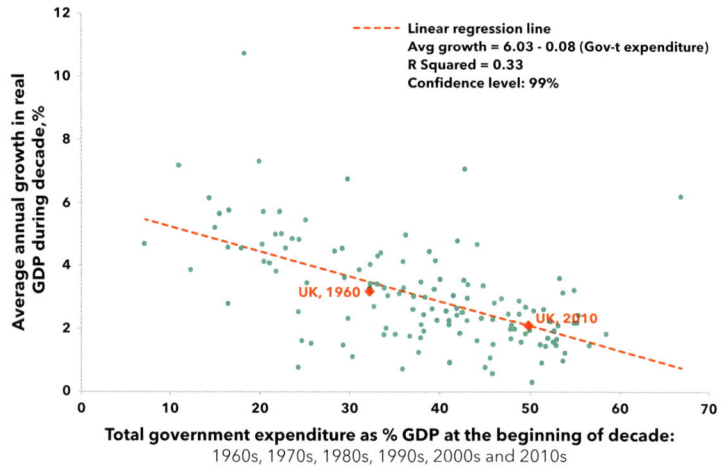

Source: *International Monetary Fund, moyniteam analysis*[6]

Beyond these several studies and confirmed analyses, is there evidence to make us even more sure of the link, and indeed of causation, between small government and economic growth? There is. Matt Palumbo and Corey Iacono, in their excellent *In Defense of Classical Liberalism*, review a number of other studies, all pointing to the same conclusion.[7] They review, for example, the work of two Swedish economists, Andreas Bergh and Magnus Henrekson, who conducted a wide survey of the academic literature on the relationship between government size and economic growth.[8]

The studies Bergh and Henrekson examined had to meet the following criteria:

- published in peer-reviewed journals after 2000
- used panel data
- focused on rich countries (i.e. EU, OECD or equally rich countries)
- measured total government size (i.e. total taxes or total expenditure)
- examined the effect of government size on growth of real GDP per capita

The findings were:

> The most recent studies find a significant negative correlation [between government size and growth]: An increase in government size by 10 percentage points [of GDP] is associated with a 0.5 to 1 per cent lower annual growth rate.

This, Palumbo and Ianoco said, confirmed that countries with smaller governments grow faster. However, Bergh and Henrekson had added an important note: government spending typically increases during economic downturns, so the relationship *could* be partially driven by slow economic growth causing government spending to rise (reverse causality), not the other way around. The left-wing economist Paul Krugman, they said, subscribed to that explanation.[9]

Three of the studies, however, had addressed this issue; all three found that *government size is the driving factor behind the negative relationship*.

The fact that these studies utilised different methods of determining causality and came to the same conclusion led the authors of the study to state, 'The research is rather close to a consensus: the correlation [between government size and economic growth] is negative, and the sign seems not to be an unintended consequence of reverse causality.'

This important final point means the authors had found causation, not just correlation.

Palumbo and Iacono reviewed the work of other economists who have sought to come up with an optimal size of government as a percentage of GDP (taking both societal and growth desiderata under consideration).[10] In particular, they quoted Livio di Matteo:

All other things given, annual per capita GDP growth is maximized at 3.1 per cent at a government expenditure to GDP ratio of 26 per cent; beyond this ratio, economic growth rates decline … Over the course of a decade, an economy with a public sector size of 30 per cent could see its per capital GDP (in US PPP$) grow by over one-third, while an economy with a public sector size of 40 per cent would see smaller per capita GDP gains of only one-fifth.

Palumbo and Ianoco denied that having a small government results in undesirable social outcomes. They quoted research by the Centre for Policy Studies that found countries with small governments (less than 40 per cent of GDP) have similar or better social outcomes than countries with big governments. According to the CPS and the researchers, Ryan Bourne and Thomas Oechsle, small governments have better educational outcomes and higher life expectancies, while big governments have slightly lower infant mortality rates.[11]

Helena Cenc, based at the University of Maribor, has analysed the issue, particularly for euro area countries.[12] She concludes by positing a somewhat startlingly large size of impact: 'Based on the econometrics model applied, the author established that in panel data, government expenditure has a negative impact on economic growth, more precisely, if government spending as a share of GDP increases by 1 per cent, economic growth decreases by 0.509 per cent.'

In her paper, Cenc cites numerous other authors (most not covered in the papers previously reviewed here), most of whom came to a similar conclusion. In view of her findings and the large proportion of GDP that government takes up in most of the large euro area countries, it is not surprising that growth within these countries is so anaemic.

Palumbo and Iacono go further by looking at the size of government versus unemployment. While a superficial thought process might assume that more spending leads to less unemployment, if, however, the extra spending provides a cushioning (that is to say, an economic incentive to remain unemployed) for the unemployed, then the opposite is more likely to be the case. And indeed, that is what the two economists found.

Palumbo and Iacono quote Abrams and Wang's finding of causation between small government and high growth; the authors estimate that stimulus spending actually *increases* unemployment. They then quote economist Horst Feldmann of the University of Bath, who comes to similar conclusions.

Feldman's words:

I find that a large government sector is likely to increase unemployment. It appears to have a particularly detrimental effect on women and the low skilled, and to substantially increase long-term unemployment. It seems that dominant state-owned enterprises, a large share of public investment, as well as high top marginal income tax rates and the low income thresholds at which they apply, are particularly detrimental.[13]

Palumbo and Ianoco go on to emphasise that other studies have also shown the counterintuitive (to some) conclusion that extra government expenditure leads to more, not less, unemployment.

• • •

All the evidence implies therefore that as government grows in size (as a percentage of an economy), growth slows and unemployment rises. The impact is greatest on those groups that are most marginal. The impact on social good is also negative.

What are the particular reasons as to why large government is so damaging to growth, and what are the channels of causation that these studies deduced? Intuitively, true economic growth comes from the creation of new businesses and the expansion of the existing ones – all in the private sector. Adding more civil servants or increasing government spending does not create wealth and cannot fuel sustainable growth. The larger the government, the less easy it is to create needed private-sector growth because:

- *The larger the government, the greater the opportunity for rent-seeking*: those citizens of an entrepreneurial bent will, rather than starting up new businesses, be drawn to the easier pickings of government subsidy, given the tough sledding of starting, winning with and maintaining a successful business in the cut-throat competitive environment of the private sector (where true growth comes from).

- *The larger the government, the larger and less productive of growth are the entitlements that it hands out*: the growing level of expectation that the government will step in whenever there is a problem – regardless of whether a citizen has the ability to pay to resolve the problem for themselves and regardless of the true severity of the problem – can be especially damaging to the work ethic that creates economic growth.

- *The larger the government, the greater the propensity to regulate*: it often seems that spending money on any new perceived societal problem must nowadays be accomplished or accompanied by a new law, rule and regulator. In turn, such regulation adds more and more of a burden to businesses, thus preventing them from growing. It also discourages new businesses from emerging, thanks to higher entry barriers, which thus prevent competition.

- *Public-sector expenditure is almost always less efficient than private-sector expenditure*: lacking, as it does, the essential component of price and delivery competition, with little downside for any personal failure and little pressure to complete in any given timeframe, any activity in the public sector becomes vastly more costly and inefficient than if it had been in a properly competitive private sector.

- *Too many talented individuals will be sucked into the public sector*: this will particularly be the case when, as in the UK, civil servants are paid 6 per cent more than private-sector workers after accounting for differences in employee characteristics, bonuses and employer pension contributions.[14]

These points are in some parts the same as, and in some parts go beyond, the well-known 'crowding out' argument but with more precision.

If we turn our attention to the UK, in Chart 2.7 we see that unfortunately, the size of our government has steadily grown from 35–40 per cent – the level where it was most of the time during the second half of the 1900s (the period covered by Barro's analyses) – to over 50 per cent during Covid-19. It is now, in 2024, still around 45 per cent. Until recently, changes to the size of government could be seen as a see-saw between profligate Labour governments and prudent Conservative governments; since the May, Johnson and Sunak regimes, this is no longer a valid differentiation.

Chart 2.7: UK Public Spending as a Share of GDP

Apart from intermittent periods of sobriety under earlier Conservative governments, UK public spending has grown incontinently over recent decades.

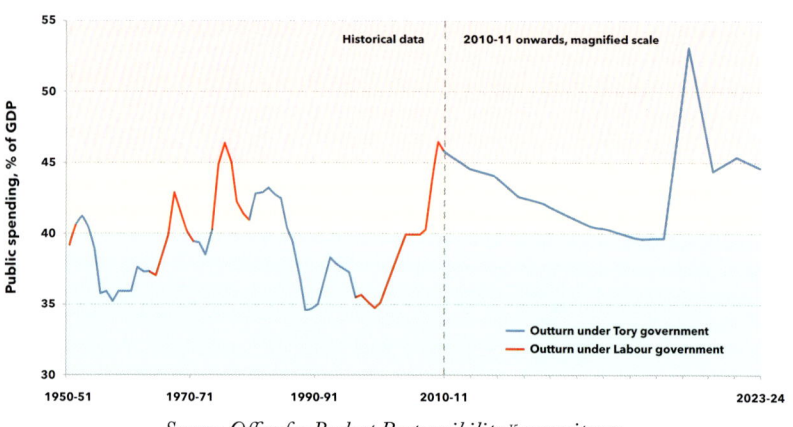

Source: Office for Budget Responsibility,[15] *moyniteam*

• • •

In business, they say that the only way to manage is towards a target – however vaguely calculated that target might be. It's no different for a country. The problem can be seen in spades when we look at national expenditure. How big should it be? How much can we afford? And at what point is our national expenditure at a level that is really foolish? Without a well-derived target, experiences indicates that our expenditure will just drift up and up without much real restraint.

One way of finding the right target is with the rule in mind, as discussed in the previous pages, that the smaller the size of government, the faster the growth. Even for a state that wishes to be generous in its payments to various parts of its population, it seems counterproductive to target a size of government greater than the low to mid-thirties as a percentage of GDP; arguably, a target of 33 per cent of GDP seems to fit the bill. In the rest of this book, we discuss aiming for that 33 per cent of GDP as a long-term target for the UK.

But to get to that 33 per cent from the 2023/24 level, the government would, at the current size of the economy, have to spend a full £324 billion less than it currently does. Clearly, cuts of that level would be impossible to accomplish overnight – for a start, the electorate would not wear it. Getting to 33 per cent of GDP will therefore require combining cuts with more rapid economic growth in expenditure. So, what level of cuts would be justifiable and acceptable in the short term? What level of cost should we target? An indication can be derived from an analysis or estimate of how much spend a country of the UK's wealth can afford. So, how much is that in our case? Well, it would seem fair to agree that the amount that can be spent per head each year should be related to the country's GDP per head. Clearly, the lower a country's GDP per capita, the less it can afford to spend per capita.

The UK is the sixth-largest economy in the world by overall size, but, as we have discussed earlier, it is not so high-ranking when measured on GDP per capita; currently, on that, we are only seventeenth among the thirty-eight OECD countries (see Chart 1.14). Accordingly, one can expect that the UK cannot afford to spend as much per capita as other countries might. Chart 2.8 shows the OECD countries (and a few others) on both measures (GDP per capita and spend per capita) with a regression line plotting the relationship between the two measures – as predicted, the richer the country, the more it spends per capita. The regression line could be said to show what countries in general seem to believe they can afford to spend at a given level of GDP per capita. Groups of countries that are above the regression line (in other words, that spend more per capita than the average country at that wealth level seems to think they can afford) grow at much lower rates than countries below the line (countries that are prudent in spending relative to others).

Chart 2.8: Living Within One's Means
Actual Versus Average Expenditure for a Given Level of National Wealth Per Capita

If the UK wished to spend only as much per capita as the average country that has an equivalent level of GDP per capita, today, it would need to be spending £112 billion less.

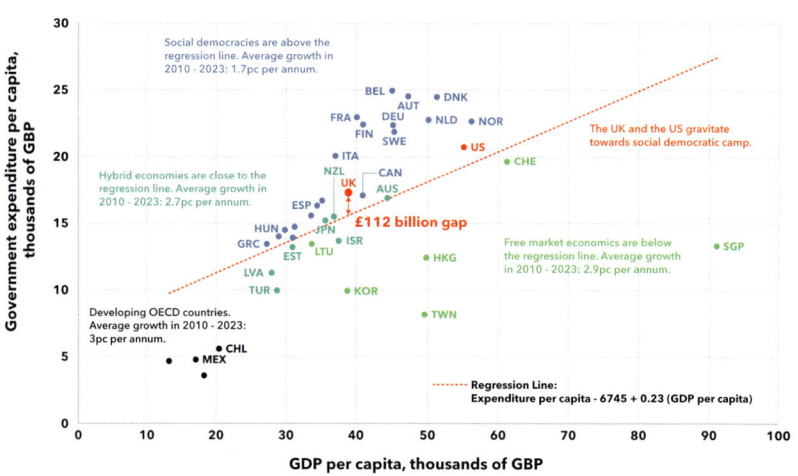

Source: International Monetary Fund[16], moyniteam analysis

The UK is, as the chart shows, spending quite a bit more than the average equivalently wealthy country in the sample and this is a factor in our low level of economic growth. Were our expenditure such that we sat exactly on the regression line, we would be spending £112 billion less than we are now.* This £112 billion figure is a mark of how much we are spending, over and above what the average country of the same wealth level as us is spending: i.e. we are spending £112 billion more than the average country of our wealth level sees itself as able to afford or is anyway prepared to spend. Even reducing our expenditure by £112 billion won't guarantee us a high rate of growth; it would only reduce our expenditure, as a percentage of GDP, from 45 per cent to 40 per cent. If we want to get down to a growth-promoting expenditure level of just 33 per cent of GDP, we would thereafter need to ensure that our growth in expenditure was at a considerably lower rate than our growth in GDP per capita.

SPENDING MONEY ON THE WRONG THINGS SHRINKS GROWTH EVEN MORE

We have seen that the less a government spends, the faster the economy can grow. But what about *what* the government spends money on? Does that separately impact growth too? Some expenditures will, for a given overall size of government, help economic growth to some degree. Others can hinder growth from the get-go. A further group of expenditures may, of course, be neutral.

At the same time, any given nation will consider certain expenditures to be essential, regardless of their association or otherwise with growth; these are dubbed 'core' expenditures. A particular problem

---

* Note that since most advanced economies are spending more than they can afford to, this merely sets a short-term target that makes us still feckless: just no more feckless than equivalently rich countries.

comes when inessential expenditures that don't help growth come to be seen as essential (the logical outcome of Wagner's Law).

In the UK, for example, total public-sector expenditure prior to Covid was running at around 40 per cent of GDP.* With Covid, it briefly rose to 53 per cent of GDP. It dropped back only as far as around 45 per cent in 2022/23 and is now forecast (as of March 2024) to have remained at that level in 2023/24.[17] Despite recent government statements indicating a desire to drop further, expenditure is not, in 2024, showing much sign of dropping. There has been very little public discussion or analysis of why the shockingly high level of UK government expenditure seems now to be pretty much embedded into the economy.[†]

The subject of 'core' expenditure was reviewed in both Gwartney et al. (1998) and Connors and Norton (2012). What are these 'core' expenditures, and how much do they add up to in the UK?

Chart 2.9 offers a view of the overall 'core' versus 'non-core' concept in relation to the US, which we show here to illustrate the concept and also to illustrate the fact that in all advanced countries, 'core' expenditure is becoming less and less of total expenditure.

Various estimates, such as Connor and Norton's, indicate that expenditure for these core activities sits at around 15 per cent of GDP. As shown in Chart 2.9, this 'core' number does not seem to increase over time (as a percentage of GDP) as the economy grows – though in the US that static level may in part have been an artefact of the reduction in defence spending (the imagined 'peace dividend') that occurred in the 1990s, coincidentally balanced out by the increase in education spending.

---

* Figure for the financial year 2019/20.
† The lack of debate on this point led to allegations during the recent election that Labour and the Conservatives together comprised a 'uniparty'.

What is the right mix of spend? To start with, that 'core' spend of 15 per cent of GDP – which, in the US, was one half of government spend in 1960 and in 2010 was a little over one third of all its government spend – comprises those expenditures which are generally seen as essential items, the ones that keep society working – police, sewage, highways, education etc. Note that in the US, healthcare has traditionally been seen (although less so in recent years) as being a matter of private concern, rather than a 'core' spend. In the UK, that is, of course, not currently the case. We discuss healthcare extensively later.

Chart 2.9: Core US Government Expenditures (federal, state, local)
As a percentage of GDP, 1960–2010

In the US, 'core' government used to be half of overall government spending. With growth in overall spending (Wagner's Law), 'core' government is now only around one third of overall spend.

Budget categories	1960	1970	1980	1990	2000	2010
Police, judicial, prisons etc.	0.6	0.8	1.0	1.3	1.6	1.6
Defence and diplomacy	9.7	8.3	5.3	5.4	3.1	5.1
Education	3.5	4.7	4.6	4.8	5.5	6.3
Highways	1.8	1.6	1.2	1.1	1.2	1.3
Sewage, sanitation and environment	0.5	0.6	1.0	0.8	0.8*	0.8
Total 'core' government	16	16	13	13	12	15
Total 'all' government	30	35	37	40	38	42
'Core' as a percentage of 'all'	53	46	35	33	32	36

Data for this item are no longer available. The author assumes data for 2000 (for this item) at the level of 1990. • Source: Connors and Norton[18]

So, as far as the US is concerned, the 'core' expenditures needed to keep the country running, excluding health expenditure, are some 15 per cent of GDP. Expenditures beyond that are discretionary – the country can, in theory, carry on without them.* Democracy (with Wagner's Law) is unlikely to allow as low a level of expenditure as that, but it is worth noting that some democracies spend not hugely higher than that.

What other expenditures, beyond the necessary 'core', are more likely to promote growth and which ones are likely to hinder it? One key paper on the effect of the public-spending mix on the long-run growth rate is from Norman Gemmell, Richard Kneller and Ismael Sanz (2015). Chart 2.10 depicts their overall findings.

Chart 2.10: Impact of Public Spending Mix on Long-Run GDP Per Capita

Investments in infrastructure and education, and to some degree housing, were found to improve standards of living in the long run, whereas spending on other categories had either a relatively small or a statistically insignificant impact. Others had a detrimental effect on economic growth.

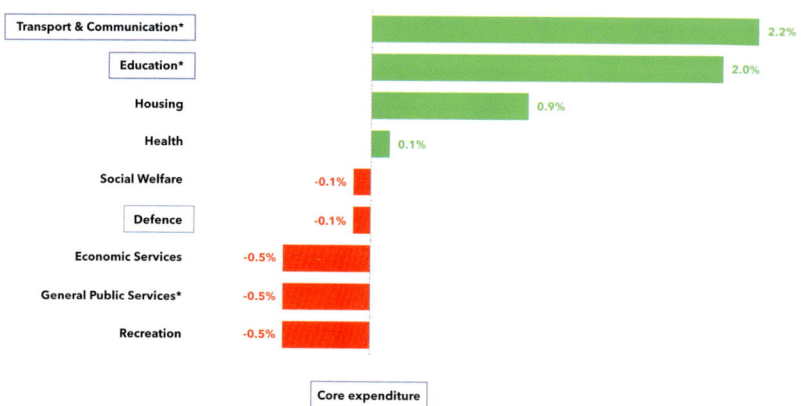

*Statistically significant at the 1 per cent level • Source: Gemmell, Kneller and Sanz (2015)[19]

Gemmell et al.'s results show that reallocating resources to transport,

---

* Leaving aside for now the question of health expenditures.

infrastructure and education spending – all 'core' areas – has a strong *positive* impact on economic growth; the same is true for housing, although with only half of that strong impact. Health, social welfare and defence have pretty much a *neutral* impact when spending on them is increased, relative to other categories – although we have to bear in mind that, as we have shown, in general *all* overall increases in expenditure have a negative impact on growth. Reallocating resources to economic services (which includes government involving itself in the economy e.g. with labour affairs, agriculture and forestry), general public services (which include such things as expenditure on government itself and overseas aid) and recreation (which includes broadcasting, culture and religion) all have a *negative* impact on growth.

Gábor Kutasi and Ádám Marton (2020) offer a useful summary of recent findings by other researchers on this topic and then report on their own analysis, which they performed on twenty-five EU economies between 1996 and 2017 (a useful comparison set for the UK).[20] They have a stronger conclusion regarding Gemmell et al.'s findings on social protection (which Gemmell et al. call social welfare), saying such expenditures have 'a negative, statistically significant and robust impact on GDP growth', by which they mean that higher expenditure on welfare is robustly found to lower economic growth. Apart from the fact that Kutasi and Marton didn't include transport and communications as a separate item, their results are much the same as Gemmell et al.'s but with stronger negative results. As opposed to Gemmell et al.'s negative 0.1 per cent for welfare, their estimated impact is negative 1.6 per cent. One of the major improvements Kutasi and Marton bring to research in the area is that they analyse carefully the *lags* in impact of particular expenditures, specifically for education and health; by analysing these lags carefully, the authors show that each has a positive, albeit delayed – as one might expect – impact on GDP per capita (as did Gemmell et al., although when it comes to health, only to a small degree). This validates that their findings show the impact is causal, not just correlative.

Chart 2.II: UK Core Government Spend as a percentage of GDP, 2000–2023

'Core' spending in the UK, excluding health expenditure, is some 12 per cent, compared to 15 per cent in the US. Even when we include health, 'core' expenditure in the UK is still only 20 per cent of GDP – only 44 per cent of total government spend.

CATEGORY	FY2000	FY2010	FY2020	FY2023
Public Order and Safety (Police etc)	1.7	2.2	1.5	1.7
National Security/Defence	2.7	2.9	2.4	2.5
Education	4.0	5.7	4.0	4.2
Transport	0.7	1.5	1.5	1.7
Environment Protection	0.5	0.7	0.5	0.5
Public and Common Services	0.8	0.9	0.5	1.1
Total 'Core' Government excl. Health	10.4	13.9	10.4	11.7
Health	4.7	7.5	7.3	8.4
Total 'Core' Government	14.3	20.5	17.2	19
Total 'Non-Core' Government	20.5	25.8	22.3	26.6
Total 'All' Government	34.8	46.3	39.5	45.6

KEY: Productive Unproductive

Source: HM Treasury[21]

As noted earlier, different countries have different, and differently effective, education and health systems. A blanket conclusion that willy-nilly spending in either area (or indeed in any area) will increase growth is unlikely to be correct. For a start, as we have seen, all overall increases in government expenditure have a basic negative impact on growth. Secondly, expenditure on an area can be effective or ineffective. In the UK, for example, we spend a lot on education with, as we shall see later, good but not great results, and despite our general good results, we have created an uneducated 'underclass' of 25–30 per cent of our citizens – immiserating for them and increasingly costly for the economy. In the field of health, our NHS, designed as a socialistic structure that is not copied by any other country I am aware of, we deliver – again, discussed later – more and more woeful results, despite ever-increasing amounts of expenditure. The same effect, and presumably therefore the same impact on growth, could be created with somewhat lower expenditure.

How does UK spending per capita compare with the US in key 'core' spending areas? Chart 2.11 shows HM Treasury's view of 'core' spending in the UK.

Total 'core' expenditures by the UK are, as we can see from this chart, some 12 per cent of GDP, excluding health. This compares with, as discussed, some 15 per cent in the US. So, the US is (excluding health in both cases) 25 per cent larger on the 'as a percentage of GDP' measure of how much it spends on essential matters and spends even greater per head on an absolute basis when you take into account the US's larger GDP per capita. As GDP per capita in the US is some 67 per cent higher than in the UK, we see that US 'core' expenditure per capita (excluding health for both countries) is around twice as high as that of the UK (1.25 x 1.67 = 2.09). Breaking that down in detail:

- The two countries have very similar levels of public order expenditure as a percentage of GDP (1.6 per cent UK versus 1.7 per cent US). So, because its GDP per capita is much lower, the UK spends some 60 per cent of the US's absolute expenditure per head on this item, or, put the other way round, the US has 67 per cent higher spend per capita on public order.
- The UK has somewhat higher expenditure on transport and infrastructure as a percentage of GDP than the US (1.7 per cent

UK versus 1.3 per cent US), but, because of higher GDP per capita in the US, absolute spend on transport and infrastructure in the US is about 30 per cent higher per capita than in the UK.

- The UK has somewhat lower expenditure than the US on the environment as a percentage of GDP (0.5 per cent UK versus 0.8 per cent US). As a result, in absolute terms the US spends nearly three times as much per capita as the UK does on the environment.

- The UK spends significantly less on education than the US as a percentage of GDP (4.2 per cent UK versus 6.3 per cent US). The US's spend per capita on education is therefore two and a half times that of the UK.

- The UK spends around half what the US does on defence as a percentage of GDP (2.5 per cent UK versus 5.1 per cent US). So, the US's expenditure per capita on defence is a full three and a half times that of the UK.

Should the UK seek to be spending US levels per capita on 'core' government activities? No: it can't afford to. It can do so only if it grows its GDP per capita by a significant amount. When determining how much it can spend, a country must cut its coat to suit its cloth. The UK – having ordered its economic behaviour over the past decades as to now have a significantly lower level of GDP per capita than does the US – spends a similar percentage of its GDP on some 'core' sectors as the US, while in absolute amounts it spends only a fraction per capita of what the US spends in other 'core' areas.

Reducing expenditure in any of these 'core' UK areas seems difficult – and, judging by history, to *some* degree unnecessary because the US was able to grow its economy well in the past while leaving 'core' expenditure at a similar absolute per capita level. But spending less can, of course, be done if a more efficient or less costly way of achieving the same result can be found.

Moving beyond core expenditure, where do we spend our government's money and how well? To answer this question, we now break up UK government expenditure into its individual major components in Chart 2.12.

Chart 2.12: UK Public Spending on Services 2022/23
£ billion/per cent of total (100 per cent = £1.07 trillion)

Over 90 per cent of UK government spend is in just eight areas. The two largest areas – social welfare and health – are around one half of expenditure.

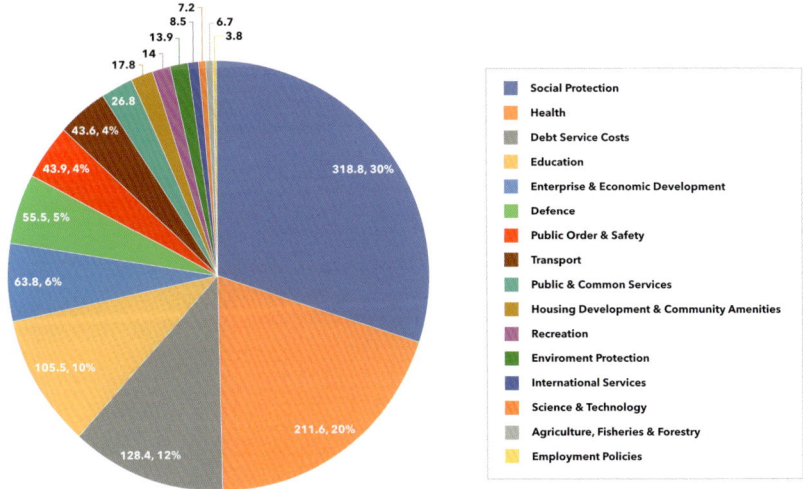

Note: 100 per cent of spend = 46 per cent of GDP. So, each percentage point of spend shown in the chart represents 0.46 per cent of GDP. As an example, health spend is 9.2 per cent of GDP. Source: HM Treasury[22]

As we can see, almost one third of government expenditure in 2023 was on social protection (mostly welfare); health takes up a further fifth. Together, these two comprise half of all government spend. Shockingly, the third largest expenditure is now debt service – £128 billion last year.[*] Education takes up a further 10 per cent of spend, economic development 6 per cent and defence 5 per cent.

In the following sections, we take a deeper look at those top areas of spend that comprise over 80 per cent of total government expenditure, plus some of the smaller areas of cost:

- welfare
- health
- debt service costs
- education
- enterprise and economic development
- defence
- other

Welfare

The term 'welfare', in the US sometimes termed 'entitlements', relates to different items in different countries. For example, sometimes health is included as part of welfare. In this book, however, in accordance with the international classification,[†] I cover health separately in the next section.

As we saw in Chart 2.12, welfare takes up one third of all government expenditure. If we cannot lower welfare costs in the UK, we have little hope of shrinking the overall size of government in a meaningful way.

Clearly, the largest change in UK government spending patterns

---

[*] This will continue to rise as old, cheap debt is replaced with new debt issuance.
[†] Classification of functions of government, or COFOG, developed by the OECD.

in recent years has been on increased benefits. The pervasive 'big government' model in the UK has resulted, as in all big-government countries, in major ongoing redistributions that, among other things, try to make up for any perceived lack of economic opportunity. As Baroness Dambisa Moyo, quoted by the Centre for Policy Study's Robert Colvile, has pointed out: Europe plus America comprise 12 per cent of the world's population and half its GDP but 90 per cent of its welfare payments.[23] This surely has to make the reader pause and think: this 90 per cent statistic is likely to have considerable negative implications for our competitiveness against the rest of the world and thus on our ability to grow our way out of our current troubles.

Welfare costs have risen drastically this century across the developed west. Previously seen as a safety net, benefits have more and more turned into social redistribution. A recent Civitas paper showed that 'a record 54.2 per cent of [UK] people (36 million) now live in households that receive more in benefits than they contributed in taxes'.[24] 54 per cent clearly goes well beyond the economically disadvantaged and now reaches well into the middle classes.

The evidence suggests that the primary reason for governments that are too large in western economies (and specifically the UK government) is from having a level of entitlements/benefits – including pensions, with a particular nod to public-sector pensions – that is too large. The areas of welfare and social protection are the prime reasons why we have such a large-sized government, and therefore, most likely the prime contributor to our lack of growth. Wagner's Law was presumably formulated by Adolph Wagner out of his expectation that politicians will vie with each other to offer 'free stuff' at each election, so that the spending bill will inevitably ratchet up and up and cannot thereafter be ratcheted down. This seems to be what has happened. But unless the spending is lowered, growth will remain at a low-to-no-level, with all the negative consequences flowing from that, as described in Part I.

Addressing welfare overspending is, therefore, clearly a *sine qua non* for any UK government if overall expenditures are to be significantly lowered. Realistically, a good part of that would have had to be found in reducing the level of benefits paid. Much of these savings would need to have come from removing some benefits from a large swathe of the population, including the middle classes.[25] Critics of the welfare state, such as myself, cannot, if they are to be honest with their audience, merely disparage that such a large percentage of people are net beneficiaries of the welfare state. We have to point explicitly to what (inevitably difficult) steps must be taken to reduce this very high net dependency ratio. What's more, the steps to be taken have to be quite significant if the public finances are to be transformed and the creation of a growth economy enabled.

The key argument for those who, like me, challenge the need for as large a welfare state as we have, is the principle of self-reliance and the belief that human beings are capable of individually responding to challenge or adversity in a constructive and successful way, rather than so frequently needing state intervention to help them through difficult times. Countries that encourage a self-reliant approach have better outcomes for individuals *on average* – not always, of course, which means that *as with all approaches*, individual hardship will frequently occur. Such an argument is always complicated and difficult to put forwards, in the face of what is, not infrequently, undeniable and real distress, but it is a view that prevails in most of the successful economies of the world: the view that the less is the safety net, the more will individuals pick themselves up, and, conversely, that the greater the safety net, the more inclined individuals

are to misuse it and in doing so often lose the incentive or willingness to work to change their own circumstances, ending up stuck
on society's floor. When a population embraces self-reliance, the
long-term positive impact on national wealth and, as a result, the
reduction in poverty for all (through eventually additional available
tax revenues, as well as through self-help) can be very large.

This is not to say that anyone is advocating that there should be
no safety net, or that there is *no* level of distress that the state should
not respond to. Rather, it says that a lot more than 45.8 per cent of
the population should be net contributors to the state's financial
needs. A relatively small change downward in how much welfare is
paid to or income tax paid by, say, the twentieth to the seventieth
percentiles would go a long way to taking the pressure off. Careful
attention has to be paid to ensuring that for all who are capable of
work, the financial incentives to claim any out-of-work benefit are
lower than the significant financial incentives to get a job and earn
money. (Income taxes and the further myriad distortive taxes that
suppress growth will be discussed in Chapter 7.)

What, as a policy target, would we like to see as the right percentage of individuals to be net recipients from, rather than contributors
to, the state? The particular percentage level that we choose will necessarily be somewhat arbitrary, but let us, for the sake of argument,
choose an ambitious – but not, I would argue, a particularly cruel –
target that no more than 30 per cent of the population should be net
takers from the state. This would mean that the ~36 million people
in the UK who are takers drops (*ceteris paribus*) to ~19 million. Some
17 million individuals would be newly required to be net contributors rather than net takers. This would mean reversing the boasts of
politicians that they have 'taken X thousand people out of the tax
net'. Why should that be a boast? Is it not far better to make sure

that as many voters as possible have a stake, even if it is only small, in ensuring the government spends as little and as wisely as possible? Why should we seek to train our citizens into thinking that the tax system is something for others, not for them?

Dispiritingly, modern UK governments and aspirant governments pride themselves on removing more and more people from the tax net. As a result, the middle classes are turning from contributors to takers. According to a recent *Telegraph* article on this very topic, 'In 2016/17, middle earners paid over £3,300 more in tax than they received from the state.' By 2023, they were receiving £563 more than they were paying.[26]

Chart 2.13: UK Welfare Spending 2023/24
£ billion/per cent of total (100 per cent = £292 billion)

Over 50 per cent of the UK's population receive more in benefits than they pay in tax. The puzzle is how to compassionately reduce these payments.

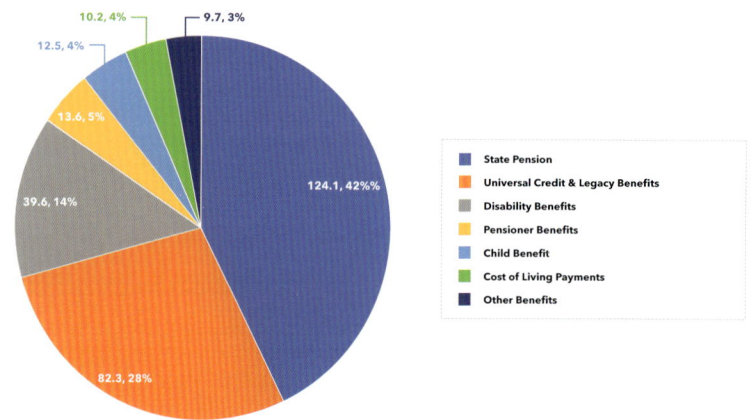

A full breakdown of welfare spending can be found in Appendix D. In this chart, Personal Independence Payments and the Disability Living Allowance for pensioners have been included in disability benefits rather than in pensioner benefits
Source: Department for Work and Pensions[27]

As regards the tax angle, this line of thought is pursued further in Chapter 7. Meanwhile, there remains the question of how to remove, streamline, or rightsize the very large amount of benefits payments in our country.

What are the components of the UK's welfare bill? Chart 2.13 breaks them down for 2023/24.

In the following pages, I look at the chief components of the welfare bill listed here:[*]

- state pension and pensioner benefits
- universal credit (including housing)
- disability benefits
- cost of living payments

State pensions and pensioner benefits

As Chart 2.13 shows, the biggest expenditure in the welfare area is the state pension, which has risen *in real terms* by some 29.4 per cent in the thirteen years since the Conservatives came to power and a full 84 per cent since 2002.[28] Increasingly, commentators say we cannot afford these payments.[29] Yet governments, terrified of losing the pensioner vote, insist on sticking with their high-spending pension plans, increasing the amount ever further each year.[30]

The ever-spiralling cost of the UK's state pension expenditures is due to two things:

- the fact that people are living ever-longer and that our population keeps growing

---

[*]   I do not discuss child benefit.

- the ever-increasing amount we annually pay each pensioner through the 'triple lock' mechanism

Longevity

The state pension was originally introduced in the UK through the Old Age Pensions Act 1908 for those aged seventy and above and with annual incomes below £21.* At the time, the expected lifetime of a newborn boy was 48.5 years and that of a newborn girl was 52.4 years. For anyone who actually reached the age of seventy (and not many at that time succeeded), the anticipated period over which they received their pension before dying was, on average, 8.4 years for men and 9.3 years for women. Today, the pension age in the UK is sixty-six years old for both sexes, four years lower than it was set initially in 1908, and the vast majority of citizens are reaching pensionable age. Life expectancy at birth is now around eighty years, and upon reaching the pension age, men and women are currently expected to live another 17.5 and 19.9 years respectively. Although the pension age is set to rise from 2026, there have been many calls to go beyond this. Those making such calls argue, almost certainly correctly, that the existing age-increase schedule is financially unsustainable.[31] Of course, there are those who are not interested in worrying about the cost of pensions to the nation; they decry the idea of any increase in the age before qualifying for the pension as being 'brutal'.[32] But those of a more analytic bent point out: the money is just not there. The age qualification must be raised higher and sooner.

---

* For those who earned between £21 and £31 10 shillings, a reduced rate could be claimed.

The triple lock

Why have basic pension payments seen such a considerable increase in recent years? The answer lies in the wonky working of a little-understood mechanism, the triple lock: a device that David Cameron and George Osborne came up with to secure the over-sixties vote. The triple lock is not a well-understood calculation (it increasingly seems as if it was not even understood by its progenitors). Most people think, wrongly, that it's a mechanism designed to ensure that pension payments keep up with the highest growing of three measures: inflation, salaries and GDP. In fact, because the basis of the calculation starts anew each year, increasing pensions by whichever was the highest that year, *the absurd effect is to increase pensions to a far higher level over time than any long-term rise in any one of the three measures.*

This phenomenon is shown in Chart 2.14. As can be seen, pensioner pay growth since the triple lock was introduced has way outstripped any of the three measures.

Why, how, does the triple lock work this way? It is not intuitively obvious, but when each year you take the highest of three different measures, switching back and forth from one to the other each year as one or the other becomes the highest that year, you end up with an amount paid out to pensioners that is enormously higher than the growth in any individual one of the three measures. As a result, over the past thirteen years, the cost to the country of the amounts paid out is a full £15 billion higher than the amount that would have been paid out had we relied solely on just one of those indices – even the highest rising of the three. Did those who invented the triple lock (some of whom now benefit from it) understand that this is what would happen? Do taxpayers understand it? Do any of them realise that pension payments will, if the triple lock is kept in place, continue to rise dramatically?* When you think about it, that outcome is bound to be the case. It comes about because each year the index that fell behind last year tends to bound ahead this year, so the pensions amount is boosted even further. The game is totally rigged. There has never been any discussion of this (admittedly counterintuitive to some) point from what I have been able to discern.

Chart 2.14: State Pension Triple Lock
Updating Factor and Reference Indices, 2010/11 – 2023/24

Because of the (little understood) mathematics of the triple lock, pensioners have, over the past decade, benefited dramatically relative to the average of the three growth measures.

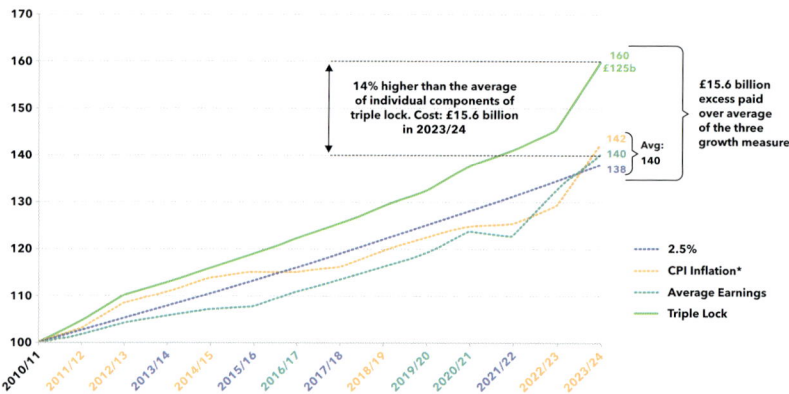

First year: RPI • Source: House of Commons Library,[33] moyniteam analysis

Before the 2024 general election, the Prime Minister announced that the Conservatives would maintain the triple lock for the rest

---

* To be clear: the UK state pension is significantly below the average of the OECD, although not much different from that of Switzerland or Ireland. But as we have seen, the UK's GDP per capita is also below that of the OECD average, and the average UK citizen lives, as it happens, longer than the average OECD citizen. From the point of view of cost, the money is not there to keep increasing pensions so rapidly and faster than any of the three indices.

of the decade. Labour has not yet indicated it will resile from that. This is the same as saying that pensioners will be more and more subsidised – as they have increasingly been over the past decade or more by other parts of society – by some totally random but large amount, whose size depends upon the idiosyncratic changes each year of these three measures. As there will be ongoing switching, on many or most years, between which measure does best, it can be expected that pensions will soar even further and even more randomly above the three measures.

The Institute for Fiscal Studies guessed that keeping the triple lock would add a further unintended amount of anywhere between £5 and £40 billion to the national bill, in present terms, in 2050, relative to if the state pension were increased in accordance with average earnings.[34] My own estimate, based on more recent demographic projections from the ONS, implies under current plans an additional £58 billion per annum, which is clearly unsustainable.* The triple lock must be eliminated urgently. Does the new Prime Minister and do his Chancellor and the Treasury actually understand how the triple lock creates this enormously costly effect? Or was the promise by both sides to keep the triple lock a cynical electioneering ploy, made despite the knowledge that it will likely create an unaffordable level of cost (but comfortably far away in the future)?

Worse: under the assumptions about pension age previously mentioned, we will have another almost 3.3 million pensioners in 2050. The cost of these new pension payments, even if the state pension doesn't increase in real terms, is £32 billion in today's money.

---

* The £58 billion is derived from assuming the following: the triple lock will increase according to the historical average of 3.68 per cent per annum, average earnings will grow at a historical average of 2.62 per cent per annum, inflation is kept at its 2 per cent target, and the pension age is increased to sixty-seven from 2026 and to sixty-eight from 2044.

If the triple lock were kept on, this would add a further £12 billion or so to this amount. That's a significant additional demand on the already stretched public purse.

In the following pages, which review potential cost reductions in national expenditure, we look at each issue through the lens of 'we can't afford this'. Therefore, rapid elimination of the triple lock is crucial. People living mostly or entirely on their pension will have meagre resources – that is already the case. But we cannot afford the triple lock, particularly if longevity continues to increase, and most expect it to.

Recent analyses claim the state pension, on the scheme as is, will become 'unaffordable' just one decade from now.[35] The rapidly ageing profile of our population throws up an even bigger problem than the triple lock. By 2040, over one in twelve retirees will be over eighty and the number of centenarians will rise six-fold to 83,000.[36]

The UK working-age population will itself only grow over that period by 4 per cent.* [37] The ratio of those of pensionable age to those of working age (the 'dependency ratio') will rise by some 25 per cent. There will, per retired citizen, be fewer and fewer working citizens to earn a salary and pay the taxes that will fund the pensions of those increasingly numerous retirees.

In these circumstances, the best that can be hoped for is to keep pensions from increasing to a greater share of GDP. Accomplishing that, in turn, can only realistically be done by increasing the pensionable age to seventy and doing that as soon as possible.

---

* And, of course, the health implications are equally bad – the number of people with serious illness is projected to increase over that period by 37 per cent.

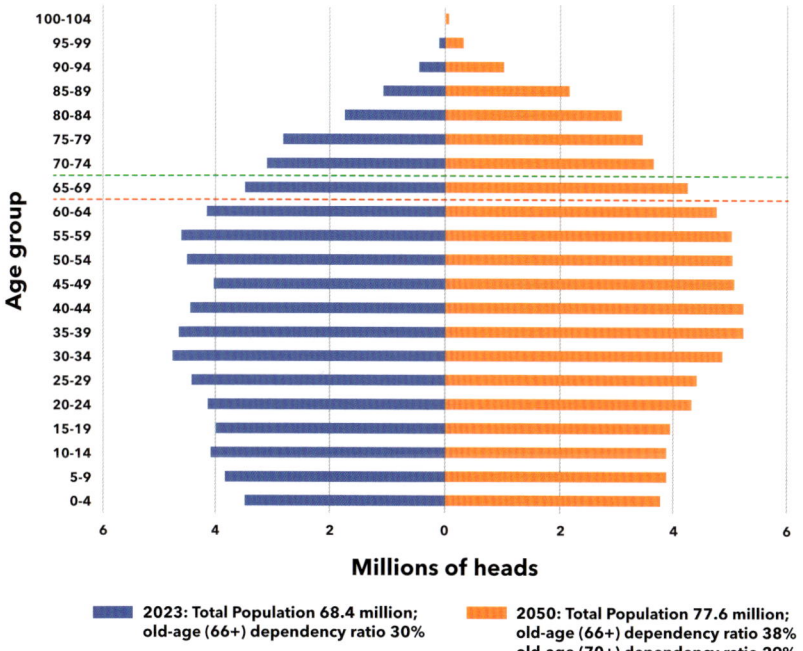

Chart 2.15: Age Pyramid/Dependency Ratios, 2023 and 2050
To keep the dependency ratio at 2023 levels, the pensionable
age needs to rise to age seventy within a very few years

2023: Total Population 68.4 million; old-age (66+) dependency ratio 30%

2050: Total Population 77.6 million; old-age (66+) dependency ratio 38% old-age (70+) dependency ratio 29%

Source: Office for National Statistics[38]

To curtail the overall and growingly unaffordable level of pensions, my proposal would be to:

- Remove the triple lock and replace it with average earnings growth, thus tying any increase in pensioner benefits directly to what increase the average worker gets each year.
- Increase the pension age to sixty-eight in 2031, sixty-nine in 2035 and seventy in 2039 for both sexes (compared to the current plan to get to sixty-eight sometime in or after 2044).*

---

* These proposals are, coincidentally, the same as suggested by the International Longevity Centre, whose report warns that future pension costs will be unsustainable.

By doing this, three complementary things happen: first, the growth in payments goes down; second, there is an increase in taxes paid as people stay in work; and third, as they do so, GDP also goes up. The triple lock and the demographic impact together will add up to an estimated (and unaffordable) £118 billion in extra annual pension costs by 2050: these suggested steps would reduce that increase by £78 billion, meaning the pensions bill will be relatively flat, relative to GDP, if we can grow a little faster.*

Note that even with these draconian steps, all we have succeeded in doing is keeping the old age pension to a level where it has a chance of staying at much the same percentage of overall national expenditure; longer term there will be further demographic change, which means that pension costs will start rising again and further hard decisions will have to be made. In any event, under these proposals the cost of pensions to the nation as a percentage of GDP does not at all decline.

We conclude that drastic steps need to be taken immediately on the state pension but that these steps will not save anything on total expenditure – it will merely prevent expenditure from going up even further.

Pensioner benefits

In addition to the state pension, pensioners also get almost £20 billion in various benefits, as follows:

---

* Moyniteam estimates.

Pensioner benefits in 2023/24[39]	£ billion
Pensioner housing benefit	6.1
Pension credit	5.4
Winter fuel payments	2.0
Personal Independence Payment (PIP)	3.7
Disability Living Allowance (DLA)	2.4
Total	**£19.6**

There is money to be saved on these benefits. Some of them are per-haps too small to bother with for the purposes of this book: others are significant.[*] The point is, again, that we have been incontinent in offering these to one and all, whether they needed the benefit or not. And, if a person is on disability payments prior to their retirement, why should they proceed into retirement with full PIP being paid, as can currently be the case?[†]

If there was a means test for pensioner benefits, focusing only on the truly in need, at least 50 per cent of winter fuel allowance goes (£1 billion) and let us say (moyniteam estimates) 40 per cent of PIP and DLA (£2.4 billion).

> For pensioner benefits, £3.4 billion could be saved

What other diminutions in welfare spending could be achieved? The rapid post-Covid growth in the next two items – universal

---

[*] For example, the winter fuel payments cost the taxpayer £2 billion in 2023/24. They are intended to help pensioners with heating bills. It would, of course, make much more sense to avoid these energy bills being so high by having a sensible energy policy in place, without the massively distortive subsidies to 'green' energy providers. (This subject is discussed in more detail in Chapter 8.) But in any event, these payments are only truly needed for a minority of pensioners; a majority do not suffer from fuel poverty.

[†] PIP can only be claimed by working-age people. However, once claimed, it may continue on into the pension age. If a retired person needs significant support because of their disability, there are other payments available, such as attendance allowance and carer's allowance. Disability benefits are discussed in more detail later.

credit and disability payments – has been puzzling. Let's examine each in turn.

Universal Credit (including unemployment and housing)

Universal Credit is a safety net for claimants on low income, unemployed or unable to work. It was introduced in 2012 to replace six means-tested benefits for working-age people.* As shown in Chart 2.13, in 2023/24 these benefits cost British taxpayers £82.3 billion.

Universal Credit was an excellent reform that in some ways works but in others is now proving too generous in disincentivising the unemployed from going back to work. Families on Universal Credit can now be better off than those earning £70,000 a year.[40] This is crazy and a massive disincentive to get a job.†

Let's look at three issues related to Universal Credit:

- unemployment
- housing benefit
- fraud

Unemployment

About £11.4 billion, or 14 per cent of that £82.3 billion bill, is spent on unemployment benefits. If benefit spending had been used only to soften the effects of unemployment, the level of expenditure on benefits should have fallen post-Covid. However, as Chart 2.16 shows, it did initially fall but started to rise even pre-Covid, and

---

* Those benefits, usually referred to as 'legacy benefits', were income-related Employment and Support Allowance, income-based Jobseeker's Allowance, Income Support, Child Tax Credit, Working Tax Credit and Housing Benefit. A portion of these costs still remain in the system.

† And on top of that, you don't have to repay your student loan.

apart from the one-year Covid bump, is now much higher, despite the major fall in unemployment.

Chart 2.16: UK Welfare Spending and Unemployment
£ billions in 2024/25 terms, 1997/98–2023/24

Welfare spending now seems increasingly untethered from unemployment levels.

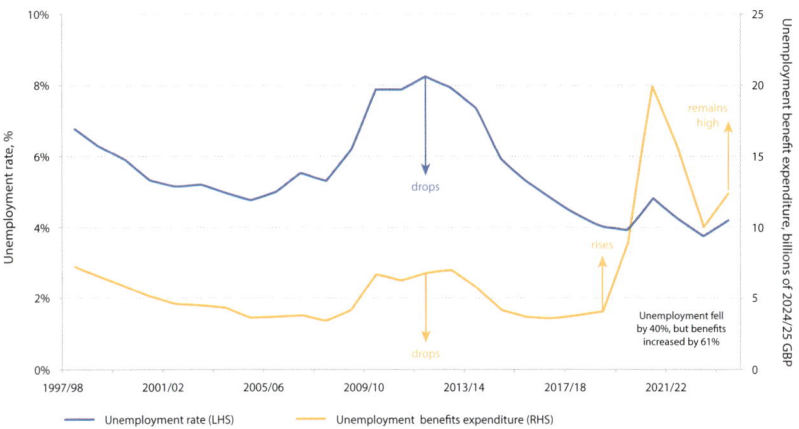

Source: Department for Work and Pensions [41], *moyniteam*

In 2023, 3.7 million working-age people were being paid jobless benefits while being exempted (because of claimed and accepted ill health) from any need to find a job (meaning the taxpayer will have to pay these benefits indefinitely), out of an overall out-of-work benefits roster of 5.2 million people (by 2024 this rose to 5.6 million).[42] The annual cost of paying those 3.7 million people is around £25 billion. The numbers not engaging in the workplace continue to rise: by March 2024, there were 9.3 million working-age adults neither in work nor looking for a job.[43]

As can be seen from Chart 2.16, when unemployment shrank

and then as the Covid emergency receded, benefits stayed at the same high levels that we saw after the financial crisis and the Covid era. Unemployment is now much lower, yet unemployment benefits are over double the amounts the UK was paying out not so far in the past.

In the 1990s, President Bill Clinton had massive success in reforming welfare in the US. The centrepiece of the reform was the time limitation of welfare payments: you were given two years to get a job, after which welfare payments ceased. Some denounced this as cruel, but Clinton was making this change from the left, so was able to ride out the criticism better than if a presumedly uncaring right-wing government were to have done it. In the end, the Clinton reforms were a major success. By 2016, the number of those receiving cash assistance from the government had dropped to 3 million from 13 million in 1995.[44] Payments had dropped by some 36 per cent.

Recently, Rishi Sunak proposed a similar approach with a limit of twelve months.[45] As with so many Tory initiatives, there seemed to be no follow-up, and then the announcement of a premature election ensured that, yet again, the announcement was just words rather than serious intent. A Labour government, coming like Clinton from the left, is well positioned to initiate a similar type of welfare reform that could bring back the pleasure, pride and sense of contribution that having a job will provide to many of the currently unemployed. Reforms could include a time limit on payments and no longer incentivising people to work two or three days a week.

The task that welfare reform has to perform in our model is not ambitious: we just aim to return benefit expenditures on unemployment to pre-Covid levels. This would save £8 billion (Chart 2.16).

Chart 2.17: Numbers Claiming Unemployment Benefit and Average Cost per Claimant 1997–2023

If we can reduce the number receiving unemployment benefits and inflation-adjusted cost per unemployed to pre-pandemic levels, then some £8 billion will be saved.

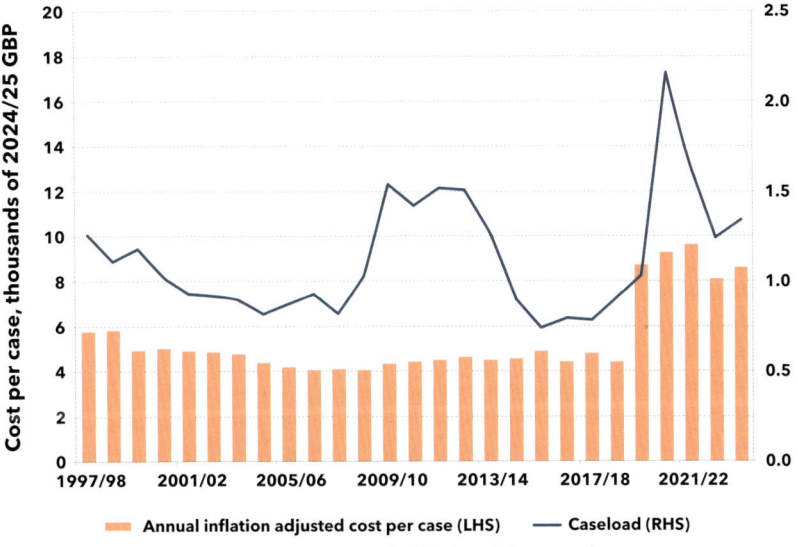

Source: *Department for Work and Pensions*[46]

By taking steps to return unemployment payments to pre-Covid levels, some £8 billion can be saved.

Housing benefit

As a further component of Universal Credit we have housing benefit, which was some £15.4 billion in 2023.* Can any of this be reduced?

---

* This figure includes the pensioner part of housing benefit.

It is another area where human rights law constrains what a local council or other authority can do. Were it possible for the provider to be more flexible in what was provided, more could be done for more people, offering:

- *Cheaper-built housing.* Encouraging cheaper ways of building – more modular/prefabricated houses, for example – could significantly increase the housing stock and lower rents.
- *Housing in cheaper parts of the country.* Schemes for building large numbers of houses in cheaper parts of the UK to accommodate need have come up against aggressive condemnation as being 'social cleansing' of richer areas. As a result, many are left homeless.
- *Smaller or less comfortable housing.* Minimal space standards for housing in the UK are another example of regulations inhibiting growth. The Housing Act 1985 requires minimum standards and sizes for social and other housing. The Nationally Described Space Standard (2015) has been adopted by most councils, including all London councils. Those who are seeking but not yet getting council accommodation would of course *prefer* something bigger, but if they got something smaller, they would get something – which would be much nicer for them than the nothing they are currently getting. As in so many areas, we need to stop telling ourselves that we are richer than we are. If standards were to allow smaller housing to be provided, then more housing would be provided. Smaller accommodation would certainly be appreciated by those who currently end up getting nothing or who have to wait for years to get anything. Options range from slightly lower size and standards of rooms, all the way down to

receiving disability benefit. This cost the nation £18.7 billion in 2023/24. *The Economist* editorialised, 'Too many mild cases are being medicated.'[54] The magazine argued in that piece that it was a mistake to treat every case as a 'mental health issue'. Something termed a 'mental disorder', they said, may be best – if mild – worked through, rather than the person being given a referral to a doctor who then certifies their disability. One hazards a guess that currently, the attractions of disability payments and no need to work will, to many, appear (superficially) superior to having to hold down a job and earn a wage. But, as we know, joblessness and a disability payment very often do not end in either individual or societal happiness.

Disability is a category that includes individuals with daunting personal circumstances: some citizens suffering from severe disability need all the help they can get. But there seems to be agreement that the majority of disabilities eligible for benefits are not severe, a view that is supported by the fact that the number claiming disability payments has in the past fifteen years shot up, with the number of recipients rising by 62 per cent and the total bill escalating by 126 per cent in real terms. In the next years, these numbers are expected to grow at an even higher pace (Chart 2.18).

Since 2013, the main disability benefit has been the Personal Independence Payment (PIP), a tax-free cash remittance intended to help working-age people with long-term physical or mental health conditions causing difficulties in everyday life. PIP is not means-tested, does not depend on whether the claimant is employed or studying, does not affect the amount received in other benefits, can be spent with no restrictions or control *and is a lifetime ongoing benefit*. PIP was introduced to replace the Disability Living Allowance (DLA) and was aimed at cutting disability spending by one fifth. Instead, however, and, as the Institute for Fiscal Studies has reported, 'Spending on disability benefits has in fact markedly increased – and at a faster rate than before the policy change.'[55] Clearly, something has gone badly wrong. Anecdotally, one reason for the boom in PIP claims is that it appears ministers were assured by civil servants that checks on claimants would be stringent and would weed out those malingering.* In the event, it seems that over 50 per cent of claimants succeed with their PIP claim, often helped by YouTube advisers and the like.[56]

Chart 2.18: Number of People Claiming Main Disability Benefits* and Their Cost in Real Terms

The number of working-age recipients of disability benefits has risen by over a million since 2008/09, while the cost to the taxpayer has increased by £10.5 billion in real terms and is expected to continue growing.

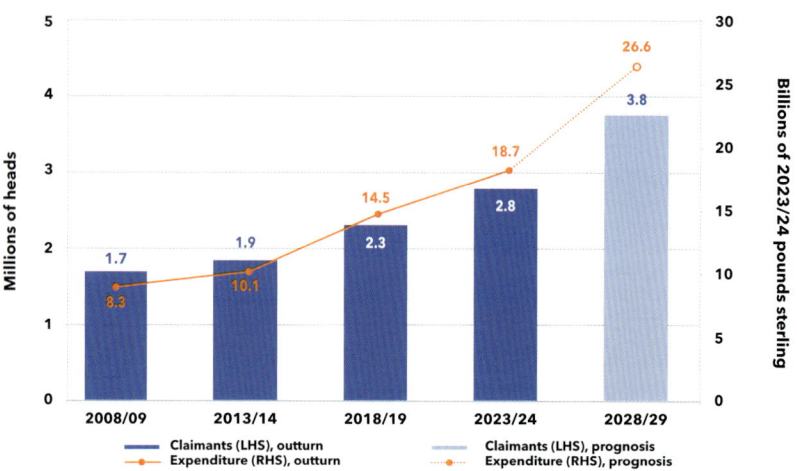

Personal Independence Payment and Disability Living Allowance administered by DWP
Source: Department for Work and Pensions,[57] moyniteam analysis

Some recipients of PIPs very much deserve and need them. But

---

* Recounted to the author by one of the senior Conservatives involved in setting up Universal Credit.

many others don't and strong financial incentives exist for people to seek diagnoses that enable them to obtain a PIP. In 2023/24, the average PIP recipient was paid £6,842, a substantial addition to most UK citizens' income (wages or other benefits). Some citizens get significantly more than the minimum. Others receive payments for conditions that are not necessarily lifelong or crippling. For example, according to the *Telegraph*, '14 people in Britain qualify for £9,500 in PIP per year to help them live with haemorrhoids.'[58]

The key peculiarity of PIP, which allows quite a lot of people to claim it successfully, is that it is equally designed for those with either physical or mental health conditions. This makes PIP readily available for someone who claims to have anxiety, depression or stress, all of which are subjective, and in many cases, relatively mild conditions. By the end of 2023, those with anxiety, depression, and mood disorders accounted for almost 16 per cent of the PIP caseload, a staggering 543,544 individuals.[*]

Disability payments are projected to rise *even further* in real terms, leading the benefits system to hoover up an ever larger proportion of the working-age population (Chart 2.19). Chastened by the blunt fact of unaffordability, not to mention the need to cut costs in order to improve economic growth, we really have no choice but to scale back.

The Institute for Fiscal Studies states that the disability bill for working-age people was already, pre-pandemic, 70 per cent higher than expected, at some £14 billion rather than an expected £8 billion.[59] If the number of working-age claimants was the same as in

---

[*] Anxiety, depression and mood disorders include agoraphobia, generalised anxiety disorder, panic disorder, social and specific phobias, bipolar affective disorder, depressive disorders, mood disorder and other (including unknown) types of anxiety disorder. See https://stat-xplore.dwp.gov.uk/webapi/jsf/login.xhtml

2013, there would be a saving of over £6 billion. If, in addition, we stuck to and achieved the intention in 2013 to reduce the incidence of accepted disability by 20 per cent, a further £4 billion would be saved: in all, a saving of £10 billion. Month by month, however, the number who are claiming disability benefit, many of whom can be forecasted never to return to work (if nothing is done to prevent that), climbs ever higher. Instead of a rational, perfectly humanitarian level of £8 billion a year, we are climbing ever nearer to an astounding £27 billion or more a year (Chart 2.18).

Chart 2.19: Proportion of Working Age Population Receiving Disability Payments and Average Paycheque in Real Terms

Both the proportion of the working-age population claiming disability benefits and the average payout are forecast to balloon.

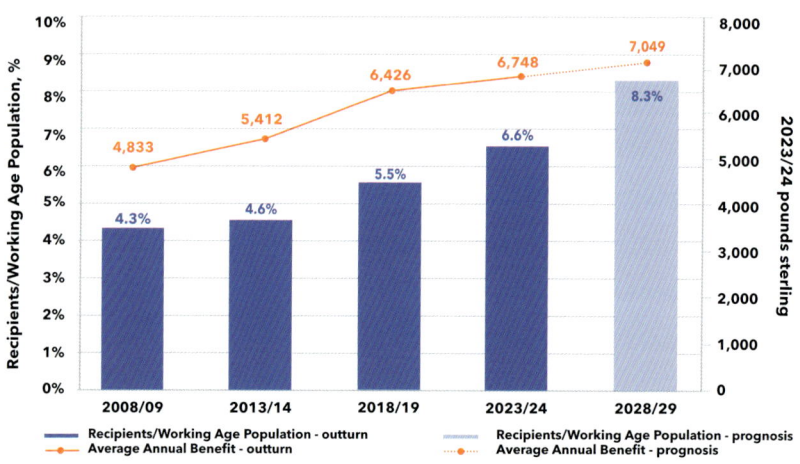

Personal Independence Payment and Disability Living Allowance administered by the DWP
Source: DWP,[60] moyniteam analysis

What this rise shows is that the UK is a country that believes it is right, appropriate and humane to have moved in recent years to paying incapacity payments to three times as many of its citizens (from 2 per cent to 6 per cent of the population) as before. The question of affordability has taken secondary place to considerations of what is felt to be 'fair' or 'humane'. But to repeat: we can't afford it.

Since the start of the Covid period, over a million people have joined the ranks of long-term economically inactive. Chart 2.20 shows that much the largest contributor to that was the number of long-term sick.

Chart 2.20: Reasons Behind the Change in UK Economic Inactivity
Changes since February 2020 in economic inactivity level by reason

Almost 1 million people have been added to the inactivity list since the beginning of Covid.

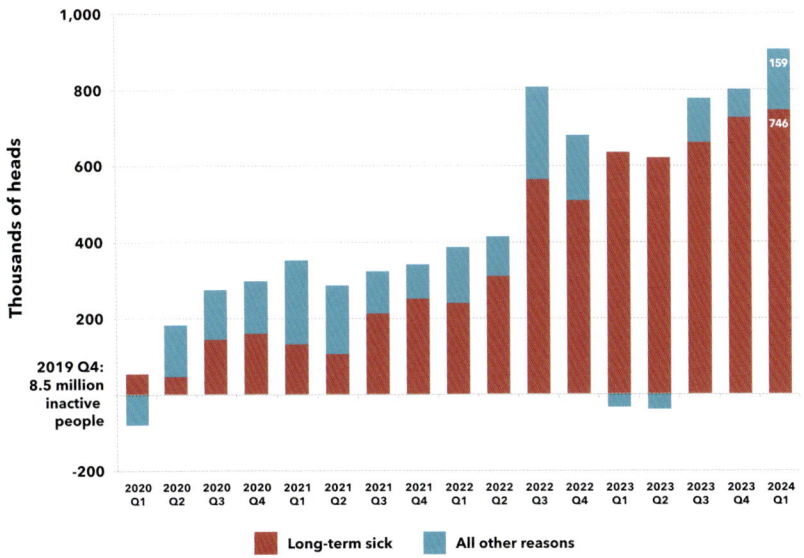

Source: ONS dataset release date: 11 June 2024[61]

One of the frontier issues on controlling incapacity levels is stress. Suffering from stress is not a recognised incapacity, but it can quickly result in the individual claiming other symptoms that in turn are then deemed incapacity.[62] All the way back in 1995, *Walker vs Northumberland County Council* resulted in a cost to the county council of £174,000 for, according to the employment court, failing to deal properly with the stress – stated as leading to two nervous breakdowns – that the employee suffered.[63] £174,000 awarded to one individual suing their employer for the repercussions of 'stress', make employers understandably chary of hiring any employees they think might ever claim to suffer from stress, while, to make it worse, GPs around the country are, it seems, increasingly happy to sign stress sufferers off onto disability benefit.

Clearly, in the quoted case, the individual suffering from stress could have been given the challenge to find themselves a new, less stressful job. If the onus were put on the individual by law to manage their career, rather than creating incentives to go off work and sue the employer, it is likely that many of the 6 per cent of the working-age population suffering from 'incapacity' might still be in the workforce.

Over half of sickness claims are for 'depression, bad nerves or anxiety'. *The Spectator* claimed that the increase in incapacity was the chief reason for the UK slipping into recession in 2023. Had we had figures more along the lines of the US, Canada or France, a million or so more people would currently be working in the UK.[64] *The Economist* believes, plausibly, that the primary cause of this upsurge is that 'there are very strong incentives to apply for this benefit' and our 'black and white system encourages gaming'.[65] They say, 'Those deemed severely ill by a work-capability assessment do not care to look for work; they receive more than double the standard allowance.' So, do we believe the incidence of disability has shot up, or that gaming and weak gatekeeping has?

In the centre of this joblessness crisis, we have the problem of 'mental health'. Theodore Dalrymple, a former prison doctor, describes it as 'a hypochondriac's, narcissist's, shirker's and social security fraud's charter', and says the entire concept should be eliminated.[66] Matthew Parris, normally seen as a socially liberal commentator, points to the fact that this 'mental health' epidemic is, above all, a phenomenon of younger people, who sincerely believe they have a right to a mental health disability claim (and they can go on YouTube to find out how best to be successful with that claim).[67]

The point is that the moral panics I describe later, in Chapter 8, have taken so much hold in schools and encouraged vulnerability, suggestibility and a search for medicalisation of all youthful concerns. This has led to an epidemic of self-diagnosis of mental health issues – mostly among younger people coming out of schools and in their twenties but extending increasingly to older ranks too. All of this would not matter were there not, because of the state of the law, a significant financial incentive to put yourself into that class. The fact that a nine-to-five job is one of the best cures for depression or anxiety goes by the board.

The more benefits society offers, and the more compassionate it is in making it easy to claim those benefits, the more we open ourselves to much larger groups of citizens deciding – whether in a knowingly fraudulent manner or through disposition – that they wish to claim the benefits. It should not therefore be surprising that disability claims have recently soared. And in the digital age, there are plenty of people to lend a hand. We read that Charlotte Anderson, on YouTube, has thirty plus clients a month paying her £650 each to fill out their disability payments – and 'has only lost one claim in six years' and has a '100 per cent success rate at winning PIP'.[68] In the same article, we find that we are paying £292 million a year to people claiming to have ADHD (a controversial condition that may not be helped by the individual getting bene- fit), *up from less than £1 million a year a decade ago.* We are paying £1.8 billion a year for depression and anxiety claims (again, usually not helped by unemployment) and £1 billion for autism claims, all helped with online coaches and form fillers. In severe cases, help and money are indeed needed, of course, for those. In a growing number of cases, however, the intervention does not help soci- ety – nor, in the main, does it help the individuals receiving the benefits.[*]

Official estimates suggest that many school leavers in the UK (variously measured at between 20 and 30 per cent) depart from their school functionally illiterate or innumerate or both.

Of course, and inevitably, these failings in our education system have life-changing repercussions for the future life chances of these children and there are inevitable consequences for the benefits system. I have not seen any comparable analysis in the UK, but in the US, it has been found that the recent decline in participation in the workforce and the consequent movement from there onto welfare, is almost entirely confined to low-wage individuals.[69] In the general absconding of millions from the workforce that we have seen in the last few years, much is spoken of 'house husbands' and 'eternal students', but in the US, those categories represent, togeth- er, only around 20 per cent of that 'great resignation'. Almost all of the rest leave the workforce to claim disability and almost all of those are from the low-wage bracket.

---

[*]   It does massively help those online form fillers.

It is not possible to know how equivalent these trends might be in the UK because we are less informed here in analysing these trends. We know that in the UK there is a different dynamic between the workforce and the jobs market than in the US; a great deal of the commentary on the 'great resignation' in the UK is (relevantly or not) about middle-class withdrawal, not that of the lowest paid. However, that commentary is mostly anecdotal. It is more likely that much of the move from employed to claiming disability benefits is in the lowest-paid categories of worker. The connection in the UK between poor educational attainment and lack of participation in the workforce is both intuitively obvious and frequently documented.[70] This is particularly important when one appreciates that the UK economy is 80 per cent services and only 20 per cent manufacturing; services increasingly require educational skills, while even the remaining manufacturing jobs increasingly require high levels of literacy, numeracy and other skills of the educated.

Clearly, we need to restructure the disability benefit programme to coax as many as possible, whose disability is not preventing them from working, back into the workforce. Much as an individual may feel that their mental or physical health suffers from having to work in a job that they may not like, the alternative of not having a job is hardly any better for a person's mental health.

Much of this problem could go away if we were to give a better education to all of our children (including adult education), teaching them reading, writing and mathematics to a standard that will give them proper life skills and altering the structure of the British educational system to provide training in multiple practical skills for those teenagers not of an academic bent.

In any event, if we removed just 1 million from the 2.8 million working-age individuals currently on disability benefits, then some £10 billion in payments would be saved annually.[*]

To argue for lower benefits payments is not out of the mainstream: the OBR, not usually noted for right-wing policies, agrees that the UK should cut benefits.[71]

Savings of £10 billion from lower disability payments

Cost of living payments

In May 2022, the Chancellor announced a package of measures to help households mitigate the impact of the rapid rise in price levels (it is important to remember here that high inflation had largely been a result of monetary policy mistakes made by the Bank of England). The package contained additional lump-sum cost of living payments for the recipients of certain benefits, including Universal Credit and most legacy, disability and pensioner benefits. According to the DWP, these payments amounted to £8.2 billion and £10.2 billion in 2022/23 and 2023/24 respectively.[72] The Conservative government insisted it had no plans to extend the scheme and the new Labour government has not said it will extend it, so annual savings of some £10.2 billion should be available from 2024/25.

Savings of £10.2 billion from ceasing cost of living payments

---

[*] In spring 2024, the government announced reform of disability payments, which, they said, would otherwise double in cost (from some £30 billion to some £60 billion a year) by 2030. Reforms proposed included creation of a requirement for a second doctor to sign off, not just the GP, plus legislation that depression or anxiety would no longer count as a disability. Note that to pass such a law it is likely that the UK would have to leave the EHCR. It's not clear how fully committed the Conservative government ever was to pass this reform; in any event, they called an election rather than making it happen.

Health

The UK is proud of its NHS: in recent decades, NHS-worship has become something of a religion.

Is that pride justified? Personally, coming from a family of a long line of doctors, I admire the medical profession tremendously and see the vast majority of healthcare workers as dedicated, selfless, empathetic heroes. But having travelled the world, I've seen those heroes performing better or worse depending on the medical system they work in. The NHS would appear to be among the least effective healthcare systems in the developed world. In the following pages, I look at the evidence:

- We spend a lot

- Outcomes are poor and are getting worse

- Attempts at reform are unsuccessful

- Our socialist approach is a tried-and-true recipe for failure

- There are more effective ways of organising healthcare provision

- There are better ways that cost less

In the UK, we currently spend some £282 billion a year and rising on health, £211 billion of it through public spending (Chart 2.12) – almost 20 per cent of all government spending. The overall spend level has risen almost 30 per cent since 2019, when we spent some £223 billion. An astonishing rise in spending, yet health outcomes do not seem to have benefited much from the increase.

The money for healthcare spend (in 2022) comes from:[73]

- government-financed schemes: £230 billion
- voluntary health insurance schemes: £7 billion
- non-profit institutions/charities: £5 billion
- enterprise financing schemes: £0.6 billion
- individual expenditure: £39 billion

How does that level of expenditure compare with other countries with similar levels of wealth to us? Chart 2.21 indicates that we overspend, compared with the average country that has the same level of wealth per capita as us, by about £25 billion a year.

This conclusion – that we are spending more than what the average country at our wealth level would conclude it can afford – can be argued in terms of both pros and cons, as can be deduced from the chart. On the pro side of the argument, it is striking that just about every country that falls above the indicative line (i.e. they spend more on health than their wealth per capita indicates) has a higher GDP per capita than the UK and that almost all countries as poor as, or poorer than, the UK spend much less per capita on health than the UK does. On the con side, France and Germany, the big social democracies, spend far more – France at much the same level of GDP per capita as the UK, Germany at a higher level of GDP per capita.* But our argument is that those big social democracies are cutting off a brighter future for their people by spending so much. Arguing to spend at levels that high or higher carries

---

* Note in Chart 2.21 the enormous amount per capita spent by the US government (federal and state). This is over and above the private health insurance that 90 per cent of US citizens take. The implication is that the money the US government spends on health is spent inefficiently, but it is not ungenerous.

the further negative that the amounts are long-term unaffordable. Moreover, I argue in a few pages that by choosing the worst, most socialistic of health systems for our country, we are spending more to achieve worse health outcomes for our people.

Chart 2.2l: Government Expenditure on Health by GDP Per Capita

Indicatively, the UK spends more than it can afford on health.

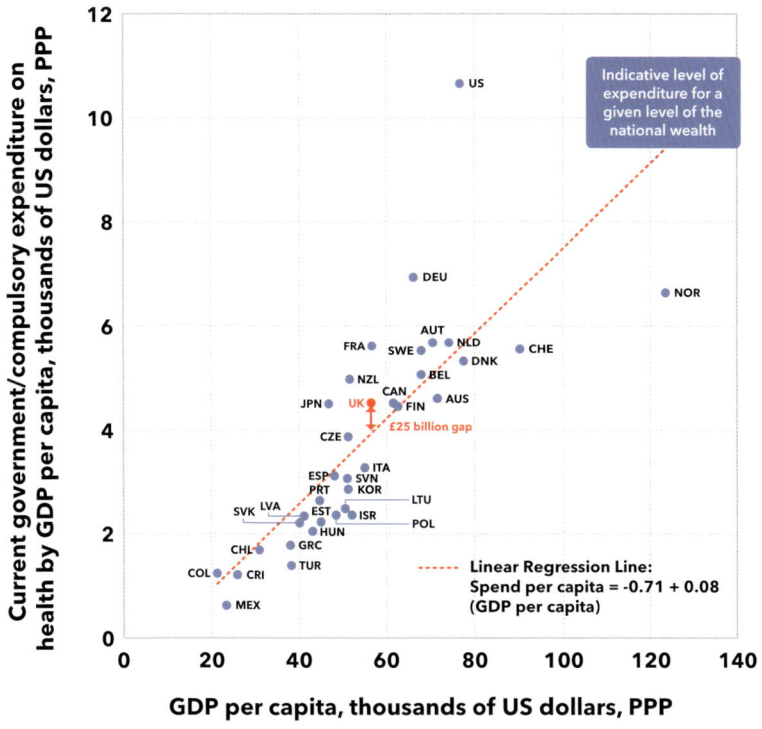

Source: OECD[74]

The fact is that in recent decades, the UK has massively grown its population, and thus the number that needs healthcare, from 58.8 million in the year 2000 to 67.9 million in 2024 – an over 15 per cent growth in headcount.[75] At the same time, we have not grown our GDP overall fast enough to be able to meet the demands of that growing population. And anyway, spending more doesn't, as I soon discuss, seem to be leading to better outcomes.

To be clear: this is not about health *needs* – if we spent per capita what we thought our citizens *needed*, our health spend per capita could be up there with that of Germany or even the US. What this discussion is about is how much a country of our size can *afford* and, in particular, what we can afford if we are to get out of the low-to-no-growth trap. As we have seen, countries that spend more than they can afford are not growing and so remain unable to afford any improvement in their health services.

The UK can't, Chart 2.21 would imply, afford its current level of health spend. The good news, however, as discussed in the following pages, is that we have one of the most inefficient and ineffective ways of spending money on health anywhere in the world – so there is a lot of opportunity to improve health outcomes while not spending more, or even spending less.

Let's note first, from Chart 2.21, that we spend £25 billion on health over and above what the average country at our level of wealth spends.[*][76] Noting from this that we need to better cut our coat to suit our cloth, it becomes crucial to find a better way to spend our NHS money, one that will produce better outcomes.

It is clear from Chart 2.21 that the amount a country can afford to spend per capita on health is very much a function of its GDP

---

* Incidentally, since 2016, the UK has increased its annual spending on the NHS in real terms by some £39.4 billion (adding in the planned £2.5 billion increase for 2024/25). The 2016 level was, therefore, well below the level of expenditure currently indicated for countries of our wealth per capita. If we returned to 2016 levels, and even if we added Vote Leave's promised £350 million a week (£18 billion), we would be spending near to £25 billion less on health than we are now. See endnotes.

per capita. So, again, a country that has achieved decent economic growth can afford far better healthcare for its citizens. A country like Switzerland, with a high absolute GDP per capita, can afford to allocate a *lower* share of its GDP to health yet still outspend almost every other major OECD country. For the UK, as discussed earlier, the key seems to be to increase its GDP substantially and then it could afford to spend more on health.

During the Covid period, the Treasury did authorise a large increase in healthcare staffing and expenditure. Since then, that higher level has been maintained. According to the IFS, 'There were 10.2 per cent more consultants in July 2022 than in July 2019, and 10.7 per cent more nurses and health visitors.'[77] Overall, according to the ONS, the number of doctors in the NHS has increased by 37 per cent in the last decade and other health staff by 23 per cent.[78] So, the steady deterioration in results in the past decade that we will go on to list cannot reasonably be claimed to be a function of the number of medical staff.

Health outcomes from the NHS are poor and getting worse
That the NHS has poor outcomes is becoming more and more unarguable. For example:

- Waiting lists are exploding.[79]
- 40 per cent of urgent cancer referrals are seen on average after sixty-two days, relative to 10–15 per cent a decade ago.[80]
- Mortality rates are the worst among comparator countries for seven key cancer areas (oesophagus, stomach, colon, rectum, pancreas, lung and ovarian cancer).[81]
- Infant mortality rates are one of the worst among comparator countries.[82]

- British five-year-olds are increasingly stunted, with their average heights now ranked ninety-eighth out of 200 countries.[83]

But that is just a small starter example of the poor results the UK gets from its health services. Overall, the NHS shows entirely unsatisfactory performance against its key targets. No wonder that public satisfaction with the NHS has fallen to an all-time low.[84]

As a result of this much-discussed decay of the NHS, the UK has dropped from an already poor nineteenth in health outcomes among all countries in 2013 to a somewhat shocking thirty-fourth, just one above Uruguay and just below the UAE in 2023 (Chart 2.22).

Chart 2.22: The Legatum Prosperity Index Health Outcomes, UK Versus Free-Market Economies
Ranking among 167 countries 2013–23

The UK's healthcare outcomes have been rapidly falling further and further below the results of the free-market economies.

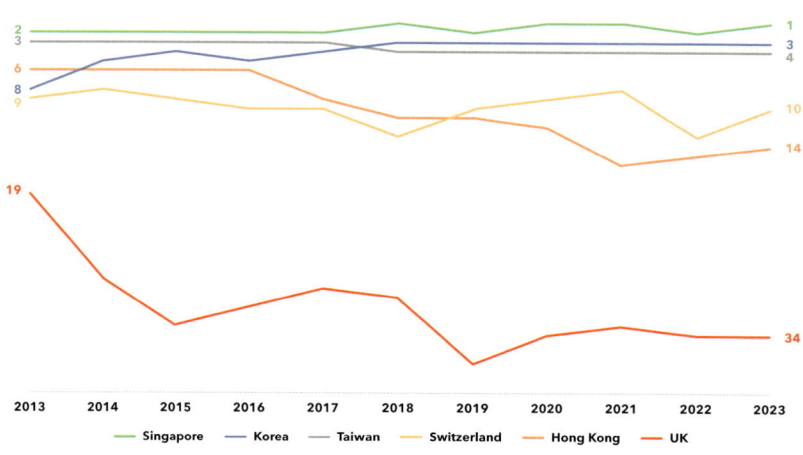

Source: The Legatum Prosperity Index[85]

From this chart, it is difficult to avoid the conclusion that the NHS has something fundamentally wrong with it.[*][86]

Attempts to reform the NHS have been unsuccessful

Over the years, there have been multiple attempts to reform the NHS. Every decade or so, it seems, a new report upends everything. All that seems to happen as a result is what always happens in collectivised entities: the bureaucracy and administrative burden grows and the apparatchiks, not the medical staff, are more and more in charge. In the Lucy Letby case, doctors were, enragingly, forced by administrators to write apologising to her for accusing her of possible complicity in multiple infant deaths.[†] In the infected blood inquiry, medical staff were suppressed from raising the alarm. In case after case, medical whistleblowers have been attacked, traduced, and required to sign NDAs. Administrators suppress all rational dissent, just as happened with the Post Office scandal, another centralised state function.

The NHS suffers from all the problems that may be expected from a socialistic, centralised, state monopolistic, employee-captured organisation.

The key issue that needs to be confronted when planning the future of healthcare in the UK is the apparently paradoxical fact

---

[*]   The US scores even worse than the UK. While many healthcare results are measured differently in the US than in other countries, certain poor outcomes of the US are undeniable. The unacceptable record is a combination of multiple differences in approach, much greater spend overall (legal fees and malpractice insurance), much worse performance on preventative medicine (particularly pre-natal), a major negative impact from mortality from violent assault (some twenty-five times the rate of the UK) and deaths from the ongoing opioid/fentanyl crisis. See endnote. The US is, however, much better in curing cancer and other mainstream diseases. For an adult with decent health insurance (90 per cent or more of the population), the place to be sick still seems to be the US – if we are to judge by the many ill foreigners flying there to be treated. This book does not, however, advocate a full-scale adoption of the American system of healthcare, although there are many components of it that the UK could benefit from.

[†]   Lucy Letby is, at the time of writing, appealing her case. My point is not about guilt or otherwise – it is about the suppression, and indeed victimisation, of whistleblowers.

that more money spent on the NHS does not overall seem to lead to an improvement in efficiency or to a reduction in suffering. Confronted with the undoubted distress and human anguish caused by a failing health service, we pour ever more money into it (even by 2018, we had increased NHS funding by considerably more than the £350 million a week posited in 2016 on the side of the Brexit bus during the referendum campaign).[87] Yet despite this compassionate and popular allocation of funds, the NHS service, even with Covid now pretty much in the rearview mirror, gets worse and worse – in GP availability, in hospital waitlists and in health outcomes.

Why should this be? In Volume Two we will be talking about the attractiveness and success of free markets compared with socialism. But the NHS, as constructed, is the opposite of a free-market approach; it is a classic state-run socialist monopoly. By delegating everything to the state, the system ends up the victim of employee capture, stultified and rigid one-size-fits-all solutions, major reduction in innovation, more and more pressure on the few good souls whose shoulders are put to the wheel to keep the dysfunctional juggernaut moving, and little competition to highlight deficiencies or spur better performance.

As we will see in Volume Two, the monolithic structure of the NHS is perfectly suited for employee capture. The pay and working conditions of staff are such that doctoring, for example, is among the highest-paid jobs in the UK, especially with its generous pension scheme (and especially given the high cost of training doctors who sometimes, soon after qualifying, take that costly qualification of theirs and go part time, retire or leave the country to practise elsewhere).[88] Administrative staffing and pay in hospitals seem also to have run riot.[89] There are indications that negative attitudes toward increasing, or even maintaining, productivity are now prevalent in parts of the NHS.

Socialised systems are inherently inefficient and badly managed: a privately managed system would be unlikely to result in individual GPs being paid, as happened in 2021–22, over £1 million a year.[90]

This dysfunctionality of the NHS is nowhere better illustrated than by the large changes to doctors' working practices achieved by militant unions in the NHS, whether in the lowering of maximum weekly hours or concessions on part-time working – and above all, by the fact that doctors now routinely go on strike.

A typical feature of a collectivised system is employee capture; this now extends beyond the service's administrators, being embraced more and more by the medical staff. The practice of medicine is a vocation and a very special one at that. Throughout history, the concept of the Hippocratic oath was that every doctor and nurse recognised that when they entered into the profession, putting themselves forward as individuals who will take responsibility for the health and lives of their fellow beings, they took on a solemn duty to do what it takes when faced with urgent medical needs. 'Is there a doctor in the house/on the plane/in the crowd?' goes up the cry. The response of the conscientious medical professional is not 'Sorry, I'm off duty', or 'Sorry, I'm on strike'. It is 'Here I am'. Being a doctor is not a lifestyle; it is a vocation. Thus, while the UK's NHS is undoubtedly in a mess and that's not the fault of doctors, nonetheless, if right now there are crowded waiting lists for GP surgeries, then it should be seen as morally unacceptable that so many GPs are choosing to work only four or three days a week. Same with hospitals. If all of those part-time doctors came back to full-time work for a year or two, the waiting lists would disappear rapidly. Yes, the government has a duty to sort the GP and hospital problems out as rapidly as possible, but in the meantime, patients are suffering and dying, whether because of part-time doctors or doctors on strike or because many doctors are not putting their shoulders to the wheel in the way that doctors of previous generations always instinctively did.*

How is it that there has been such a major change in personal attitudes and so many in this generation of doctors seem so indifferent to such considerations? Presumably, it is a failing of our education system, where a moral approach to education, such as that taken by Katharine Birbalsingh's Michaela Community School, seems nowadays to be a rare exception among schools. Without a well-established moral compass, why would doctors do other than seek to maximise their pay and working conditions, regardless of the impact on patients?

In consequence, the productivity of the workforce, especially relative to the cost of developing that workforce, has been going down and down in the NHS. This is mostly due to improved working conditions. Doctors are, on average, among the highest paid professionals in the UK.[91] This was the case originally because traditionally they worked very hard and had undergone many years of training. Now this is changing. During the training years, particularly for junior doctors, the amount of hours worked has been negotiated down dramatically, but their pay is still as high as before. Then, for GPs and hospital doctors alike, the average number of hours worked per week has declined dramatically because so many doctors moved to four- or three-day weeks, and many retire altogether, even when still in their thirties. So, both the efficiency (yield per

---

* I was warned that references to doctor strikes and waiting lists could result in this part of the book becoming quickly outdated. Let us hope so – but maybe it won't…

£ spent on doctor training) and effectiveness (knowledge and skill of those doctors who have spent much fewer hours practising in their formative junior years and therefore are less well trained) have declined significantly.

Above all, the government and the NHS seem to make decisions based mostly on grounds of compassion or good feelings, rather than expected outcomes. The NHS becomes a system structured for the least self-sufficient in the community. The result is that elements of personal effort that patients might employ are removed. True, pushy middle-class patients often find ways to jump the queue, but only at the expense of others: a zero-sum game.

The NHS's socialistic approach is a tried-and-true recipe for failure

All this is entirely predictable to any political historian worth their salt. If you adopt socialistic structures, you get inefficiency, capture by administrative staff, suppression of attempts to dissent or reform and calamitous outcomes.

In former days, 'privatisation' of the NHS was a 'third rail' of British politics that no one dared touch. Now, a recognition that the NHS is just another failed socialist experiment means that calls to abolish the NHS entirely grow more frequent.[92]

Taking a larger number of citizens out of the NHS for much of their needs would remove all sorts of strain from almost every point of the NHS, from GPs to hospitals. Widening the number of those around the country who take private insurance would, for example, permit development of the same kind of private hospital networks across the rest of the country as we are now seeing in London. Increasing the number of private hospitals in the country will put moral pressure on those (not all) NHS hospitals that are falling behind to be as efficient and effective as private hospitals.

This gradual commingling of private and public in the health sector would lead to all sorts of opportunities for the NHS to avail itself of provision from the private sector and for private-sector approaches (in areas such as patient records and digital appointments) to be adopted by those parts of the NHS that are currently struggling with modernisation.

However much or little money governments spend, however big or small the size of that government is, the degree to which it spends efficiently or inefficiently will impact the cost of what it is delivering. A government spending inefficiently would, if it rationalised itself, deliver the same service and benefits to its citizens at less cost, shrinking the size of government and thus (since the size of government clearly impacts economic growth) having a better chance of the nation's economy growing faster.

There are more effective ways of organising healthcare provision
As will be discussed in Volume Two, competition and price mechanisms improve the product or service being offered and drive cost efficiency.

The implications of this are that the more competition that can be inserted into the NHS, the more efficient and effective it is likely to be, and if a clear price is placed upon any particular health benefit that is delivered, more careful attention will be paid by the user to whether they need it or not. As has been pointed out by many, the NHS, with its ethos of comprehensive health provision free at the point of delivery, is in many respects unique relative to other systems spread around the world. In removing both competition and the price mechanism from most of its activities, cost efficiency and effectiveness are removed from the equation. This is such a basic and obvious point that it is surprising that it is not more widely discussed.

What might an NHS with competition and a price mechanism that challenges users with the economics of what they are receiving look like? It might look a little more like the French system in some way, where users must pay a small amount for each appointment with their doctor; or like the German system in another way, where insurance is compulsory and multiple insurers compete on both medical outcomes and cost; or probably a bit like the US system in yet another way, where Medicare and Medicaid provide free health-care and free prescriptions to all over sixty-five. Health outcomes in the UK are poor relative to other countries. Mostly, this is an inevitable outcome of an overly socialistic system with inefficient and overly costly practices. An NHS with competition introduced, rather than one with hospitals that look entirely to the government for ever-expanding expenditures and ever-larger annual budgets, would be different and better.

Ara Darzi, Lord Darzi, generally given much of the credit for a previous reduction in waiting lists under Labour's government, has recently called out the failure to budge the current woeful waiting list figures.[93] Calling for operations to be performed seven days a week, greater productivity and swifter turnaround times, he recalled his Blair-era efforts, which included bringing in European surgeons for weekly stints, clearing '3,000 cases in about three and a half months'. Such a can-do attitude is gradually being seen in some parts of the NHS. For example, in the use of F1 'pit-stop' techniques to slash waiting lists, between three times and five times the usual daily number of patients were operated on in this process.[94] Unfortunately, these new approaches are not yet gaining widespread traction, so are not as yet making any big difference. As in the rest of the public sector, productivity is given low priority.*

Other obvious efficiencies that need to be implemented are dedicated surgical hubs: theatres, possibly privately run, dedicated to one specific procedure (hernia, hip replacement, whatever) and run on a seven-days-a-week basis.[95] Community diagnostic centres could also bring scanners and efficiency to the people at far lower cost. Opening up these areas to the private sector would result in more investment being made, more capacity created and more efficiency: all putting greater pressure to improve on NHS hospitals.

The better ways can cost less

The issue of the nation's health and the role of the NHS in it is so emotive that it is unlikely that *any* specific proposal to cut costs will be received with favour. It won't be until there is more general recognition that we are living above our means, in particular with respect to the NHS, and that we are spending at least £25 billion a year more than we can afford at our current level of national wealth, that savings can start to be enforced. Sooner or later, though, this problem will be recognised, at which point it will be seen that there are plenty of opportunities to cut cost without worsening – indeed, in many cases improving – services. Much of the benefits could be a result of moving large parts of the NHS to a more privatised regime.†

By how much could costs be reduced? What elements of privatisation or commercial discipline should be introduced into the NHS? First, we might note that the NHS is already being privatised

---

* Incentives and a focus on the finances play a large part here. In a competitive private sector, both the director and the hospital are incentivised to maximise the use of the expensive surgical theatre. Administrators, and indeed medical staff in the NHS, have little direct incentive to behave in the same way.

† I persist in my pious hope that the British electorate are not so endlessly gullible that they will continue to respond forever to the dog whistle that says 'privatisation' of any part of the NHS is the equivalent of selling our souls to Satan.

– by stealth, as it were. In just the past five years, the number of people in the UK using private health insurance has gone from 12 per cent to 22 per cent of the adult population.[96] In what way the NHS can be seen to have benefited from this huge reduction of pressure on it is a further mystery, but if this trend continues, the UK's health system is, in a few decades, going to look much more like the US's, with more private hospitals and GPs than NHS ones. The process could be accelerated by adopting various and somewhat uncontroversial privatisation steps:

- State-funded insurance: Germany, widely praised for its health-care outcomes, uses forty-six private insurance companies, which citizens can choose from and through which healthcare is delivered.[97] Such an approach carries obvious opportunities for efficiency, if only because it ensures competition between organisations, both for better outcomes and for cost control.

- Compulsory private health and privately funded insurance for the wealthy and for new immigrants: Private insurance in the UK doesn't cover all health expenditures for those who have it – some costs and activities are still picked up by the NHS. Nonetheless, the fact that so few in the UK take private insurance puts a significant strain on the NHS. Arguably, anybody earning above a particular level of salary should be *required* to take private insurance. Wealthy citizens who boast that they always and exclusively use the NHS should be encouraged to start thinking of that action as making themselves either free riders on society or as mistakenly thinking virtue signallers who are making waiting lists longer, rather than what many of them, not really plausibly, claim to be: rich citizens exercising solidarity with the (poorer) rest of the populace. As mentioned earlier, pre-Covid only 10 per cent of Britain's population were privately insured. Post-Covid, the number has nearly doubled to 22 per cent.[98] But the number of insured in the US is 92 per cent.[99]

- Small fees for visiting the doctor: Countries such as France – despite it being, in general, far more committed to social equality than the UK – charge a minimal, non-refundable fee for each visit to the GP. The amount of doctors' time that is wasted is thereby reduced because more people then actually turn up for their appointments. Objections to this approach, claiming that it hurts the poor, can be overcome by creating exceptions. Objections that adopting the same approach would subvert the egalitarian ideals of the NHS should be countered with estimations of how much the approach would save the NHS, thus freeing up funds for needed improvements to the NHS. Rishi Sunak had this as part of his pitch in the Conservative leadership race, but never resurrected the idea once he became Prime Minister.

- Recovery of training fees from NHS-educated doctors who fail to stay in the NHS: As doctors' earnings have sky-rocketed following some highly generous wage settlements throughout the 2000s, the amount of hours worked has simultaneously collapsed. In particular, many doctors go part-time within a few years of qualifying or retire altogether (while still in their thirties), and, of course, there are also the many doctors who immediately go private (or emigrate). Any or all of these doctors should be required to pay back some or all of the between £175,000 (junior) and £500,000 (consultant, including surgeons) that it costs the taxpayer to train a doctor in the UK.[100]

- National, privately run centres of excellence: Better outcomes are achieved from specialisation and economies of scale. An example would be in screening and in treatments and surgical interventions, such as for hernias, prostate cancer, breast cancer, hip replacements and cataracts. There is no reason why we could not create privatised national entities in a way that ensures that a sufficient number of these are created to ensure that there is price competition between them. This would be in contrast to the monopolies of our privatised utilities, where there is currently insufficient competition to create a good and cheap service.

- Privatisation of the part of the NHS that most blame for the ever-worsening performance: its administration. As Sam Ash-worth-Hayes put it, 'Let Amazon run the NHS. That would cut the waiting lists.'[101] In practice, the best way to do this would be to outsource the administration of each NHS trust, by open tender, establishing a number of private-sector providers.

- Restricting 'luxury' or controversial healthcare procedures and benefits from the NHS mantra of even inessential care being available to all: in the US, while almost all citizens are either privately insured or under Medicare or Medicaid, the suite of basic medical coverages doesn't cover, say, elective cosmetic surgery.

The biggest shibboleth is, or course, the phrase 'Free at the point of delivery for all citizens'. Why? A large proportion of citizens in the UK are among the wealthiest in the world. If we know that free, competitive markets deliver the best results, why do we force one of the OECD's most socialistic health systems on generally wealthy and intelligent consumer-minded UK citizens? If Germany, France and other EU countries, not to mention the US, have approaches where people pay something into the system, if only to improve consumer discipline, then why not the UK? Why not take a huge strain off the NHS by, say, requiring the top 40 per cent of earners in the country, along with all (non-asylum) immigrants for, say, the first six years of their life in the UK to take private health insurance? Again, the amount of healthcare cost paid for by citizens, as opposed to by governments, varies widely across different countries. France charges a small amount for every medical visit. In Germany, 11 per cent is paid from private insurance, but the remaining 89 per cent, paid for by the (privately run) sickness funds, is funded by private contributions (fifty-fifty by employees and employers).

The advantages that could be obtained from privatisation of large swathes of the NHS are amusingly captured in a recent letter to the *Telegraph*:

> I recently phoned my local hospital to inquire about an appointment for an investigation requested two weeks earlier … After evenually being put through to the correct department, I learnt that no request had been received. A visit to the GP's surgery established that the request had not, in fact, been made.
>
> The same afternoon my cat became unwell following a bite from one of his acquaintances. His vet was able to offer an appointment three hours later, the abcess was drained, and medication commenced … The contrast between the two treatment experiences could not be more stark.[102]

Weirdly, however, many well-off individuals in the UK ostensibly take pride in sticking with the NHS. In this, they use up NHS resources that could otherwise be available for those less wealthy, they renounce agency in looking after their own health and that of their families, and they perpetuate the creaking, failing state of the NHS. Virtually no country – not even among the social democracies of the EU – goes as far as the UK does in making its healthcare system so socialistic.

What would an alternative be? There are a variety of options to be seen around the world. The most obvious one to emulate without controversy is the German insurance-based system (using both statutory and private insurance funds).[103] We would, however, have to come up with a way of doing it less expensively. Or, ignoring the 'Singapore on Thames' jibes, Singapore might be the way to go. EPICENTER, the European think tank, reviewed how Singapore's healthcare system is the most efficient in the world, with the second-best healthcare performance and fourth-highest life expectancy at birth globally.[104] They achieve this, says EPICENTER, through 'uniquely' combining individual social responsibility with a government safety net. If Wes Streeting, Labour's Health Secretary, can visit Singapore before the election and find things to emulate there, why did successive Conservative Health Secretaries consider doing that too hot to handle?[105]

And then there is the US, the most privatised of major systems. Around 92 per cent of US citizens under the age of sixty-five have some form of healthcare insurance paid for individually, by employers or by the US government via Medicare, Medicaid, veterans' or children's schemes.[106] All over-65s are covered by the federal Medicare programme. This leads to excellent healthcare outcomes for the majority of medical fields with, as mentioned earlier, a relatively small but definite number of problematic areas.[107]

Hospitals and other services are springing up in places where there are a large number of privately insured individuals, such as London, providing better and (from the insurance companies' point of view) cheaper services than NHS hospitals. In London, a number of private hospitals, including the Cromwell, the Lister and London Bridge, have advanced IT systems that interact with private GPs and the insurance companies to allow easy bookings of appointments, swift transfer of test and scanning results, transfer of medical records, documentation of historical interactions and the like. While these hospitals may not be at the leading edge of, for example, every type of cancer treatment or some other major disease,* it is indubitable that within the London catchment area these generalist hospitals take away from the NHS an enormous amount of strain and activity.

Breaking the emotionally driven and damaging shibboleths of 'our NHS' could have an enormous impact on healthcare in the UK – costs reduced, results up, UK citizens living longer, cancer and other major health issues dealt with quicker and more successfully.

Are there parts of health we should not be doing at all?
The major obstacle to moving the NHS away from its increasingly dysfunctional, state monopolistic approach seems to be a psycho-logical – quasi-religious, even pathological – veneration of a social-istic approach. That approach hasn't worked well in any other sector of the economy and it doesn't in the healthcare sector either. Should there be things that the NHS shouldn't be doing? Yes – and they are things that the private sector can do and does cheaper, more efficiently and with better outcomes.

However, even raising the issue of privatisation has come to be seen as something that is well outside the so-called 'Overton window'; instant death for the politician who raises it. It is depressing that the commentariat and mainstream politicians have allowed this doctri-naire rhetoric of 'no privatisation of the NHS' to occupy the high ground. For a start, the concept of 'privatising the NHS' is far too muddled to have any coherence; there are so many different parts to the NHS that privatisation could refer to a multitude of different

---

* In the US, they have separate hospital complexes (e.g. Sloan Kettering) for those individual diseases.

possibilities. Many parts of the NHS are, indeed, already 'privatised' (within any meaningful sense of the word): the network of general practices; temporary nursing agencies; the building of hospitals; private hospitals; rehab and many other parts are run by private companies or, as with the case of GPs, by sole proprietors.

If the shibboleth of 'no privatisation' can be put aside, there could be many opportunities to introduce the discipline of free markets and competition into the provision of healthcare in the UK. For example, routine operations such as hernias, hip replacements and cataracts could be opened up across the country to competitive bids by specialist centres, rated on cost, speed and health outcomes. Lower costs, no more waiting lists, better outcomes for the patients because of the concentration of specialist expertise.

So, and given that large parts of the NHS are already 'privatised', the issue is: what other parts of the NHS might usefully be privatised and which parts should remain entirely within the public sector? In discussing this, we should surely be prepared to look at health services around the world that are more successful than the UK's, regardless of their level of expense or degree of 'privatisation' or otherwise, and seek urgently to learn from their success: how it is accomplished and which parts of that success could be adopted by us.

And there is one further area of savings: the £2.64 billion (up from £900 million a decade ago and rising rapidly every year) in compensation payments made annually by the NHS. Even the House of Commons saw this as excessive and produced a report as to how to reduce it.[108] As soon as a compassionate society creates a framework for compensation, two things happen: unfairly injured patients get remunerated but the legal profession flocks round, and claims balloon. If the recommendations of the Commons were implemented, around £1 billion could be saved.

- Take the top 30 per cent of taxpayers and, for their first six years in the country, immigrants out of the NHS full-care safety net, requiring them to take private healthcare from a recognised health insurance provider.[*]
- Privatise all hospitals under an agreed German-style insurance system, creating private sector-run surgical centres for routine operations
- Outsource the admin for each NHS trust, while removing all diversity, equality and inclusion (DEI) training and similar distractions
- Bring pit-stop-style scheduling management to hospitals
- Issue vouchers for procedures and operations, with assistance to the patients to find alternative providers
- Require all doctors to contribute seven full-time equivalent years to the NHS or repay part of their training
- Limit 'luxury' NHS health provision and encouraging supplementary private insurance that provides upper-tier services and procedures
- Take the top 30 per cent of taxpayers and, for their first seven years in the country, immigrants out of the NHS full-care safety net, requiring them to take private healthcare from a recognised health insurance provider.[†]

These reforms would save, at a minimum, 10 per cent of NHS spend. Half of this should be used to plug various current spending holes in the NHS, the other half becoming part of overall cost savings: at a minimum, some £13 billion. (This would mean that the UK was still spending some £12 billion per capita more than other countries of similar wealth.)

Further, £1 billion a year could be saved from excessive compensation awards.

Total savings: £14 billion

---

[*] Excluding asylum seekers and low-paid occupational exemptions.
[†] Excluding asylum seekers and low-paid occupational exemptions.

Debt-service costs

The startlingly large size of debt-servicing costs incurred by the UK for 2022/23 (some 11 per cent of total government receipts or 4.4 per cent of GDP for that year) had a cause: the major, although temporary (one hopes), payments that the government had to make on its inflation-linked gilts, caused by the high level of RPI inflation in 2022–23. For 11 per cent of our government revenue to be on debt-servicing costs is clearly unsustainable. It can be hoped that such a level of cost is not going to be repeated. At a more normal level of inflation, one that is close to the long-term 2 per cent inflation target, the 11 per cent drops to 8–9 per cent (2 per cent or more of spend, 1 per cent of GDP lower).[109]

So, as and when inflation dies down, that second payment (inflation-linked) shrinks.* However, we will then still be at the unconscionably high debt-service level of 8–9 per cent of government revenues or slightly over 3 per cent of GDP. And lurking around the corner is a new danger that will inevitably increase this amount. As older, expiring government bonds are replaced with newer bonds issued in our now-higher interest rate environment, the cost of debt service rises again (think of the analogy of the increased cost to a house owner whose mortgage deal has come to an end and who has now to pay a new higher rate on their borrowing).

So, as can be seen in Chart 2.23, with these two opposing items, the level of our debt-service cost looks to remain, pro-forma, much at that same high level. And then, of course, on extrapolating the status quo (Chart 1.29), each year we will add more to the pile of

---

* To the naïve onlooker, this could lend a spurious element of plausibility to any future narrative that would claim the government had significantly reduced the overall level of national expenditure by a full 2 per cent of GDP. It won't have really. It would be because we had become the beneficiaries of the worldwide drop in inflation – in our case, from very high levels.

national debt, so the level of debt service costs will go on rising steadily over the coming fifteen years.* [110]

Chart 2.23: Total National Debt Servicing Costs
2007–2023: percentage of government expenditure

As debt rises, so do payments – turbocharged by having issued so many inflation-linked gilts.

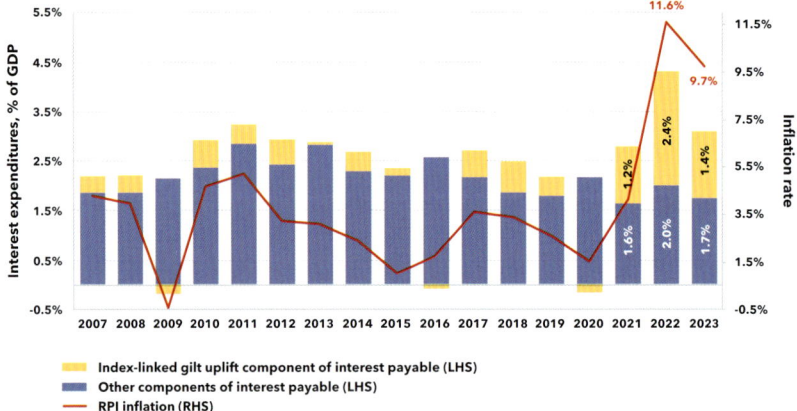

Source: ONS, [III] *dataset identifier codes NMFX, MW7L, YBHA, CHAW, moyniteam analysis*

But wait (as they say) – there's more! Thanks to the misguided Keynesian obsession with quantitative easing (QE) and the mistaken conclusion that a 'great moderation' would give us a never-ending era of cheap money, the Bank of England, in its QE programme, purchased almost £1 trillion of gilts and corporate bonds, with any future losses on that portfolio guaranteed by the government. Well, those losses have arrived and are running – last year, this year and the next few years these losses are expected to cost HM Treasury

---

* The OBR says they 'expect public sector net debt to rise to a peak of 103.1 per cent of national income in 2023–24, which is equivalent to around £2.7 trillion or £95,000 per household, and then fall gradually to reach 96.9 per cent in 2027–28. In cash terms, we expect it to stand at almost £3 trillion by then'. (See 'A brief guide to UK public finances' from the OBR at the endnote.) This book's models, as we have seen in Part I, beg to differ; they think debt will carry on rising to much higher levels than that unless something drastic is done.

(i.e. us) some £104 billion until all gilts are sold back to the market – let us say, some £10 billion a year, for the next five years, in monies paid from the government (i.e. us) to the Bank of England.[112] Once all the bonds are sold back into the market, that cost will cease. These short-term costs are left out of the model.*

Even if we avoid future inflation but fail to take the radical steps advocated in this book, then national debt continues to grow and the annual debt payments continue to rise, until we get control of our deficits. There is nothing we can do to get this baked-in cost of debt service down until our debt recedes or GDP significantly grows. Government debt is reviewed extensively in Volume Two.

In summary, if inflation can be kept under control, annual interest costs will be reduced by over £20 billion relative to 2022/23 levels. But there are the added costs of refinancing our maturing debt at higher interest rates that shrink the savings somewhat – perhaps reducing the savings from £20 billion to £15 billion. But still there will be that large and growing (approximate) £100–115 billion a year of debt service costs, and if we carry on as we are, it will just get worse and push the number back up again. Over time, only by reducing the deficit and growing more rapidly can the debt service cost be prevented from getting greater and greater as a percentage of GDP.

---

* One popular view claims there is no cost to the government in selling these bonds back into the market after having purchased them at a higher cost. That's odd: the bond traders who sold and then repurchased these bonds have made, overall, hundreds of billions of pounds in profit from those trades. If the money had been given to a sick mother, it would have been government expenditure. So why is that any different if the money is given to a rich bond trader? Some say that to avoid acknowledging the losses, the Bank of England should hold these bonds to expiry, at which point they disappear. This view is chimerical: many of the bonds were bought above par so there will be a loss when they expire, while the interest gained from holding them will be less than the interest needed to pay on reserves funding them. So, losses eventuate there too. The economic losses must, by definition, be identical.

Total annual savings from drop in inflation-linked payments, less refinancing our debt at higher interest rates: £15 billion

Education

Education is another sector where there seems to be a disconnect between spend and outcomes.

The UK, regardless of what is often claimed, spends a lot on education: it is at the upper end of spending levels on primary and secondary education when compared with other OECD countries.

Chart 2.24: Public Spending on Education
Primary to post-secondary, non-tertiary and tertiary,
as a percentage of GDP, 2020 or latest available

The UK spends above what other OECD countries spend.

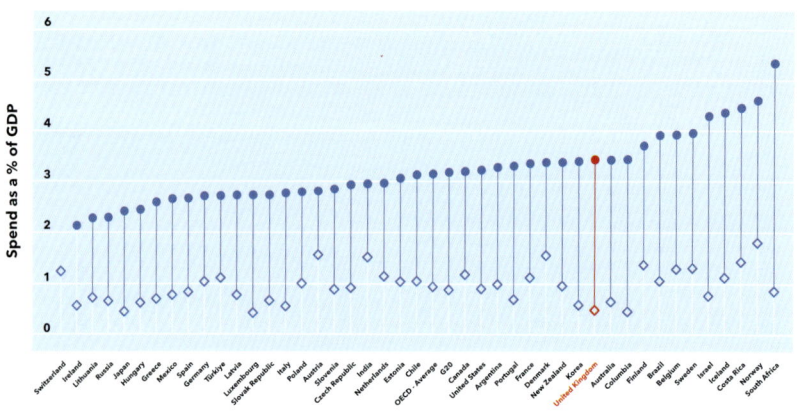

● *Primary to post-secondary non tertiary*
◇ *Tertiary*

Source: OECD

As can be seen from the chart, our high spend is for schools; at the university level, we are one of the lower spenders (as a percentage of GDP).

In the following pages, we split our discussion into two:

- Schools (primary and secondary): costs and results
- Higher education (tertiary): costs and results

Schools: costs and results

In Chart 2.25 we see that for countries that spend below the OECD average on schooling (in dollars per student), an increase in expenditure leads to a significant improvement in scores. However, for countries already spending above the average, the more you spend, the (very slightly) worse your educational outcomes become. This – at first sight paradoxical – result may be because high level of spend is often driven by high teacher wages. Such high levels are a marker for the grip the teachers' unions have on the education system in that country; the main focus of teachers' unions is on improving the pay and working conditions of the teachers. The improvement of conditions (reduction in hours worked etc.) can often be to the detriment of the children's schooling. Hence, more money spent is correlated with slightly worse educational outcomes.

How do the UK's educational results compare internationally? Not bad; those results are one of the few bright spots in the past decade. England has risen dramatically in the PISA educational tables.[*] In Scotland, the more they spend per child, the worse they

---

[*] Education is a devolved power in the UK, so Scotland, Northern Ireland and Wales have different systems to England's. England's improved position is more due to other countries' post-Covid results falling back while England's results stayed much the same.

do; they are now, in terms of results, the equivalent of a full year of teaching behind the UK.[113]

Chart 2.25: Reading Performance and Spending on Education 2018

Additional spending on education after a certain point is (mildly) negative if correlated with educational outcomes. Spending more than the OECD average (as the UK does) doesn't improve outcomes.

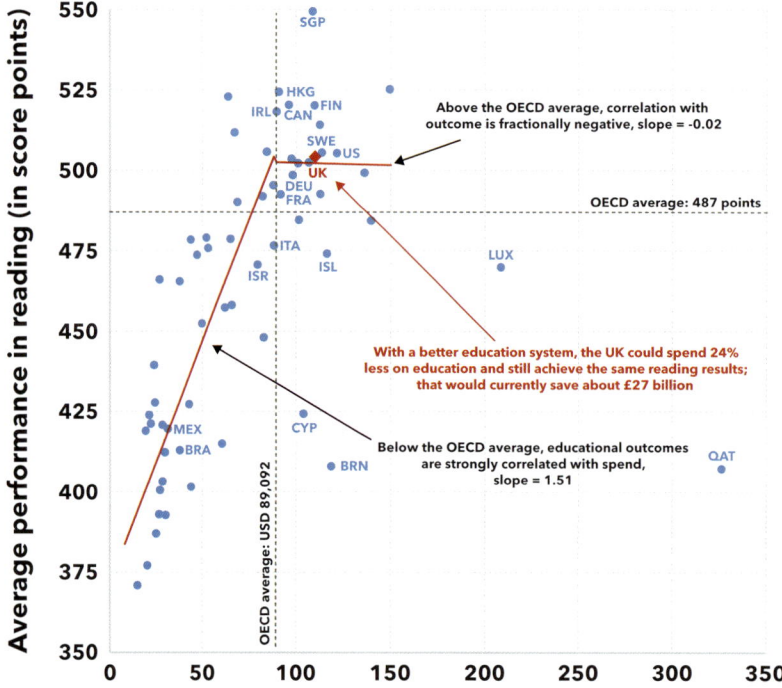

Source: OECD, PISA 2018 database[114]

The UK's improved results are a function of two key changes to England's approach to education since the early 2000s. For maths, we adopted the Shanghai teaching method and for reading, the phonics approach.[115] Anecdotally, it is said that a very large proportion of the UK's schools either have failed to comply with the requirement to adopt these approaches or have such bad levels of classroom discipline that they cannot teach much at all, but schools that adopted those two approaches and have good classroom discipline have seen startling improvements. The schools who don't adopt these approaches see, correspondingly, poor outcomes – so we still have many children leaving school illiterate and innumerate, but this is a consequence of poor teaching approaches and poor classroom discipline, not of insufficient money.

Chart 2.26: Educational Costs and Outcomes
England, Scotland and Wales

Spending per head has not been the key to academic performance.

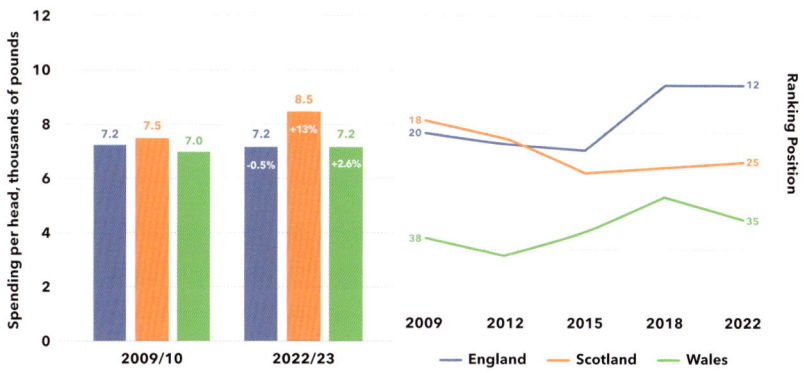

Source: Institute for Fiscal Studies and OECD (PISA)[116]

As a result of the reforms mentioned here, the number of those leaving school both reasonably literate and reasonably numerate has increased, as Chart 2.27 shows.

Chart 2.27: Level 2 Attainment in English & Maths
by Ages Sixteen and Nineteen
2004/05 to 2021/22

Spectacular improvements have been achieved at both age sixteen and age nineteen.

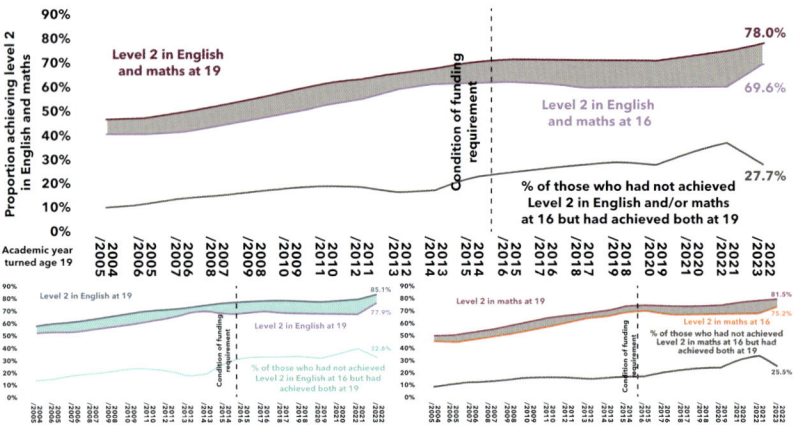

Notes: Figures for English and maths are based on those educated in the mainstream state-funded sector in Year 11, therefore overall attainment rates differ to headline measures. Trends are comparable.

'Condition of funding' (requirements for a school to get its state funding) changes for young people were introduced by the Education and Skills Funding Agency from 2014/15 onwards. This has resulted in most students having to study English and/or maths as part of their programmes between the ages of sixteen and nineteen if they are yet to achieve qualifications at GCSE level (level 2).

Source: National Statistics[117]

We see in this chart the rate of literacy and numeracy for sixteen-year-olds rising from 40 per cent in 2004 to 69 per cent in 2022 and for nineteen-year-olds from 47 per cent to 78 per cent.

The bad news is that leaves 30 per cent of sixteen-year-olds either illiterate or innumerate or both; a well-functioning school system could reduce that to 10 per cent or even 5 per cent.

Chart 2.25 lends confirmation to the argument that the cause of this is not that our schools have too little money to spend but because they teach the wrong way. In particular, the examples of Singapore (who spend the same as us per pupil but get far better results than we do), the US (who spend much more than us but get the same outcomes) or Ireland (who spend much less than us and get better outcomes) suggest the problem is one of wrong teaching rather than too little expenditure. The UK only ranks twelfth in the 2022 PISA tables. This compares to Singapore at number one – and Singapore spends only 2.5 per cent of its GDP on education compared to 5.2 per cent for the UK. This is, admittedly, in part because Singapore's GDP per capita is so much higher than ours – but that is yet another incentive for us to grow our economy. We could do so much better – and it is not necessary to spend more money to do so. Rather, as Chart 2.25 implies, we could be spending some £27 billion less and still get the same results.

The private education sector in the UK certainly takes some of the strain from the state budget and gets good results: shrinking private education (e.g. by imposing VAT on private school fees) is going to further overload state schools, as parents who can't afford the cost return their children to the state sector, thus imposing economic self-harm on the country.

One bit of good news, though: there are going to be more than half a million fewer children in England in the school system by the mid-2030s, saving around £1 billion in school costs.[118]

It is clear that some aspects of the UK's schooling are being badly managed by our educational establishment: deteriorating buildings, fewer and fewer playing fields, fewer evening and other extracurricular activities.[119] All of these (excluding attempts by teachers to move to four and a half or four days per week) could benefit from having more money.

The governments of Tony Blair and Gordon Brown doubled the amounts of money spent on education.[120] On what did the schools spend that money? Not, it appears, on the money-starved areas listed above. There is evidence that much of this extra money, still swimming around the system, was squandered by many schools on hiring a huge new class of employee to our schools: teaching assistants (TAs).[121]

In 2023, there were 282,925 FTE teaching assistants in the UK's school system.[122] This compares with some 468,693 teachers – more than one TA for every two teachers (and bear in mind that many schools don't have any TAs at all). A small proportion of these TAs are, and always will have been, needed for severely disabled pupils. In 1996, pre-Blair, there were some 60,000 TAs; now there are 283,000.[123] So, when the money came in from Blair, TAs almost tripled, and by now, post-Blair, their numbers have almost quintupled.

Chart 2.28: Number of Teaching Assistants in England
Full-time equivalent, 2000, 2011 and 2022

Why are there almost 300,000 teaching assistants in the UK, costing us some £8 billion? It's an example of misdirected spend.

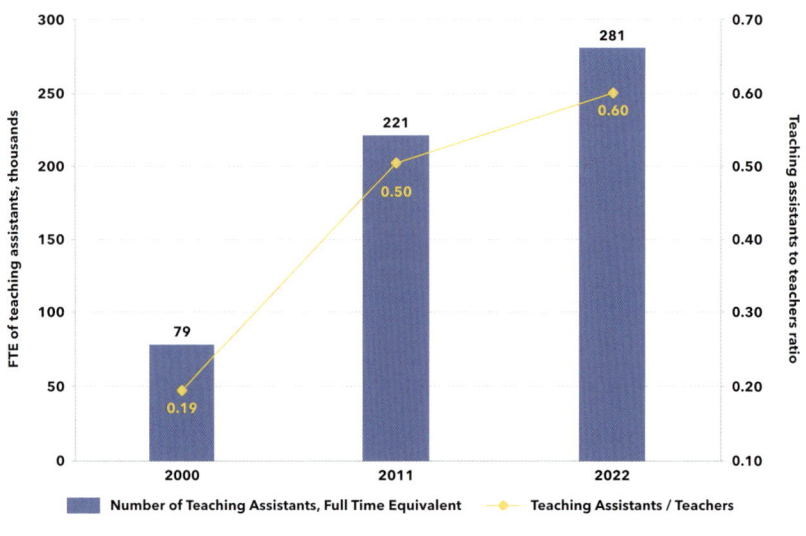

Source: Gov.uk[124]

At an average salary of £23,400, and adding in an additional (min-imum) non-salary cost of 20 per cent per load, the overall cost of this TA workforce is around £8 billion.[125] And yet, observant senior educationalists believe that the presence in the classroom of most of these TAs actually *worsens* academic outcomes (the reason being that their presence distracts the child from paying attention to the teacher at the front of the class). While the number of TAs in some schools is large, in others it is almost zero – so it cannot be said that their presence is imperative.[*] The claimed need for TAs is nowadays based on the alleged and increasing number of school children with special educational needs or 'mental health' issues. I argue, along with others, that this number is massively overblown and is damaging the very children it is meant to help by medicalising bad behaviour and preventing children from developing traits of self-discipline.[126] Proper classroom discipline, not TAs, should be used to address the problem.

Hiring too many TAs is possibly the most egregious – although not the only – example of poor cost control in schools, where savings could be made without negatively impacting educational attainment. A further possible area for savings is if each school were to become part of a Multiple Academy Trust (MAT), where not only significant economies of scale savings on administrative costs are achieved but also the school can be administered far better by using specialists within the MAT structure. Most importantly, head teachers can focus better on the school's core task of teaching, rather than on administrative faff.

So, it is clear that there is a degree of poor spending in many schools: TAs, schools not in MATs, generally poor financial management.

---

[*]	In admittedly non-rigorous, non-published analysis by this author, the more TAs a school has, the (slightly) worse (non-statistically significant) will be its academic results, presumably because TAs distract the pupil from focusing on the teacher as the teacher tries to teach, and the more likely that school will be to run a financial deficit, presumably because of the cost of the TAs putting pressure on the rest of the school budget.

Non-salary spend cannot be lessened by much, particularly given the dire state of many school buildings.* Moreover, as discussed, there are plenty of areas where not enough is spent to give our children a rounded and fully life-enhancing education. For example, only 12 per cent of state schools have orchestras and, as stated earlier, the number of school playgrounds and playing fields is ever-shrinking.[127] If money were to be saved on school budgets from some of these points, some of those savings could and probably should be spent on these problems. A reduction in TAs and an increased requirement to ensure economies of scale through MATs could result in at least £5 billion in savings. These savings could be used on such pressing needs.

Are there parts of education where we can be more efficient, accomplishing the same or better at less expense? As I discuss later, in Volume Two, education, being mostly a government monopoly, suffers, as all such sectors do, from employee capture. Any such sector ends up being run primarily for the benefit of its employees – the teachers and other staff, rather than its customers, the schoolchildren.

Data from 2023 reveal that, even before recent favourable pay settlements, England's teachers are among the best paid, for the fewest hours, in Europe.[128] † And yet they are required to work for less hours than any other country that gave data to the OECD (apart from Luxembourg).[129] Savings can, over time, be achieved by reducing some or all teacher salaries or, at the very least, allowing them to grow less fast over the coming decade.

---

* Conservative government plans in 2024/25 were to increase spend on school rebuilding from some £700 million to some £1.2 billion. It's not clear whether that new amount enlarges the school budget or is taken from other parts of the budget. At the time of writing, Labour government plans on this item are unclear.

† Part of the problem is the failure to distinguish sufficiently on pay for teaching different subjects. With a teaching salary of £36,000, a maths graduate earns far less than they could get in other sectors. Higher pay for qualified graduates teaching maths or science, with perhaps lower pay for some others, could have a significant impact.

The introduction of free schools under Michael Gove has exploded the myth that under-par educational attainments are inevitable and that more money is needed to get great results. Katharine Birbalsingh's non-selective Michaela Community School, in a poor part of London, with the same level of funding and socioeconomic cross-section of pupils as other Brent schools, has within a decade come to outperform *every single school in England* in terms of 'progress 8' improvement in its pupils' skills and capabilities. She and her other teachers at Michaela have published extensively on the methods and approaches that have led to this achievement. Michaela School is, famously, open to any curious educationalist to come and thoroughly inspect all parts of the school. Yet, shamefully, the UK's education establishment, and in particular many schools with very poor results, have by and large turned up their nose at this opportunity for them to learn how to transform the lives of the around 10 million other children in the UK school system. You would have thought that Michaela's results would have compelled our rest of the school system to change; it hasn't.

In conclusion, schools in the UK could achieve more by ensuring that the Gove/Gibb* reforms are practised in every, rather than just some, schools: by following the teaching methods (in particular, warm/strict and knowledge rich) of successful free schools such as Michaela Community School or West London Free School or the many other successful schools around the country;[130] by forming more such free schools; and by ridding themselves of unnecessary cost, whether that be too highly paid teachers or unneeded TAs. We have shown that, in theory, the UK's schools could spend £27 billion less without diminution in academic results, and we have shown

---

* Education Minister Nick Gibb, who during eleven years in the post delivered much of the promise of the original Gove reforms.

ways to achieve those savings. But we have also shown considerable gaps in our schooling approach (deteriorating buildings, shrinking playing fields, shrinking curricula, less after-school and extracurricular activities). Accordingly, it seems wrong to advocate taking too much of the money from potential savings out of schools at this time; rather, I advocate here tight restraint on school budgets but transfer of budgetary amounts from the unproductive spend to the needed productive spend.

There is an exception: the number of school children in the system has peaked.[131] In the coming years, schools, if they wish to spend the same per pupil, will need to spend £1 billion per annum less than they do now. We put this £1 billion into the list of money to be saved going forward.

Tertiary and higher education costs and results

What of tertiary and higher education? This can be a greater or a lesser expenditure for a particular country, depending upon whether or not the country charges its students for it. The issue of whether the UK should be charging students for their tertiary education is important. In the modern world, tertiary education is key for improving productivity in an economy. Charging for it ensures it can be consumed more intelligently, so helps drive better colleges and universities. That incentive is, however, lost if to help the student with that cost, the government, as is the case now, extends a loan that is, in the most part, forgiven.[*] Many students therefore pay little attention to the economics, reckoning (possibly incorrectly) that if they make a lot of money after university, they won't mind repaying the loan and if they don't, they won't be required to repay it.

---

[*] Certainly though, putting the cost of the university straight back onto the government would be inimical to the objectives of shrinking government size.

Should all types of higher education be equally emphasised? Given the importance of having a citizenry that is increasingly educated in science, technology, engineering and mathematics (STEM) if we are to grow the economy, it could be argued that more subsidy should be given to these and related subjects, such as medicine, and less to others – particularly those that do not have a good record of employment or good wages for their graduates. As we shall see later, we do the opposite and are subsidising the most economically useless causes by the biggest amounts.

The following relates only to the largest segment of the tertiary education sector: the cost of undergraduates at English (not UK) universities.[132] Overall potential savings are therefore somewhat greater than what is indicated here.

We spend some £18.5 billion in this segment. £1 billion is spent on non-undergraduate staff, £8 billion is carried by the government in non-repaid loans and the rest is paid for (eventually) by students through loan repayments.[*]

The university sector has expanded mightily, mostly as a result of the Blair government aiming at 50 per cent of pupils going on into higher education, a target that was reached in 2019. The objective has been successfully attained, primarily because, due to student loans, higher education is free of cost to the student *at the time*; it only has to be paid back later and in 54 per cent of cases it isn't ever paid back, as over half of later earnings fail to reach the level required for repayments. Young people are very happy to study free for three years, especially as they are told university is a good thing; the problems of repayment are in the future and for now can be safely ignored.

---

[*] The £9.5 billion paid for by students is equally worthy of inspection: much of it is (economically) wasted, as discussed later.

The issues in the university sector

First, as we have seen, there is a large cost to the government of £8 billion in this sector. Can this be reduced? Well, is it value for money? Apparently not, as we will go on to discuss.

As Chart 2.29 shows, a good number of courses see only a third or less of the students completing the course or otherwise staying economically active.

Chart 2.29: Bottom Twenty Courses by 'Proceed'* Rate

Some courses see only 15 per cent of students completing the course properly.

University	Subject	Proceed rate (%)
University of Bedfordshire	Business and management	15
University College Birmingham	Performing arts	15
University of Bedfordshire	Sociology, social policy & anthropology	22
University of Wolverhampton	Psychology	25
University of Wolverhampton	Sociology, social policy & anthropology	25
University of Wolverhampton	Business and management	26
University of Bedfordshire	Psychology	27
London Metropolitan University	Business and management	31
University of Central Lancashire	Sociology, social policy & anthropology	31
Nelson College London Limited	Business and management	31
The University of West London	Business and management	32
The University of Bolton	Business and management	32
Birkbeck College	Business and management	32
London Metropolitan University	Education & teaching	33
Staffordshire University	Education & teaching	34
University of Wolverhampton	Creative arts & design	34
Buckinghamshire New University	Sociology, social policy & anthropology	34
University of East London	Business and management	34
Middlesex University	Business and management	35
University College Birmingham	Sports and exercise sciences	35

Proceed rate is defined as completing the course and getting a job or further study etc.
(including retiring, becoming a carer or going travelling)
Source: Centre for Policy Studies.[133]

Second, an astonishing 20 per cent of students, the IFS reports, will actually end up worse off for having gone to university, while for many more, the economic benefits of their three years of study are negligible.[134] Few first-year undergraduates will have the slightest clue that is likely to be the case for them.

Chart 2.30: Total Long-Run Government Spending by Subject

Over £1 billion in unrepaid loans for creative arts courses.

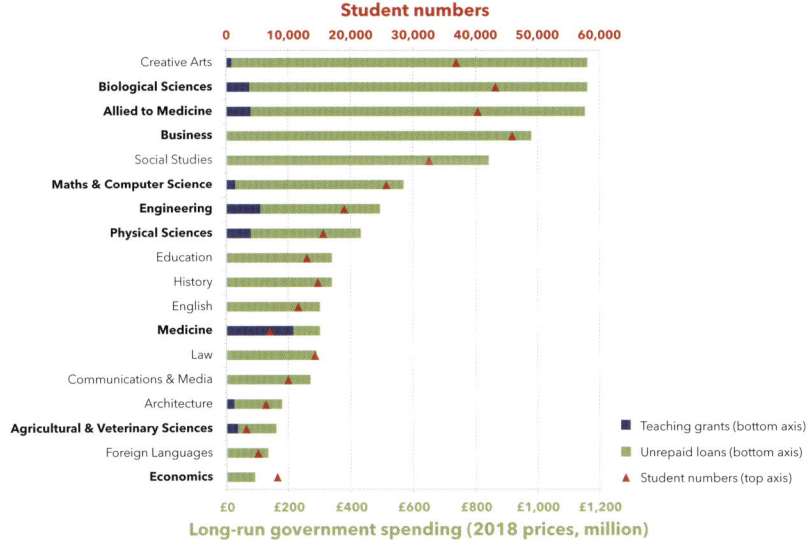

Bolded subjects are STEM or near-STEM
Source: Centre for Policy Studies[135]

Third, the highest subsidies are, as shown in Chart 2.30, for the least valuable courses, such as creative arts (which has the highest number of students on its courses). Subsidies to creative arts students (who can overall expect to get zero economic benefit from their course) are on average some £37,000 per student; the overall cost to the taxpayer of these courses (net of repaid student loans) is some £1.2 billion. Many creative arts students go on to great, productive, growth-generating careers, but there are too many students overall and many are on those courses because they didn't realise that their economic benefit may be zero or worse.

A further problem occurs, generated by the number of overseas students at our top tier universities. A somewhat fatal confusion exists on the topic of tertiary education in the UK: is it best seen as an essential part of our national fabric (in which case it should focus on educating UK students) or as just one out of the many different sectors of the economy (in which case it should merrily bring in as many overseas students as it likes)? I would argue the former. Undergraduate and graduate degrees, particularly those in STEM, are crucial if we are to maintain our ability to innovate, in particular in the sciences. It is (or should be) a self-feeding mechanism: the top academics who live and teach in our top universities should be training their successors, as well as the potential innovators who will leave university to work in the UK, either in the research and development departments of major companies or as entrepreneurs in start-ups that will become future successful companies.

Well, that's the plan anyway, but in what I consider to have been a somewhat shortsighted approach, we have decided to charge all our undergraduates to attend university while keeping universities short of money (in part by limiting what they are allowed to charge UK undergraduates). Thus, universities are reliant on attracting more and more high-paying foreign undergraduates and graduates, who they can charge as much as they like. A large proportion of those foreign students – many of whom usurp places in elite UK universities so that UK citizens are shut out of those universities – leave the UK after graduation, taking their precious and valuable knowledge with them.

The outcome of this approach has the potential to destroy our nation's leading status as an academic and scientific powerhouse. There are twenty-four institutions in the Russell Group of universities in the UK: four of these are in the top ten global universities, fifteen of them are in the top 100 and all of them are in the top 250. But 24 per cent of their undergraduates are from overseas. Graduate students are in an even higher percentage so that overall, 57 per cent of the Russell Group's fees come from overseas students. The author was, a while back, informally told that 80 per cent of certain STEM graduates at Oxford are from overseas. Thus, 80 per cent of the available graduate places in those STEM subjects are not available to the talented aspiring UK STEM students who would like to do graduate studies there. What results from that? Given that around two thirds of overseas students return to their own countries,[136] we will soon have a dearth of home-grown academics who can go on to be future STEM teachers at Oxford; we won't have a base of STEM-educated brainboxes to be our future research and development and entrepreneurial leaders, and, possibly worst of all, all of our science knowledge base is being exported aboard. One look at Imperial College London, a top ten global university, where some 60 per cent of *all* students are from abroad, tells us where the results of all that teaching and knowledge transfer will end up.

A final problem, related to the 50 per cent target, is that as we have already seen, 22 per cent of our nineteen-year-olds are functionally illiterate or innumerate or both. Beyond this 22 per cent of our school leavers, there are many who are not much better. What is the point then of sending 50 per cent of nineteen-year-olds to university? As the Centre for Policy Studies has pointed out, both our literacy and our numeracy skills at school-leaver age are fifth worst among twenty-three OECD countries yet we are fifth highest in the number who graduate from universities (Chart 2.31).

Chart 2.31: Basic Skills of School Leaver Versus Size of University Sector

We have among the highest innumerate and illiterate school leavers… and among the highest attendance at university.

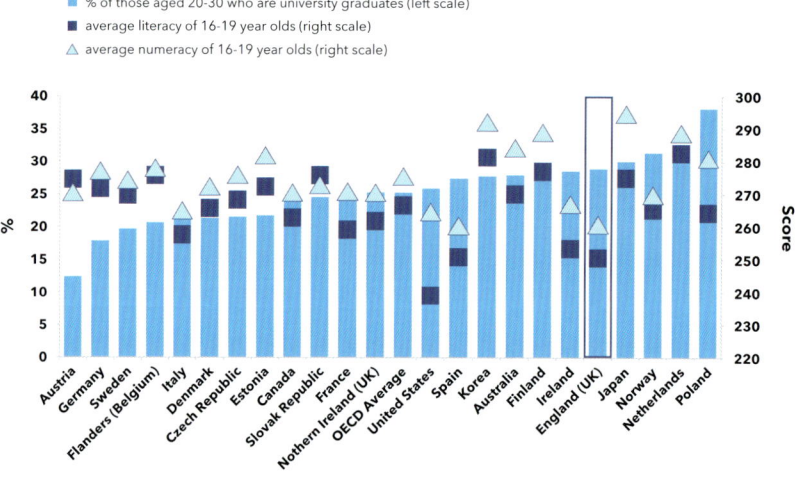

Source: *Centre for Policy Studies*[137]

The solution

I would argue, therefore, that we need to accomplish the following:

- Have fewer university courses: eliminate all courses with a three-year average of less than 50 per cent 'proceed' rates. (Rishi Sunak, in yet another policy announcement not followed through on, proposed cutting 130,000 university places.)[138]
- Subsidise the worst courses the least: make universities pay the cost of 15 per cent of estimated losses from 'low' employment rates. Use 50 per cent of the resultant money to subsidise STEM and near-STEM courses with high economic outcomes and keep the rest as savings.
- Make students better consumers of courses: require universities

to send, with their acceptance letters, full details on expected economic outcomes of all courses (UK-wide) in that subject and the economic outcomes from their own particular course in that subject. Require stark, factual wording, akin to that on cigarette packets.

- Have fewer overseas students on key STEM and near-STEM courses at our top universities: require at least 75 per cent of all STEM and near-STEM course undergraduate and graduate places to be given to UK passport holders for all Russell Group universities.*

The expected outcome

The savings from these actions are not easy to estimate precisely, but the proposals here are to eliminate some courses and change the number and mix of courses by having better-informed students. This returns income from money lost to loan defaulters. There will also be fewer loan issues because students will be directed into more economically productive courses and less courses overall. (We will also get a more productive economy from all of that.) This should mean overall that we could save half the annual £8 billion we lose on defaulting debtors: so savings of £4 billion.

After that, though, some of that money – say, £1 billion – should be spent on improving our technical education colleges. So, a net gain on higher education spend of £3 billion.

---

* The universities will have to absorb the loss of income from having fewer high fee-paying overseas students: the nation cannot afford the loss of knowledge and economic benefit that arises from denying places to some of the country's most capable and intelligent students.

Without compromising quality – in fact, improving it – we can
reduce the overall education bill by £4 billion:

- Save £5–10 billion from fewer TAs and introducing better-run
  MATs.
- Spend these savings on buildings, curriculum expansion etc.
- Keep future wage rises for teachers low.
- Save £1 billion from a future where there will be fewer school
  children in the system.
- Save £3 billion from rearranging further and tertiary educa-
  tion funding.

Enterprise and economic development

We have seen from Gemmell et al. earlier, that economic development – think Crossrail, HS2, the Heathrow expansion, public
housing development or last decade's mooted Boris Island, among
others – aids economic growth in general. Anyone who has seen
London's new, excellent Elizabeth Line in action can see why that
is so.[139] But here in the UK, we see, compared with dynamic economies such as Switzerland or Norway, very little such development
going on.

Why should this be so? The obstacles are multifold:

1. Byzantine planning processes are the key obstacle. A bureaucracy
   has taken grip and is now imposing insufferable delays for reasons like protection of animals e.g. bats and newts, to health and
   safety concerns, to NIMBY coddling.

2. Sluggard civil servants make it worse, with little sense of urgency or cost efficiency and a tendency to be hostile to enterprise.

3. 'No money', which means our economy is in even worse shape than we would otherwise think.

4. Hesitant, unimaginative, changeable politicians who are not prepared, Churchill- or Macmillan- or Heseltine-like, either to energise or to inspire – or in any event, somehow drive – the bureaucracy to make what is needed happen; nor are they prepared to go in any way against NIMBY opinion in the way they do in France.[*]

It's easy to see why this item of expenditure has such importance for economic growth. The calamity of HS2 overruns (in both money and timing), the endless saga of the third runway at Heathrow[140] and many other minor and major infrastructure issues – as well as the significant success of that recently completed, even if delayed a couple of years, Elizabeth Line in London – make it easy to see how important, and how difficult, the topic of infrastructure is and how easy it is to turn this from a growth-creating to a growth-destroying expenditure.

An excellent report from CapX reveals that 'it costs more to build new roads, railways and tramlines in Britain than it does anywhere else in the world'.[141] Expanding underground lines is 97 per cent more costly per mile than in France and a full 405 per cent more than in Spain. Manchester built a mile of train track for £203 million; the French city of Besançon spent £260 million for a full nine miles. Electrification of rail lines costs four times as much as it

---

[*] Famously, Charles de Gaulle was alleged to have disdainfully remarked, 'When you plan to drain a swamp, you don't ask the frogs.'

does in Switzerland. Building a new lane of road is 23 per cent more expensive. For French towns of greater than 150,000 in population, every single one has a light-rail system, while thirty such English cities (including Leeds, Liverpool and Bristol) lack one. Thus, 90 per cent of workers in Marseilles can get to their city centre in thirty minutes; only 40 per cent of Leeds workers can do the same. HS2, of course, was off the scale: ten times the cost of similar in France, and now mostly abandoned, with an extraordinary £100 billion of mostly wasted expenditure to date.

We know it's the planning bureaucracy and system that does this to us; why don't we change it? If we managed to do so, we could spend less and get more. But no, instead we keep doubling down on regulation with new, massively obstructive laws coming faster and faster. The nutrient law, the biodiversity requirement, putting a strong environmentalist, Tony Juniper, in charge of Natural England: all this has led to gridlock on economic development in the UK, including, to take just one random example, 150,000 houses not built.[142]*

As Chart 2.32 shows, the UK is below the middle of the OECD pack as regards the size of our infrastructure investment. Other advanced economies, such as France, Germany and the US, are equally low in their expenditure, but we can assume that they get far more bang for their buck than does the UK. Yet it is the enormous difference between the UK's level of expenditure and that of China (or indeed South Korea, Switzerland or Norway) that is in particular worthy of more discussion.†

---

* The new Labour government says it will attack planning: will it?
† It is interesting that all of these last three countries have high economic growth compared to others. More reconditely, each has a major focus on tunnelling – possibly partly for geographic reasons but likely also showing a forward-looking view on economic potential, finding new ways to improve the economy.

Chart 2.32: Investment in Inland Transport Infrastructure
2010 and 2020, as a percentage of GDP

The UK spends less on infrastructure than the average OECD country and a lot less than a number of successful economies do.

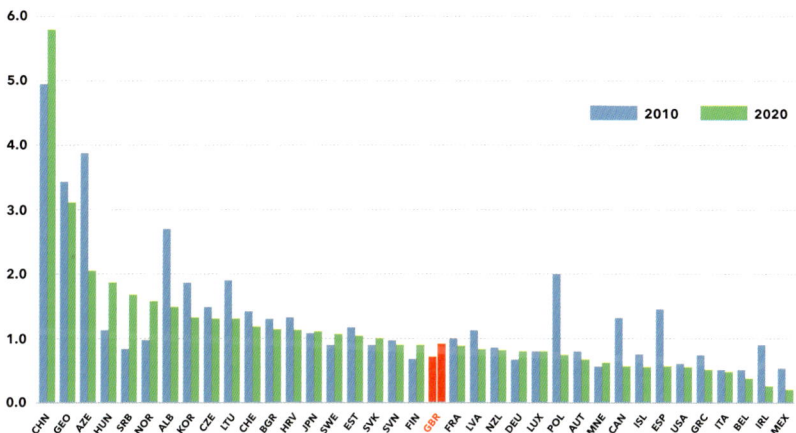

Note: 2019 data used for Belgium, Canada, Georgia, the UK, Ireland, Italy, Japan, South Korea, Montenegro, Norway, Serbia, Switzerland and the United States
Source: International Transport Forum[143]

Are there parts of infrastructure we should be doing less of?

While one has to be cautious in equating low spend with low success in infrastructure (the 'bridge to nowhere' scandal in the US and the decades-long focus in Japan on often valueless infrastructure projects come to mind), one does end up suspecting that we in the UK are too much constrained in our expenditure on infrastructure because we spend too much of our limited money on other, non-growth-enhancing items of government expenditure.[144]

This low level of expenditure implies we probably should not spend much less than we currently do on infrastructure, but then again there is the fact that our planning system and other incompetencies mean that we get far less bang for our buck from infrastructure spend than do other countries. HS2 had to be cut right back because it was looking as if it would cost a whopping ten times what similar projects cost in France; even its reduced scope is expected to show costs of between £45 and £54 billion.[145] The planning stage for a new downstream crossing of the Thames has cost £300 million and after twenty-two years, it is nowhere near even getting permission to start.[146] The crossing is just 2.4 miles long.

Are there parts of infrastructure we shouldn't be doing at all?
A piece in *The Economist* in February 2024 laid bare the full horror (to date) of the HS2 fiasco.[147] At the end of the project, the remaining 'rump' line from London to Birmingham will be one of the most expensive in the world, while travelling by train from Birmingham to Manchester will – due to an ordering calamity – actually take longer than it does now once the rump HS2 is complete. Clearly, as things stand, it would have been far better never to have started the HS2 project.

Certainly, the UK's infrastructure is in fairly woeful shape; our schools estate is a good example of that. But for most major infrastructure projects in the UK, we just shouldn't be starting them until such time as we have reformed planning law and become more confident that we can deliver these projects on time and at the sort of cost level that other major European countries can deliver at.

There will, of course, be exceptions where there is major benefit to be gained, such as with airports or new runways, new bypasses, or the North–South equivalent of the highly successful Elizabeth Line (which itself was delayed and overspent but not by nearly as much as was the case with most major UK infrastructure projects).

But in general, and most importantly, we urgently need to get rid of much of our overwhelmingly growth-destructive planning laws.

Reining in our infrastructure spend until such a time as we have a better planning regime – and have achieved a structure and staffing within the civil service that is capable of delivering projects in a timely and cost-efficient manner – will keep the infrastructure budget flat in the meantime. As costs are reduced to more reasonable levels, more projects can be taken on without growing the budget excessively from the current level.

I have, however, for the purposes of this book, assumed there are no savings to be had from the infrastructure bill.

We forecast no savings from infrastructure but offer a pious hope that the spend will be deployed far better than currently. The chief obstacle to cost effective spend is our appalling planning system, discussed further in Chapter 8.

Savings: Zero

Defence

Defence, as a 'core' spend, is particularly difficult to argue cuts for: a defence capability is something you either need or don't. You either have enough capability or you don't and must spend more. For so long as there are powerful bad actors in the world, the issue of national defence must take precedence over any left- or right-wing ideology. Moreover, without security in a nation, investment and entrepreneurial activity will be limited.

Even peace-minded individuals agree at the moment that the

world is a less safe space and that our opponents – Russia, China, Iran, North Korea, among others – are gathering strength and capability. The more hawk-minded among us (the more realistic, some would say) are shouting that we are woefully underprepared for a war that may be much nearer than most realised. Defence Secretary Grant Shapps stated that we have left the 'post-war' world and have entered a 'pre-war' one. But the way we carry on in the defence sector shows little sign of that. We seem to be badly unprepared, having cut our defence expenditure over and over in the past fifty years. The Labour government has ordered a defence review.

Chart 2.33: UK Health and Defence Spending 1995–2022

Health spending has increased as defence spending has halved.

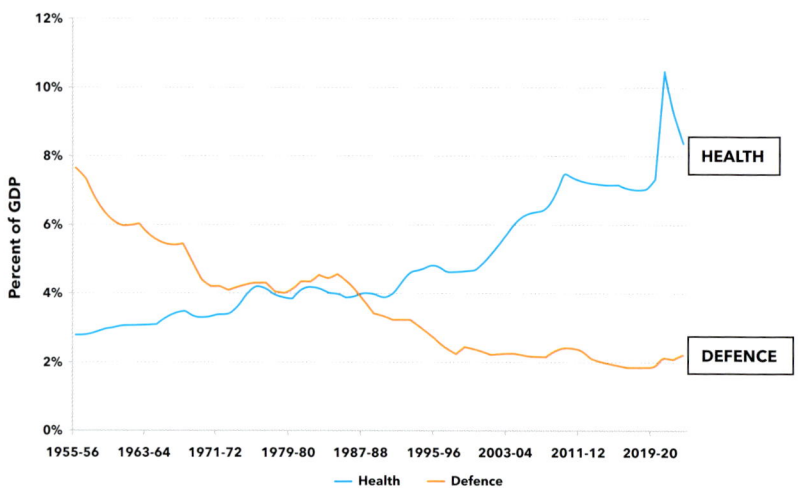

Source: Institute for Fiscal Studies[148]

Having traditionally spent at a higher level than the other major European countries (although one eighth of that spending was on the nuclear force and if you take that out, we were in the middle of the pack), the UK is now at similar levels of expenditure.

Chart 2.34: Military Expenditure as a Percentage of GDP, Major Western Economies Versus Russia, 1960–2023

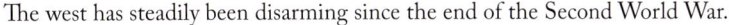

The west has steadily been disarming since the end of the Second World War.

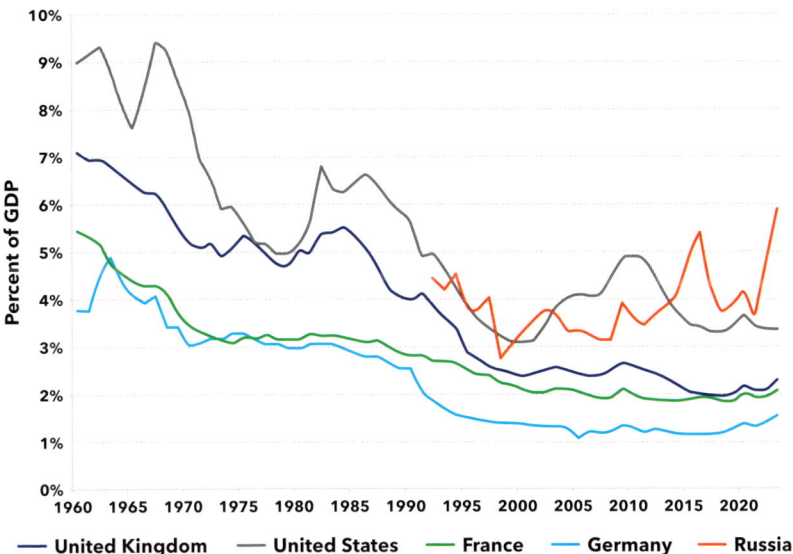

In 2024, Russian spending under the 'national defence' category will hit 29.4 per cent.[149]
Source: SIPRI Military Expenditure Database[150]

In the new global environment, there is a growing imbalance of arms. With Germany proving reluctant to engage in military confrontation, China and particularly Russia are growing their military capabilities at a rapidly expanding pace. None of that might matter too much if the US preserved its military hegemony, but the US is, at the time of writing, prevaricating on providing sufficient military assistance to Ukraine. The potential re-election of Trump to the

White House in November 2024 could, at the worst, lead to Europe being left, as Trump has threatened, to face Russia alone.*

Were Ukraine to fall (or even be forced to accept a ceasefire on current lines of battle) and the US to abandon Europe, the temptation to Putin to keep going west, especially when faced with the current state of military unpreparedness in western Europe, would be significant. As Chart 2.35 shows, there is a growing disparity of arms in Europe, with Russia benefiting from further military support from Iran, North Korea and, above all, China (who might react to Russia's successes by concluding that an invasion of Taiwan and other expansionist moves could be successful).

Chart 2.35: Defence Spending 2013 Versus 2023
$ billion, constant 2022 prices and exchange rates

The west is now totally reliant on the US for its defence.

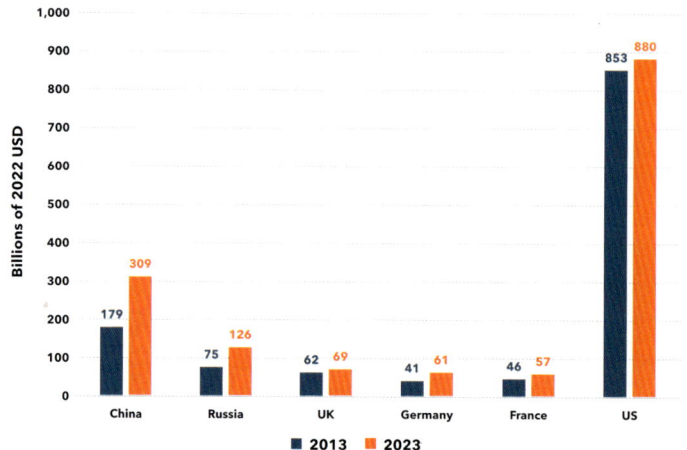

Source: SIPRI Military Expenditure Database[151]

<hr />

* Europeans, particularly Germans, may have cause to regret deeply the open derision with which they greeted Trump's 2018 remarks to the UN General Assembly about the Russian threat. Trump is unlikely to have taken kindly to such behaviour.

At the same time, according to the National Audit Office, the UK now faces a massive £17 billion shortfall on equipment, indicating lack of preparedness for war.[152]

Part of the problem is that, somehow, 'woke' culture has infiltrated the Ministry of Defence (MoD); it would seem that woke's inroads into our defence establishment have been actually worse than in many other departments of state. The recent stories include a group captain resigning over 160 white men being discriminated against, white males refused consideration for pilot training, navy personnel required to introduce themselves with pronouns, and recruitment ignoring security concerns in their search to promote 'diversity'.[153] The entire MoD is seemingly obsessed with diversity, resulting in the sidelining of the pressing needs of our military and defence capability.[154]

So, we need to spend more, not less, on defence, and we need to get serious about it, eliminating anything in our defence establishment that does not exclusively focus on improving our country's preparedness for war. Labour has, commendably, agreed a defence-spend target of 2.5 per cent.

I go further than that: if, as a down payment on building our defence capability back, we increased our defence spending to, say, 3 per cent of GDP, then spending would grow from some £52 billion to £67 billion – a £15 billion increase.*

The problems with our military expenditures are not limited to their paltry size: the MoD's ineptitude at procurement is

---

* This extra money would soon be used up in extra planes for our two aircraft carriers, no early retirement for C-130s, purchasing the originally planned five E-E Wedgetails, sorting out the Morpheus and Ajax problems, and massively expanding our unmanned/autonomous land, sea and air drone capability, including swarming, jamming, counter-swarm, counter-drone and counter-jamming capabilities.

legendary, ranging from aircraft carriers that can't go to sea to armoured vehicles that vibrate so much they damage our soldiers more than they do damage to the enemy, from submarines and planes whose costs have ballooned to cancellations of C-130s and E-7 Wedgetails that have led to major gaps in our basic defence capability.[155]

There are rules about procurement that seasoned project managers consider sacred, such as 'whenever possible, try to use a pre-existing platform' or 'never change a spec after starting the build'. The MoD seems adept at utterly ignoring these rules: for example, with the Ajax armoured fighting vehicles where the procurers imposed 1,200 new 'capability requirements', plus a gun no one else had asked for, all piled on to the original spec. The result seems to have been the military equivalent of Norman Foster's infamous bouncy millennium bridge. The MoD's procurement group, a huge bureaucracy itself (overall, some 62,000 employees in the MoD), seems irretrievably inept. Andrew Neil has proposed that the procurement group should be replaced with an arm's-length procurement agency (not within the MoD).[156] This proposal could in fact be extended to include most or all arms of government – a unit which focuses on value for money and in delivery, buying from existing platforms, alliances and proper specs with none of the post-procurement 'tweaks' that cause the massive delays and cost overruns.

Defence needs £15 billion more in spending (and within fifteen years should grow further to 4 per cent of GDP).

Other

The previous sections covered some 83 per cent of government spending – around £888 billion. That leaves some £182 billion left undiscussed, covering a large gamut of services – public order, transport, public services,* housing, recreation, environment, international services, science and technology, agriculture, fish and forestry, and employment policies. Even the last (the smallest) of these adds up to £3.8 billion of expenditure, while the largest (the first) of these is more than ten times larger than that – £44 billion.

Clearly, individual books could be written about each of the individual items of expenditure within this £182 billion; for each, there would be separate conclusions made about their potential for cost savings. For public order (£44 billion) the state of crime and our prisons makes it difficult to argue for a cut in this area. This is a 'core' spend that should be left alone. Ditto for transport, another £44 billion; housing, £18 billion; international services, £8.5 billion; and science and technology, £7 billion. However, it seems reasonable to say that for the remaining £60.5 billion, any incoming government that was bent on rightsizing overall public expenditure would have to insist on doing, overall, 10 per cent less than currently – say, £6 billion in current-year money. The following pages discuss how to go about achieving such cost cuts, including adopting a leaner way, i.e. with fewer people and fewer resources.

Other savings from smaller government departments: £6 billion

---

* Spending on public services reduces economic growth – see earlier.

BEYOND THE FACT OF THE PUBLIC SECTOR BEING TOO LARGE, A FURTHER KEY DRIVER CHOKING OFF ECONOMIC GROWTH IS THE INEFFICIENCY AND INEFFECTIVENESS OF THE SECTOR OVERALL

In the previous sections, we discussed areas of potential savings in the different areas of government spend. At the heart of the need to lower the cost of government is, however, the issue of the efficiency of those who deliver government: the public sector. Here we find one of the largest obstacles to delivering growth, both in failing to implement government policy swiftly or well and in failing to do so at an acceptably low cost. The obstacle is the overall inefficiency and poor working habits of the public sector – inspired in large part by the poor performance of the sector's central part, the civil service itself, from whom the rest of the public sector tends to get its working attitudes and policies.

The high cost of government is due to doing too many things and doing things so badly, with so little oversight and so little ability to make the government's public servants do things in an efficient, effective and, above all, cost-controlled way. If we were to persuade the public sector to focus only on the essential things and to improve efficiency, then by how much could we reduce the overall cost of these bodies, while simultaneously delivering better services to the British people?

How big is the government payroll?

Official figures indicate a total public-sector workforce of some 5.8 million in 2023. Only 521,000 of these are actual civil servants, as we see in Chart 2.36.

Chart 2.36: Number of Public-Sector Employees in the UK as of 2023 by Industry (in thousands)
Total = 5,827,000

Civil servants are less than 10 per cent of all reported public-sector employees.

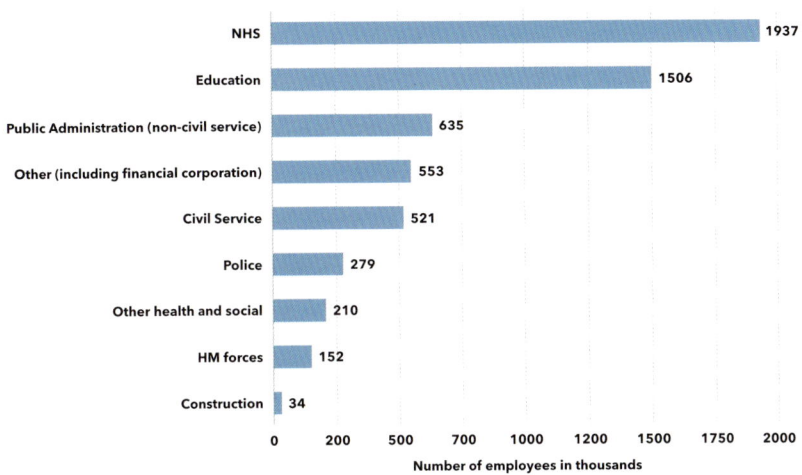

Source: *Office for National Statistics 2023*[157]

The number of 5.8 million significantly underestimates the true figure because it fails to take into account a large number of workers that produce services for the public sector but are not classified as employed by it. Examples are outsourced government workers, consultants, bin men, all the way down to self-employed speech and language therapists at schools. An analysis by the National Institute of Economic and Social Research points out that 'it is not who employs the labour that matters for resource allocation, but what the labour produces'. It concludes that a more accurate estimate of the public-sector workforce would be the number of people who 'work in industries that are traditionally regarded as the public sector': public administration and defence, social security, education, human health and social work activities.¹⁵⁸ The point is that these workers are all, ultimately, *paid* by the state – so they are indeed public-sector employees. Thus, the more correct number is – as the reports states and as Chart 2.37, taken from that report, shows – actually 10.6 million. This is one third of all UK workers, a number that is up from one quarter in 1997 – four million extra workers added during what we might call the 'social democracy era' of the UK, some 62 per cent higher than it was in 1997.

Chart 2.37: Share of the UK Workforce Employed in Public Sector-Dominated Industries
Quarterly, 1997–2023

The share of those employed in public sector-dominated industries rose from a quarter of the workforce in 1997 to a third in 2023.

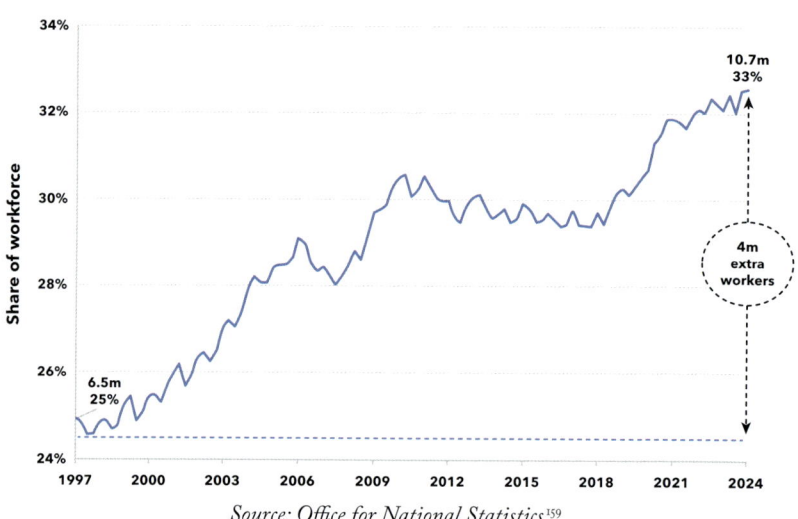

*Source: Office for National Statistics*¹⁵⁹

This should be a salutary statistic: since Tony Blair came to power, an extra 4 million workers, an increase of 60 per cent, have been employed into the public sector, squeezing the private sector while at the same time requiring ever-higher tax monies to fund them. Much of this was during the reins of May, Johnson and Sunak.

About a third of the total people in employment in the UK are now engaged in providing public services. How can free enterprise survive and how can the economy grow when the state gobbles up more and more of the available resource?

Shrinking the size of the government substantially would presumably require shifting at least two million workers into the private sector over time. A formidable task that would take several years and one that would have to be accomplished in the teeth of grinding pressure from Wagner's Law.

But, as we discuss next, doing this, accomplishing the same or more with fewer staff, as is continuously done in the private sector, is crucial. Even with all the modern-day productivity tools at their disposal, the public sector – and here we are back to talking about the 5.8 million officially classified as public sector – fails to improve. In fact, it is currently going backwards on its productivity. Almost all public-sector services are, or are next to, a monopoly, so, and as we have seen in recent years, many of them can strike to improve their pay and working conditions, almost at will, without reference to providing more value for the money we already pay them. And that threat to strike is dreaded by the unprepared politicians; keeping the public-sector strike tiger in its cage is important to every government.

The scope for free enterprise to work its magic on economic growth in the UK is becoming more and more limited, way beyond that third of the economy. The automobile industry is now essentially nationalised, with 780,000 workers who will, in a few years from now, only be allowed to make electric cars.[160] The same is true for the home-heating industry, which will only be allowed to make heat pumps, not gas boilers. High street banking is essentially now nationalised – comprising 581,000 workers.[161] All in all, less and less entrepreneurial scope.

Because many are essentially self-governed, public-sector workers have little incentive to improve their productivity. While private-sector companies face competitors who force them to improve, year after year, the public sector mostly doesn't have or experience that competition. So, even though their pay goes up, their productivity doesn't – as Chart 2.38 shows.

Chart 2.38: Total Public-Sector Productivity and Pay
UK index 1997=100, 1997–2022

Public-sector productivity has remained flat for twenty-five years. With ever increasing rises in real wages, the cost becomes unbearable and the ability to expand services unfeasible.

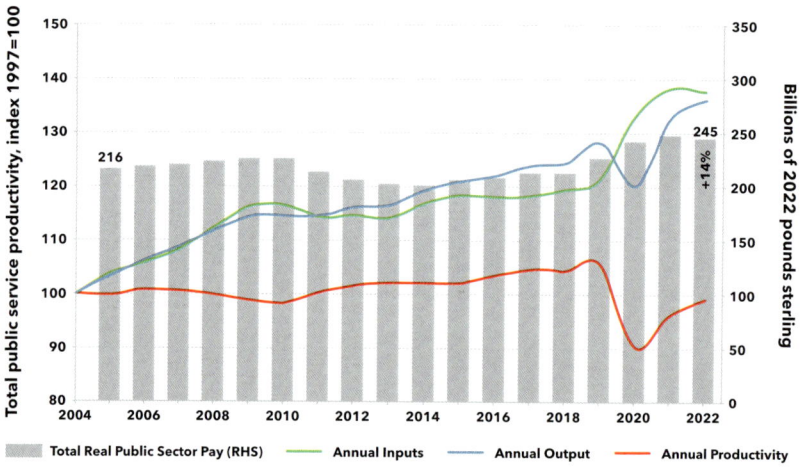

Note: Estimates for 2020, 2021 and 2022 are experimental statistics.
Estimates 1997–2019 are national statistics.
Source: Office for National Statistics, moyniteam analysis[162]

An illustrative anecdote: in 1992, I was minding my own business, working as an adviser in New York and contemplating early retirement, when I received an offer to come back to the UK and become CEO of a venerable British institution, PA Consulting (a company that all knew was unsettled but it was still, they told me, thriving). I thought 'Why not?' and headed back to the UK, never dreaming at the time that this would result in my settling back long-term into my homeland.

What I found at this company was nothing short of astonishing. PA was, as our bank swiftly informed me on my arrival, bankrupt. Its travails were almost entirely due to its having succumbed to a very early form of 'wokery'. The most radical, non-commonsensical ideas had been implemented at PA so that, at the end of the day, it was impossible under their system to make money and survive. We had a grim few years before the company finally turned around and was ready to grow. (Cutting briefly to the end of that story: PA has now, thanks to its great people over the years, returned to being a thriving, tremendously successful organisation.)

Just one small exemplary problem that immediately confronted me was that around the world, in any of PA's fifty offices, it was impossible to find out how many staff the company employed (in the end, it turned out to be about 4,000 staff, but it took an entire year to find that out). In addition, and amazingly, all job titles had been abolished – so I had no idea who did what. The combination of knowing neither how many employees we had nor what any given employee did made it bewildering to try to manage the company, or to manage its costs of employment, or its people's performance.

I encountered similar problems across just about every aspect of management. I still remember what it was like to thrash around, making guesses as to what we should do to improve performance enough to survive in the absence of any hard numbers.

Well, lo and behold: our government is in much the same position.

For civil servants, numbers are available for particular departments, but there has been so much outsourcing that it is impossible to know whether we have more or fewer people doing the work now than we used to. During the Covid era, we added over 100,000 civil servants and they don't seem to have disappeared now that Covid is over. It seems as if nobody can say who these new civil servants are or what they are doing.

Not just that: as a parliamentary public accounts committee reported, the civil service doesn't monitor what happens to their underperforming staff and the Cabinet Office queries the usefulness of doing so:

> Further, most departments do not monitor or report what happens to staff identified as underperforming. Monitoring outcomes for underperforming staff is essential if departments are to understand how effectively their performance management systems are supporting people to move out of underperformance or identifying alternatives for those individuals, such as changing roles. The Cabinet Office noted there is a balance to be struck between the time departments spend on collecting and reporting data and the time they spend on supporting managers and teams to improve performance. However, this is slightly at odds with the Cabinet Office's own civil service performance management framework, which sets the expectation that departments 'must track and be able to report on the progress being made with each individual' identified as underperforming.[163]

And the actual civil servants are only a fraction of the problem. We have, in addition, all the public service bodies such as the courts or the NHS. We have the quangos. We have the regulators. We have all sorts of other bodies that seem not to fall within any of these categories. We have no clue how many people are involved; we can, of course, be pretty sure that the expectation is for the number to go up and up, even if we exclude the NHS's plan to massively increase the number of staff working there.[164]

You can't manage what you can't measure. In the private sector, the need to compete on the world stage means that any organisation must improve the productivity of its workforce year after year after year; the alternative is bankruptcy. In the public sector there is no such constraint, so that from what we can see (Chart 2.38) productivity never improves (yet pay does increase year after year after year).

To make improvements sufficient to bring the public sector up to private-sector levels of productivity – which, from Chart 2.38, would imply firing some 27 per cent of public-sector employees or 1.6 million workers – is, at first sight, a daunting task. Fortunately, however, the tools are at hand to accomplish this. In the private sector, large organisations routinely use a tried and tested process. It's known by various names, one common name being Overhead Value Analysis (OVA). It is used to identify where productivity is low due to poor practices, which therefore lead to overstaffing. By improving processes and reducing staff, productivity is improved.

Having seen OVA, or its variants, applied to organisations many times, I have never seen it fail to reduce staff by between 10 to 20 per cent. This was often in companies that were, before the process was applied, far leaner than the civil service, which from what I know has rarely, if ever, tried the OVA approach. A simplified description of the OVA process is that each area within the organisation is asked to identify opportunities to reduce costs by, say, 20 per cent. (The cost reduction will not necessarily be of people costs but much of it necessarily will.) Each area of the organisation has to present their proposals to senior management, who choose, out of the proposed actions, a number of them that collectively add up to at least 15 per cent cost reduction.

When any attempt is made to cut costs within the civil service, albeit on rare occasions, it notoriously responds with proposals to close clearly indispensable activities and, of course, senior management then decide not to implement those cuts – Sir Humphrey remains undisturbed. In the private sector, managers who try on anything like that are swiftly canned and someone is put in their place who will offer up more realistic proposals. Doing that in the civil service is much harder because the civil service, in the main, controls its own hiring and firing. So, in my view, it is crucial that the civil service's HR department needs to be separated out into a unit that is independent of the civil service hierarchy, so that a more 'proactive' stance can be taken toward obstructive middle managers and staff movement can be structured around the needs of politicians and policies, not around civil service manoeuvrings.

In the 1990s and 2000s, large organisations in developed countries went through several waves of rationalisation using approaches such as OVA. At the end of that period, on average, these organisations probably carried 25 per cent less staff than before but produced more, even with that reduced workforce.[*] There is absolutely no reason why similar productivity gains could not be quickly achieved in the public sector, were politicians and the senior management of the civil service to be determined and forceful enough. The steps that all organisations in the private sector have to take – consolidation,

---

[*] With the working from home phenomenon, those companies that have indulged their workforces too much have, in many cases, given up much of those gains and are consequently facing difficult and dangerous competitive headwinds.

simplification, refusal to accept low productivity – are just as easy to take in the public sector. In schools, as discussed earlier, Multiple Academy Trusts (MATs) have been an extraordinary and growing success and have brought massively improved education to their pupils at lower cost. One major contributor to their success is the fact that top capability from one expert can be spread across a few dozen schools, rather than just confined to one; administrative functions (finance, property, HR) can be concentrated into one centralised unit with a professional. MATs often have few or no TAs.

Again, a similar process of consolidation for general practices in the NHS is yielding significant improvements in both cost and efficiency, but so far, multiple general practice groups are the exception, not the rule.

A further example: our courts are antiquated and massively inefficient. Privatising part of their back offices and possibly introducing competition between courts to speed up and streamline their services would likely bring the golden benefit of faster and cheaper justice.

We see, over and again, the public sector being incompetently managed from the point of view of the customer, the British public. So, it's hard not to conclude that it is managed primarily for the benefit of its employees and not for the people and customers it serves. This leads to two conclusions:

- An activity is almost always qualitatively better and more efficient if it is performed by the private sector. Outsourcing or eliminating some activities and benefits from the public sector – by saying we won't pay for them any more, regardless of all the special pleading – will enormously improve the public finances as well as the delivery of some public services.

- For those activities that remain in the public sector, the low productivity of public servants will remain a problem, as they fail to
focus on delivery to the customers, until a truly determined several-
year OVA plan is agreed and implemented. This would sweep
through every part of the public sector – requiring the kind of determined effort to decrease staff and improve productivity that any
private-sector organisation would routinely have to deploy. This involves separating the HR function out from the civil service itself.

Why is the productivity of the public sector so low?

In 2023, public-sector employees of many stripes were threatening
to strike, demanding higher pay and getting it. By contrast, in the
private sector, higher pay can only be afforded if productivity improves. If public-sector employees are to be paid more without any
improvement in productivity, then the taxpayer has to come up with
extra money – while getting nothing extra in return. As the *Telegraph*
reported, Douglas McWilliams, founder of the CEBR, calculated
that were public-sector productivity to have climbed just back to its
(already very low) pre-pandemic rate, spending on public services in
2023 could have been a full £73 billion lower. This money could have
been used, for example, to double the budget of the MoD, made it
unnecessary to raise the corporation tax rate to 25 per cent *and* could
have lowered the deficit by a further significant amount.[165]

· · ·

How is the public sector organised beyond the twenty-four ministerial departments (Downing Street, the Cabinet Office and the
various departments of state) that employ those half-a-million civil
servants? Government documents tell us that beyond those central

government entities there are 317 local authorities and 576 other agencies and public bodies, comprising:[166]

- twenty non-ministerial departments, such as the Charity Commission, CMA and OFGEM
- 421 agencies, such as the Arts Council, Bank of England, Kew Gardens, Atomic Weapons Agency, British Wool
- 113 high-profile groups, such as Border Force, Welsh Language Commission, Defence Academy, Flood and Coastal Erosion, National Cyberforce, Race Disparity Unit, Submarine Museum
- nineteen public corporations, such as the BBC, National Nuclear Laboratory, Post Office
- three devolved administrations: Scotland, Northern Ireland, Wales

As can be seen, the categorisation of different entries seems beyond random. The distinctions are nevertheless important because each category has a different form of governance, which to some extent defines how much at arm's length that entity is from the government and therefore how easily the government will be able to stretch in and interfere with it. But the muddle of categorisation shows how randomly this enormous number of separate bodies has been thrown together. Worse, the list is not at all complete: each of the departments of state works with scores of 'executive agencies', 'executive non-departmental public bodies', 'advisory non-departmental bodies', 'public corporations', 'ad-hoc advisory groups' and on and on.

Overall, the creation of this legion of separate and semi-independent arm's-length bodies has been an exercise in sloughing off responsibility from an elected government to various semi-independent entities so that if something goes wrong, the government can fold its arms and look pouty, just like the rest of us do. But the unintended yet inevitable consequence of all this abdication of responsibility means that democratic control of these entities becomes – apart from turning the money spigot on or off – harder and harder.

For local authorities, who take up some 20 per cent of all government spending, there is the democratic control mechanism of local elections. But for arm's-length bodies (ALBs), which took up a further 21 per cent of spending in 2023, finding out and controlling whether or not they are doing the right thing, and at an efficient cost, is much harder.[167] And it doesn't stop there: these ALBs then go on to pour much of their money into charities, whose own activities are shrouded at yet one more remove from democratic control. As early as 2012, the Institute for Economic Affairs (IEA) was able to reveal that an astounding 27,000 charities were 'now dependent on the government for more than 75 per cent of their income'. The entire 'voluntary' sector, the IEA revealed, receives more money from the state than from voluntary donations.[168] This is a far cry from the 'charity' idea that most of this country grew up with. (We explore the issues and opportunities with this a little later.)

Each of these entities is represented as a separate, semi-autonomous ALB. But the difference between the civil service and the ALBs is not as large as it might seem. Personnel, particularly senior personnel, flit back and forth between the various bodies. Networks exist between the bodies so that usually a unified front is presented among the various relevant bodies whenever an issue arises with the government. Above all, the civil service – as we can see, only about 10 per cent of the overall workforce of all these bodies or even as low as 5 per cent if you include private-sector companies working primarily for the public sector and then even less than that if you include those self-perpetuating charities – exercises significant control on the style, attitudes and efficiency or effectiveness of the entire sector through its tradition and training, its control of access to ministers and its patronage.

In the following section, therefore, we review the opportunities for improvements and cost savings, first in the civil service itself, then in local government, then in all the other ALBs and, finally, within public sector-wide opportunities.

EXPLORING SAVINGS AND OTHER IMPROVEMENTS IN THE CIVIL SERVICE ITSELF

The mood music of the public sector comes from the civil service, a self-described Rolls Royce operation. The structure of the civil service in the UK is fascinating. It runs itself. It hires and promotes its workers with very little input from its alleged bosses, the politicians – except in a tiny proportion of positions at the very top. Memoirs and books on current affairs by recently retired senior mandarins reveal a culture of self-regard, complacency and little self-awareness.[169] The civil service has no owners, no shareholders to act as a control on how its people behave. Whitehall departments do have boards (a recent innovation), but, as even a brief perusal of the compendium annual report from these boards reveals, the activities of these boards are misdirected, their outputs are risible and their supervisory function is, in the main, non-existent.[170]

This situation is exactly analogous to an idea that is much beloved of various idealistic left wingers: a factory that is run by its workers. The outcome is precisely what most non-left-wing thinkers would expect.

As an example, Martin Stanley states, 'It is a firm rule that ministers cannot dismiss civil servants that displease them or offer unwelcome advice … If a minister cannot stand a particular official,
the latter is usually moved to a different job … Where possible,
this leads to two or more Permanent Secretaries swapping places.'[171]
So, right there, you have the problem in a nutshell. Certainly, if
the civil service is (a) competent and (b) at one with the minister
in their objectives then, as Michael Heseltine boasted in a recent
letter to *The Times*, much can be achieved and indeed numbers can
be reduced.[172] But what if the permanent secretary is opposed to a
Conservative, say, or to a Brexiteer government? Or, worse, what if
the minister and the permanent secretary are disagreed about what
constitutes good performance? Or, heaven forbid, if the permanent
secretary is incompetent?

The civil service has a pervasive influence on the overall working
environment for all other public-sector workers, because it sets and
directs policy for the other 90 per cent of the sector and because its
middle and senior managers transfer back and forth from the civil
service to manage the other parts. So, singling out the civil service
for close review, as I do in the following pages, sheds a light also on
the further reaches of the public sector.

What do we find? Where to start? Conquest's second law states
(in my version at least) that any organisation not explicitly right
wing becomes, by default, left wing over time. Agency theory says
that the weak governance implicit in most public-sector organisations (especially because they have staff whose views are primarily
with the left of centre) results in those organisations being run
on behalf of their employees, not their customers.[173] The civil service has, over the past few decades, built an almost impenetrable
thicket of protection against interference by its notional bosses,

the politicians. It now runs itself autonomously – and not, in most cases, for the benefit of its customers.* This is seen in a variety of dimensions:

- The civil service (and the public sector generally) has failed to improve its productivity in twenty-five years.
- Civil service working conditions now represent a joke upon the public.
- The civil service manages itself for its own benefit, paying no regard to its political masters.
- The civil service, in the main, now sets political policy for the government and politely ignores ministers who want to set any different policy themselves.
- The civil service now dominates and frightens its political bosses.
- The civil service is masterful at seeing off even small attempts at reforming it.
- The civil service is now an organisation that abides in a different universe from private-sector organisations.

I discuss each of these in the following pages.

The civil service (and the public sector generally) has failed to improve its productivity in twenty-five years

All public-sector workers in the UK are able to take advantage of belonging to an 'extractive sector' where pay, terms and conditions of service come to be for the benefit of the worker, not of the

---

* This is not a diatribe against *all* civil servants. As we will show later, some are appalled at the overall trend and are seeking to reverse it. But, in general, the overwhelming trend (in the face of pusillanimous weakness from politicians) is to keep going down the road I have described, of enjoyable working conditions, zero outside oversight and zero improvement in productivity. The situation has been the same for decades and has not as yet been reversed; indeed, as discussed earlier, it seems to be worsening.

populace. Of many available examples, an article in the *Telegraph* entitled 'The "laid back life" of a £67k train driver and how it compares with other jobs' is a good illustration of the unwarrantedly superior conditions of the public-sector worker.[174]

During the Covid pandemic, the civil service's productivity crisis was subsumed into the general pandemonium, to a degree because a not dissimilar problem, working from home (WFH), was occurring in both the public and the private sector.* Since then, in the private sector, former working patterns have been returning (albeit slowly), forced by the productivity imperative created by competition. Reality is asserting itself. However, not so in the UK's public sector.

On top of the WFH problem, claims of sickness both physical and mental have increased, sometimes attributed to the stresses of modern life, sometimes (but increasingly less so) to long Covid. 'The absence epidemic has struck – welcome to sick day Britain' said a *Telegraph* headline towards the end of 2023.[175] Sickness absence is up by a third in the UK, the article stated. A 'wellbeing and benefits director' (what that?) is quoted as saying, no doubt with complete objectivity, 'There are also around 700,000 people who have had long Covid for two or more years or more.' Various managers are quoted as approving of individuals staying away from work if feeling in any way sick.

Some companies who enjoy monopoly-style status in the world of

---

* Whatever self-interested workers say, productivity almost always plummets when WFH is indulged. The stakes are high: a battle continues to be fought by employees and their representatives on the claimed benefits or disbenefits of WFH. All sorts of extravagant claims have been put up by workers hoping to retain WFH as to how work could be conducted remotely and how hours of work could be lessened. In the private sector, however, bosses are bit-by-bit forcing employees back into the office. In the public sector, so far, government bosses have singularly failed to do so – so much so that agreements that employees will work in the office on just Tuesdays, Wednesdays and Thursdays are seen as a victory for management. (Plot spoiler: they aren't.) Anecdotally, many government departments still see their employees working from home most, or even all, of the time. The opportunities for downsizing staff, while making the remainder work a full week in the office, seem considerable.

business (say, Google) can afford to have quite relaxed HR policies and benefits for their employees because their profit margins are so wide and they are way ahead of the competition. Most others, however, are in more competitive environments and have been forced to turn their backs on Covid-era relaxations of policy. *The Economist* reported in mid-2023 that 'remote working has a target on its back'.[176] Influential business voices such as Jamie Dimon, chair and CEO of the most successful bank in the world (JP Morgan Chase), are 'intent on making WFH a relic of the pandemic'. The article cites data, ranging from IT workers in India to Wall Street bankers, that document the significant drop in productivity (of around 20 per cent) when people work at home. As the founder of Punch Taverns, Hugh Osmond, put it:

> Any team worker who has ever sat at their laptop in their kitchen during the working day knows everything takes longer … away from the scrutinising eyes of their bosses, employees pick the kids up from school, walk the dog, and get their hair cut … with leisure services up and down the country reporting a surging demand for weekday bookings … the amount of money spent mid-week in the hair and beauty industry was up nearly 5 per cent last year … fitness instructors and golf courses have all reported spiralling bookings during normal office hours.[177]

The thing about the private sector is that, for most companies, they are always up against competitors who they will ultimately win or lose to. That's how over time we get cheap food, better cars and better phones. A dominant player in the industry can hold competitors off, occasionally for decades, but sooner or later all private sector companies must face fierce competition and thus have to up their game if they are to survive and thrive. Consequently, the private sector as a whole always has to create sustained and steady improvements in productivity. In turn, that allows those improved companies to pay their workers more, in real terms, every year. No productivity improvement and over the long term you can't pay your employees more, because if you did so your profit margins would shrink and shrink until they turn negative and you go bankrupt. Employees in private-sector firms that have not managed to improve overall productivity are aware that rises in salary will be thin on the ground for all until they do. Private-sector managers know that the quickest way to improve productivity today is for their organisation to return their employees to the workplace, get rid of WFH and have a less relaxed sickness policy.

For the civil service and other public-sector workers, there is no compelling driving force equal to competition. Civil servants expect to get pay raises each year that will keep their salaries competitive with the private sector, regardless of any improvement in productivity or not. The evidence is unequivocal: the public sector in the UK doesn't just not do productivity improvement. Rather, it gets *less and less* productive over time. Civil Service World reports that public service productivity is down 5.7 per cent from pre-pandemic levels.[178] Overall productivity, boosted by a strong increase in private-sector productivity, improved fractionally in that same period.[179] And prior to that, as we have seen in Chart 2.38, the sorry tale is one of essentially zero public-sector productivity improvement over the past quarter century.

The civil service shows little sign they know their lack of productivity is an issue. The private sector isn't seen as the paradigm they need to emulate. Indeed, it is difficult for an outsider to look at the world that the UK civil service now lives in without wondering whether or not the public sector is perpetuating, possibly even consciously, a giant mocking leg-pull on the rest of the country. For example, HMRC recently announced that their response to ever-longer waiting times and widespread failure to get through to their phone banks – calls from thousands of frustrated private-sector callers, many of them self-employed – was that they would close these self-assessment helplines for half a year.[180]

Chart 2.38 showed that while inputs and outputs have both increased by some 40 per cent since 1998, there has been zero improvement – in fact, a small decline – in public-sector productivity over the entire eighteen-year period. So, given the vast 40 per cent increase in inputs, what did the British public get for their money? Not much, it would seem. As the chart showed, outputs basically tracked inputs – more people doing much the same stuff, at higher salaries, with no overall change in productivity. It's even worse than that, in my view. I'm entirely unsure why 'outputs' were shown as going up by 40 per cent. What were these increased outputs? And for those outputs that were indeed real, why did they need an even larger rise in inputs to deliver them? To take an example: the 26 per cent increase in pension payments, presumably an output, required, more or less, no increased effort to pay it out.

Inputs are, presumably, the employees and their compensation and other costs. As we have seen, headcount in the public sector has increased by at least 24 per cent since 2016 (an increase of 101,440) after there had been a steady decline from 2009.[181] And each of these heads has been paid more each year, so the inputs got bigger. It is remarkable that there has been only muted outrage at these two increases at a time when there is little discernible increase or improvement in public services.

In 1999, soon after Labour took over from the Conservatives, there were some 477,000 full-time equivalent (FTE) civil servants. In 2010, when the coalition government took over, the FTE head-count of civil servants was 481,000. Over the next six years, the government reduced this number by almost 100,000 civil servants, under an initiative by Francis Maude MP (now Lord Maude), to 384,000 – a compelling achievement.* [182]

Then, subsequently, the reported civil servant FTE number rose during the Theresa May regime to a reported 423,000 in Q1 2020 and then during the Johnson and Sunak regimes to 511,000 by Q1 2024. [183] Add in some portion of that reduced 100,000 from the Maude reforms (see footnote), and we are now anywhere up to 550,000–600,000 civil servants – significantly higher than at the height of the Gordon Brown follies. And, of course, even though the Covid crisis has now gone, the number of civil servants has not been dropping. It continues to increase – and prior to the election, the Conservative government, while paying lip service to the idea of reductions, hadn't succeeded in denting that number at all.† [184] The extractive institution had again triumphed over the elected politicians.

---

* There was, though, a glitch. The coalition government had outsourced and privatised numerous parts of government. This was, in itself, no bad thing if, as a result, the area that had been outsourced became more efficient and effective. But it did not mean that the civil servants had completely gone away. Instead, they were now employees of various outsourced bodies or new quangos, regulators or other ALBs. The government didn't lose the cost of their activities. (The cost of that outsourcing may feasibly go down over the decades if these outsourced entities are able to become more efficient, and the government negotiate cheaper contracts.) For outsourcers, instead of paying the civil servant directly, the government paid the outsourcer, who in turn paid the civil servant, but the government potentially had to pay even more than it had before for the activity because the outsourcer, of course, took a profit on top. The government didn't even lose the enormous cost of civil servants' defined-benefit pension obligations – in the outsourcing negotiations, the outsourcers, in all cases that I know of, forced the government to keep paying that enormous cost itself, which, as far as I know, it does to this day. What this means is that, in truth, the number of public-sector employees didn't drop by 100,000 in the period 2010–16 but by a lower number. How much lower? The data is unavailable, although the numbers still enrolled in the lavish public-sector pension schemes could be a good indicator, were that data to be uncovered.

† A recent edict by Conservative Minister for the Cabinet Office John Glen stated that 66,000 civil servants must go. It was one of many such edicts in the past few years from the Conservatives; nothing happened. It will be interesting to see whether the new Labour government will continue or abandon the initiative. The civil service is adept at seeing off such optimistic public pronouncements.

Compare this with Javier Milei, President of Argentina: in the past half year, in a country with two thirds of the UK's population he has reduced the number of government departments from eighteen to nine and fired 30,000 public servants already – and that's without even having a parliamentary majority.[185]

Chart 2.39: Civil Service Staff Numbers
Full-Time Equivalent, March 2009 to March 2024

After half a decade of careful pruning of the civil service, led by Francis Maude under David Cameron and George Osborne, the hapless governments of May, Johnson and Sunak proved incapable of preventing the civil service from ballooning back up again.

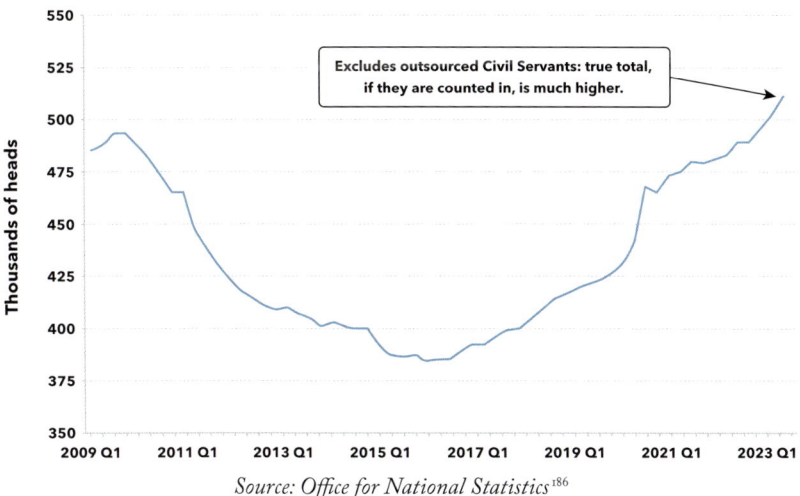

Source: Office for National Statistics[186]

And it's not just numbers: civil servants have also decided that their pay levels should be munificent. They have implemented that decision by means both fair and foul, as we will see in the following.

It has always been the case that, with the exception of the highest grades (important for those top civil servants but irrelevant for all others), the salaries of civil servants have been higher than in the private sector (and this is before we get to pensions, discussed later). The ONS's conclusion in 2011 was that 'allowing for job differences as far as possible, in April 2010, public-sector employees were paid, on average, 7.8 per cent more than private-sector employees'.[187] It is against this background that the 'austerity' of the Cameron governments as regards civil service remuneration should be viewed.

This situation hasn't really changed since: the House of Commons Library reports that in 2023 'median weekly earnings for full-time employees in the public sector were 8 per cent higher than in the private sector'.[188]

Chart 2.40: Percentage of Civil Servants in the UK at Each Grade
Percentage change in share of total in parentheses, 2012–22

There has been a massive shift towards the more senior civil servant ranks in the past decade, presumably by swift promotion since there has been no massive cull nor hiring pause in the junior civil service ranks. If so, the increase in the civil service wage bill is driven in large degree by indefensible excessive promotion.

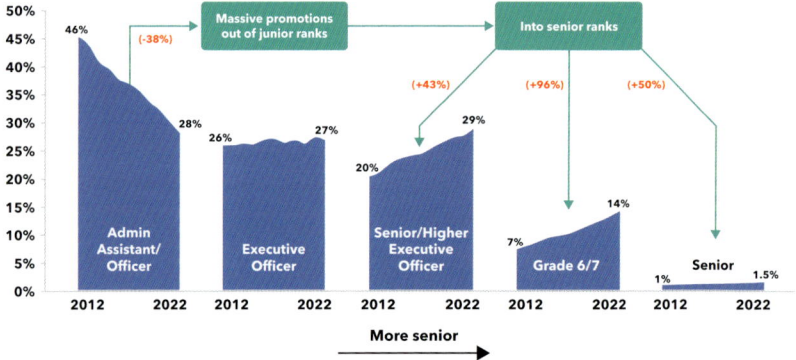

Source: Cabinet Office [189]

But, as Chart 2.40 shows, the unwarranted salary gap is as nothing compared to a brilliant coup that the civil service has in recent years pulled off: they have circumvented allegedly red-lined pay limits through massive numbers of promotions into higher pay grades. Most of these are surely unjustified; there really hasn't been any significant change in what they do. However, now these same people proudly carry different, more senior, better-paid titles – which has to mean that despite strict pay restriction protocols, the average civil servant is now paid way more than before *for doing the same job*.

The effect of this has been to almost double the number of civil servants earning over £100,000.[190] What do you think? Do you think that since 2015 the *needed* number of senior mandarins earning over £100,000 has doubled and the *needed* number over £75,000 has tripled, with 200 senior civil servants earning over £150,000? This dodge has led to the civil service pay bill rising by £5.8 billion in a short seven years.[191] A lot of this cannot be anything but, it seems, a wheeze to get around pay restrictions.

A precedent even exists for such tricks, going back to the time pre-2010 when the defined-benefits scheme for civil servants was a 'final salary' scheme; in the last year of their employment, many civil servants would see their final-year salary bumped up a considerable amount, thus massively increasing the pension that they received on their retirement – an amount that was index-linked for life. The reforms of Lord Hutton's report put an end to that particular game, but it would seem that an alternative way of bumping up remuneration has now been found.

How much would be saved if the civil service ranks were proportionately returned to their former pay grade levels? This could be done by imposing pay freezes on each department until the right proportions had been reached. A back-of-the-envelope calculation implies that the salary savings would be some £5 billion and assuming the 40 per cent on-costs add an additional saving of £2 billion; a total of £7 billion in savings per annum.

Public sector defined-benefit pension schemes

Even that outrageous manoeuvre, however, fades into minor significance when we introduce into the picture the rights to defined-benefit (final or average salary) pensions that the public sector, some 5.3 million workers, continue to enjoy almost alone in the UK. Neil Record, an expert on this topic who started his career at the Bank of England, asserts cogently that the schemes are steadily pushing the country into bankruptcy.[192]

The full cost, moreover, is hidden; the Institute of Economic Affairs recently reported that the real annual cost of public-sector pensions is an extraordinary £57 billion per annum more than is declared.[193] This would be a hidden full 30 per cent addition to the entire public-sector payroll. The overall *unfunded* current liability for the pension promises that have already been made – let alone the unfunded new liabilities that are being added every year – is now actually larger than the entire GDP of the UK.[194]

It is quite extraordinarily unjust that the public sector – with its many failings, low productivity, its efficiency falling further and further behind the private sector every year – should have managed to extort, and keeps on extorting, this enormous luxury benefit from the nation. If scientists in the coming years were to invent a pill that extended average life by twenty years – an entirely possible event – the new additional cost of these public-sector pensions would, quite certainly, immediately bankrupt the UK. The most obvious reasons for politicians not having removed this pension benefit – at a time when almost all private-sector companies have been forced to remove such schemes – are twofold. First, politicians have insufficient determination to face down the massive tantrum that the public sector would throw, were the benefit to be removed. Second, possibly even more important, MPs themselves have these wonderful, golden-plated, defined-benefit pensions. As it stands, if challenged on that, they can hide behind the rest of the public sector so as to avoid having to strip themselves of this benefit. I don't know of more than a handful of (very honourable) MPs who are prepared to discuss reforms that would change these schemes to be the same as the rest of the country, so that they, and all the rest of the public sector would have a defined contribution rather than a defined-benefit plan.

Steven Cameron, of Pension firm Aegon, states, 'Employer contributions to the civil service pension scheme can add more than a quarter to salaries.'[195] This is correct with the employee contributions that adds up to the mid-thirties as a per cent of salary. But the true cost is much larger. Using the scheme actuaries' own calculations, the true annual cost of some of these schemes are as follows:

- civil service: 80 per cent of salary[196]
- NHS: 82 per cent of salary[197]
- armed forces: 128 per cent of salary[198]
- teachers: 82 per cent of salary[199]

The cost to the taxpayer of the defined-benefit civil service schemes, and other similar public-sector pension schemes, is astronomical. However, much of it is hidden, particularly because the majority of such schemes are unfunded, carrying the quaint label of 'pay as you go'. That phrase actually translates, in more crude but meaningful language, as 'Ponzi scheme' – by which we mean that future generations will have to pay those pensions, regardless of the eventual cost. The full unfunded, undeclared, future cost of these pension schemes is some £2.6 trillion – just under 100 per cent of GDP and equal to the entire existing UK debt mountain.[200] In other words, counting just this one item, the UK owes twice as much money as we say we do – our debt is not 100 per cent but 200 per cent or more of GDP (and that number gets worse when we take into account the further items shown in Chart 1.28).

The reason why defined-benefit schemes have virtually disappeared from the private sector is that they would, if they had been continued, have bankrupted the firms that offered them. Dubbed 'an immoral bet on an uncertain future' – because no one can say how long any of us will live in future decades, so it's impossible to know the full cost of the promise – a defined-benefit scheme can be afforded only by those who have the unlimited purse of the state (aka the taxpayer) behind them. The problem of this exponentially growing yet unaffordable liability is so extreme that it should not go on, but it does. The allegedly poorly paid top civil servants and other public-sector employees receive, on retirement, up to 60 per cent of their final salary for the rest of their (increasingly lengthy) lives. To the outsider, all this seems to be happening because the civil service has impunity; these arrangements, which received no more than a cosmetic alteration when the Conservatives came to power in 2010, seem untouchable. Those mortals from the private sector who encounter retired civil servants at play can only marvel at their comfortable retired lifestyle.

No wonder that the *Telegraph* was able to report a beaming 34-year-old who stated, 'I took a pay cut to get a public-sector pension.'[201] A large final-salary pension is a wonderful thing; it gives fantastic lifetime security. Basically, after retiring you don't have to worry about money for the rest of your life. It would be wonderful if we could all have such comfort. But recipients should be aware that it is fundamentally immoral to accept a defined-benefit pension because the cost is already entirely unaffordable. None of us know what the cost of money is going to be in the future; we don't know what medical breakthrough marvels will occur that could have future generations living to 130 or more, drawing their final salary pension all the while and thereby bankrupting the country. None of us know what the state of the economy will be then, nor whether future generations will be of a size, or our economy rich enough, to be able to afford paying our current generation of civil servants these fabulous, index-linked amounts.*

We have known for at least twenty years that the already impossibly sized liability that we are building up could well break the 'national bank' at some point in the future.[202] No reason has been given as to why public servants should have a particular moral claim to being, on top of what they already get, the only ones who are allowed to benefit from such lifetime schemes of retirement – except for the fact that they are close to the politicians and the politicians have also awarded themselves these defined-benefit pension schemes, so each group benefits from the cover provided by the other.†

Worst of all, the public-sector defined-benefits schemes are, as I've already said, a giant Ponzi scheme, where people put in contributions that are insufficient to pay their future pensions. The government says it is putting in contributions – but in most cases it doesn't. And *all contributions are used to pay amounts out, the same year, to existing pensioners* – no fund is being built up to pay for future pensioners. Yet there is a very clear attempt to make it look

---

* Yet another plot spoiler: the demographics are not favourable to this working out well, nor is our current level of economic growth.

† Of course, the matter seems entirely different to the public-sector employee, who if any of them read this, will be utterly indignant at the above words. Don't we know how hard they work, how deserving they are? In some cases, those words will be true – but that's not the point. Defined-benefit schemes are implicitly immoral and besides, *we just can't afford to go on with these schemes*. Sooner or later, the UK will go bust if we carry on with them. Better to be honest and stop them now before we reach that point. Better to make our public servants face the same financial circumstances that the private sector faces, rather than being allowed to be a gilded, privileged elite.

as if the monies 'going in' to the scheme (the 'contributions' made by the state and by existing employees) are somehow what is funding the 'benefits' paid out to existing pensioners. They aren't. Not a penny of the 'contributions' – purely notional in the case of the state, subtracted from taxpayer-funded salaries in the case of employees – goes into a pension pot. Instead, they go into general funds. No pot is created. Let's take the armed forces scheme as an example. After a member reaches age sixty, they're due a certain percentage of their average annual earnings, depending on how long they served for. Each year they serve, the actuary says, 65.5 per cent of their salary *should* be put into a pot to fund that future pension. However, as Neil Record has demonstrated, the numbers to be found further on in the same actuary's report actually show that for these armed forces, an extraordinary 128 per cent of salary is what really needs to go into that pot each year. And in any event, not 128 per cent, not 65.5 per cent, *not anything* is put into a pot. And the only indication of that is hidden in the text of the 'Report of the Pension Managers', referenced earlier, where with commendable discretion, they slip the word 'unfunded' into a mass of verbiage. Does your average armed forces member know what that means?

So, there is no pot of money being built up to pay for future pensions and each year, the future, entirely unfunded, payment obligations get larger and larger. It's a complete scandal. To be very clear, if this was being done in the private sector, the illegitimate conflation of two separate things (contributions in from one lot of *future* pensioners and payments out to a completely different set of *current* pensioners), plus the failure to fund any of the legally obligatory pensions, would result in people being sent to prison, twice over – Ponzi schemes are illegal, as is any failure to properly fund a pension scheme. In the extreme, it's almost inevitable that some of the younger public servants expecting these pensions won't receive them – even if by then they have spent decades paying into their scheme.

Chart 2.41: Public-Sector Pensions Annual Payments for Existing Pension Liabilities

Forecast 2023–2103, if all schemes closed at end 2024. Note: all payments unfunded

We are already committed to making annual public-sector pensions payments of around £112 billion by 2058 – an amount that is over 10 per cent of current government spending.

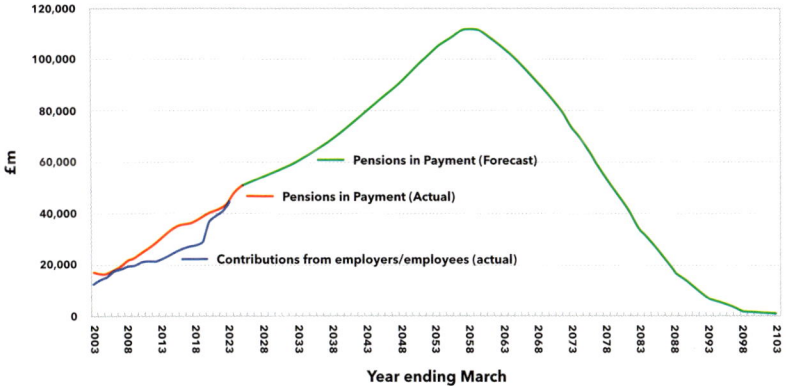

Assumes no new contributions and new pension accruals from 2023–24.
CPI 2 per cent per annum, salary growth CPI +1 per cent.

The fact that 'contributions in' almost exactly equal (in current years) 'pensions out' is only meaningful to the extent that it allows the national accounts to improperly portray (for a brief few years) an implied little-to-zero cost for these schemes. In fact, the two numbers relate to entirely different sets of pensioners; within a few years, payments out will significantly exceed contributions in and the Ponzi scheme will no longer be possible.

Source: Neil Record's analysis of government accounts, public-sector pension liabilities and scheme resource accounts; moyniteam

This ploy won't last for much longer. As Chart 2.41 shows, annual payments to pensioners have been shooting up. Contributions also increased at a rapid rate for a few years recently, partly because staffing and salaries have increased and partly because the reforms of 2010 did increase overall reported contributions. However, payments will continue to increase rapidly, while contributions will now not increase, because the impact from the 2010 reforms is now incorporated and because staff and salaries should not grow in future – indeed, if we take the needed steps on reducing numbers of civil servants and reforming their pay, contributions will shrink. So, one way or another, a disparity between the contributions and the payments is emerging and will now grow rapidly; the Ponzi scheme will be revealed and the drain on the national exchequer will become more and more glaring. Every year we continue the scheme this disparity will be made worse and worse – making it more and more difficult to hide the scheme's true Ponzi nature. All we are doing by keeping the Ponzi scheme going, rather than closing it down immediately, is to make the eventual reckoning, year by year, worse and worse.

Any Ponzi scheme always gets worse as time passes. Therefore, this scheme, as with all Ponzi schemes, must be stopped as soon as possible to prevent the ultimate funding catastrophe from being even larger than it is now. Annual payments for existing retired public-sector workers currently in receipt of their pension payments will be, in 2024–25, £51 billion.[203] *Even if we agreed to end the schemes right now* (which is difficult to envisage), payments to retired public-sector workers will, by 2058, peak at a stupendous £112 billion a year (Chart 2.41). That number is already far beyond what we can afford, yet we have *already promised* that in 2058 we will be paying it to employees turned pensioners. That £112 billion high point will increase for every year that we continue with these public-sector defined-benefit schemes.

And it is even worse than that! Stopping the schemes, necessary as that is, would make the reported situation much worse. To lay out the full problematic magnitude of both the reported and the economic situation, let's portray the individual financial aspects of those public-sector schemes. Chart 2.42 shows the true economic situation that currently exists.

Chart 2.42: The Public-Sector Pensions Ponzi Scheme

Public-sector pensions are astonishingly costly to the nation, which is maybe one reason why most of that vast expense is concealed.

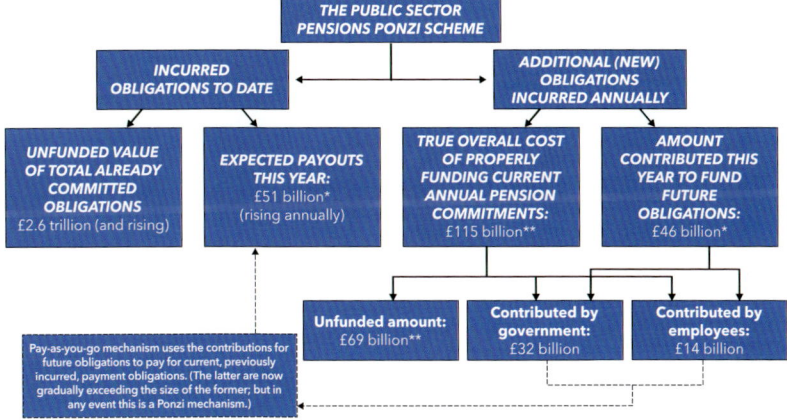

PESA 2023 chart D1: number for 2024/25

**2022/23 actuals. Taking into account that needed payments in are separate from payments out, then the true annual unfunded amount, including government contributions in, is £152 billion.*

Source: Neil Record's analysis, moyniteam analysis

The chart shows first the already incurred, but unfunded future obligations that the country has already committed to. These are £2.6 trillion – an undeclared debt equal to around 100 per cent of GDP.*

---

* Note that all numbers quoted here are only for 'unfunded' civil service defined-benefit schemes. 'Funded' schemes (for example at the Bank of England) are not included; in theory, those don't need any future money from the government. In practice, though, they will need more money if longevity increases beyond what is forecast. And they will need more, as has happened quite a bit recently, when their pension fund investments are badly managed. Any additional liabilities from that are over and above the numbers quoted here.

The chart then shows the obligations we are piling on top of that, whose true economic cost are currently some £115 billion a year.

For the already incurred amounts, it is clearly impossible to fund this £2.6 trillion undeclared debt in the short term; a new government bond issuance of that amount, to create the needed funds for an inviolable pot to cover future payments, is inconceivable. The only practical way to deal with this colossal obligation is to leave the undeclared debt hanging there; shut the scheme down as quickly as possible; painfully, over the years, pay (assuming that we cannot renege on) these excessive pension payment obligations; and hope that our economy grows fast enough to find the money to pay for them. And remember, if we don't close these schemes down immediately then for so long as we keep them open, that unfunded £2.6 trillion is increasing, rapidly every year, as we continue to pile up more and more of these expensive and unfunded pension commitments to our public sector workers.

If we then look at the second, ongoing, issue of newly incurred obligations each coming year, then we see in Chart 2.42 two new, to date mostly unpublicised, numbers:

- The (unfunded) payments each year to existing retirees. This year that is forecast at £51 billion and it rises every year.
- Properly funding each year's new pension commitments for existing employees.

How large is the second of these? Neil Record's analysis indicates that, as is shown in the chart, the current level of new committed pension promises is approximately £115 billion (for 2022/23). The combined current contributions of government (£32 billion) and employees (£14 billion) is £46 billion, leaving an unfunded amount of £69 billion.

As the chart shows, the amount of government money that is actually paid out is the £51 billion to retired employees. What is depicted as paid out is far less, because of the implied claim that the (totally separate) £14 billion and (not actually paid in) £32 billion can somehow be netted off against that. So, both the £32 billion and the £14 billion are, as the dashed lines in the chart show, swallowed up in the Ponzi scheme. These amounts are some £69 billion short of covering the current annually incurred new obligations. The overall annual new cost of £115 billion, when added to the £51 billion payments for past-incurred pension obligations, creates an overall annual cost of £166 billion a year, with only the £14 billion of employee contributions to net off against that, giving a net cost of £152 billion a year. By 2058, if the scheme is not closed, that annual needed number will have risen to a cost that most likely will be *over £220 billion a year, unfunded* – or even more, if we take into account probable longevity improvements, inflation and similar changes.

Clearly, £150 billion a year just to pay past unfunded and newly incurred public-sector pension obligations each year is unsustainable, with £220 billion even more impossible. Future governments will inevitably be tempted, though probably will be unable, to renege on even the current, let alone any future, promises. In any event, £150 billion a year is the true current obligation and over £220 billion a year the true upcoming future obligation: they are the *true undeclared cost of the current set of public-sector schemes.*

These numbers are of mind-boggling magnitude, but they show the true situation, rather than the fake one currently presented in the national accounts. A parade of governments have failed to recognise any of this publicly; the size and generally outrageous nature of these numbers account for why governments choose to leave it as a future, massive and growing, problem for their successors.*

When looked at like this, we can see that the already too high public-sector salaries are, when augmented by the pension schemes, taken into stratospheric levels – and are ruinous for our public finances.

A sensible solution is in the first place to turn these defined-benefit schemes into defined-contribution schemes, thus avoiding the additional risk that the defined-benefit construct contains (large changes in longevity inflation etc.).

What kind of defined-contribution scheme would we arrange for these employees? I would propose that the government pay only what is paid on average in the private sector – say, 6 per cent employee contribution and 6 per cent employer contribution. Difficult as imposing such a change would be, doing it would reduce the annually incurred obligation to a fraction of what our national finances are currently taking on. It would leave us still with the black hole of our payments for unfunded past liabilities (the £51 billion for 2024/25, rising to £112 billion by 2058), but could lower the annual payment for new obligations to, say, £10 billion. Moving to such a scheme would not only be fair (both for these employees and for the taxpayer who has to pay for them) but would limit the current annual cost to some £60 billion a year now, rising to some £120 billion (minimum) by 2058 and then declining.

Any responsible government must immediately put an end to this defined-benefit Ponzi scheme: step away from having such a scheme for themselves, divert the current pension contributions

---

* As said earlier, the main reason that politicians don't get rid of these outrageous schemes is, most likely, the fact that they themselves are beneficiaries of them. A realist, let alone a cynic, can predict that nothing will be done for reform of these schemes until the elected politicians themselves renounce them. How likely are they to do that, do you think?

servants were 'working from home'.[206] Few employees can do their job properly, stuck away at home, with no office facilities and no colleagues to discuss things with. Government figures show that, bit by bit, some departments are improving.[207] The point is, though, that if some ministries can manage to get their employees to come into work, so should the others; the failures to do so are almost certainly down to bad management. And those that are the lowest – HMRC, the Home Office, the Foreign Office – are, unsurprisingly, the ones with the worst reputations for failing to deliver on government policies.

- Whitehall civil servants took 2,100 man-years of stress-related sick days off in 2022. The Guido Fawkes website reported, 'In 2022, more blobsters bunked off for "stress and other mental health problems" than ever before – they took a stonking 771,433 days of mental health sick leave between them, a rise of 38 per cent on the year before. That works out 2,113 of man years lost… all funded at your expense. Labour reckons the "shocking" figures show there is "a mental health crisis at the heart of Whitehall".'[208] Hmm. Is the crisis one of mental health or of bunking off? In the private sector, many employees take pride in never having taken a sick day in their life.

- Over a third of staff in the civil service have a 'hybrid' work week (i.e. some days per week working at home).[209] Most likely, for most of these it is the Tuesdays, Wednesdays and Thursdays arrangement – since that is what is most agreeable to the employee. What price on those individuals getting much work done on Mondays and Fridays?

- Cambridge Council have agreed to let staff work a four-day week (like all such policies, this would have been primarily formulated by the workers themselves, not the councillors – who have, nevertheless, fecklessly agreed to this).[210] Specious excuses have been made based on the alleged extra intensity of effort that the employees will bring to their four-day week. Why couldn't they instead be required to bring their best game to work every day in the first place and thus do an extra 25 per cent of work above what they were delivering previously on each of the five working days – which would enable elimination of 20 per cent of the workforce? The government intervened to prevent this barefaced cheek but apparently without avail.[211] The taxpayer, of course, is paying for all this, including for the legal disputation on the matter between local and central government.

- Civil servants now have costs for their home offices paid (i.e. a direct incentive to work at home and thus be less productive). £450,000 for domestic fuel bills was paid by eleven councils, £700,000 for home internet was paid by forty local councils, £246,000 for 'light and heat' was paid by just one council, Wealden.[212] Related to that, as the *Daily Mail* reported, 'Michael Gove's Department for Levelling Up, Housing and Communities agrees to spend £160,000 to provide furniture to Civil Servants so they can work from home in comfort.'[213] This story includes the revelation that the government has now given into the WFH trend and designs its offices assuming only half the workers will be in at any given time, down from 66 per cent before the pandemic.

- Civil servants are being allowed to work abroad for two weeks a year.[214] This one is about as egregious as it gets – what does it mean except paying for a civil servant's vacation?

- From the *Daily Telegraph*: 'More than 1,000 healthcare workers have been invited to a three-day diversity conference that will feature discussions on pronouns and gender … The conference will include lectures on "pronouns, language and LGBTQ+ allyship" and "gender and LGBTQ+ sessions for colleagues working with children".'[215] Does anyone think that the NHS will improve its productivity as a result of this? Or as a result of the 'mandatory unconscious bias training'* that healthcare staff, the article says, are required to undergo?

- In response to a Freedom of Information request, the Cabinet Office spelled out their policies for annual leave, and employees going through gender reassignment get an especially good deal: 'Up to 13 weeks' special leave with pay may be considered for absences directly related to gender reassignment or intersex variations, in any 12-month rolling period.'[216]

Note that such policies are overwhelmingly decided by the civil service themselves, not by their political masters. Woe betide the minister who tries to stop it!

The whole concept of 'training' as practised in the public sector, when viewed from a competitive private-sector perspective, is either puzzling or risible. The belief seems to have grown in the public sector – self-managing, autonomous, shielded from effective criticism as it is – that the way to manage your workforce well is constantly to take them off on 'training' sessions, away days, team building events. But that's not how it's done in effective private-sector companies. There, the training focuses on imparting the skills needed for the person to do their job well; 'away days' and the like are for the David Brents of this world, not for serious companies. Yet in the public sector, drinking sessions are justified under the excuse of 'team building'. Costly and valueless 'away days' take staff away from their proper work for lengthy periods to be bombarded

---

* A now thoroughly discredited woke theory.

with irrelevant, politically correct, often counterproductive information. For example, they are given training that warns them that they are in danger of sending, or being in receipt of, desperately dangerous 'microaggressions' (£160,000 spent by the government on that).[217] Or that we must all fight, or be on the alert to recognise, 'unconscious bias' (a now-discredited concept).[218]

Even when back at work the counterproductivity doesn't stop: employees must announce their 'preferred pronouns' or tell other people how their name should be pronounced.[219] This more recent feature phenomenon of 'say my name' involves putting the phonetic pronunciation of your name alongside your 'pronouns' at the end of an email.[220] And now – there is always something new but this is very dangerous to the public purse – 'social value'.[221] This is a little-known but highly dangerous new concept, allowing any old activity to be embraced so long as it is defined by civil servants as having an (impossible to define) social value, which is then pursued without regard for value for money. If allowed, this would usher in a torrent of activities that few taxpayers would vote for their money to be spent on were they given the opportunity.

These are examples of the so-called 'woke woo' that is being thrown around the civil service at this time. The example of the government spending £160,000 to take civil servants away from their jobs for three days to learn about 'microaggressions' is a perfect illustration, one of many such examples that could be referenced.

None of this is needed and all of it detracts from a person being able to get on and deliver whatever it was they were hired to actually do. All of it is a useless, fanciful productivity sinker.

The problem, above all, with the new 'woke' approach is that it defines itself as the one true way, seeking to preclude any return to other management styles – which are themselves defined out of existence using terms such as 'bullying'. But this new, one true management style has led to quite outrageous excess and to ever-new heights of bonkers. It is quite fantastical that – at a time when we should be looking to prune every possible penny of excess spend in the government and when a large proportion of citizens have to budget carefully with every single penny they have to spend – we find that the government is allowing some £7 billion to be not just wasted in silly spend but to be expended on (in the words of the report that uncovered this) 'politically motivated campaigns'. Conservative Way Forward sent Freedom of Information requests to some 6,000 central and devolved government departments and local councils, universities and schools, health providers, emergency services, courts, the armed forces, and parliamentary and cultural bodies.[222] In their report, they recount an extraordinary story:

- 10,000 equality, diversity and inclusivity (EDI) officers, costing the taxpayer £427 million a year
- EDI training for staff that takes them away for *1 million working days a year*, meaning the UK taxpayer loses £150 million in public-sector staff time each year
- £212 million wasted on issues relating to race, sexuality, unconscious bias and EDI training
- £778 million a year spent on government grants to charities, who often use the money to lobby for policies that are directly contrary to government policy
- £20 billion spent on quangos, much of it wasted, with a suggested *£5.5 billion* in savings from the removal of politically motivated activities

Leaving out for now the last two of these, we find, in the first three, a direct savings opportunity of £1 billion.

The problem is in large part a consequence of the recent rise of importance of the HR function. Originally a department whose job was just to hire, fire, pay and train (in actual work-relevant skills), HR has been infiltrated in many organisations by nouveau-Marxists, adept at displacing the latest moral panic into the workplace. Thus, it is not enough to have an effective intelligence community working to protect Britain from the machinations of some very dangerous individuals and state actors: no, let's set off on a wild goose chase to complain that there are not enough female or ethnically diverse spies, sending the community into a roil of navel-gazing that detracts it from its proper purpose and pushes it into diversity hires that simultaneously ensure less effective employees *and* create the risk of importing security risks into the organisation *and* cruelly leave many employees doubtfully wondering if they were hired for their ability or because of their gender or skin colour.[223]

As a result of it all, productivity – already impacted hard – gets further hammered by steps that are taken primarily to benefit the employees, and that disbenefit the customers. Four-day weeks; allocating massive amounts of time, that could otherwise be productively used, to useless training or 'staff morale' activities; and enormous swathes of individuals promoted above the appropriate rank for their tasks so as to get around pay constraints, with consequent higher than necessary salary bills and yet another hit to productivity. The obvious solution to this problem is to outsource the pay, hiring, and firing activities of the civil service; limit the training function to skills actually needed for the day job; and then fire anyone left in the HR department, apart from a small, professionalised personnel. But locate that HR function *outside* the civil service organisation and have it report to ministers, so as to avoid the civil service running itself. This is the kind of action a CEO taking over a dysfunctional organisation would take; this is what is needed across the entire public sector. At the end of it, the civil service would be more productive and a large number of civil servants from the HR function would no longer be needed. With these changes, we might stand a chance of a responsive, effective, productive civil service emerging from the current disastrous situation.

While it is clear from earlier pages that, throughout the most recent run of Conservative governments, those with unconservative views have been pretty much calling the shots across the public sector, that is not at all to say that *all* civil servants are happy with the situation that has been described here. Recently, the Cabinet Secretary was sent a letter, signed by forty-two staff from sixteen departments, saying that ideology on gender, promoted by trans activists, has become embedded in the civil service in a 'significant breach of impartiality'.[224] Depressingly, it took two months for the signatories to get a reply, sent to them by the government's 'chief people officer' – indicating who is actually running things (hint: not the politicians). The problems are, of course, far wider than this one wedge issue. But this evidence of a certain degree of fightback from within the civil service is gratifying. However, looking back over what has been discussed here, it is difficult not to draw the conclusion that, in general, a massive and very expensive joke is being perpetrated on the public by the civil service – a joke that imposes an enormous drag on the economy, ensuring that all public-sector work directed by the civil service is likely to be inefficient and overly costly.

The civil service manages itself for its own benefit, paying little regard to its political masters

What are the outputs of the civil service? According to Chart 2.38, shown earlier, their numbers have increased by at least 40 per cent. But what outputs do they produce? Are they outputs that the British public needs or even wants? Advantageously for the civil service, a lot of what would constitute an output in civil service land is nebulous. One wonders what outputs were claimed to have been achieved in the following incident from the early 2000s, which I recollect taking place a few weeks before a general election. It involved a (private sector) team from my then company that had been seconded into one of the central government departments. An urgent, time critical issue arose that the departmental client needed to be consulted on. To my team's consternation, not a single civil servant could be found in the government building; the team were told that the entire department had gone into Saint James's Park for the day to have a 'purdah picnic'.*

While that purdah picnic event is just one example, it is a good illustration of how time constraints and urgency to deliver any output get relaxed by the civil service at any opportunity – indeed, routinely. Charles Moore caught the mood perfectly in a *Spectator* article, describing how the famed British inventor and entrepreneurial icon, Sir James Dyson, sought to meet Thérèse Coffey, the DEFRA Secretary, to discuss and show her some of his innovative approaches. His office made numerous approaches to hers. Time went by. Her office said they'd lost his letter. Nothing transpired when it was resent. Dyson's office enquired whether he was being snubbed – over

---

*   Purdah is the multi-week period prior to elections when politicians are prohibited from much interaction with their civil servants. Apparently, the view is that during this fairly lengthy multi-week period, the need to get anything at all done is low to non-existent.

four and a half months and ten interactions had then gone by in this outstanding display of civil service incompetence. After that, more promises were made. Still nothing happened.

This story is not at all exceptional, although in the private sector it would most likely have led to a number of people being fired. But surely, one asks, this is not just a fault to be laid at the feet of the civil service employee. Any employee who could wangle a public-sector gig – one that offers high pay, a fabulous pension and a relaxed work environment – would take it like a shot. So, don't blame the employee. Blame the politicians who have been elected to sort such messes out. They have the requisite legislative tools at their disposal, just as employers in the private sector have employment law, to rectify this problem – so why don't they? The answer lies in the fact that we have increasingly 'professionalised' politicians, who can appeal to the public, and even occasionally formulate policy, but who can't manage, can't impose their intent on a department, and are anyway comprehensively outmanoeuvred by civil servants. Lenin famously declared that the only important question was: who got to say what the rules were and enforce them, and who got told what the rules were and had to endure the draconian consequences if they failed to follow them? In Vladimir Ilyich's words: 'Who, whom?' It is clear that the civil service is laying down rules for themselves, while politicians watch helplessly, fearing the consequences should they be so foolish as to interfere.

The civil service now sets political policy for the government and politely ignores ministers who want to set policy any differently

Watching the government during 2023 and 2024, it was hard to see any successful actions being taken that would not have been approved of, or at least tolerated by, our officials. Secretaries of State and ministers are happy to announce initiatives that have been worked up for them by their civil servants, but any deviation from officialdom's approval can be met with obstruction and outright refusal. And even those whose political outlook is likely to meet with approval from civil servants must not deviate. An example of that is Rory Stewart, whose 2023 book *Politics on the Edge* in general reveals him, despite his having many good ideas, as a true centrist in the social democrat mould, mostly concerned, it seems, with how to extract more funds from the Treasury and hand them out to various interest groups and not really showing any interest in how to grow the economy so as to make such funds available.[225] But despite his location in the soft middle, Stewart experiences obstruction after obstruction from his civil servants. Over and again, his civil servants presume to tell him they are right and he is wrong. As a minister he is given a small desk behind a glass wall in a corridor; visiting the Permanent Secretary of his department, he finds himself in a large, luxurious room. He does not complain that the elected boss is subservient to the unelected servant. His civil servants patronise him. Trying to find out to whom a given unit reports, so that he can ensure that the unit is ordered to do something, he is given the runaround over and again, just on that single point of who was the unit's boss, and in the end, the thing that he wants to get done by that unit doesn't quite get done.

It is clear that the civil service currently runs the government. Over the years, politicians have allowed this to come to pass. The politicians are notionally in charge of Parliament, which could pass laws overriding the basis on which civil servants manage to rule the roost. If they wished, politicians could restore control to themselves. But there is no sign of that happening. Why? Is it because MPs have to be nice to be electable and can't switch off being nice whenever the opposite is called for? Or are they just scared of civil servants and afraid of being removed? Changing the power structure in government is an essential first step to trimming back the costs and inefficiency of the civil service.

The list goes on, showing over and again that it is the civil service who decide what will pass, what policies will be implemented and what regulations will be enforced:

- Civil servants threatened to go on strike rather than implement the government's migration policies.[226]
- Officials 'run down the clock' when they know a reshuffle is coming.[227]
- A former Cabinet minister claimed he was told 'that may be the minister's policy but it is not the department's'.[228]
- 'Eye-rolling civil service leaders block reform': proposals to reform Whitehall have been met with eye-rolling, disengagement and aversion tactics by top civil servants.[229]
- According to former Trade Secretary Liam Fox, 'Britain's civil service leaders are sabotaging elected ministers.'[230]

But if all this is the case, what is it that prevents politicians from exercising their legitimate governing powers to impose their political will on the civil service? A possible answer can be seen in the following section.

The civil service now dominates and frightens its political bosses

In the early days of the Cameron government, Sue Gray, at that time director general of propriety and ethics, was described as 'the most powerful person in government you have never heard of'.[231] This shows how even then, the civil service was in the habit of exercising the whip hand over the politicians. Since then, the problem has become much worse. Draconian impositions such as the 'ministerial code' or convoluted interpretations of Tony Blair's Human Rights Act, along with the creation of disciplinary offices run by civil servants such as the one referred to above, mean that politicians with ambitions to change things will be out of luck (and if they persist, out of office) unless the changes they want are also approved by their officials (hint: most civil servants tend to be not warmly supportive of Conservative Party policies).

In the past few years, there have been further striking examples of civil servants effectively firing their bosses, by calling on various bodies and 'codes' that they themselves originally initiated to propel the politician out of office.

Priti Patel was regularly accused of bullying and had to endure an eight-month investigation, which found bullying but whose findings were rejected by the then Prime Minister Boris Johnson – a great, albeit rare, example of how a show of spine can see the woke warriors off. This, however, led to a row in which the depth of the civil service establishment's opposition to their being governed by elected politicians was on full display.[232]

Dominic Raab had been universally praised as a soft-spoken and effective stand-in Prime Minister when Boris Johnson was in hospital for two weeks. Nonetheless, the following year, he was accused of bullying. All of the complainants remain anonymous. Raab incautiously vowed to step down if the enquiry found that he had bullied. *The Guardian* reported allegations of 'individuals being physically sick before meetings, regularly in tears and, in at least one case, left feeling suicidal as a result of the alleged behaviour'.[233] Two of the eight accusations were upheld in a 48-page report by investigating KC, Adam Tolley, who stated that Raab's behaviour was 'intimidating … and persistently aggressive in the context of a workplace meeting'. He quoted a definition of bullying as 'intimidating or insulting behaviour that makes an individual feel uncomfortable, frightened, less respected or put down'.[234] Note that these definitions make the concept entirely subjective – all it takes is for one oversensitive individual to feel uncomfortable or frightened for you to be guilty of bullying. Tolley made it clear that he had based his finding on subjective evidence; saying, 'I recognise and accept that the impacts communicated to me had genuinely been experienced.'

Any private-sector boss would tell you that on that subjective standard of bullying, it would be virtually impossible to demand good performance from your team because you'd risk losing your job if the weakest personality in your team decided to allege, truthfully or not, that they had felt intimidated. But if you fail to call out that weak player for poor performance, the keener elements of your team will probably leave, disgusted that poor performance is not being called out. A private-sector company could not survive under such constraints. In the case of Raab, he found a civil service machine that was not fit for purpose, did his level best to make it perform better and was ousted by that machine. Additionally, Tolley's finding seems to have been even further removed from the feelings of the allegedly abused public servants; apparently the conclusions were mostly based on the feelings of those *observing the behaviour* i.e. not those who were the *recipients* of the alleged bullying behaviour. Truly Orwellian.

Other Conservative MPs have been forced to resign after allegations of bullying, drunkenness and sexual shenanigans (both small and, admittedly, large). Some of the sexual behaviours certainly cry out to be dealt with, but it is a shame that Zac Goldsmith's proposal

– surely the constitutionally correct approach – to allow the electorate to recall MPs, rather than unelected bureaucrats ruling on these matters, was not adopted. Boris Johnson and various of his allies were imposed upon by relatively new parliamentary oversight bodies. Many of these contain unelected lay members and use standards of evidence taking and 'balance of probability' decisions, rather than 'beyond reasonable doubt'.

The argument that politicians – who are, constitutionally, supposed to be on top – can sort the civil service out should have force. But here, a further beauty of the situation reveals itself. Because the civil servants have created and mostly run the processes that regulate and discipline the politicians' behaviour, it seems that they are able to see off even a determined political boss from stepping in and forcing them into a different mode of working. The Raab episode brings the point home forcefully. The result of that is that every minister is now stuck entirely at the mercy, and under the thumb of, their civil servants. A definition of bullying now exists that enables the flakiest of snowflakes to bring down an elected politician. There will be civil servants who continue to do great work for their minister, but for civil servants who feel they righteously oppose any particular government policy and want to obstruct it, there is nothing much the minister can do if they turn to oppositional behaviour. The Raab outcome was a triumph for that extractive institution, the civil service, and a tragedy for our nation. The Truss and Kwarteng ejections contain similar elements.

The civil service is masterful at seeing off attempts at reforming it
Why have we allowed this situation to emerge, when we know from centuries of experience in the private sector that organisations that are allowed to be run by their own workers end up being run on

behalf of the employees and that they become fantastically inefficient – see *Animal Farm* for an allegorical description of how that happens. In the private sector, CEOs and other senior positions are hired by owners or governing bodies. Hirings, firings and promotions in the private sector are performed by an HR function that is clearly under the thumb of the CEO; the size of the workforce and its remuneration is constantly under review.

Sir Humphrey, however, feels pretty secure in his job – possibly because of his apparent ability to threaten the career of any politician who wishes to reform the civil service. Some attempted reforms might temporarily make a dent – see the decline in the number of civil servants 2010–15 – but soon after, they get reversed, as can be seen by the steady rise in the number of civil servants since then.

An elected minister can almost never hire, fire, discipline or overly direct a civil servant. If the minister tries to manage the team, it is bullying. If a civil servant screws up, however, they are moved to another position. Promotions are decided on within the civil service, by the civil service. Those who say that reforming the civil service is impossible take two different lines. First, that productivity is hard to improve in the civil service type of work and second, that if you tell them to cut costs, they just propose cutting those exact initiatives which will cause outrage among the electorate. For the first, it's ludicrous to claim that civil service work is somehow so different from other work that productivity can't be improved. Automation, centralisation and the use of technology are all key.

The second argument reflects how civil servants dominate politicians by choosing the ground of argument; they effortlessly ensure the conversation is about what programmes to cut, and then ensure the programmes being discussed are contentious electorally. The former Chief Secretary to the Treasury, Lord Macpherson, inadvertently revealed the technique in all its glory in a recent interview with the *New Statesman*.[235] On consulting with George Osborne in the runup to the 2010 election, he drew up a menu of potential cuts of £30, £60 or £90 billion: 'Once you've got to £90 billion of cuts, you did quite serious things, like abolishing the Navy.' Right. And all those 'serious things' were about cutting programmes, not about making remaining existing staff more efficient or changing ludicrously expensive working conditions. In the revealing words of Martin Stanley, a former top mandarin, 'It is a firm rule that ministers cannot dismiss civil servants that displease them or offer any unwelcome advice.'[236] (Gosh.)

Employees inside any organisation usually can't see the opportunities for efficiency, for working harder or for doing with less. That's why outside governance is always necessary. The civil service hasn't got that. They can't see that the major issues are not just about cutting programmes but, in addition, should be about *delivering the same programmes with 15 per cent or 20 per cent fewer civil servants* – that's what productivity improvement means!

The civil service is now an organisation that abides in a different universe from private-sector organisations
Pusillanimously, politicians go along with a structure that includes:

- *Weak, badly supported politicians*: ministers, usually inexperienced, are thrown into departments and expected to accomplish something. Civil servants dominate them with ease. The minister is given no training in how to impose their political will. They are not supported by government lawyers who could advise them how to see off attempts by civil servants to subvert their initiatives.

- *Weak governance*: the boards of departments of state mostly seem to preside over and nod along with whatever the civil servants put up as their agendas; there is usually almost no attempt to challenge and push the department to accomplish the government's programme.[237]

- *Multiple frameworks and strictures*: these are drafted by civil servants and can be exploited by them too. For example, the ministerial code, the civil service code, the 'seven principles of public life', which are all vague enough to make it easy to attack an office holder.

- *Supervisory and disciplinary bodies that constrain the politician.* The list is longer than already mentioned: the Committee on Standards in Public Life, the Office for Ethics and Responsibility, the Independent Complaints and Grievance Scheme and on. Possibly most of these contain lay members, not many of whom are of a right-wing disposition and who swiftly can do for an elected minister or other recalcitrant politician.

- *Responsibility sloughed off by activities being handed over to ALBs*: ranging from the NHS being separated from the Department for Health and Social Care, to the Treasury handing its responsibilities to the Bank of England and the OBR, to the many hundreds of quangos and regulators.

- *Decisions delegated to the civil service or outside bodies* on who is appointed or deputed to those ALBs (these decision makers will be, as mentioned, inevitably mostly left-wing in disposition). As a classic example, until the mid-1990s, ministers and senior civil servants were responsible for appointments to quangos and other similar public bodies. But the Nolan Committee on Standards in Public Life was created and it then said that a commissioner of public appointments (currently, at the time of writing, the excellent William Shawcross, but he is an exception, not the rule) should regulate these appointments. So, now the politicians, having foolishly created these ALBs responsible for all sorts of aspects of government, no longer in many cases have a say in who runs them. It was said by Nolan that the appointments must be 'free from undue political or other influence' – why on earth should that be a requirement? How else can an elected government make sure that its (necessarily political) programme is going to be implemented but by appointing its own people to run organisations? Another example: a special independent commission now oversees the appointments processes within the NHS, so that government can't intervene autonomously when they need to put some tough turnaround person into, say, a failing part of the NHS without being overseen and/or challenged by that outside commission. This is no doubt very convenient if the government wishes to avoid taking blame for the NHS's failings, but how can a government possibly then implement any hard-hitting strategy for reforming it?

Today's modern civil service marches to its own drum, with its own view of what is needed, spending much of its time ensuring that the imperatives of ideological diversity requirements are scrupulously attended to and coming up with demeaning, demoralising, increasingly ridiculous, ever-new requirements. These include forcing ('encouraging') employees to go on training courses in recondite concepts such as unconscious bias or microaggressions; enforcing (whether overtly or subtly) the use of pronouns or 'speak my name' nonsense at the end of emails; and an obsession with hiring and promoting in ways that balance identity categories such as race, gender, or sexual preference (rather than in more important dimensions, such as skills, critical thinking ability or psychometric profile). None of these fad obsessions have much to do with the fulfilment of the job of each department of central or local government. Many of the fads get in the way of a good job being done. All are championed by an out-of-control, identitarian-focused HR function that sees itself as the champion of the worker, or of millenarian societal goals, rather than the taxpayer.

Clearly, over the previous decades, there has been a shift in the way the modern civil service and its companion public-sector organisations understand the world, how to behave in it, how to accomplish things (or not). What was the cause of this shift? Why has it happened so comprehensively in the public sector? Aside from the growingly powerful role of HR departments, importing woke woo beliefs from the US and universities, a further factor seems to be the significantly changing psychometric profile of civil servants. The civil service was, at earlier stages of its existence, brisk, decisive, efficient – and famously small. A shift in the profile of employees and management, to some degree reflecting changes in society overall, but nonetheless creating a cadre with different movers and behaviours in the private sector, has taken place.

The civil service seems to have its greatest focus on process – that is, whether a job is being done the right way, whether the formalities are being properly observed, whether the team is working harmoniously, using interpersonal skills – rather than having the focus be on outcomes (meaning getting to the right result or end product in a timely, cost-efficient way, using rational analysis rather than emotional sentiment).

Traditionally, nine (or more) out of ten CEOs in the private sector are, in the language of Myers–Briggs personality types, thinkers (head), not feelers (heart).[238] How about the civil service? Are its leaders and its employees primarily thinkers or feelers? Most of the descriptions and anecdotes in this book point to the civil service being stuffed at all levels with feelers; short on thinkers.

The thinker, in this context, focuses on using facts and logic to get swiftly and efficiently to the right *end product*, one that is seen as objectively satisfactory. The feeler, however, focuses more on values, emotions and intuition and is concerned most of all with the *process* and whether everyone is happy and feels good about what they have done. Famously, an entire industry has been built around explaining people who have differing types of psychometric profile to one other and, in particular, it has been observed over and again that while thinkers seem to understand feelers but tend not to understand *why* they are that way, feelers don't really understand, and often have a violent dislike of, thinkers. A thinker will see feelers as kind-hearted but misguided; a feeler will often believe that thinkers lack values and make heartless and harsh decisions.

So, is there a dominance of feelers in the civil service? It seems plausible that in most parts of our civil service, feelers significantly dominate over thinkers. See, anecdotally, the confession by the Permanent Under-Secretary of the Foreign Office at the time, Simon (now Lord) McDonald, that his staff were crying and in a state of 'mourning' the day after the Brexit vote, and that to comfort them, he informed his colleagues that he had 'voted to remain in the European Union'.[239] A very feeler response to such a situation; a thinker response would most likely be 'please would you all stop moaning and get back to work'.

The feeler versus thinker distinction is also, to a degree, an indicator of left-wing versus right-wing views. An abiding problem, not just with the civil service but with regulators and quangos, is that for whatever reason, they seem to end up getting staffed by people with left-wing leanings. These, in a self-reinforcing way, convince themselves that redistribution should be the predominating economic guiding principle, that the principle of more regulation and direction-setting from the centre is good, and often that the doctrines of the various 'woke' movements represent an urgent moral point of view that should be imperatively adopted. Even if the majority of the population doesn't particularly agree with those sets of principles, that is how the civil servants and regulators and quangos will behave. Thus, it is right-wing think tanks that get most aggressively attacked by the charity commission, it is GB News that OfCom seems to get into a perpetual lather about and it is regulators, the civil service and quangos where the most ludicrous woke seems to thrive.[240] It may be that people of a right-wing-ish disposition just aren't attracted to government jobs, but the end result is that across society, the left-wing viewpoint – so different from what the electorate voted for 2010–19 – is able, through the state power these government servants possess, to rule the roost and thus have a stultifying effect on any innovative, freedom-promoting, libertarian-style initiative. And, on more than one occasion, be able to threaten the job, position or livelihood of outspoken right-wing types.

So, where does this all take us? Feelers, it seems, increasingly dominate the public sector.* If all that counts in the civil service is ensuring that teams are working in a cuddly, wokey environment

---

* A recent tale of a whistleblower in Whitehall being forced out of the civil service for denouncing woke activities is instructive. She is a PhD in engineering – a profession almost exclusively thinker. Her insistence on logic and discipline appears to have led to swift ejection by the organisation. See Camilla Turner, 'Whistleblower "forced out" of Whitehall over gender beliefs', *Daily Telegraph*, 18 May 2024, https://www.telegraph.co.uk/news/2024/05/18/whistleblower-forced-out-of-whitehall-over-gender-beliefs/

and that the processes they use tick all the woke boxes, then that, by definition, will have massive negative repercussions for productivity, precluding making the unproductive public sector more like the productive private sector. A feeler would probably think I was being beastly by pointing out that the civil service displays feeler-type behaviour and by my claiming that it needs a large injection of thinkers – especially among its leaders. A thinker, however, would probably just assume I was trying to come to a logical conclusion and treat the idea on its merits. Regardless, my conclusion is that over recent decades, the civil service has become a 'feeler' organisation and that very serious problems derive from that.

I end this matter on that note, except to say that for those who find this topic interesting, Appendix B has a lengthier discussion on it, with a few more interesting details.

• • •

At the end of the day, we have a civil service that thinks it is like the private sector and deserves to be paid at the same level as (or, in fact, at a much greater level than) the private sector. Yet it is much less efficient than its equivalents in the private sector. The public sector is run by people who are very different in outlook and temperament from people in the private sector. As attempts to put them into high-level private-sector jobs reveal, they don't do at all well there.[241] Major transformation of the overall makeup of our civil service's HR and leadership is needed if the civil service is to return to being a lean, efficient, effective organisation, one that is focused on delivering the agenda of the elected government of the day – and especially so if that government's agenda is opposed by left-leaning mandarins.

In summary, civil service costs could be cut by:

- 20 per cent staff reduction, returning to 2015 levels: £4.2 billion
- returning remaining civil servants to proper pay grades: £0.8 billion
- on-costs of 40 per cent saved for both: £2 billion
- moving defined-benefit pension schemes to defined-contribution: £0 savings but prevents later disaster
- removing all EDI/ESG staff and all non-skills training, away days etc.: £1 billion

Total expenditure savings: £8 billion per annum

EXPLORING SAVINGS AND OTHER IMPROVEMENTS IN LOCAL GOVERNMENT

At £205 billion in 2022/23, the cost of local government – basically the 317 local authorities in England, plus the cost of local authorities in the three devolved administrations – was some 18 per cent of the total £1.2 trillion of overall government spend.[242] £71 billion was in salary and on-costs.[243]

These amounts are contained within the numbers in Chart 2.12, shown earlier.

Local government spend is primarily focused on social welfare, education and public order (Chart 2.43).

Given that the largest categories of spend are social welfare, education and public order, it is difficult, from the helicopter-view level this book necessarily takes, to argue for cost-saving changes in all of what local government does. What we can argue, however, is for changes in *how* that money is spent. The TaxPayers' Alliance, in the twenty years of its existence to date, has sent out tens of thousands of Freedom of Information requests to local authorities, that have resulted in the uncovering of waste, high salaries, poor procurement and generally extravagant expenditure.

Chart 2.43: Major Components of Local Government Spend 2022/23
100 per cent = £199 billion

Local government spends nearly £200 billion a year and rising. Some of this would be difficult to cut, but some of it is crying out for cost reductions.

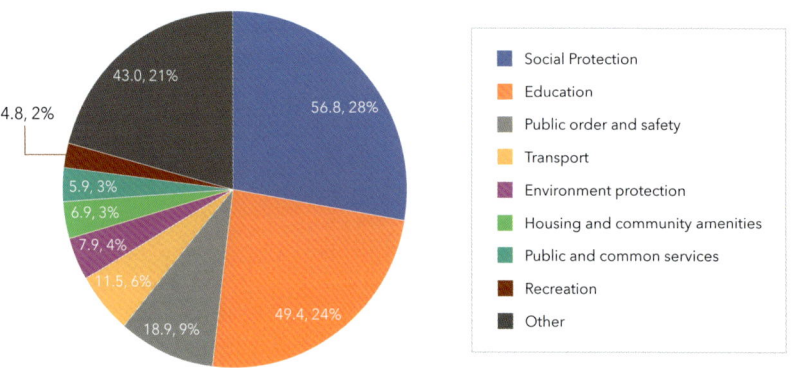

Source: HM Treasury[244]

One of the most egregiously wasteful actions a local council has taken, already discussed earlier, is the proposal by South Cambridgeshire County Council to allow staff to work for only four days a week with no loss of pay or benefits.[245] To admit, in essence, that the council is allowing its staff to goof off for 20 per cent of the time is to say that the council is deliberately squandering public money. If the council workers are failing to deliver at full productivity, the answer is to have more demanding management, not to give out bribes. That's what managers are for; managing people so as to get top performance from them is not a discretionary task. Again, it seems that in most councils, local councillors, instead of acting as owner-managers on behalf of the electorate, are usually too scared to intervene in personnel or disciplinary matters; they get sternly told by senior council staff to butt out and they are told it is illegal for them to interfere. What is needed is for the central government to change the law (assuming they can find no existing laws that serve) to put the elected officials back in charge and then provide a central legal resource to support councillors who wish to take back control of their council.*

On the assumption that local government can, just as with central government, be 10 per cent more productive (but applying that to only 50 per cent of local government workers and leaving alone the three big categories of spend discussed earlier because they would be regarded by most as essential), then a saving of £3.5 billion in local government remuneration seems achievable.

Savings from local government: £3.5 billion

EXPLORING SAVINGS AND OTHER IMPROVEMENTS IN QUANGOS, REGULATORS, CAPTIVE CHARITIES AND OTHER ARM'S-LENGTH BODIES

For quangos, the think tank Civitas offers an entirely different taxonomy than the one we showed earlier for the types of body

---

* In the case discussed above, it does not appear that Cambridgeshire councillors wished to stop the four-day initiative; rather, they enthusiastically supported it.

that make up overall government. Its 2023 breakdown identifies 295 quangos, divided into:[246]

- non-departmental public bodies (NDPBs): 237
- executive agencies: thirty-eight
- non-ministerial departments: twenty

The quango landscape described here has changed significantly from the late '70s when there were 2,167 of them. In the Civitas report, we find that the National Audit Office has claimed that a lot of this was due to reorganisation, with various quangos 'reclassified outside boundary' (what's that?), 'no longer an NDPB' (what are they now then?) or 'closed'. However, many that they claimed as closed weren't, such as the civil service appeal board or the Alcohol Education and Research Council – now an 'independent charity' which states it is 'under government supervision' and still gets tax-payers' money. The number of staff in the remaining quangos has halved since 1979. The cost has, at £15 billion, halved since 1979 and is a quarter of 2009's £60 billion (all in today's prices).

But quangos, in that Civitas taxonomy, are only a fraction of the non-governmental landscape. Chart 2.44 gives the government's version of major components of ALB land and its overall spend of £224 billion. (Some people refer to every body on that chart as a quango but Civitas, clearly, didn't.) Furthermore, that £224 billion isn't the entirety, since some ALBs are not on this chart – the BBC, for example.

The following case example, the Bank of England, illustrates how regulators, along with various other ALBs, are no slouch when it comes to replicating civil service follies.[247]

Chart 2.44: Arm's-Length Body Landscape by Gross Resource
Expenditure figures 31 March 2020

Around 21 per cent of all government expenditure is through ALBs.

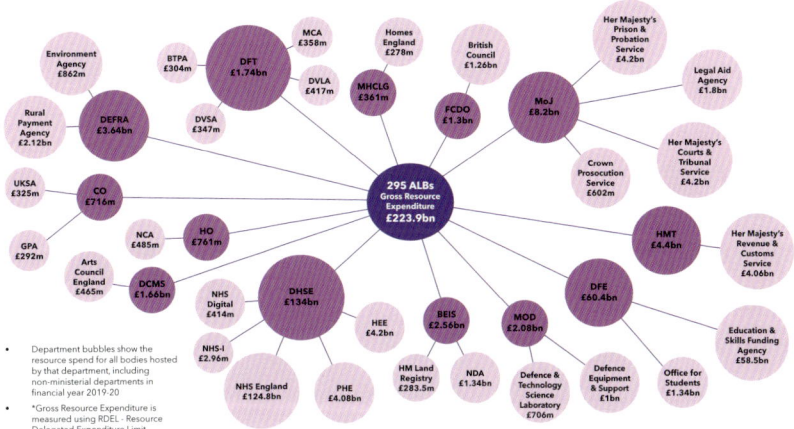

Source: Gov.uk [248]

Case example: Bank of England

The Bank of England – which the naive observer would presume to be a fairly 'dry' bunch of people, sternly presiding over the nation's finances and worrying only about inflation and the banking system – seems to have turned itself into a warrior of woke. The bank, in 2021–22 and beyond, utterly failed in its primary, almost its only task – to keep inflation at 2 per cent. The bank itself was deeply entangled in the leveraged LDI funds scandal in 2022, where it, apart from failing to prevent the loss of tens or even hundreds of billions of pounds across various pension funds, lost a large amount in its own leveraged LDI pension fund.

The Bank of England and its leadership are accused of having failed to control the money supply and thus to have caused the high level of inflation that the UK has experienced; to have made the decision, some years ago, to not even *publish* the money supply figures that could have raised concerns that excess money was going to cause inflation; to have unpardonably put the entire £5 billion of their pension fund into the highly risky and now busted LDI approach; to have raised short-term interest rates 2021–22 too little and too late; and even to have precipitated the demise of the Truss administration by failing to raise interest rates enough to prevent 'chaos' in the markets while simultaneously, out of the blue, announcing £80 billion of quantitative tightening. This last point further roiled the bond market the day before Truss and Kwasi Kwarteng's mini-budget, and the bank then failed to support the markets enough following the mini-budget, directly creating a crisis when the collateral calls on the leveraged LDI funds caused a run on gilts. All this ultimately led to the fall of the Truss government.* 249

You would think there would be an awful lot on the bank's plate already, with its rather highfalutin mission 'to promote the good of the people of the UK' having clearly fallen by the wayside given destructive levels of inflation. The bank's primary remit is to control inflation and financial stability. And yet we now discover that during 2021 and 2022, the Bank of England was spending a lot of time and money attempting to curry favour with Stonewall, the LGBT

---

* The Bank of England itself has published a paper saying that two thirds of the run on gilts at the time was caused by the risks taken by LDI funds *prior* to the time of the Truss government (see endnote). If we split the responsibility for the remaining one third of the interest rate rises between the Bank of England's actions and the mini-budget, then Truss's actions were clearly of too small effect to have brought about the crisis. Rather, it was the failure of the regulator to have controlled the risk level in the LDI funds – plus the failure of the Bank of England to continue its market support until the LDI funds had sorted themselves out. The Bank of England paper also makes it clear that the bank's extensive and excessive quantitative easing in 2020/21 added significantly to the risk in the LDI funds by pushing interest rates down in those earlier years. Much of the pressure on the LDIs was already known to the bank prior to the mini-budget, but they did not warn the Truss government of that. The run on gilts was therefore *not* the international bond market's verdict on Truss; it was, rather, a result of a rolling series of collateral calls being made on the irresponsibly risky and catastrophically regulated LDI funds industry, which led to a vast dumping of gilts and thus a tanking bond market.

lobby group, submitting a 103-page application in an attempt to be ranked high on Stonewall's list of favoured companies. They did well, coming fifty-seventh in Stonewall's annual list of all employers in the UK. Success! Or so you might have thought, but the BBC's Stephen Nolan has created a superb podcast showing how deeply wrong and misguided it was and is for any public organisation to attempt to curry favour with Stonewall in this manner.[250]

And how did the bank succeed in getting to be the fifty-seventh best organisation in the UK on Stonewall's favoured list, one wonders? *The Times* revealed that staff were 'encouraged to include their pronouns in email signatures' and to be 'allies' to the LGBT community 'by wearing a rainbow lanyard and displaying the same symbol at their workstation'.[251] Note the word 'encouraged'.

The list of nonsense – any gender can get pregnant, LGBT targets, every department required to submit and be assessed on their annual 'diversity and inclusion objective' and on and on – is seemingly endless. The woke stuff was not just something done on the side by the Bank of England's HR department. It used up a major part of senior management's time: 'Five governors and executive directors attended a meeting of the "LGBT plus and allies" steering group, and eight signed up for reverse mentoring.' Reverse mentoring, in case you haven't come across the term, basically represents an abdication of leadership in which the bosses submit to being told by usually rather youthful – and in this case, it appears, LGBT activist – workers what their attitudes and actions at work should be. A sort of reverse pyramid of management – utter foolish wokery, but typically 'feeler' in approach.

And the bank, of course, breezily uses the term 'birthing parent' and promises that one floor of its offices will have only gender-neutral bathrooms.[252] Are employees 'encouraged' to use them?

Nor does it stop at the gender wars; the bank fights our climate battles for us as well. We learn, among other things, that the bank is going to 'install heat pumps' in a 'net zero drive'.[253]

All this is quite a litany. Given the horror and damage that inflation has inflicted on the UK over the past two to three years, not to mention the LDI fund crisis and the bond market meltdown, you would have thought that the Bank of England would be feeling a bit sheepish and certainly not wanting to draw attention to itself at this time. But instead, it doubles down on fighting the woke wars, just as the public's backlash against those questionable positions begins to swell. Over and again, we are told that the government doesn't have the money for basic needed services such as childcare, social home care, the NHS in general, teachers' salaries, whatever. And yet institutions such as the Bank of England have no compunction or shame in charging off in any direction they like, spending any money they want, on any woke topic. This, however, is far removed from the one prime job they have, the job they have singularly failed on: controlling inflation.

As this chapter has discussed, the Bank of England is just one out of numerous such extractive, out of control institutions, spanning the breadth of the public sector in the UK.

If other ALBs are in much the same shape as the civil service, then similar savings can be made from them. Even taking only a fraction of those potential savings:

- If all EDI activities were to be eliminated, then according to the Conservative Way Forward report quoted earlier, around £1 billion could be saved.
- Even if we assume, prior to a thorough cost review of each ALB and quango, that only 5 per cent of cost could be cut in

an overhead value analysis-style exercise, that is still £11 billion saved.

- Note that much of the spend by ALBs (culture, aid, religion, recreation) is exactly the sort of spend that at the beginning of this chapter was shown to be negatively correlated with economic growth.

- A determined government could also cut back significantly on regulatory overreach (discussed in Chapter 8). Christopher Snowdon of the IEA, in a report discussed further in the following section, reviews how an 'iron triangle' between politicians, pressure groups and the civil service drive the constant enlargement of the bureaucracy and how that doesn't just enlarge government involvement in charities but also helps balloon the quango sector. While regulators are only a subset of ALBs, a determined effort could cut (say) a further quarter of the costs from a quarter of the ALBs: approximately £12.5 billion.

Which, in total, offers immediate savings of £24.5 billion.

Total savings from ALBs and quangos: £24.5 billion

Politically motivated campaigning

There are numerous calls for cost cuts in this area, such as the paper from Conservative Way Forward previously mentioned, which shows that a full £7 billion of saving could be realised just by ceasing to fund politically motivated campaigns.[254] There are frequent complaints about aggressive, politically motivated advertisements calling for expenditure on this or that need or promoting the latest piece of wokery: it is doubly frustrating if our taxes are paying for it.

There is clearly enormous room, and public appetite, for shrinking that area without harm to our electorate and polity. An incoming government with determination could just edict that this activity was banned and save that £7 billion.

Worse, many charities are given money by the government and use it to campaign *against* the government. A classic example of this dysfunctionality is the news in early 2024 that some 265 charities, the prior recipients of some £209 million in taxpayers' money, were lobbying against the Rwanda Bill – official government policy.[255]

'Sock puppet' charities, those that get given money by the government to lobby for government policy or to lobby for more money for themselves, are one of the most egregious manifestations of a civil service controlling itself. A rule should be created that only exclusively operational (not campaigning) charities can be funded, including that their effectiveness in delivering value should be stringently monitored; that their contracts should be regularly open to competition, not just from other charities but from the entire private sector; and that they should not be engaged in any sort of lobbying or political activities.

Total savings from eliminating all grants for politically motivated campaigning: £7 billion

---

Charities

The proliferation of captive, sock-puppet charities can be seen as having become a way of further cocooning counterproductive entities within our public sector; such charities are one more step away from effective oversight by the democratically elected government and are well insulated both from scrutiny and control. A useful, although now old, paper by Christopher Snowdon of the Institute of Economic Affairs revealed that 36 per cent of the income of the voluntary and community sector, or £12.8 billion, was at the time coming from statutory sources.[256] As of 2020/21,* this number had risen to £16.8 billion, with over 16,000 voluntary organisations currently supported by the government† as their majority funding source (i.e. over 50 per cent of their income).[257] Snowdon identified a sinister fact: that much of the money paid to these charities was used by them to lobby the government and the public for policies, thus creating 'the illusion of grassroots support and pressure' for new legislation. 'State-funded activism' therefore deludes civil society into thinking there is more support for a policy than there is – and we pay for it. However, we have already elsewhere assumed savings from removing politically motivated campaigns so we do not discuss that here, to avoid double counting.

An interesting aspect of this is the way that government subvention of these charities outlasts the particular administration. Snowdon, writing in 2012, pointed out that the rise in funding for charities occurred during the Blair/Brown years. He predicted that once the party funding the charity had lost power, the contributions would continue and the charities would 'become a "shadow state" using public money to promote the political causes of its original funders'. This prediction appears to have come triumphantly true, with the added bonus for the original funders (the Labour Party) that the charities, post-Labour's defeat in 2010, became an employment refuge for many who had worked in the Blair/Brown administrations.

Accordingly, a new government should institute a review of all

---

* Latest data available.
† Includes a small proportion of funding from EU or international governments.

funded charities and withdraw funding to all but the most productive. Even then, most activity run by funded charities should be pulled back into the government to ensure qualified, not leftist refugee, staffing. In view, however, of my lack of detail here as to which charities to go after, I leave any amounts that would be saved outside the plan given in this book.

> Pull back on funding charities: no further savings (some could be found, but more detailed analysis would be needed).

OTHER SAVINGS

In housing illegal immigrants, we find savings of £3 billion to be made.[258] According to the Home Office, housing illegal migrants in hotels across the UK in 2022/23 cost the taxpayer around £8 million a day or around £3 billion annually. When the backlog of asylum claims is cleared and illegal migration into the UK falls drastically,* booking hotels for illegal migrants will be no longer required and that £3 billion would be saved.† However, it is open to us to follow the example of the new Dutch government of Geert Wilders and offer only an 'austere' environment to asylum seekers. Shock horror for the tender-hearted among us, but these would be far superior conditions to what these refugees were experiencing before and it would reduce the incentives for anyone who comes to the UK solely for the benefits.‡

---

* The book does not provide enough room for a comprehensive discussion of the issue of migration and the potential remedies for the problem of the influx of migrants across the English Channel.

† The hotels are just part of the accommodation set aside for these immigrants; we assume only the cost of the hotels is saved.

‡ Actions of this sort might make it necessary to leave the ECHR and to amend the Human Rights Act, but such considerations don't seem to have deterred the Dutch.

Chart 2.45: Savings Identified in this Chapter

A determined government could eliminate some £118 billion of expenditure (some 4 per cent of GDP) in its first term.

Component of government expenditure	Savings, £b	Action
Welfare: state pension	0	Abolish the triple lock, use the increase in average earnings instead Increase pension age to sixty-eight in 2031, sixty-nine in 2035 and seventy in 2039
Welfare: pensioner benefits	3.4	Only to be for the truly needy
Welfare: unemployment benefits	8	Reduce the number receiving unemployment benefits, and inflation-adjusted cost per unemployed, to pre-pandemic levels
Welfare: housing benefit	1	Get more in employment and less claiming benefit
Welfare: Universal Credit fraud	3	Halve the fraud rate by reimposing checks on claimants and tightening the eligibility criteria
Welfare: disability benefits	10	Reduce incidence of accepted disability by 20 per cent
Welfare: cost of living payments	10.2	No actions, payments to stop from 2024/25
Health	14	Various measures, including some privatisation
Debt-service costs: inflation uplift	15	No action required if inflation is kept at 2 per cent target
Education: primary and secondary	0	Save £5–10 billion from less TAs and more MATs. Spend these savings on buildings, curriculum expansion etc.
Education: less school children	1	In the future, there will be fewer school children
Education: tertiary and higher	3	Save £4 billion from removing the worst courses and reallocate £1 billion to technical training
Enterprise and economic development	0	Optimise regulations and processes
Defence	(15)	Increase to 2.5 per cent of GDP, up to 4 per cent within fifteen years[*]
Other government spending	6	Doing less of growth-reducing activities
Civil service: 20 per cent staff reduction	5	£4.2 billion plus 20 per cent on-costs
Civil service: return to proper pay grades	1	£0.8 billion plus 20 per cent on-costs

---

[*] An increase in spending is a 'negative decrease' in spending, so increases are shown in brackets to denote a minus sign. I hope this is not too confusing.

Civil service: remove defined-benefit pension scheme	0	Prevents future financial catastrophe
Civil service: work practices	1	Abolish EDI/ESG, similar training, away days etc.
Local government	3.5	Require reasonable working practices and reduce staff by 5 per cent
ALBs and quangos	24.5	Similar changes to the rest of the civil service: ban political campaigning, abolish many quangos, reduce the scope of remaining ALBs
Political campaigns	7	Depoliticise and eliminate sock-puppet charities.
Housing illegal immigrants	3	Introduce an austere environment
Foreign aid	1	Eliminate non-essential spend
Green subsidies	12	Abolish entirely
Total savings	**£117.6 billion**	

In foreign aid, we find savings of £1 billion. All actually useful aid grants could still be made. There is a wealth of saving opportunity here: we should stop donating money for 'climate change', which only encourages countries to immiserate themselves, and we should stop handing money to the agendas of other countries and bodies (the EU, the UN etc.). Having dropped aid from 0.7 per cent to 0.5 per cent of GDP, we are already spending some £5 billion less.

In green subsidies, we find savings of £12 billion.[259] Renewable energy in the UK is subsidised through a triad of programmes: feed-in tariffs, contracts for difference and renewables obligations certificates, with the latter being the largest scheme, costing around £7 billion annually. The total cost of these handouts, including the expenditure for rebalancing the grid due to the intermittent nature of renewables – the wind is not blowing and the sun is not shining all the time – is around £12 billion per year and is expected to rise. These funds could be saved if the government stops recklessly pushing the country towards net zero. The claim is that wind is now as cheap as gas. If so, why is a subsidy needed?

CONCLUSION

To summarise, even the relatively high-level view taken in this chapter has identified very significant sums that could be saved – not without difficulty but doable – and without much loss to national efficiency or services. How big the amount would be that the new government resolves to cut in its first sweep depends on its level of willingness to confront and conquer institutional resistance and special pleading.

As shown earlier, the larger the government, the lower the growth rate. A government sized at 30 per cent per annum of GDP is associated (at a 99 per cent confidence level) with growth rates that are at a minimum over one and a half percentage points higher (per annum) than a government sized at 50 per cent of GDP. A first set of steps to achieving such savings can be taken with net savings from the items discussed in this chapter, as seen in Chart 2.45, at some £118 billion. This takes the UK, as a first step, to parity of expenditure per capita with countries that have equivalent levels of GDP per capita as we do. Those cuts are only a start: at the current size of the economy, the remaining expenditure would still be greater than 40 per cent of GDP and our target is 33 per cent.

Clearly, even this tightening of the belt would be met with uproar; it is a fraught and herculean task. But it is entirely necessary in getting our economy to return to growth mode. Any government preparing to set out on the road of expenditure reduction would need to plan for it, ideally several years before achieving power. In Volume Two, we discuss how such a plan could be pulled together and executed. The task is not impossible, and similar achievements around the world and in the UK, both in the private sector and in individual parts of the public sector, have shown that it can be done. The prize would be great.

CHAPTER 7

THE HIGHER THE LEVEL OF TAX, THE LOWER THE ECONOMIC GROWTH

In the previous chapter, we discussed the negative correlation between government expenditures and economic growth and suggested a list of measures to cut the former with the intention of boosting the latter. In this chapter, we focus on taxation, which, of course, is tied to expenditure since spending has, long term, to be funded with tax revenues – although, see Chart 1.20, showing how the more you spend, the harder it is to raise the needed money through tax.

The UK's tax regime, having previously been assessed as fifth best, is now astoundingly thirtieth out of thirty-eight countries in the Tax Foundation's annual international competitiveness ranking.[1] Only our cross-border tax rules (the second best in the OECD) prevent the UK from being ranked even worse than that, but the new Labour government may attack those rules and has anyway said it will increase a few taxes further.[*] The direction of travel is clear.

It's not just that our tax rates are so high. In addition, the real property burden is the highest in the OECD and the VAT rate of 20 per cent applies to less than half of the potential consumption tax base, distorting

---

[*] During its campaign, Labour kept carefully quiet about capital gains tax, fuel duty, council tax, corporate tax, road tax and alcohol and tobacco taxes.

the economy significantly. Our tax system is unbelievably complex. Even by 2009, the UK had the longest tax code in the world – and it has only got worse since.² High, complex, uncompetitive, unfriendly tax rates – do our uniparty politicians really think this is such a good idea?

Worse, relative to the thirty-seven other countries, the UK will increase taxes the most, out of *all* those countries, as a percentage of GDP 2019–29.³ The UK is travelling fast to a new location, a destination with potentially devastating economic consequences.

These points raise questions not only about the size of our tax bill but also about the way in which it is structured and what we think we are doing by burdening our citizens and businesses so highly and so distortedly. We seem not only to have become addicted to taxes but also now see increasing taxes as the default action to take whenever there is a fiscal problem.

Governments face a conundrum: Wagner's Law. Those demanding ever-increasing benefits and services in developed countries reflect little on the fact that over 80 per cent of the world's population lives in economies that cannot afford even a fraction of the services that are demanded in, say, western Europe. Yet western Europe's services are frequently seen as a humanitarian imperative, rather than as a choice that involves consideration of whether the money is there to pay for these services and what happens if we spend money we haven't got.

So, political parties that advocate reducing the quantity and level of benefits we provide to the population tend not to get elected – or, as in the case of the coalition government of 2010–15, they get attacked aggressively for their so-dubbed 'austerity' policies. Most actual or would-be governments therefore come to believe that the benefits they provide must continue to grow and that 'cuts' of any sort will be seen as unacceptably unpalatable, resulting in electoral defeat. But the money isn't there to provide everything that is demanded.

What to do? The answer for the past three decades, under both Conservative and Labour governments, has been to increase benefits and to pay for them by pushing taxes ever-upward by first increasing tax *rates* and second, introducing new *forms* of tax.

What level of tax take is optimal for economic growth? What impact does our current level of tax take have on the economy? What is the right mix of taxes and how does the UK's system stack up against that? In the following sections, I show:

1. High taxes inhibit growth. The larger the amount of tax that is collected as a percentage of GDP, the slower is the country's economic growth. The UK badly needs to reduce its overall tax burden.
2. Some taxes hit growth worse than others, but the UK government has implemented precisely those growth-hitting taxes. A major change in the UK's overall mix of tax is needed.
3. Taxpayers respond dynamically to tax increases, so that planned-for hauls of new tax revenue do not always result in as much tax revenue as was expected.
4. The negative dynamic response to tax increases can come close to overwhelming any expected positive impact on tax revenues.

HIGH TAXES INHIBIT GROWTH

Countries with large-sized governments have to somehow pay for their costly activities or in the long run they will go bust. Therefore, we can expect that countries whose government expenditures are high will also be high-tax countries. This in turn needs a rapidly growing private sector to provide the necessary higher level of tax revenue because proper, sustained growth of an economy is only created by proper, sustained growth in the private sector.* And yet, as I will show, the two most effective ways to inhibit private-sector businesses from starting up and growing and thus creating economic growth are:

- high taxes (reviewed in this chapter)
- high regulation (reviewed in the following chapter)

As Chart 2.46 shows, the higher the amount of tax that a country extracts from its citizens, the lower (by a significant amount) is its economic growth rate. The UK used to be a low-tax, high-growth country; now it is a high-tax, low-growth country.

Chart 2.46: Impact of Size of Tax Take on GDP Growth
Twenty-three OECD countries, 1960–2019

Larger taxation is significantly associated with a slower growth rate for the economy.

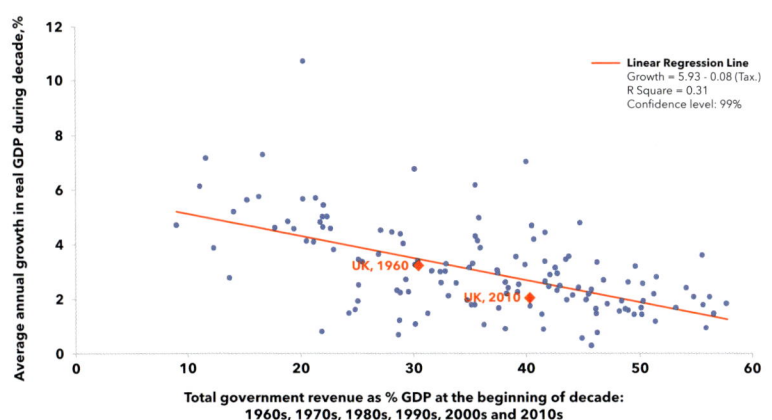

Government revenues = tax revenues + other government income. 'Other government income' for the UK has in recent years been around 4 per cent of GDP.
Source: International Monetary Fund,⁴ moyniteam analysis

---

* Income and other taxes from public-sector employees are not genuine tax revenues. Rather, the government is just taking back some of the money it just gave them – money that originally came from taxes contributed by the private sector.

The difference in growth associated with high taxes is substantial: every additional 10 per cent of GDP worth of taxes is correlated with a reduction of almost 1 per cent of GDP per annum in economic growth.[*] Economists Patrick Minford, Yue Gai and David Meenagh provide a more rigorous analysis of this point, showing that lowering taxes significantly increases economic growth.[†][5]

There is, of course, no one-to-one correspondence between size of government and level of tax revenue; apart from all the other influences on growth discussed throughout this book, one major reason for that is because any government can put off raising taxes for some years, even when that government's spending is taking up an ever-larger share of that country's economy.[‡]

The annual growth rate of high-tax economies is, in general, several percentage points lower than that of low-tax countries, and those large-government countries that don't succeed in raising tax revenues to levels equal to or near to their outgoings will, sooner rather than later, run into financial difficulties.

The evidence that high taxes inhibit economic growth goes way beyond Chart 2.46. In recent years, many studies have reviewed the impact of tax increases on different countries' economies. Palumbo and Ianoco have collated ten such studies showing how tax increases reduce GDP. From that list, the work of Christina Romer and David Romer (2010) is typical and often quoted: like all the studies,

---

[*] The issue of 'correlation versus causation' is addressed throughout this chapter. There will of course be an inevitable and large correlation between large government and high taxes, so the potential impact on growth of changing to a smaller government, combined with changing to lower taxes, is not 100 per cent additive, but nor is it 100 per cent duplicative.

[†] They also address the issue of correlation versus causation, observing changes to tax rates that *precede* changes in growth.

[‡] Most large-size governments have the flexibility to borrow for many years (until, one day, they suddenly lose that flexibility). So – at least for as long as their borrowing flexibility lasts – they can put off the day when taxes need to be raised to a level that is commensurate with expenditure. In consequence, many large sovereign countries manage, *at least for a while*, to keep their taxes lower, but as a result, they run up large deficits, which means that one (low taxes) or the other (high expenditure) will eventually need to be abandoned.

it finds a negative impact on growth from tax increases or, vice-versa, that lowering taxes increases growth.[6] Romer and Romer concluded that these studies show that the effects of higher or lower taxes on growth are astonishingly large, finding that a tax increase of just 1 per cent shrinks the economy by 2.5–3 per cent.[7] The results detailed in the studies examined by Palumbo and Iacono are crucial, in particular because several of them help rebut the 'correlation not causation' narrative. They show that in many different and differing countries and economies, a change (upward or downward) in the level of taxation is followed by a change in economic growth (downward or upward). The studies observed this over a long time period; the finger points to causation.

Of course, some social-democrat ideologues insist that high taxes can correlate with high economic growth. Martin Wolf, writing in the *Financial Times*, recently claimed that, looking at the past few years' data for a smattering of countries, tax levels made no impact on prosperity.[8] This is not a widely held view: the consultancy CEBR, for example, made a relatively detailed analysis of Chancellor Jeremy Hunt's 2022 business tax increases and concluded that 'Jeremy Hunt's Britain will stagnate on the world stage'.[9] They predicted that the budget would derail previously forecasted growth that, if the tax increases had not been imposed, would have seen the size of the UK's economy eventually overtake that of Germany.

Wolf's was an anecdotal-style analysis, with only ten countries analysed. As can be seen in the chart within his article, his conclusion relied heavily on just two outliers:

- South Korea, which not long ago had low GDP per head with very low taxes so it counted as a low tax/low GDP country from

Wolf's perspective. But, probably in part because of its low taxes, it has been growing rapidly from its previously-low GDP base. If this continues for only a few more years (and it is expected to), South Korea will, quite soon, sit comfortably in the low tax/high GDP per head quadrant.

- France, which traditionally has had high GDP per head (a good part of which is from its large share of subventions from the EU, for example from the EU's Common Agricultural Policy) but is now hardly growing at all – so France is moving smartly in the direction of the high tax/low GDP per head quadrant.

Remove those two countries, or just readjust their position for their forecasted future position in a few years, and even Wolf's chart proves the point that higher tax equals lower growth.

Pace Wolf, the conclusion that high taxes depress economic growth is by no means only dependent on Chart 2.46 or on Romer and Romer; it is, in fact, one of the most proven in business academia. The conclusion cannot be avoided: the higher the level of tax, the lower the level of economic growth.

Tax incomings, even when rates are raised to high levels, reliably prove insufficient to the task of feeding the burgeoning size of governments, with Wagner's Law remorselessly enlarging the size of peacetime governments of developed countries. Taxpayers obstinately refuse to cough up as much taxes as were hoped for, year after year, and the story shown in Chart 2.47 is that not only have existing tax rates had to be increased, but all sorts of new taxes – requiring increasing creativity on the behalf of government – have had to be invented. This has led to a myriad of ever increasing, government-imposed new taxes. Often these taxes are disguised as pious attempts to inhibit undesirable economic activity, but let's face it, the underlying reason for them is to get more tax revenue. Green charges, airport tax, van tax, stamp duty, windfall tax and on and on – and we can expect new taxes to continue to be invented until the paradigm of more and more spend, more and more tax is finally abandoned. Many of these new taxes create an immediate and significant lowering of economic activity – to take an example, high street footfall dropping due to ever-increasing parking charges, 20 mph, ULEZ and other similar taxes.

Chart 2.47: The Tax Implications for Over-Large Governments

More, and more novel, taxes must be introduced in the (vain) hope of paying for bigger and bigger government. But the burden on the private sector grows and grows.

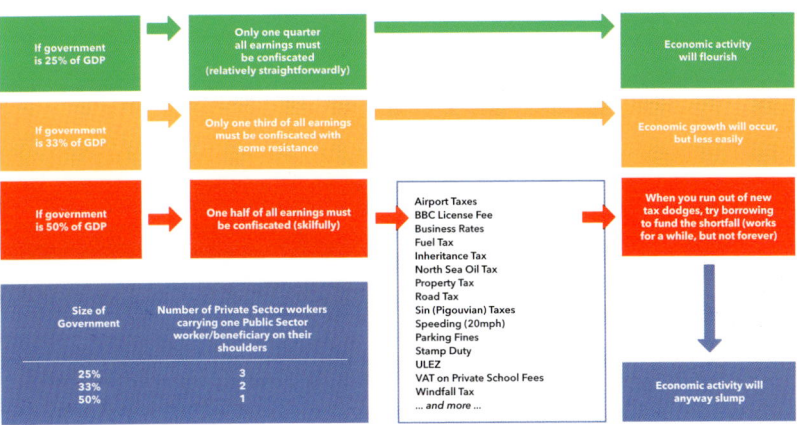

So, if we in the UK are to have high, social-democrat levels of expenditure, we also need similarly high levels of tax revenue (as a percentage of GDP). Inevitably, if so, we are condemning ourselves to a continuation of the low to no growth that our economy has seen for almost two decades and continued depredation of our pockets by ever more inventive, ever more ridiculous taxes. Part I already showed how such a future would be both deplorable and unsustainable. The UK, at the same time as abandoning its high-spending regime, badly needs to reduce its overall tax burden.

SOME TAXES HIT GROWTH WORSE THAN OTHERS

What are the taxes that pay the costs of running the UK's modern state? There are many ways to characterise the different types of taxes in society. The categorisation I use in this chapter – not perfect and with some overlap between categories but nonetheless useful since it creates a view on what each category's impact on economic growth might be – is as follows:

Income taxes:

- corporate income taxes (corporation and 'windfall' taxes)
- individual taxes (income tax and employee NIC)

Production taxes:

- employer NIC and multiple other levies on business – green apprenticeship etc.

Capital taxes:

- capital gains tax
- inheritance tax
- stamp duty

Consumption taxes:

- value added tax (VAT)
- Pigouvian 'sin' taxes
- other consumption taxes.

Let's look at how much each of these taxes contribute to the overall tax revenue (Chart 2.48).

Chart 2.48: UK Tax Receipts, 2023/24
Billions of GBP, share of total tax receipts. 100 per cent = £979 billion

Taxes in the UK were, most recently, around 36 per cent of GDP (and rising).

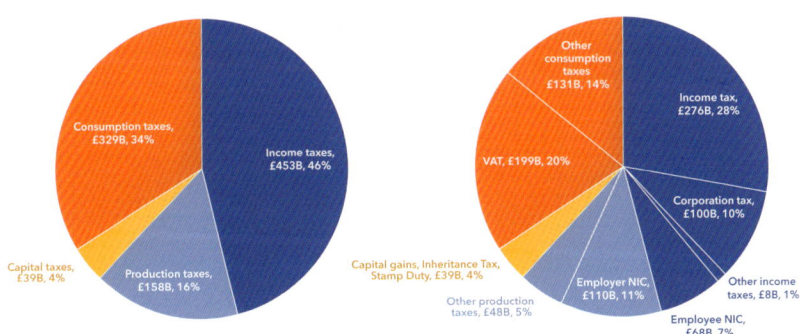

Data in this chart are presented on an accrued basis and do not represent actual cash receipts in the financial year ending March 2024

National Insurance is split between income taxes (NICs for employees and self-employed) and production taxes (employers' NICs). Includes other social contributions.

Source: Office for National Statistics[10]

As can be seen, 46 per cent of taxes in 2023/24 came from taxing business and personal income (income tax, employee NIC, corporation tax), 16 per cent from production taxes (mostly employer

NIC but also green levies and the like), 4 per cent from capital taxes (capital gains and inheritance tax) and 34 per cent from consumption taxes (VAT and sin taxes). The large proportion of the burden, almost two thirds, is therefore on business (supply) activity; only a third is on consumption (demand) activity.

Total taxes of £979 billion took up some 36 per cent of GDP. Other government revenues added a further 4 per cent to that, so total public sector current receipts (excluding public-sector banks) were some 40 per cent of GDP. In the coming years, the OBR expects tax revenue as a share of GDP to rise further because of tax increases and fiscal creep, and because economic growth is highly likely to be low. Later in this chapter, I show how growing taxes as a percentage of GDP beyond 36 per cent is an objective with uncertain achievability.

Now, let's examine whether these proportions are desirable and where we can get the most benefit from cutting taxes. Which of these are the most damaging taxes, which are the least damaging to society – and, in particular, to economic growth? Let's review each category and the major tax items within each and then discuss possible reductions. Remember, we've already found £118 billion of potential spend reduction in the previous chapter.

Income taxes: corporate and individual

As we've seen from Chart 2.48, some 46 per cent of the UK's tax revenue comes directly from taxes on income. Any tax, by increasing the cost of something, reduces demand for that something – that's basic economics. Tax the income of corporations more, and investors and businesses are less disposed to start up new business initiatives, build new plants and hire more people. Tax the income of individuals more, and they are less disposed to work and more inclined to work somewhere else in the world and work 'off the books' or for cash.* So, income taxes are bad in general for economic growth.

Corporate income taxes

The following paragraphs review multiple studies that empirically support the reasonable expectation that high corporate taxes will be the most likely culprit in holding back economic growth in a given country. This point has been proven by a plethora of economists over the years, especially in the last decade or so. Palumbo and Ianoco list twenty-three separate studies that looked at this.[11] Very few of these studies show anything other than a negative impact on growth from increasing corporate tax.

A typical finding is that of Djankov et al. who analysed tax rates in eighty-five countries. Their conclusion was, 'The effective corporate tax rate [has] a large adverse impact on aggregate investment, FDI, and entrepreneurial activity.'[12] All of this is consistent with what basic economic theory would suggest: that higher corporate taxes crush economic growth.†

In all the gloom of the UK government pig-headedly insisting in 2022 on raising the corporate tax rate by an astonishing 32 per cent (by 6 points to 25 per cent, from a basis of 19 per cent), with predictably negative economic consequences swiftly following (see later for detail), it was refreshing to read a positive, almost inspiring recent article by Isabel Díaz Ayuso, president of Spain's Madrid region, showing how a low-tax *rate*, low-regulation economy in

---

* And more inclined not to report, or to underreport, their earnings.
† Yet despite this plethora of evidence, never mind the obvious common sense of it, the OBR insists on producing forecasts that brightly assume that growth of the economy will not be negatively affected by a large rise in corporation taxes, and Liz Truss was, when Prime Minister, forced by (allegedly) Conservative colleagues to go through with the previous government's planned massive increase in corporation tax.

Madrid has led to higher tax *revenues* and to higher economic growth.[13]

So, tax on business is, as recounted here, generally agreed to be the most damaging tax to impose or increase, in terms of its impact on economic growth. And yet, revenue-hungry governments continue to see business as a tax revenue piñata, with taxes on business activity around twice as large as on consumption.

A business will prefer to invest elsewhere if it knows of a friendlier business environment, one that has lower taxes and smaller regulation. The overall attitude of a country's government toward business is crucial. For example, one massive turn-off for business has always been any retrospectively introduced 'windfall tax' – the introduction of which at any time signals that in future, you will not be able to trust that country's government to keep its word. If your business is well run enough or lucky enough to make a good return, then the government, in a country that thinks 'windfall taxes' are a good thing, may step in and confiscate large parts of your profits. So, if you're a company that wants its investment to pay well, you will steer well clear of that country if you can! This indeed is what has now indeed transpired with the government-introduced Energy Profits Levy, which has led to 'severely dampened' investment in the North Sea according to Upstream, the energy industry news site. Ithaca Energy, for example, who had to pay £223 million in total tax for just the first six months of 2023, has consequently decided to defer or cancel multiple projects in the North Sea, the consequence being lower forecasted flow of North Sea oil and therefore less future tax revenue to the Treasury.[*][14]

---

[*] And, of course, businesses right across the economy, from multinational down to entrepreneurs, are not slow in absorbing the potential implications.

Business growth comes in large degree from existing companies making their new business investments within the UK, as well as from companies bringing in investment from abroad. But to an equal and possibly greater degree, it comes from entrepreneurs. Even without consideration of windfall taxes, entrepreneurs are less likely to start up a new business if they see the prospect of success being lessened in other ways; for example, if much of the potential rewards from that startup will be absorbed via the tax regime. As for the investors who provide capital for new businesses, they are disincentivised from doing so when they have reason to believe that if things do go well, the returns they make will then be diminished by high taxes or unnecessarily restrictive regulations. That, in turn, makes it harder for entrepreneurs to raise money from investors and it diminishes their incentive to take a risk and create something new.

Research from 2008 has found that a 10 percentage point increase in the effective corporate tax rate reduces the investment-to-GDP ratio by two percentage points from the average of 21 per cent – that is to say, it leads to a 10 per cent overall reduction in business investment. It also lowers the entry rate of new business by 1.3 percentage points from the average of 8 per cent – that is to say, it leads to a 16 per cent lower rate of business formation.[*] [15] This is precisely the dynamic response I alluded to earlier.

Raising corporation tax to 25 per cent therefore turned the UK singlehandedly into a high-tax economy, while being unlikely over time to result in significantly increased tax revenues. Keeping corporate tax low would have encouraged businesses to move

---

[*] It is very odd that these well-known, intuitively correct and respectable academic results seem to be not just ignored but denied by the previous government, the Treasury, the OBR and even, on occasion, in various allegedly informed commentary from newspapers such as the *Financial Times*.

to, or stay in, the UK. But now, if you were planning to locate a prospective company on the island of Ireland, where would you place yourself? In the Republic of Ireland at 12.5 per cent corporate tax or in Northern Ireland in the UK, where it is 25 per cent? The answer has to be the republic; AstraZeneca's CEO explicitly said that his decision to locate a $400 million plant in the Republic of Ireland rather than the UK was because of UK tax rates.[16] The UK is shooting itself in the foot (and in particular, gratuitously punishing Northern Ireland's economy) by adopting a 25 per cent corporation tax rate. That 25 per cent tax resulted, in 2023, in 'dozens' of US multinationals 'shunning' the UK; many other less visible companies will have made similar decisions.[17] The loss to the UK economy overall will likely be significantly larger than any gains in revenue (if there are any) from the tax increase. Now that's what you call dynamic response…

But beyond these points, an even greater negative comes from specific taxes that seem designed to put businesses off from expanding or entrepreneurs from starting a business up in the first place. There are a number of anti-growth business taxes in the UK.

'Windfall' taxes, an income tax recently imposed on energy and other companies, is an example of using tax policy to manage the political news cycle and another example of an anti-growth business tax. When companies do the maths, they withdraw their potential investment. If any possible big gain by a business is potentially going to be taxed as a windfall, with a big loss still possible but the big gain no longer possible, the calculus of the decision changes. A recent significant example is Shell deciding to pull out of major UK investments.[18] Yet another is Harbour Energy, the biggest producer of oil and gas in the North Sea and a British success story, which had its entire profit for 2022 wiped out and has now shut down any new exploration. Even in mid-2024, two years after the introduction of the tax, the world's third-largest oil company, Chevron, announced it was pulling out of the North Sea.[19] Predictably, and in yet another example of the Treasury's foolish failure to understand dynamic Laffer-style effects,* the windfall tax was forecast to bring in £5 billion but only realised half of that, bringing in £2.6 billion.[20] Plus so much future tax lost.

The introduction of any windfall tax is enormously damaging to an economy, both short and long term, because it signals that the country's promises (in this case, not to tax retrospectively) cannot be relied on. The damage can last for decades. Windfall taxes should be removed immediately and forsworn by any and all UK governments (as should the UK's attack on North Sea oil). This demonisation of hydrocarbons is beyond unintelligent. It will not lower the UK's use of them; we will merely import them at the same volume from some other (most likely more polluting) part of the world, with attendant carbon costs to transport them to the UK. The departure of various oil companies will certainly lose the UK more corporation tax, employment taxes and hydrocarbon taxes – not to mention putting a big dent in our balance of payments. Even President Biden hasn't made such a colossal mistake; in mid-2023, he gave the go ahead to a vast new oil field in Alaska.[21] The recent decisions/threats of the new Labour government on North Sea drilling just increase the damage to our international reputation done by the Conservatives.[22]

Corporate income tax is the tax that governments and voters are often most eager to impose (excepting perhaps the desired extra taxes on 'millionaires and billionaires'), yet it is at the same time the most damaging of taxes to economic growth and, therefore, to

---

* The famous (or infamous) Laffer curve is mentioned repeatedly in this chapter. The concept is discussed in more detail towards the end of this chapter.

future prosperity for all. Do we have such foolish voters that they can't elect a government that is prepared to support business, to remove and ameliorate many or indeed any of these taxes? Or is it that there are no longer any major political parties that will do so? Are we collectively less insightful than, for example, the Argentinians, who elected Javier Milei when he stood very frankly on a pro-business, neoclassical economics platform?

A series of actions are needed to make starting up and growing businesses in the UK more attractive. I propose the following initial changes towards accomplishing this:

- Take corporation tax back to 19 per cent: the increase to 25 per cent was disastrous and significantly reduced our economic competitiveness and potential economic growth.
- Remove windfall taxes: cancel badly thought through imposts such as the bank levy and the energy profits levy. Both distort the economy, and constrain growth.

These items are the first part of any proposed overall programme of tax reductions. (We show the full schedule of these at the end of this chapter.)

Income taxes for individuals: income tax and NIC

As per Chart 2.48, personal income tax is the largest (30 per cent) individual source of tax revenue in the UK.

Income tax and NIC are structured in the UK in such a way as to fall heavily on the upper half of earners. As quoted earlier, a record 54.2 per cent of (UK) individuals, 36 million of them, now live in households that receive more in benefits than they paid in taxes; the highest percentage on record.[23] Straightforwardly, if you increase the income tax rate and/or the employee NIC rate, you disincentivise people from working or incentivise them to emigrate or to move into the black economy.*

A mostly undiscussed corollary of this point is that the nation, to a large degree, runs itself on the net tax contributions of 46 per cent of its citizens (plus businesses). Chart 2.49 shows how a large proportion of even these net positive contributors contribute quite small amounts.

Chart 2.49: Share of the UK's Income Tax Paid by Percentile Groups 2019/20

The top 10 per cent of the UK's earners contribute over 60 per cent of income tax revenues.

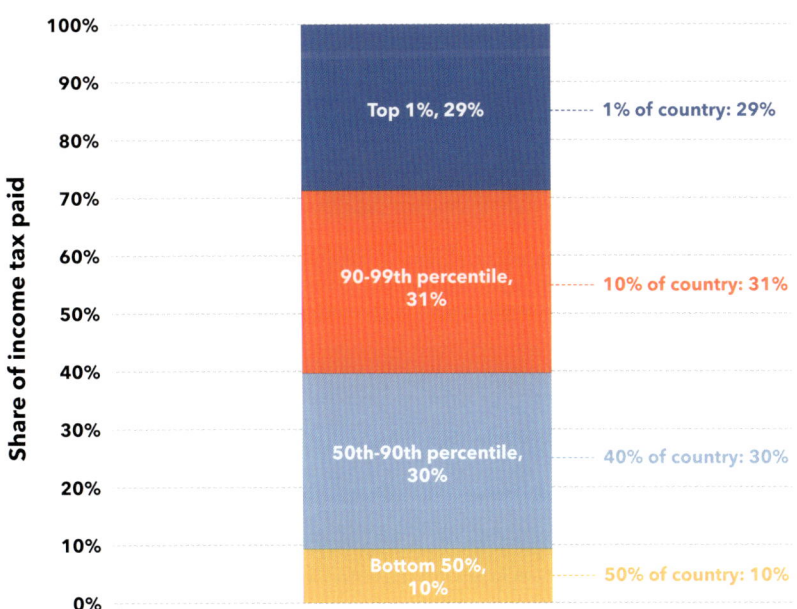

As noted by Civitas, the tax payments paid by the bottom 50 per cent are cancelled out by the benefits they receive
Source: House of Commons Library[24]

---

* Employee NIC is nothing more than a poorly disguised income tax. Thus, *actual* income tax rates are significantly higher than the headline numbers imply. Having employee NIC as a separate tax becomes more and more difficult to justify.

As shown in Chart 2.49, just over 60 per cent of income tax is paid by the top 10 per cent of the population, and half of that, or 30 per cent of income tax, is, shockingly, paid by the top 1 per cent.

Beyond the impact on high earners, the government has been waging war on the self-employed. The self-employed are the most entrepreneurial, risk-taking part of the workforce. The Association of Independent Professionals and Self-Employed has detailed the devastating impact on the number of self-employed once major tax changes were introduced for this sector – because, as usual, no one was paying attention to the likely dynamic response.[25] The number of self-employed people fell by 14.6 per cent between the beginning of 2020 and the beginning of 2022, from 3.5 million to 2.9 million.[26] Much of that loss of self-employed workers would have been individuals withdrawing permanently from the economy – which will only slow business growth.

The emphasis on finding money to pay for more benefits has led to many responding, as might be expected, to the incentive to live off benefits rather than working a job. As of 2024, a non-working family in London could expect to get over £50,000 a year untaxed in Universal Credit, plus council tax support, plus child benefit, plus discounted social housing. This is the same as what someone earning £70,000 a year will get after tax.[*] Only 4 per cent of UK adults earn £70,000 or more.

Clearly, and as discussed in the previous chapter, the emphasis has to be on reducing benefits. But there is a strong argument also for reducing the level of taxes on all middle-level earners. Eliminate

---

[*]   And that's only if they are not repaying student loans: if they are, their net earnings are way below £50,000. See Sam Ashworth-Hayes, 'Families on benefits can be better off than those earning £70k', *Daily Telegraph*, 31 January 2024, https://www.telegraph.co.uk/money/tax/income/families-benefits-better-off-earning-70k-london/

employee NIC, reduce the additional rate from 45 per cent to 40 per cent, and get rid of the absurd cliff-edge removal of childcare allowances at £100,000 of earnings and more enterprise will be the result, leading to higher economic growth, less dependency and less departures from the UK.[27] As the burden on high earners increases and the rewards to them for staying diminishes, many high-earning, high-tax-paying citizens are leaving, putting the UK very near the top of the list of countries in the world that are losing millionaires (Chart 2.50).

Chart 2.50: Millionaire Migration 2022
Countries Gaining and Losing the Most Wealthy People

It is crazy for the UK to be losing its millionaires – 1,500 of them left in 2022.

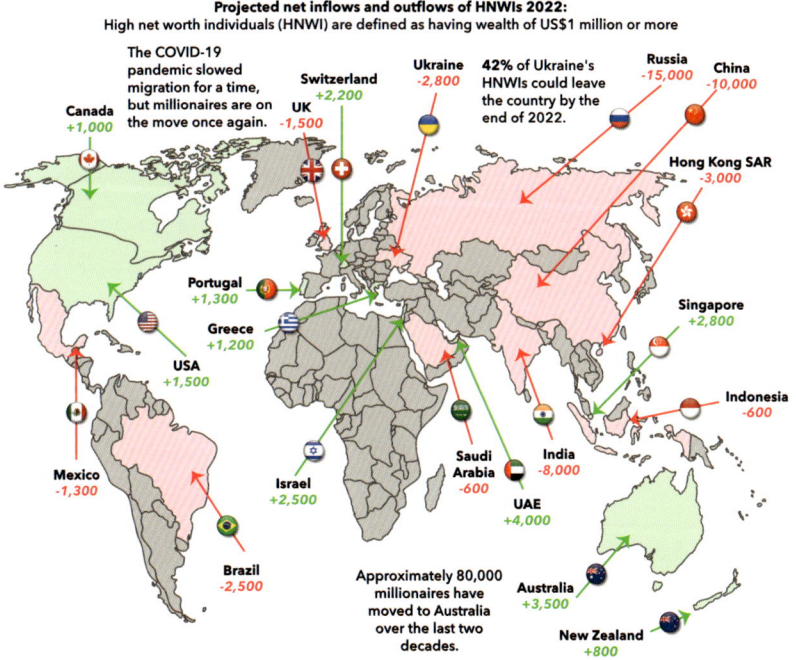

Source: visualcapitalist.com[28]

As shown in Chart 2.50, 1,500 millionaires left the UK in 2022. A probably greater number of rich or high earning, but not quite millionaires, left with them.

The implications of these departures for our economy long term – not to mention the medium-term impact on tax receipts – are troubling. The comparison with California, whose citizens are emigrating and whose economy is imploding, is clear.[29]

The point goes well beyond the impact from millionaires and billionaires. Because our top 1 per cent of income-tax payers, 320,000 souls, pay 30 per cent of all income tax, then if the UK could attract just 100,000 more such earners in the top tax bracket, it would add a full 10 per cent to income tax receipts. Likewise, if 100,000 of our top earners left the country, income tax receipts would *fall* by 10 per cent. And remember, over 500,000 people left the UK last year. How many of them were among the top 1 per cent of earners?

Should a government's policy be to have as many as possible in the income tax net, or as few as possible? On the one hand, we don't want people being put off from working by being penalised with an income tax bill. However, I would argue that it's more important to spread at least *some* of the tax cost across society and to not enrage the top 10 per cent of earners, who are currently paying 60 per cent of all income tax and surely, as a result, feeling somewhat put upon by the rest of society. It must be good for *all* wage earners to feel that they are contributing to society in some way.* So, I feel it was not totally right for the TaxPayers' Alliance to complain that fiscal creep had pulled 4.5 million more citizens into the tax net relative to 2010.[30] I believe it good for all to should pay *something* – however small. (Of course, fiscal creep throwing existing taxpayers

---

* I am retired. I don't claim income from my current position in the House of Lords. I don't pay much income tax any more. I have no personal dog in this fight.

into higher-rate tax brackets is pretty unequivocally a bad thing; we want people to contribute, but we don't want them to be, and feel, fleeced.)

With individual income taxes, we must create incentives for high-value workers to stay in work and to move to and remain in the UK. Thus, needed changes to the tax regime are:

- abolish both employee and self-employed NIC – one third soon, one third later, the last third when we can
- abolish the 45 per cent rate of tax – get it back to what Gordon Brown charged, 40 per cent

Production Taxes
For Corporations

Taxes on corporations include business rates, climate change levy, green charges and employer NIC. The apprenticeship levy is a classic example of such a tax. I dubbed the scheme a 'farce' several years ago in a submission to a government cost-cutting initiative; now, in 2024, we read that far from promoting apprenticeships, the introduction of the scheme has actually led to a *drop* in the number of apprenticeships by some 40 per cent. The Treasury, therefore, has snaffled £4 billion in 'unused' levies, so in the end it was just yet another disguised punishment tax on business.[31] All these taxes increase the cost of doing business and as a result, they discourage economic growth (as well as increasing prices to consumers). Production taxes are a category that should be high on the list of what needs to be abolished or minimised if we are to return to growth.

The green levy, the climate change levy and other crippling imposts are production taxes disguised as subsidies for rent seekers, designed to make companies, and ultimately consumers, pay for the net zero adventure.[32] They keep energy prices far higher than they would otherwise be, providing subsidy to so-called renewable companies and concealing the true cost of renewables. All this is gradually shutting down the UK's industrial economy: Britain now has the highest energy prices in Europe.[33] Again, the impact is that energy intensive companies will shut down in the UK and open up elsewhere, whether in China, Hungary, Czechia or Germany (the German government still subsidises companies – energy intensive or otherwise and both directly and covertly – often with coal-generated electricity). The global level of CO_2 in the air that the net zero agenda seeks to eliminate will continue as before – indeed, it will increase – because the goods are still being manufactured. The soot and the sulphur and the CO_2 will be put into the atmosphere elsewhere, using dirtier energy and with added transport costs for taking the goods back to the UK. The UK's economy and its people are impoverished, while China's, Germany's and others' economies are enriched and the world is more polluted. The levies must be removed.

Keeping business rates and employer NIC high only serves to cripple small businesses up and down the country. With high rates and NIC, businesses don't expand and don't hire, and they don't make any money, so they will be paying less in corporation tax to HMRC at the end of the year. Business rates should be halved and employer NIC eliminated at the same rate as employee NIC.

Capital taxes

Tax on capital is a tax on money that has, in the main, already had tax paid on it. That is to say, if I save 10 per cent of my salary after tax and after ten years have built that up to a pot of, let's say, £100,000, much of that pot will be from money I already paid income tax on. So, if you tax my capital in a wealth tax, say through inheritance tax after I die, you're taxing me at least twice (and some of it may be money I have already paid income tax and then later capital gains tax on, so thrice) on the same money. The two capital taxes in the UK, capital gains tax (CGT) and inheritance tax, are particularly pernicious when the asset has been held for a long time and its value cut down by inflation, so that you are maybe paying more than 100 per cent tax on your real gain (were it to be adjusted for inflation).

Capital gains tax

On individuals, the biggest capital tax is CGT. A more wide-reaching form of capital tax – a wealth tax – is sometimes threatened but has yet to be imposed in the UK. France tried a version of one recently but had to mostly withdraw it when an estimated 42,000 millionaires left the country in reaction.[34]

The problem with CGT as it is currently structured is that if an individual has a large business gain, there is a major incentive on them to leave the UK before the gain is realised. Whenever one such individual leaves, it means that any hope of *some* tax from the gain is then lost to the country, as is the ongoing entrepreneurial drive of that individual – who would potentially reinvest their gain into a new UK startup. To counteract that, 'entrepreneur's relief', halving the CGT to be paid, can be claimed by some individuals on their capital gains – but it's allowed only up to the first £1 million of gain, so it's of no interest at all in any large transactions, which are the ones that move the level of tax receipts significantly. So, you are left with the problem that entrepreneurs are incentivised to leave the country as soon as they start seeing a large gain on the horizon. This is likely to be one reason for the large number of millionaires leaving the country recently. Further capital gains (and other) tax relief are available through the Enterprise Investment Scheme, where investments are income-tax deductible and gains are not taxed. However, this is only for the more risky investments and is only for outside investors in the company, not the business entrepreneurs who start companies up.

In any event, both for individuals and in general, the higher the CGT rate, the less people will want to invest and the more they will want to move to jurisdictions with lower, more reasonable CGT rates. If CGT was reduced to 10 per cent from 20 per cent, many of the large transactions would no longer be sited offshore and individuals would no longer be so incentivised to leave the country. As a result, we can expect that CGT receipts would not fall.

CGT on property is 24 per cent: such assets cannot be moved out of the country, so they are not as much as a threat. For corporations, capital gains are in the main treated as revenue and are taxed accordingly – the business rate is therefore much the same as the personal CGT rate. Because of the incentive not to invest that is created by CGT, an opposing business incentive is offered in the UK currently – so-called 'full expensing' of investment cost for corporations, meaning that the more a company invests, the more its income tax bill is lowered. So, with gains taxed at 25 per cent for corporations, there is a sort of pushmi-pullyu deal for them, but at the end of the day they have to pay tax, whether on income or gains. At 25 per cent of gains and of incomes, the level of those taxes is now too high to make investing in the UK particularly attractive.

Inheritance tax

A second major tax on capital is inheritance tax (IHT). Again, a tax that is popular with governments because it's fairly easy to collect.

IHT is widely disliked, despite the fact that most in the UK will never (under the existing scheme) have to pay it.[35] The main reason for it being disliked is that the dead person's wealth is money that tax had already been paid on, sometimes several times – it's seen as unjust for tax to have to be paid yet again on that money. But the same thing can of course be said about most taxes on capital – and indeed on consumption taxes. So disliked is inheritance tax that Prime Ministers and Chancellors (Conservative ones, anyway), scenting electoral advantage, persistently hint that they plan to abolish it; yet so far they never have and the unfulfilled hints got tedious. Unless you find a loophole, then above a certain threshold, 40 per cent of your wealth will go to the government. Enter Laffer: loopholes are indeed available and the rich avoid, in the main, paying IHT because they can afford to take advice and, after doing so, adopt one or more of the various loopholes that get you round paying IHT. It's yet another classic example of the dynamic impact of people's responses to increases in tax rates. In consequence, IHT is a tax that, as they say, 'only the poor pay', although in this case it's the middle classes who pay it; rich people avoid it and poor people fall below the threshold to pay it.*

If you took a rational, rather than punitive, attitude to inheritance tax and wanted to get some tax revenues from people dying – while not driving those people out of the country or incentivising them to pay accountants to keep the money out of the hands of the taxman – what would a sensible inheritance tax regime look like? My own view is that most people would accept an IHT rate if it was sufficiently low that most people wouldn't choose to dynamically react against it. Such a number would be, say, 10 per cent – the

---

* As a deeply aged person not too far off from meeting the grim reaper myself, I claim the right in this discussion to sound dispassionate, nay even callous, when talking about death taxes.

traditional tithing amount. Tax on land and family businesses or buildings, inherited within the family, could be at the same 10 per cent amount but potentially on a deferred basis until they are sold.

What would the impact be of dropping IHT to such a low number? Inheritance tax revenues run at between £5 and £7 billion per annum at this time. (The more normal level of around £5 billion jumped up to £6 billion and then £7 billion during the Covid period. It's not clear whether that higher level will continue now that Covid has declined and normal international travel has resumed.) Let's assume the normal level of revenue is around £6 billion at the 40 per cent rate. If we drop the rate down to 10 per cent from 40 per cent, we at first sight lose 75 per cent of the £6 billion – that is, we lose £4.5 billion.

But that calculation ignores the dynamic impact of dropping the rate to 10 per cent. Take a billionaire whose long-term planning includes hopping it out of the country or putting their money into a complicated trust structure at some point before they die. If they successfully do either of those things before they die, we get no inheritance tax from them at all. But if they don't, thinking that 10 per cent is too little an amount to bother with the faff of avoidance, that is £100 million of inheritance tax you'd get from that one person. You'd need forty-five such people to make up the £4.5 billion. Or, if the average wealth of IHT avoiders was £15 million, you would need 3,000 such people dying each year and not evading IHT if you wanted to make up the £4.5 billion. (£15 million may seem a lot of money, but a quick look at the *Sunday Times* Rich List, where the bottom-ranked family is worth £350 million, shows that there will be a very long tail of people too 'poor' to appear on that list.) A change of this sort would go a long way to make people feel that the UK's tax code was fairer, so it would likely be net positive in terms of revenues, and it would keep those people, who spend, invest and create jobs, in this country.

Stamp duty

Taxing any transaction inevitably lowers the number of such transactions. Having 0.5 per cent stamp duty on buying shares means fewer individuals each buying fewer shares. Charging stamp duty on the sale of a house, rising to 12 per cent for houses sold for more than £1.5 million, means far fewer house sales and therefore significant dislocation on personal mobility and, of course, less building of new homes.

Stamp duty on share purchases is one of many hostile government actions against the London Stock Exchange. Analysts have estimated that, in addition to sparking economic activity, tax receipts overall would *rise* by some £600 million if stamp duty were scrapped – which it should be.[36] Capital taxes are useful for governments because they are simple to collect – particularly when registration of ownership is needed for the asset acquired. But that doesn't mean these taxes are good for growth.

Consumption taxes

Examples of consumption taxes are value added tax (VAT), Pigouvian 'sin' taxes and import taxes (tariffs).* Such taxes are easy to impose, but the larger they are, the more they encourage black markets. Economists tend to say that they are the least damaging to economic growth (out of the various options) – partly because the higher they are, the more they encourage the savings that lead to investment. They are sometimes reviled as 'regressive' because they

---

* To be discussed in Volume Two.

tax the poor at the same rate as they tax the rich (in contrast to 'progressive' taxes such as income tax, where the rate gets higher as a person's income gets larger).

VAT

Of all taxes, VAT is one of the most visible to the whole population. It applies across the economy and to many products. It is therefore perfect for 'special pleading'. When George Osborne tried to put VAT on hot food, he was assaulted for his 'pasty tax'. VAT on tampons resulted in an aggressive campaign built around the concept of 'period poverty' – what callous person would not want to prevent that?

Chart 2.5l: VAT Registration Thresholds Across the OECD, 2023
(In US$ at 2022 PPP)

The UK is right near the top of the countries that fail to spread VAT equally across the economy.

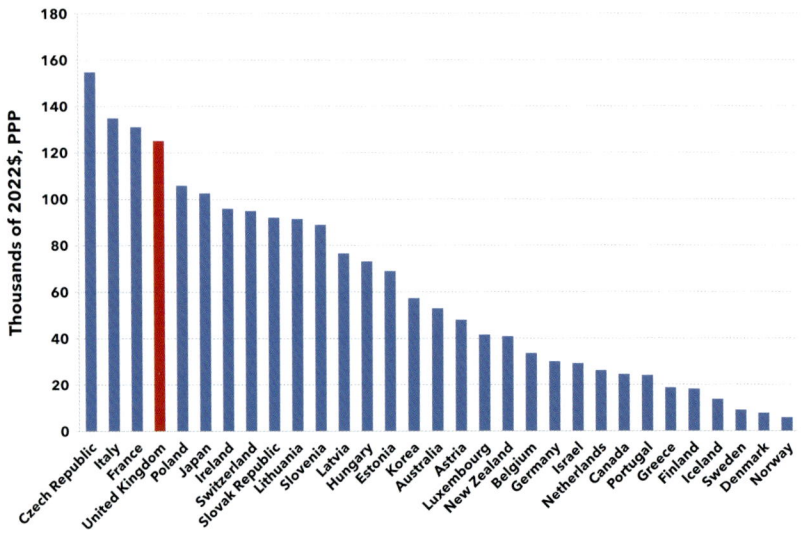

Source: OECD [37]

A range of special pleading of this sort has led the UK to have more plentiful exemptions for VAT than almost any other country.[38] Yet that long list means that the UK has to charge a 20 per cent VAT rate, higher than the OECD *average* of 19 per cent.

In addition, only companies with turnovers of £90,000 a year have to charge and collect VAT. This is way above the average (some £35,000) in advanced countries. And yet with automated charging, billing and tax reporting nowadays, VAT is no more difficult for smaller companies to charge than it is for larger companies.

The cliff-edge VAT threshold of £90,000 is, in fact, near to the highest threshold level in the OECD (see Chart 2.51). This clearly incentivises many companies not to grow beyond that threshold; yet the high threshold massively lowers the VAT base, so less VAT revenue is brought in. This economically counterproductive tax policy needs updating. In the spirit of tax simplification, the threshold should ideally be dropped to £25,000, ensuring there is no distortive incentive on business owners to hold back growth for companies sized £25,000–90,000. A further step should be to extend VAT to more products – yes, even Cornish pasties and tampons – so as to massively simplify the tax code, cease distortions and increase VAT revenue overall. This would allow other, more growth-reducing tax cuts elsewhere. In the calculations for this book, we posit only an intermediate move that increases VAT coverage from 45 per cent of the potential base to 55 per cent – just slightly less than the OECD average.

The UK tax code is enormously complex and expensive to administer. Simplification of VAT and enlargement of its reach so as to allow reductions elsewhere would go a long way to have a more rational, less lengthy code: as a result, both HMRC and the ranks of tax advisers could be significantly reduced. Many demands for VAT exemption are based in the argument of 'if his product is exempt, why shouldn't mine be?' But if *more* products incurred VAT, and companies all the way down to a much lower level of turnover were required to collect VAT, complaints would be reduced.

This book argues for overall tax reduction. It also, however, argues for a mix of taxes that will do least to stifle economic growth. Our 20 per cent rate of VAT is higher than most; our list of exemptions is longer. The OECD has proposed the UK review this.[39] *The Economist* recently asserted about such 'wholesale VAT reform' that it would 'clean up Britain's tax system, encourage firms to grow and still the cottage industry of lobbyists claiming for exemptions'.[40]

If we increased the overall amount collected by reducing the number of exemptions, and we lowered the £90,000 threshold for collection in such a way that VAT collected overall was increased from 45 per cent of the base to 55 per cent (thus bringing us just below the average of advanced countries), we could then afford to drop the VAT rate to 18 per cent from 20 per cent. This would get us below the international average VAT rate *and* bring in a further £20 billion of VAT tax revenue that would be generated despite our dropping the rate to 18 per cent.

Pigouvian 'sin' taxes

Pigouvian taxes are imposed on particular products and activities in society, in the main trumpeted as discouraging those activities but, more quietly, often because they are a tempting target for the greedy, tax-loving state. They are imposed, for example, on tobacco, vaping, alcohol and petrol and diesel. In recent times, as moral panics have taken hold, these taxes have proliferated mightily – airport taxes, carbon taxes, taxes for failing to install heat pumps, 20 mph speeding fines, ULEZ. The list increases every year. The problem, over and above the question of whether the government makes particularly well-informed decisions when it decides to act in this way, is that it is never clear how much the government was incentivised to introduce a new Pigouvian tax because of there being a true and justifiable indignation at the activity that is being censured, versus how much the incentive was the lovely tax revenues created. Given the revenue incentive, the government can't be trusted to have evaluated carefully enough whether the particular activity really needed to be discouraged and what the impact on economic growth would be for discouraging it.

A war on motorists is being conducted by local and national governments who have apparently decided that motoring is, in essence, repugnant. Thus, it is morally admirable, not to mention financially convenient for the government, to extract more and more from motorists, making driving less affordable. Motorists face vehicle excise duty; they are penalised by the insurance premium tax. The revenue from just these road taxes is expected to exceed tobacco duties in 2025.[41] Recent articles have claimed that pollution will actually increase with 20 mph limits.[42] ULEZ is a tax disguised as a climate health issue. ('If you drive that polluting car into London, you'll be killing children. Oh well, OK, it's fine, go ahead and do that, so long as you pay me £12.50 for the privilege.') It is estimated to raise £200 million a year for the next few years, for London alone – and it is to be rolled out across the country to all our major cities.[43] It's not a stretch to infer that the expectation of receiving these amounts plays a large part in the Mayor of London's decision, and the decisions of other city mayors, to impose that tax. We discuss in the next chapter how the ULEZ tax appears to have been concocted as a way of funding a radical socialist regime, not just in London but in many other cities around the world as well.

Other consumption taxes

The proposed new carbon border adjustment mechanism (CBAM) is one of the most growth-destroying, protectionist taxes yet.[44] Meekly copying the EU version, it threatens to create a new type of Smoot-Hawley era (only much more complicated and, because of related international treaties, difficult to unpick later). The tax will further massively reduce the UK's economic growth. (It will, even more importantly, also massively punish developing nations.)

The BBC licence fee is an anomalous, regressive tax that arouses much resentment and has huge administration costs, as well as the appalling criminalisation of often quite innocent non-payers. If there is to be a taxpayer-funded broadcaster, then let the government pay for it from general revenues. The licence fee should be abolished, the budget of the sprawling BBC be cut by at minimum 10 per cent and the BBC's cost transferred into the overall budget, subject to the same cost constraints as the rest of the public (and indeed the private) sector.

· · ·

So, which of these types of tax is worst for economic growth? All taxes hold back growth, but government must be paid for. Which taxes should be de-emphasised and, to the degree necessary, which further emphasised?

The general consensus seems to be that consumption taxes distort economic growth the least.[45] The major objection to raising them is that they are regressive – poorer people have a greater percentage of their income confiscated in tax for bread, or indeed booze, than richer people do. The Tax Foundation, however, asserts that larger consumption taxes actually improve tax outcomes for poorer people and 'provide an opportunity to greatly simplify anti-poverty programmes'.[46]

The taxes that hurt economic growth the most are, by general consensus, taxes on business. Unfortunately, the dynamics of democracy mean that governments will always want to placate, not irritate, the majority of the electorate. So, the temptation to politicians is to leave consumption taxes alone and hit corporations (and the rich). Despite the counterproductive impact of these tax raises, with growth hit and the expected extra tax revenues not in fact raised, social democratic politicians keep bashing their heads against that wall. The proposed changes laid out earlier in this chapter offer a different and, we can expect, more successful, approach – one that will increase economic growth and in turn unleash more tax revenues and greatly benefit our entire society.

Pigouvian taxes decrease specific 'sin' types of economic activity – some will claim rightfully so, given the alleged damages caused by the relevant activity. But for some of these taxes, the claimed damages (such as from 'climate change') are assertions of future, forecasted damage rather than proven, existing damage. No forecast, no model, is absolutely certain to be true when it comes to the reality, however much vigour and certainty their advocates employ (think Covid). Arguably, for many Pigouvian taxes, we have crossed the line where the damage done by the tax (for example, the impact of offshoring our manufacturing sector to China) already well exceeds the alleged damage created by the penalised Pigouvian activity.

So, for the tax base we need to have, consumption taxes are preferable to corporate and personal income taxes. Capital taxes need to be reformed for us to attract economic activity and grow.

TAXPAYERS RESPOND DYNAMICALLY
TO TAX INCREASES

One of the most depressing assertions to read, in any formal or informal economic analysis, is a sentence that runs along the following lines: '£x billion is currently paid in tax A; if we double the rate of that tax, then tax receipts will double to £2x billion.'

If only. Every action provokes an opposite reaction; tax is no exception. Every tax introduced or increased inevitably provokes some – sometimes a very large – reaction that results in lower tax being paid.[*] Taxes are paid by companies and individuals: both react dynamically to *any* economic incentive and tax is no exception. The reaction usually has a good level of predictability, in the sense that it can be modelled econometrically. The idea is summed up in the famous Laffer curve, which says that the higher the tax rate is on any item, the less people will engage in that activity (or report their engagement in it), until eventually, tax revenues tail off – and beyond that start to decline.

Politicians across the spectrum acknowledge that the UK tax system has become unbearably complicated, particularly for businesses beset with multiple complicated and bemusing taxes.[47] This level of complexity has primarily come about precisely because government costs have ballooned: so governments, under Chancellors Gordon Brown and George Osborne alike (both of whom were tinkerers rather than simplifiers), have identified many new and sneaky ways to increase the tax take (or so they thought).

Business taxes
When governments are in trouble and need to raise more tax, their

---

[*] This discussion is not about morality; it's about how, in practice, individuals respond to tax and regulatory changes, so that we can decide how best to grow the economy and fund public services.

first port of call is usually businesses. Nowadays, it seems, large sections of both the electorate and the commentariat encourage any government that attacks and demonises business. This superficially attractive approach can, for a while, seem unproblematic for the electorate, since the new taxes are (seemingly) being introduced against businesses, rather than directly against individuals.[*]

The counterproductive nature of this approach is that almost all taxes come, one way or another, from businesses: from their profit, from the people employed by them and from the sales of the products they produce. Each and every tax raises the cost of business, which raises prices (so the individual pays the tax in the end, through the increased price). The iron law of supply and demand says that higher prices drive down demand. The more you tax business, the less business you will get and the slower the economy will grow. Penal types and levels of tax that make it harder for businesses to sell their products, to reinvest, to grow are counterproductive, since imposing them means there will be less business to pay corporate tax and fewer employed people who will pay income tax. The ways in which the size of the business sector shrinks because of too-high taxes are suppression of entrepreneurship, emigration of people and corporations, and businesses not taking on new staff or equipment or otherwise not growing, because the additional tax costs make it uncommercial to do so or because those high taxes have removed the funds that the company needed to fund its growth.

The big-government, low-growth approach that we increasingly live under results in ever-higher taxes being imposed, in great part because of the need to pay for increased social benefits. Raising tax

---

[*] Recent governments have in particular introduced (allegedly) 'hypothecated' taxes, such as the soft drinks industry levy. In truth, the concept of a hypothecated tax is mostly nonsense: the money goes into the big government pot and can be used for any purpose.

rates not only slows economic growth but does not even succeed fully in raising the increased level of tax revenues it was aiming at.

One very obvious point to make: the more you tax business, the fewer businesses there will be because some businesses can be viable in a low-tax environment but not in a high-tax environment. These 'unseen' businesses – businesses that, because of the high-tax environment, never came into existence or fell out of existence – represent lost employment, lost tax revenue and lost economic growth.

We discussed earlier the devastating and swift lessening of inward business investment and outward business migration that was seen in the UK when the government raised corporate taxes by a third. Unfortunately, because of that rise in corporation tax, the UK is now seen as an economy that is hostile to business. Our former reputation as a country friendly to business, a reputation that took us years to acquire, has been trashed in a very short period – by a Conservative government. (The new Labour government does not seem likely to do better.) That pro-business reputation will not return overnight and not without significant changes to the tax environment. Large corporations that have the choice of country in which to invest will need convincing over a long period of time before they decide to come back to the UK. And small businesses, usually started up by UK citizens who would most obviously think first of investing in the UK, are now much more hesitant about starting up at all, due to employment taxes, business rates, the war on the self-employed or the war upon the high street shopper. Again, it will take years and major changes in the tax regime before currently discouraged potential business owners decide to beg, borrow and scrape the money together to take the risk of starting up a new business in the UK.

The larger the size of government, the more it has become

necessary to introduce these dysfunctional taxes so as to pay for the ever-bigger government. But, given their dysfunctionality, these new taxes and higher tax rates don't produce 100 per cent of the expected/forecasted additional tax revenues. Were the government to remove the most dysfunctional taxes, and lower the corporate tax rate, businesses could eventually be persuaded to return to the UK; entrepreneurs who have withdrawn from the market would return; growth would take off; jobs would increase; and in the end, *more* tax revenues (employment and corporate) would fill the country's coffers. It will, given recent government missteps, take some time to get a political environment where this view is accepted, and even longer to persuade business that the more welcoming environment would persist for the long term.

Companies considering investing in the UK will take into serious consideration the question of whether the tax regime is welcoming. France has in the past few years been beating the UK as the most attractive place for foreign direct investment. Macron gives the full glad hand to Elon Musk and other investors: the *Telegraph* describes 'how Macron stole Britain's millionaires'.[48] The last government's relations with prospective investors in the UK were pathetic. And now that our tax regime is so uncompetitive compared with so many countries around the world (and in particular with Ireland, our next-door neighbour), we can expect the number of factories being built here, the number of banking offices, the number of high-tech enterprises to decline because the majority of potential investors look at the tax code and decide to go elsewhere. There have been authoritative warnings by such as KPMG that companies are shunning Britain because of Jeremy Hunt's 2022 tax raid; the reasons for departure keep growing as more punishment taxes are imposed.[49]

Personal taxes

Just as with corporation tax, personal tax rates have inevitably in-creased. In the late 1970s, it was recognised that income taxes were at dysfunctionally high rates and led to self-imposed exile for many of our pop stars, sports heroes, and the like – George Harrison even wrote a song about it. This is a Laffer curve insight that most agreed with, but one that did not seem to prevent the left from denying the existence of any Laffer law. The situation led to a lowering of income tax rates by the Thatcher government. But as a result, consumption taxes – which originally started as excise taxes, later known by a variety of names and now in the UK mostly represented by VAT – were soon rapidly widened and the rate increased. As Wagner's Law is allowed to continue its remorseless march, the amount of tax revenues harvested proves insufficient to avoid fiscal deficits.

The growing impact of Laffer-type responses to higher personal taxes is increasingly seen. It's not just the rich who find ways to avoid ever higher taxes; back in 2021, foregone tax revenue on alcohol and tobacco (mostly as a result of smuggling) rose to an estimated £3.7 billion.[50] In 2013, the IEA estimated that the black market was some 10 per cent of the economy.[51] Perhaps the most clear signal that tax-payers are getting completely rebellious is the recent set of protest actions in London over the extension of ULEZ. In August 2023, the *Daily Mail* reported that in south-east London, nine out of ten ULEZ cameras had been vandalised.[52] The situation continues into the summer of 2024. Creative measures to avoid this tax include use of false number plates and blocking or damaging the camera vehicles that were introduced in response to the static cameras being destroyed. Meanwhile, less tax is being paid. Unfortunately, the response to such Laffer outcomes has to date only been for the government finding new ways of taxing more, and the ways they find are more and more dysfunctional.

Decades ago, I formulated several 'Moynihan laws of tax'. I have forgotten most of them now, but I remember my first law of tax, which described how people would respond when asked to say who in society should be taxed more. The answer that almost everybody gives to this question (this answer therefore became my first law) is: we should impose higher taxes on those persons who are quite a bit richer than me, or on any entity that is very much not like me.

Few people want those who are just *slightly* richer than them to be taxed more. Why? Because that could, optimistically, be them in the not-too-distant future. It was 'the rich' – people far removed from the respondents' circle of acquaintance, namely 'millionaires and billionaires' – who should be taxed more. As Senator Russell B. Long mordantly put it in the 1930s, 'Don't tax thee, don't tax me, tax that fellow behind the tree.'

And the other thing that should be taxed more, the 'entity that is not me', was, of course, business. Most people don't own a business and don't plan to own one. So, they are complacent at the thought of taxing business more. They shouldn't be; few understand, for example, that their retirement income is likely to rely on the financial success of the businesses that their pension fund has invested in. Nor do they understand that if there are no, or fewer, businesses, then there are no, or fewer, jobs and no, or a much smaller, tax base.

Those wanting others, not themselves, to pay more tax like to refer to this as those other people paying their 'fair share'. But remember, the top 10 per cent of taxpayers are already paying 60 per cent of all income tax. So, what is their 'fair' share then? 70 per cent? 100 per cent? The end result of putting more tax on 'the rich' is that we get 'the rich' working less, or just leaving the country. Indeed, the latest figures from Henley Partners show that the number of millionaires leaving the UK in 2023, forecast to be 3,200 (Chart 2.53), was in fact 30 per cent higher, at 4,200.

We are all human, so Moynihan's first law on tax is understandable if depressing. The desire by all for some *other* person to pay extra taxes is a function of an individual's dynamic response to a proposed tax increase – seeing all too clearly their own circumstances while being unable to see clearly the point of view of that richer person or business. The economist James Duesenberry wrote influentially in his 1948 PhD thesis that individuals tend to 'ratchet up' their spending as their income increases; they have a tendency to spend money towards the limits of what they are making, increasing consumption as they earn more. But this means that they then find it much more difficult to cut back in harder times. (The parallels with the difficulty of cutting back government spending are obvious.) Little surprise, then, that anyone who finds themselves in such a ratcheted-up position finds the thought of paying more tax on the same salary nigh-on impossible.* They therefore point to others to be the recipient of their desires for more tax to be paid to the government.

Balzac, the great nineteenth-century French novelist, was said to have coined the famous phrase 'behind every fortune lies a great crime'.† Nowadays, in the UK, there's a flavour of that sentiment in most people's attitudes towards the rich – wealthy people must be criminals or perhaps the descendants of criminals. It's a stupid view,

---

* Recent 2024 budgets are now busy at work testing that impossibility.

† One could be tedious and point out that he was actually quoted as saying 'behind every fortune without apparent cause lies a great crime'. But that's a more sensible statement and therefore got lost in the translation. Anyway, the saying is not considered applicable to popular sports or other media stars, who make a lot of money but have not built businesses.

of course: if we think about the contributions to societal happiness made by Steve Jobs, Elon Musk or Jeff Bezos and the crime-free way in which they achieved their fortunes, Balzac's alleged sentiment is one that obviously doesn't hold up. However, we see relentless negative propaganda against the rich by media and by politicians, which has steadily nudged a general view that rich business people are by and large unlikeable, probably criminal, and that an increase in the level of taxes they pay is the very least penalty that should be imposed on them.[*]

Unfortunately, selecting richer people and business as the ideal victims to pay more tax does not work out as expected. The rich do not respond passively when actions are taken to make them pay more tax.[†] The top 1 per cent of income taxpayers (some 320,000 individuals) pay 30 per cent of all income tax in the UK.[53] How pleased are they when demands are made that they must pay more? How many might leave the UK as a result? What will the net impact on tax revenues be from their departure: positive or negative?

Henley Partners say 1,500 millionaires left the UK in 2022 and the number rose to 4,200 in 2023; this year, they forecast it to more than double in one year, to 9,500.[54] Worse than millionaires departing, the *very* rich are now leaving in droves. The *Sunday Times*, reporting in May 2024, stated that 'this year's [rich list] edition records the largest fall in the billionaire count in [its] 36-year history'.[55] And leavers are not confined to millionaires or billionaires: a recent newspaper article was titled 'The young high-earners deserting Britain and never coming back'.[56] The examples given in the article were a hotel executive who had become a 'digital nomad',

---

[*] It is often noted that in the US, the view of the rich person by those less well-off is 'I could be like that some day', while in the UK and most of Europe it's 'Why should they be like that when I'm not?'

[†] Again, I point out, this is not about theoretical morality. It is about how people and business actually behave in real life.

a GP emigrating to Australia and a wealth manager now among the 250,000 British expats living in the UAE. All this follows on from the UK having created a tax environment that is increasingly hostile to high strivers and high earners and that is hostile to rich foreigners coming to live here: as hostile to young talent as it is to old rich. It has changed the UK from being one of the most attractive tax regimes of the advanced economies to one of the least.[57]

One particularly despised category of 'rich' people in the UK is the 'non-domiciled' taxpayer (the 'non-dom').* For centuries, the UK has been friendly to rich foreigners. The fact that they came to live here, primarily in London, was a large contribution to London coming to be seen, for a while, as the capital of the world.[58] They brought money for investment into the country and spent large amounts in our shops. One of the reasons that foreigners were attracted to the UK was the non-domiciled regime, whereby you could come to live in the UK but pay taxes only on what you earned here, not paying taxes on any assets or income that you kept out of the UK. They did pay taxes – a lot of taxes – but only on their UK earnings. This was obviously important to anybody who had, before they came to the UK, built up wealth and income elsewhere that was low taxed or not taxed. The non-dom regime, additionally, was as much a matter of convenience than of cost to many – for example American citizens residing in the UK, whom the non-dom regime helped deal with a lot of administrative faff, including recovery of double taxation. Another typical example of a non-dom might be a premiership football player: a recent analysis said that if the non-dom regime was abolished, some 200 of them might now leave the UK.[59] The better (and better paid) the footballer, the more likely

---

* By the way, many non-doms are not rich: they might be a US citizen who's a professor in a redbrick university, or a Dutch middle manager in a City bank, or even a French bartender in a London club.

they are to leave: bang goes our footballing reputation. Other typical non-doms might be executives in banking (one fifth of whom are non-doms), oil or car production.[60]

Over the years, 'social justice warriors' have sought to demonise non-doms. There seems to have been a straightforward confusion (deliberate or otherwise) between two entirely different categories, non-dom and non-resident. The former were foreigners, not domiciled in the UK but living there and paying UK taxes on their UK earnings. The latter were the opposite – UK-born individuals, resident abroad, paying no UK tax at all. Non-doms are nothing to do with non-residents. They live and work in the UK and pay tax on all their UK income, as well as on their UK capital gains.

George Osborne, as Chancellor of the Exchequer, declared a war on non-doms.[61] This was amid talk of City people 'paying less tax than my cleaner'.[62] The position seemed bedevilled by a confusion between non-domiciled and non-resident persons. Non-doms paid, from their work in the UK, far more tax than their cleaners – indeed, I'm certain they paid on average far more tax than the average UK citizen. Nonetheless they were demonised and then, in subsequent years, more and more was done to make the non-dom tax regime less attractive and then, having watched more and more non-doms stream out of the UK, in 2024 the government finally closed down the remnants of the non-dom regime almost entirely (with the new Labour government planning to get rid of the rest of the regime), so that no wealthy foreigner with low-taxed assets abroad will now want to come to live or work in the UK.

Throughout the 2010s, other countries had begun to catch on to the enormous advantages that the UK had originally enjoyed from its 200-year non-dom regime. Over the past decade, Italy has had an arrangement whereby you could go and live there and, for up to ten years, pay a flat sum of just €100,000 a year in tax, however much you earn while living there. Italy is now poised to usurp London as a playground for the wealthy.[63] Portugal had something even better but its schemes closed recently because they were so heavily subscribed (thousands of Brits fleeing to that more friendly tax regime) that housing there became expensive and locals were being squeezed out of the market. There has always been Monte Carlo, Switzerland, Ireland, Hong Kong, Singapore. France is now getting in on the act. And now, a growing destination of choice for rich earners seems to be Dubai. There is no income tax, there is very little crime, there's culture, there is a not too high cost of living (for the well-off). Incredible as it may seem for any reader who cannot imagine going to live there, Dubai is fast becoming seen as one of the most attractive places in the world for rich people to emigrate. Its economy is thriving as a result.

There is now a steady, already large and growing stream of people, who up to now had been paying large sums of tax to the Exchequer, leaving the UK. Ask any London tax adviser or major accountant. They will tell you they know of dozens of individuals in the past few years who have left the UK to find a more attractive tax environment to live in. You can rail against this or you can feel indifferent to it, but the fact is that these demonised non-doms and other wealthy individuals – who were paying large amounts of tax to HMRC and thus funding large parts of the UK's welfare state – are sentient human beings with their own autonomous decision process, and they did not just sit there and allow HM Treasury to treat them as a piñata. They left, and following the abolition of the non-dom status are, in ever larger numbers, continuing to do so. As shown in Chart 2.52, 6,000 non-doms had, even by 2022, either given up their status or had vamoosed. Goodbye to at least hundreds of millions of pounds in tax revenues.

Chart 2.52: Non-Domiciled Taxpayer Numbers, Income Tax, Capital Gains Tax and National Insurance Contributions, 2008–22

The number of tax-paying non-doms has dropped from some 130,000 to some 70,000 in the past fifteen years*.

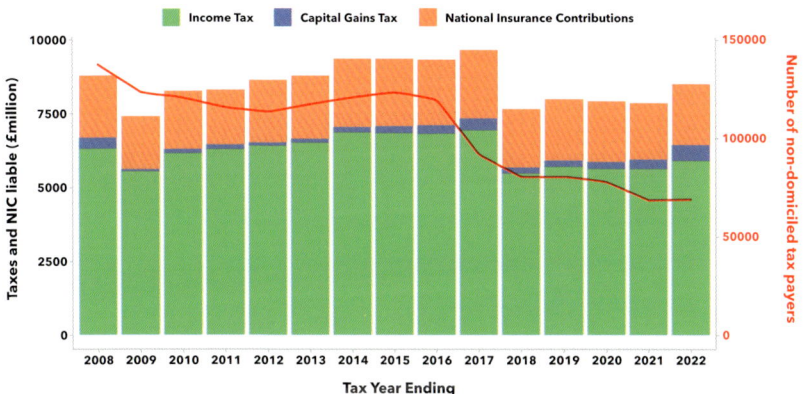

*The big drop was in part due to new laws that moved many UK residents out of the non-dom category. • Source: HMRC[64]

Well, anyway, the issue was put to bed in the 2024 spring Budget: the non-dom status has, after two centuries, been pretty much abolished. The move was greeted positively by middle- and left-of-centre publications – *The Economist* had been campaigning for such a move.[65] The University of Warwick suggested only 100 would leave the UK as a result – a truly optimistic low-ball estimate.[66] But in any case, the role of London in the world as the place to be for wealthy foreigners is now almost irretrievably dented; it will take many decades to recover and will only do so when the mistake is realised and rectified and the new posture maintained long enough to convince wealthy foreigners that they won't get fooled again. A great deal of tax and other economic activity is lost. And the new Labour government has implied it will attack non-doms even further.

To reiterate, it doesn't matter whether it is right or wrong to view rich people as bad, over-privileged or deserving to be taxed more. The point is, this view doesn't take into account that the rich, like all other taxpayers, respond dynamically to changes in the tax code. In particular, a large portion of people have the option to leave the UK, and they seem to be doing so in greater and greater numbers.

There are those, usually residing somewhat to the left in their political views, who respond to this news with a 'good riddance' to those departing non-doms and to the various others who are leaving the country.[67] These commentators seem to feel that they are taking some kind of admirable moral stance in saying that. But these are the very same individuals who will be calling for more state expenditure. How will that be paid for? Even if these moral posturers hadn't realised it, they and the rest of the country had been benefiting financially, for decades, from the presence of the non-doms before they left. The country is now poorer and less able to pay for the social goods it hands out to the population as a result of the departure of non-doms and other wealthy people. It is the poorest in society who are likely to be most damaged by this.

How much tax might we resume getting from these non-dom individuals, if we could ever persuade them to return? Around £8 billion was being received from around 7,000 non-doms, so getting 6,000 non-doms back could be worth around £7 billion, plus, say, another £3 billion from returning millionaires if we can fashion a programme to get them to return. So, £10 billion in all if we attracted rich foreigners back, but it would take an enormous amount of persuasion to get them to return in numbers.[*]

---

[*] Achieving this would be so difficult, and such a lengthy task, that in my summary at the end of the chapter, I assume zero benefit in the first years after such reforms.

The list of those declining to be fleeced of additional taxes is long. The static view, taken by those who tinker with the tax code, that those who are taxed more will just sit there and pay up has turned out over and again to be naive. Consider, as an example, the dynamic, Laffer-style reactions to changes in the following list of tax items, which in the following pages I run through:

- VAT on tourist purchases
- capital gains taxes
- inheritance taxes (already discussed)
- taxes on art

VAT for tourists

London used to be one of the top tourist destinations in the world for rich, or even just well-off, foreigners. Part of the attraction was that if you (or your spouse) were on a shopping trip to London, you could buy a handbag, suit, watch or pair of shoes and reclaim the VAT on it when you took it out of the UK. Your expenditure on other things in the UK while on holiday, on which you *didn't* reclaim VAT, would far exceed those purchases, and in any event, you would be boosting the UK economy by a considerable amount while on that trip, but you wouldn't pay the VAT on your luxury purchases. This was a small price for the UK to pay, because it attracted wealthy tourists to London.

Then, in another spectacular act of national self-sabotage, the Conservative government rescinded the VAT exemption for tourists. As hotelier after high-end shopkeeper after restaurateur will tell you, rich tourists have now dramatically fallen off in number; Paris, Milan and Rome are now the preferred destinations.[68] The overall negative impact on the economy (and thus on the tax take) has been estimated at over £10.7 billion – and the reputation that London had as being the place to go to on shopping trips and general vacations has gone.[69] It will take a long time to return, if it ever does. How difficult could it have been not to see that this would be the inevitable outcome? Is the anti-Laffer Treasury orthodoxy so strong that they refuse to admit that they were mistaken when they rescinded this arrangement?

Seeing that (all too predictable) damage – estimated by the CEBR as a hit to tax revenues of £700 million a year, not, as the government estimated, a gain of £500 million[70] – the Conservative Chancellor finally hinted he might reverse ferret and called for a review of that tax.[71] But his last chance to do so before the election passed in the 2024 spring Budget. Bang goes the luxury London tourist trade.

Capital gains tax

The capital gains tax (CGT) rate remains obstinately high.* Many of those who have built businesses in the UK, and are progressing towards the day where they will sell their business, will be careful to move out of the UK sometime prior to the day they sell – so that there will be no UK CGT income due from them when they do sell. This is a really big deal. If an individual sells their company for £100 million, they are required to pay near to £20 million in capital gains tax, depending on their circumstances. If they move beforehand to a low-tax country they can save all of that. Some won't move but – Laffer ahoy – many will. As a result, the UK's tax revenues will be much lower. Worse, at the time of writing, the Labour government has been floating the idea of

---

* The CGT rate is even higher than what a first look might imply because of the ravages of inflation: if I invested £100 in 2019 and sold the asset in 2024 for £120, I'd have to pay tax on the alleged £20 profit – but £120 in 2024 is only worth £92 in 2019 money. I've lost £8 from my investment, not gained £20. The tax on the £20 is a further loss that has to be added to the £8. For long-term investors who might have put their money in twenty years ago, the loss calculated will be far greater.

equalising capital gains and income tax rates (i.e. increasing CGT for large transactions from 20 per cent to 45 per cent) or, as a subset of that, making private equity gains be taxed as income, not capital.[72] The flood of departures will, if they do that, only swell.

Art sales: VAT and *droite de suite*

London used to be the art capital of the world. Now we impose VAT on art originating in the EU and auctioned in London, so a negligible amount of art is sent from the EU to London. Despite the fact that we have left the EU, we continue the EU's ludicrous *droite de suite* on all sales, adding a further cost for the buyer of the art. The result illustrates a depressing Laffer effect: art sales have moved to New York, Hong Kong and Geneva, where these costs aren't imposed. Now, we are no longer the centre of the art world. An entire subsector of the UK economy has collapsed. We don't collect the imposed VAT in any large amount because the art is no longer sold here, and we don't collect *droite de suite* monies in any large amount, for the same reason. As so often, we condemn ourselves in practice to be a useless, offshore appendage of the low-growth EU, and as a result, we destroy both this sector of our economy and our tax revenues.

The net result of these growth- and wealth-destroying actions, created in the first place by the UK's perceived pressing need to collect greater tax revenues to pay for its ever-greater public expenditures, is that both rich people in the UK, and market sectors formerly in the UK, depart the UK when they find it necessary for themselves, necessary for that sector, to do so. This ensures that the UK loses employment, business, footfall from overseas visitors – and, from the specific viewpoint of this particular discussion, very large sums of tax revenue that could otherwise have come our way.

How has all this happened? To be clear, it is not so much that those politicians who decide on our tax policy are stupid or overly malleable to the urgings of spiteful, left-wing tax officials. Rather, it's chiefly because we are growing state expenditures at a huge rate and have to pay somehow for the extra spend. Thus, the politicians come up with one brilliant tax wheeze after another, but somehow – that dratted Laffer again – the forecasted tax revenues never fully eventuate. So, then they come up with another brilliant idea and another. It's always about raising taxes when the needed solution is actually about cutting expenditure to grow the economy.

Chart 2.53: Top Ten Wealthiest Countries
High Net Worth Inflows and Outflows

The millionaire migrations of 2022 did, it seems, continue into 2023: only India and China are worse than the UK for losing its wealthy citizens.

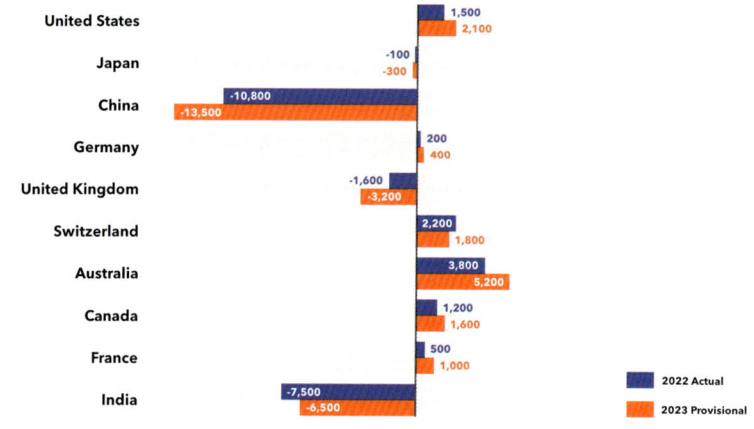

Source: Henley & Partners[73]

Codicil: Laffer curves and moynicurves

How big is the impact of dynamic responses to higher tax rates? Do these tax hikes merely not produce quite as much money as a non-dynamic analysis would predict, or is it worse than that? In this section, we review:

- one no longer controversial concept – the Laffer curve
- one slightly (as yet) less accepted concept – the moynicurve

The Laffer curve

Discussed in several places earlier in this chapter, the 'Laffer curve' concept says that increasing tax *rates* won't necessarily increase tax *revenues* as much as static analysis would suggest; indeed, past a certain point it starts reducing them. It makes logical sense that the more that people are taxed, the less hard they will work, as the higher their earnings are, the more they will be taxed. The higher a country's tax rates, the more both companies and entrepreneurial high-wage individuals leave in search of a less hostile tax environment.

The dynamic of *why* this is has been seen in so many examples over the past few pages. A further real-life illustration of the effect is what happened when NIC was increased in 2022.* That placed an extra cost on labour and all such factor inputs have price elasticity curves – price up, volume down. When NIC was increased, the owner of a small business observed to me, 'Well, that puts paid to the two extra people I was going to hire next month.' The extra NIC levied on the owner's fifty employees removed the available money needed to hire the two new employees, and had, in any event, removed any marginal benefit of hiring them. A similar dynamic likely led to business owners across the country each laying off a few people. Multiply this by hundreds of thousands of small businesses and you begin to see the malign impact of such increases on the economy and employment. This is just the impact of one small

---

* *Some* of the increase in NIC was reversed in early 2024, compounding the foolishness: business needs certainty so that they can plan. Constant change in tax is highly disruptive.

single punishment tax: there is a similar impact whenever any new tax is placed on business.

The moynicurve

There is a further phenomenon that can be found in every western economy that I have analysed and that makes tax raises even less productive; I have egregiously dubbed that phenomenon the 'moynicurve'. It offers an explanation as to why most social democratic countries never manage to raise enough tax to pay for their high expenditures. The moynicurve analysis implies a significantly worse outcome for any country that has the mistaken belief that raising tax *rates* will provide the extra tax *revenues* that are needed to fund ever increasing social democratic levels of public expenditure.

The moynicurve thesis is that Laffer curve-style responses by a country's population to any changes in tax policy are so immediate, dynamic and idiosyncratic that any country attempting to increase its overall tax take as a percentage of GDP, to a level higher than what is traditional in that country, will straightforwardly fail to achieve the higher levels of tax revenue that they predicted their changes in tax rates would achieve.

To take an example, it appears not to have been possible for us in the UK, any time in the last half century or more, to increase our tax take much beyond 34–36 per cent* of GDP.† The OBR forecasts tax revenues 2023/24 to be around 36 per cent and by 2028/29 to be

---

* In Chart 2.54, we show a moynicurve going between 32 and 34 per cent. This is because OECD numbers are lower than the ONS numbers. The general conclusions remain the same.

† I recently spotted, to my pleasure, that former Treasury mandarin Lord Macpherson made the same observation in a 2014 speech. He did not appear to have noticed that the same phenomenon can, as discussed here, be found in other western economies too. See Sir Nicholas Macpherson, 'Speech by the Permanent Secretary to the Treasury, The Treasury view: a testament of experience', HM Treasury, 17 January 2014, https://www.gov.uk/government/speeches/speech-by-the-permanent-secretary-to-the-treasury-the-treasury-view-a-testament-of-experience

a percentage point higher.[74] The moynicurve thesis is challenged by that number; will the tax take rise beyond our history's 36 per cent ceiling? Are we to be dragged kicking and screaming into social democracy land? Maybe, but if a ceiling of 36 per cent (or even 37 per cent) remains unbreakable, it will block any attempt to fund government expenditure at its current level of around 45 per cent of GDP.* My moynicurve thesis remains intact so far; the OBR forecasts tax revenues 2023/24 at 36 per cent of GDP.[75]

OK, so let's have a closer look at the moynicurve. In 2015, I wrote a paper using data originally discussed in an article I read in (of all places) *The Guardian*, examining fifty years of tax take in the UK.[76] My paper argued (along with *The Guardian*) that all the evidence shows that the citizens of any specific individual country will, in any given year, only cough up tax payments at or around a country-specific percentage, plus or minus a couple of points, of GDP.† The actual percentage of GDP varies widely for any particular individual country but – for that country – seems to stay pretty much invariant.

The key chart from my 2015 paper showing that conclusion can be seen in Chart 2.54 (updated, but only to 2019 so as to avoid distortions created from the Covid-19 period).‡

As we can see from Chart 2.54, the UK is in the middle ranks of what different countries seem to be prepared to pay. In 2015, I argued that 'UK taxpayers equilibrate the tax "take" at 34–6 per cent of GDP'. That conclusion held firm over the following years to 2019 and apparently to the present. There is no particular reason to believe that it will change dramatically from that level in coming decades, but the Conservative government of the past few years made a bold

---

* The OBR forecasts government expenditure will fall to 42.5 per cent of GDP by 2028/29. We shall see. Even at that level, there will still be an unsustainable deficit.
† Or, at least, with a ceiling – there presumably is no floor, if a country decides to cut its tax rates significantly.
‡ Note, a slightly different database has been used than in the 2015 paper.

attempt to achieve a higher level of tax take and Labour is going to try to get even more. It will be interesting to see, over the next few years, whether the UK moynicurve result of 36 per cent holds up or whether tax revenues will be up a few points as a percentage of GDP – and if they are, whether that result will last more than a year or two. History is not encouraging on that.

Chart 2.54: Tax Revenues as a Percentage of GDP

Different countries seem fated to only be able to collect relatively fixed – although for each country, very different – levels of tax as a percentage of GDP.

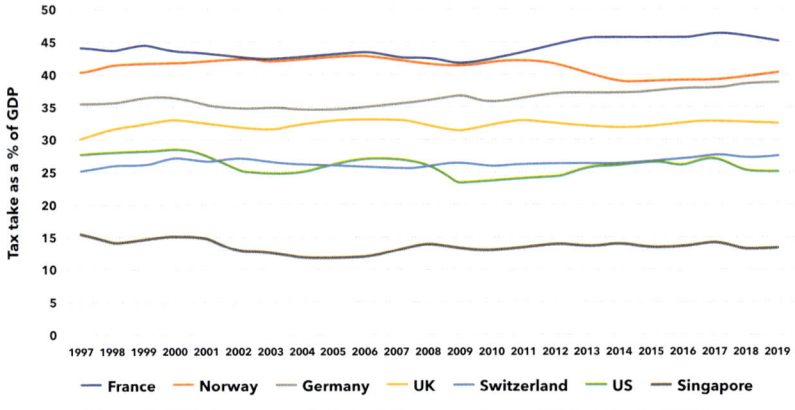

Note: the UK figures are slightly different to those published by the ONS[77]
Source: OECD[78]

We know, as discussed earlier in this book, that the size of the tax take as a percentage of GDP is negatively correlated with economic growth and wealth outcomes. Singapore, with the lowest rates in the chart, has, as discussed in previous pages, the highest GDP per capita, the best health outcomes etc.

Why should the level of tax take differ so largely and idiosyncratically between countries? After all, if there is no valid reason for the moynicurve's existence, it may be just a transient oddity. To answer this, my 2015 paper reviewed national culture as a possible influence on the level of any given country's moynicurve.

Chart 2.55: Culture Drives the Tax Take

Countries whose citizens embrace risk taking or have success-driven cultures tend to resist a higher tax burden. Thus, they have an environment that facilitates economic growth.

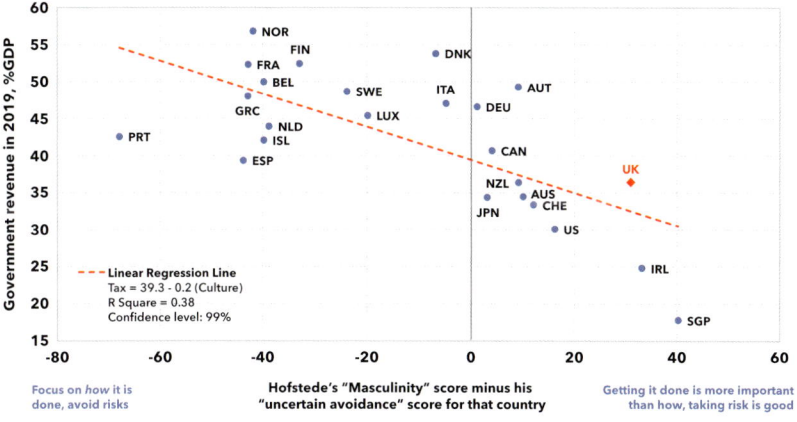

Source: Hofstede,[79] International Monetary Fund,[80] moyniteam analysis

National culture has been taxonomised and measured in different countries by the great sociologist Geert Hofstede.[81] Hofstede found various features of behaviour that vary significantly between different countries. He found Norway, Sweden and Finland to be similar to each other, Holland and Denmark to be somewhat similar to the UK, and France to be very different from all other European countries. Hofstede's differences between countries provide a plausible explanation for the differences in their tax takes. I found, as shown in Chart 2.55, a strong correlation between the moynicurve number and two of Hofstede's well-known and well-researched national characteristics. The two characteristics are masculinity/femininity (masculinity mostly meaning, according to Hofstede, favouring achievement or end product over process; femininity meaning a preference for the process over the outcome) and uncertainty/avoidance (meaning the degree to which the country's citizens have a higher or lower appetite for risk).

As can be seen, there is a strong correlation between those two Hofstede attributes and the moynicurve level of tax take, with some 40 per cent of the differences in tax take correlated with the two selected variables.

Can the UK's culture be changed to increase the level of tax we are prepared to pay? Might we become more 'risk averse'? If so, the nation might move to a higher level of tax take (and thus, most likely, a lower level of economic growth). But as the chart shows, in the UK we are far to the right of the spectrum, beyond any other country on the chart except Singapore and Ireland, on these two cultural norms: managing an enormous shift to the left on that chart would be surprising. And the Hofstede regression line currently predicts a 'norm' for our tax take level of some 34 per cent, not 36 per cent or more.

The moynicurve is not merely just an egotistic flourish; it has profound implications for every country. To understand this, let's look at why and how it works and what the impact will be of high tax raises in the UK.

When we raise tax, the key issue will be what the impact is on the top 10 per cent of UK taxpayers. They pay 60 per cent of income tax and will comprise most of the UK's entrepreneurs. If they have the same (perhaps more pronounced) characteristics as Hofstede says the overall population has, then they're not cuddly – they want to get things done, not keep things nice – and they like taking risk. If they see the UK getting in the way of their personal ambitions, they're happy to be off to greener fields. So, whether tax raises will work or not depends on the expected behaviour and characteristics of a relatively small subset: those who are paying the large part of the tax take – the wealthy, the highly talented and highly paid, the entrepreneurs and the corporations.

The dynamic (negative) reaction to higher tax levels will not just be from the current top 10 per cent – there will also be the flight of many of the potential *future* top 10 per cent, who, if they had stayed, would have created, grown and potentially sold their businesses, paying a large amount of individual income tax, transaction taxes, capital gains and other taxes over many years. All of these individuals and organisations (as I partly explained in an article in February 2023)[82] are able to alter their economic activity and, in particular, are able to switch that activity off entirely by leaving the country. As shown earlier, the brain drain has now clearly returned.[83] Millionaires are leaving in a flood. Non-doms are jumping ship. Young high achievers are off. Among our corporations, major net contributors to the overall tax take are leaving in droves.[84] Will our tax take be able to withstand all this?

The key point is that governments and quangos such as the OBR are in cloud-cuckoo land if they think that increasing tax rates will result in pro rata increases in tax revenues. The step that the Truss government took that was most attacked was the reduction of the 25 per cent top rate of corporation tax to the 19 per cent that prevailed in the late 2010s; it was alleged that reversing that back to 24 per cent would raise large amounts of extra tax. As we have seen earlier, and as also pointed out by the CEBR, so far it hasn't – the Laffer effect yet again.[85]

Assuming that the moynicurve finding for the UK persists over the next few decades, so that tax revenues of not much more than 36 per cent of GDP are extracted each year from the UK's taxpayers, the UK's current tax-and-spend policy is soon going to run into a wall. The UK had income tax rates of 83 per cent in 1980 and overall tax revenues were 32 per cent of GDP. Income tax rates went down to 40 per cent under Blair and tax revenues were 34 per cent of GDP. In the decades between, all sorts of tax changes were made and a plethora of new taxes were introduced, but the tax take as a percentage of GDP has remained, plus or minus, 34–6 per cent. But the Treasury and OBR seem to carry on assuming, in their forecasts and policymaking, that if tax rates are raised, tax revenues will increase in direct proportion to those raises. This Treasury orthodoxy implicitly assumes that the experience of the past decades, revealed by the moynicurve chart, will not persist. But Laffer – and, possibly, the moynicurve – abide.

THE OVERALL IMPACT OF DYNAMIC RESPONSES TO TAX INCREASES IS LARGE

Those plotting to raise more tax revenues through higher tax rates on the rich or on corporations presumably understand that there will be *some* evasion or avoidance of those taxes. But, implicitly or otherwise, they dismiss that point and apparently think that any concerns about dynamic responses can be ignored.* The discussion on the preceding pages has shown clearly enough, I hope, how wrong it is to ignore the dynamic effects of tax changes, but it is still something of a surprise to find officials dismissing the fact,

---

* This assumes that the setters of tax policy understand the point. I would hate to assert that Treasury officials are so unintelligent that they don't understand it or so doctrinaire that they wilfully ignore it. But if not either of these, what?

so obvious from surveying the data from many decades past, that attempts in the UK to increase overall tax revenues by increasing tax rates (or tax types) have not had a great deal of success.

Conversely, tax cuts can boost growth. In the US, tax cuts have had a fine record of producing sustained economic growth, as Chart 2.56 shows:

Chart 2.56: Real GDP Before and After Major Tax Cuts in the US
Index Year 0 = 100 (Years are 1922, 1964, 1982, 2003 respectively)

In the US, tax cuts have seen a strong record of sustained acceleration thereafter in economic growth.

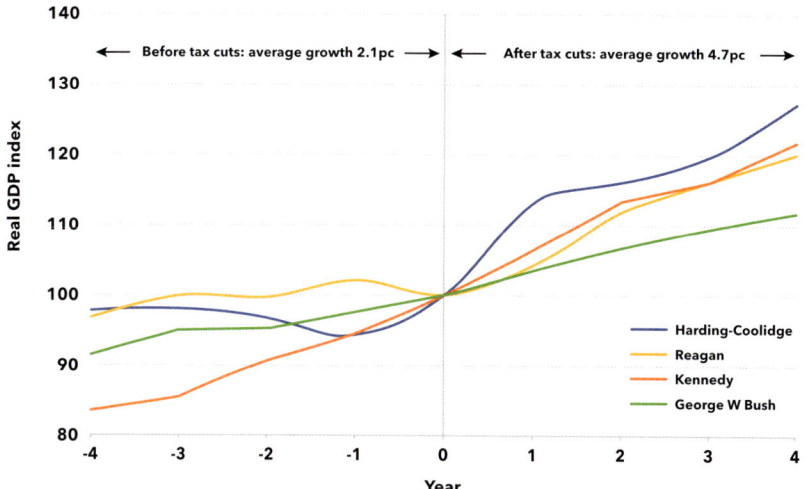

Source: International Monetary Fund,[86] moyniteam

There is little hope – whether or not we believe in the moynicurve or in the Laffer curve in general – that 2024's increases in UK tax rates will lead to a corresponding one-for-one increase in tax revenue. Increasing the tax rate may in fact overall *at best* lead to approximately zero addition to tax revenues (as a percentage of GDP). Worse, the tax rises will most likely produce slower economic growth – with all the problems that slow growth brings, as described in Part I. And, as economic growth slows, so does growth in tax revenues – an ever-worsening loop.

In light of all this, it is difficult to understand why the economic establishment continues to believe that keeping top income tax rates at 45 per cent – 5 percentage points above what pertained throughout the Blair/Brown years – and corporate tax at 25 per cent will significantly increase tax revenues as a percentage of GDP. Unless our national character[*] can be altered it is unlikely that the government's recent increase in tax rates will lead to much increase in tax revenue at all.

If true, economic growth slows, then the deficit will grow, borrowing will grow and national bankruptcy will draw ever nearer.

CONCLUSION: RADICAL CHANGE AND SIMPLIFICATION OF THE TAX CODE IS NEEDED

If tax revenues are always going to stay stable, the key question that we need to focus on is: *what will grow the economy?* There is a tax revenue ceiling that seems to hover at around 36 per cent of GDP, with additional non-tax revenues to the government adding a further 4 per cent of GDP annually to that – i.e. total revenue coming to 40 per cent of GDP.[87] This means it is clearly economically and financially unsustainable for the UK to have government expenditures at 45 per cent or so of GDP.

Spending much in excess of 40 per cent would, under my theory, mean a permanent, large deficit. Taxpayers will, of course, always be happy to contribute *less* than 36 per cent: we could, if we were to get

---

[*]   In this case, as already pointed out, it is a matter of the character of the top 10 per cent of our wealth creators, businesses and executives.

national expenditure down to 33 per cent of GDP, get taxes down to 29 per cent (which added to the extra 4 per cent of other revenues would give us a balanced budget). Getting taxes down to 29 per cent of GDP would mean, for the UK's 2024-sized economy, reducing taxes by some £200 billion. That, of course, cannot happen all at once, and expenditure reductions would have to match the tax reductions. So if, after the first few years of the plan, we had (as shown in the previous chapter) reduced government expenditure by some £118 billion,[*] then we could also cut taxes by a similar amount in that same period. This would lead to a significant acceleration of economic growth, further lowering our expenditure-to-GDP ratio, which would then make it easier to reduce taxes further, while also lowering the tax-to-GDP ratio – getting to 29 per cent needs GDP growth, not just tax cuts.

Based on the discussion in this chapter, how might this be accomplished? The set of actions for a truly radical transformation of the tax system would look something akin to the following:

- Reduce income taxes for corporations (reduce corporate tax to 19 per cent) and individuals (reduce most employee NIC and remove income tax top rate of 45 per cent).
- Lower or, when possible, abolish the rates for other taxes on business.
- Increase revenues from some, but not all, consumption taxes. Widen the base (lower the threshold but also lower the rate) for VAT and reduce Pigouvian rates.
- Reduce or abolish the different capital taxes (CGT, IHT, stamp duty).

---

[*] The amount by which the UK currently overspends, relative to other equivalently rich (in GDP-per-capita terms) countries (see Chart 2.8) is some £112 billion.

- Create a programme to bring wealthy foreigners and expatriates back to the UK and persuade discontented wealthy and high-talent UK residents not to leave.

In Chart 2.57, we outline the potential impact of such an approach, with the objectives of making the tax code more friendly to growth and effecting a reduction in taxes (to be achieved over five years, reflecting the five-year expenditure reduction programme in the previous chapter) of some £114 billion.

That initial £114 billion of tax reductions is just a down payment; it will only get taxes down from 36 per cent to 32 per cent of GDP. Getting taxes all the way down to 29 per cent of GDP, the ultimate target, would entail another (in 2024 terms) £83 billion of tax reductions, mostly to be accomplished in parallel with constraining our spending, with economic growth faster than the growth in government expenditure. The potential total cuts identified in Chart 2.57 come to £256 billion.

Chart 2.57 divides these proposed cuts into three categories:

- Cuts in the first few years: £113 billion
- Cuts thereafter: £82 billion
- Desirable but unfunded cuts: £59 billion

The third category of cuts are those that can only be implemented if GDP grows faster than our model predicts; unless that happens, we would only be able to cut two thirds of employee and employer NIC rather than 100 per cent. As shown in Chart 2.57, one third of the NIC cuts would be in the first years, one third thereafter and the final third as the fiscal position allowed.

Chart 2.57: Proposed Changes and Reductions in the Tax Code

I propose, concurrent with the initial £118 billion of expenditure cuts, £114 billion of tax cuts in the first five years, £83 billion thereafter and a further £59 billion of desirable – but since unfunded, temporarily unachievable – reductions. This is a total of £256 billion in current terms.

	Tax	Action	Cuts in first years £billion	Cuts thereafter £billon	Desirable but unfunded cuts £billon
Income tax	Corporation tax	Back to 19 per cent	13.9	–	–
	Onshore bank surcharge	Abolish	1.4	–	–
	Bank levy	Abolish (half now, half later)	0.8	0.8	–
	Offshore energy profits levy	Abolish	2.6	–	–
	Income tax	Abolish additional rate	8.3	–	–
	Employee national insurance (including self-employed)	Abolish (one third now, one third later, one third unfunded)	22.8	22.8	22.8
Production taxes	Business rates	Drop by 30 per cent (half now, half later)	4.1	4.1	–
	Green charges	Abolish	9.4	–	–
	Apprenticeship levy	Abolish	3.9	–	–
	Climate change levy	Abolish	1.9	–	–
	Employer national insurance	Abolish (one third now, one third later, one third unfunded)	36.6	36.6	36.6
Capital taxes	Non-property capital gains tax	Drop to 10 per cent from 20 per cent (pays for itself)	–	–	–
	Inheritance tax	Drop to 10 per cent from 40 per cent (pays for itself)	–	–	–
	Stamp duty on shares	Abolish	3.2	–	–
	Stamp duty on land tax	Abolish (half now, half later)	6.4	6.4	–

	Tax	Action	Cuts in first years £billion	Cuts thereafter £billion	Desirable but unfunded cuts £billion
Consumption taxes	VAT on tourist purchases	Abolish (pays for itself)	-	-	-
	Art sales: VAT and *droite de suite*	Abolish (pays for itself)	-	-	-
	Fuel duties	Cut 25 per cent now, another 25 per cent later	6.2	6.2	-
	Insurance premium tax	Halve	4.2	-	-
	Alcohol duty	Cut by one quarter	3.1	3.1	-
	Tobacco duty	Cut by one quarter	2.2	2.2	-
	Air passenger duty	Abolish	3.9	-	-
	Television licence fee	Eliminate BBC licence fee, cut BBC budget	0.4	-	-
	Soft drinks industry levy	Abolish	0.3	-	-
	Total Cuts		135.6		
	VAT	Reduce rate to 18 per cent, increase coverage from 45 to 55 per cent	(17.5)*	-	-
	Non-doms	Persuade them to come back	-	-	-
	Unemployed back to work		(5)	-	-
	Total increases		(22.5)		
	Grand total		**£113.1 billion**	**£82.2 billion**	**£59.4 billion**

SUMMARY: EXPECTED IMPACT OF SPENDING AND TAX REDUCTIONS

In Part I, I showed a dispiriting forecast for the UK's economy if present trends continued. I then worked through, in Chapters 6 and 7, large cuts in both government expenditure and taxes that could improve our potential future wealth and GDP growth.

How might the economy be expected to fare under these changes? Our model (see Appendix B for details) predicts that this re-arrangement of the economy, through reductions in both expenditure and taxes, would result in significant improvement in economic

---

* Figures in brackets denote *increases*, rather than decreases, in tax.

growth, and therefore to national and individual wealth, as shown in Chart 2.58.

Chart 2.58: The UK Economy: Scenario with £118 Billion of Spending Cuts and £113 Billion of Initial Tax Cuts

The impact of cutting both government expenditure and taxes would be profound

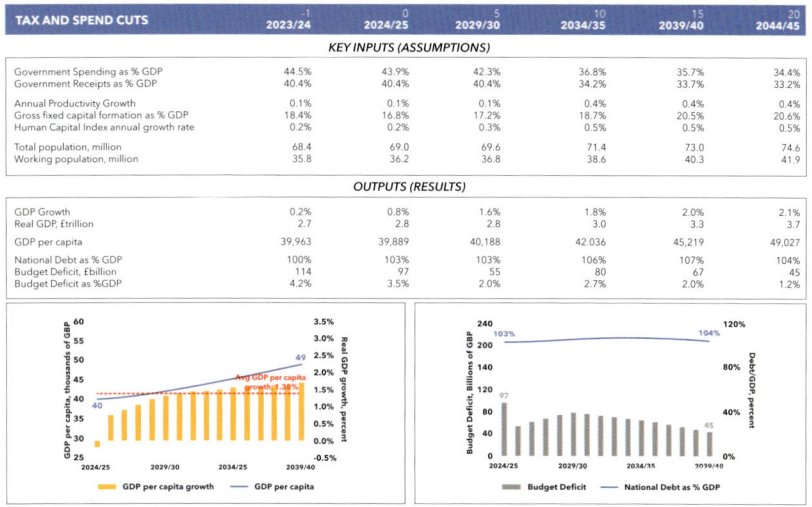

TAX AND SPEND CUTS	-1 2023/24	0 2024/25	5 2029/30	10 2034/35	15 2039/40	20 2044/45
KEY INPUTS (ASSUMPTIONS)						
Government Spending as % GDP	44.5%	43.9%	42.3%	36.8%	35.7%	34.4%
Government Receipts as % GDP	40.4%	40.4%	40.4%	34.2%	33.7%	33.2%
Annual Productivity Growth	0.1%	0.1%	0.1%	0.4%	0.4%	0.4%
Gross fixed capital formation as % GDP	18.4%	16.8%	17.2%	18.7%	20.5%	20.6%
Human Capital Index annual growth rate	0.2%	0.2%	0.3%	0.5%	0.5%	0.5%
Total population, million	68.4	69.0	69.6	71.4	73.0	74.6
Working population, million	35.8	36.2	36.8	38.6	40.3	41.9
OUTPUTS (RESULTS)						
GDP Growth	0.2%	0.8%	1.6%	1.8%	2.0%	2.1%
Real GDP, £trillion	2.7	2.8	2.8	3.0	3.3	3.7
GDP per capita	39,963	39,889	40,188	42.036	45,219	49,027
National Debt as % GDP	100%	103%	103%	106%	107%	104%
Budget Deficit, £billion	114	97	55	80	67	45
Budget Deficit as %GDP	4.2%	3.5%	2.0%	2.7%	2.0%	1.2%

Source: moyniteam analysis

As is shown in Chart 2.58, significant benefits are predicted to accrue:

- The key metric, annual GDP growth, increases by the end of the fifteen-year period from below 1 per cent in 2024 to above 2 per cent a year by 2039.
- The debt-to-GDP ratio stays flat at around 100 per cent instead of rising (under status quo) to around 150 per cent.
- Government expenditure drops from 44 per cent of GDP to 34 per cent. In absolute numbers, it grows from £1.21 trillion to £1.34 trillion; after an initial drop, it then grows in real terms at a rate of 60 per cent of each previous year's GDP growth.

Chart 2.59: Key Metrics after Reductions in Government Spend and Taxes, £ billion

By the fifteen-year mark, the economy has been truly turned around.

	Scenario after spend and tax reductions (£ trillions)		Percentage increase 2024–39	
	2024/25	2039/40	This scenario	Status quo scenario
Real GDP	£2.8	£3.7	33 per cent	13 per cent
GDP per capita	£39.9k	£49.0k	23 per cent	5 per cent
Government expenditure	£1.2	£1.3	4 per cent	16 per cent
Government expenditures as a percentage of GDP	43.9 per cent	34.4 per cent		
Government revenues*	£1.1	£1.2	9 per cent	13 per cent
Government revenue as a percentage of GDP	40.4 per cent	33.2 per cent		
Government debt	£2.8	£3.8	35 per cent	64 per cent
Government debt as a percentage of GDP	103 per cent	101 per cent		

Source: moyniteam analysis

In the next chapter, we look at the benefits that can be gained by cutting regulation, over and above the benefits gained from these expenditure and cuts.

---

* Assumes current level of 4.3 per cent of GDP for non-tax revenues.

CHAPTER 8

THE GREATER THE AMOUNT OF REGULATION, THE SMALLER THE ECONOMIC GROWTH

We have seen that as they get ever larger, both the size of government and the burden of taxes drastically squash economic growth. There is a third variable to add into the mix that goes hand-in-hand with these two in reducing growth: regulation.

One of Friedrich Hayek's better-known books, written late in life and published posthumously, is the memorably titled *The Fatal Conceit*. As with much of Hayek's writing, it's not entirely easy to read through, but its central idea, one that permeates almost all of Hayek's writing, is easy enough to understand: that the interactions between human beings and organisations are far too complex and too dynamic, as they compete and cooperate to achieve desires, wants and ambitions, for any central organisation such as government to model and order with even the most sophisticated quantum computer. If anyone believes that economic outcomes can be dictated from the centre, they are deluding themselves; they have a 'fatal conceit'. Hayek credibly explains how the whirl of human and organisational interactions in an economy is impossible to decipher in any detail; regulations that seek to direct human economic activity from the centre are doomed to fail. Hayek concludes, 'What cannot be known, cannot be planned.'

Collectivists and social democrats (and, in the extreme, communists) are seized with the fatal conceit: they are sure that desirable outcomes for the economy can be planned and dictated from the centre through laws, diktats, regulations and regulators. They believe that economic growth, jobs and even wages can and should be determined directly by a benevolent group of governing politicians and bureaucrats. Social outcomes can be predicted and managed by a far-seeing and energetic government – spurred on, no doubt, by (in the case of the UK) regulators, quangos, arm's-length bodies, academies, a benevolent BBC and so many other members of the establishment's wise men and commentariat.

The – at least implicit, usually explicit – view of those seized with the fatal conceit is that the more regulation there is, the more perfect society will become. A quick look at reality, in the scores of countries that tried the socialist or communist approach over the last century, tells us how that theory has fared. All communist countries ended with appalling economic conditions, totalitarian repression, propaganda and deception of the people, and were almost all overthrown by internal revolt. The only remaining communist countries that weren't are North Korea and Cuba, both of which have managed to brutalise and immiserate their people sufficiently to prevent them from rebelling. Because these countries have lost – or never had – any tradition of democratic governments, free markets or a competitive private sector, many formerly communist states transition to dictatorial gangster states. Russia, China and Nicaragua are good examples.

And yet in today's UK, a majority of our parliamentarians seem to have become convinced that centralised management of the economy is the best way to organise a country and its politics. Why is that? It's because they believe, either explicitly or implicitly, that they know best.

So, the question we all need to ask is: do they? Do they know best? And all experience shows us that no, they don't.

The 'we know best' mantra is at the heart of the social democratic project. It is one of the more efficient destroyers of economic progress known to man. In that mindset, all problems can be solved with an edict from the centre, a restraining law; an eager regulator. Yet the overwhelming verdict of history is clear: the 'we know best' approach doesn't work. Further, as can be sorrowfully observed, the more the centre dictates things, the more the behaviour of otherwise perfectly good private-sector companies becomes distorted, as they turn into 'rent seekers': battening onto the government, seeking to influence what regulations are passed, looking to introduce laws and rules that will favour their own business system, trying to use regulation to make life more difficult for their competitors regardless of the benefit or otherwise to the consumer. Trade bodies morph into (or, in the case of the Confederation of British Industry, always have been) channels for crony capitalism. Large organisations that can afford to lobby the government get rules passed that make it difficult for challenger companies to compete or even enter the market. Individuals also indulge in distortive behaviour when pushed from the centre: as we have seen earlier, they can be 'nudged' or otherwise economically incentivised to take steps that will hold back, rather than boost, the economy.

All of this is made possible by a misguided mindset that says that if there is the slightest societal problem then wherever possible, a law should be passed, a rule should be imposed, a regulator appointed.

In Hayek's analysis, a 'we know best' attitude leads to a distorted market and, as a result, less economic growth; for Hayek, the solution to such distortions is to replace them with a freely working price mechanism, where prices are struck directly between willing buyers and sellers in the market so as to clear transactions optimally between supply and demand. Prices are made competitive and kept low by the spurring effects of competition. The impact of individual entrepreneurs, struggling to realise their personal economic ambitions and better themselves, whether as sellers bringing new products and services to market or as buyers responding to prices, creates the conditions that further human and economic progress. Most central interference, however well meaning, only serves to hold back that progress.

And there is more to this than just the multiple mistakes made daily by those in power who think they know better, who impose harmful regulations that distort and wreck the market. Every time that a company is required to comply with any particular new regulation, it has to make its managers ensure the company is in regulatory compliance instead of focusing on the task of coming up with, and bringing to market, goods or services that customers will actually want to buy. So, yet another growth-destroying aspect of regulation is that on top of mucking up the necessarily single-minded focus that a manager needs, each company is then saddled with the extra cost of hiring additional staff for compliance departments (growing recently in some specialised organisations to 5 or even 10 per cent of all staff) to ensure the company obeys the new regulation or law. (The job of that compliance department's people is then to wander around looking for things to stop market-facing employees generating revenue.)

In recent decades, business regulation in the UK has mushroomed, placing what a company can and can't do more and more into the hands of the government. Regulators don't just sit on their hands: to justify themselves, they produce a brand-new set of regulations each year. Most of these new pieces of regulation – whatever supposed benefit they offer – constrain activity, so axiomatically also reduce growth.

In our globalised world, UK regulators can't ensure that every competitor worldwide will be required to suffer the costs of our UK regulations. So, the more regulatory costs are imposed in the UK, the more business activity will move to elsewhere in the world, looking for wherever there is a lighter regulatory regime.

The enormous and growing amount of regulation that has been imposed upon the City of London since the financial crisis of 2008 has been a very large contributor to the City's gradual shutting down over the past almost two decades. It has sent businesses fleeing to New York, Dubai or Singapore, wherever there is less regulation.

There will be those who claim that in view of the financial crisis, significant constraint on the City or on banks has become crucial. But the reasons why that 2008 crash was so extreme are threefold. The first, and most important, reason was that regulators completely failed to spot egregious leverage on overly risky borrow short/invest long (or borrow liquid/buy illiquid) strategies, leading to the collapse of financial institutions. The second reason was the insistence by the government on keeping all the failed banks' depositors and their bondholders whole, rather than making them bear the cost of having lent to or deposited with such egregious risk takers. The third was the UK's clumsy and cumbersome bankruptcy regime, which prevents a Chapter 11-type reorganisation that would allow a bank's speedy transfer to new ownership. Because of this, the UK government either had to take over (i.e. nationalise) failed UK banks or force good banks to merge with them, dragging those good banks down with the bad. The earlier S&L crisis in the US ended benignly, because only depositors with under $100,000 were protected, while bondholders and other depositors were forced (by Chapter 11 of the Bankruptcy Code) to take a haircut while becoming the new owners of the banks. For most customers of these banks, it was business as usual throughout.

Additionally, regulators are often of the type who are willing to regard the organisations or individuals that they regulate as miscreants or miscreants in waiting, who need watching and controlling very carefully. I would assert also that the majority of regulators have a mildly oppressive bent, preferring to shut things down and restrict rather than liberate and open. They tend to react against the creative elements of human nature that lead to economic growth. Once regulators get involved, a lot of sense goes straight out of the window.

To pluck just one random example from many: the Climate Change Committee have now conceded, astoundingly, that they used limited, insufficient datasets, including data from only *one single year*, for formulating key net zero recommendations; yet the very feasibility of 2050 as the net zero target date was predicated on that data, and Theresa May's government relied on those recommendations for choosing 2050 as the net zero target.[1] As a result, the data significantly underestimated the need for non-renewable energy in the mix. This alone provides a good reason, never mind all the other additional reasons that could be offered, to argue that 2050 is likely to be unachievable. To unpick what happened: the Climate Change Committee were happy to constrain the economy to an unachievable date, massively inhibiting potential future economic growth for the UK, by cherry-picking a single data point that suited their desired conclusion, and ignoring multiple other data points that rebutted the likelihood of achieving the target, *and* they have made that 2050 target legally binding.

Pulling back from that single example, how has regulation become so pervasive in the UK over the past few decades? And how bad has its impact been on economic growth? In recent years, an alarming concatenation of circumstance, involving political campaigners, burgeoning regulators and inspectors, crony capitalists and over-compliant businesses, has come together to create a perfect storm of regulation, as depicted in Chart 2.60.

Chart 2.60: The Creep of Regulation

The regulatory mindset plays havoc on economic growth.

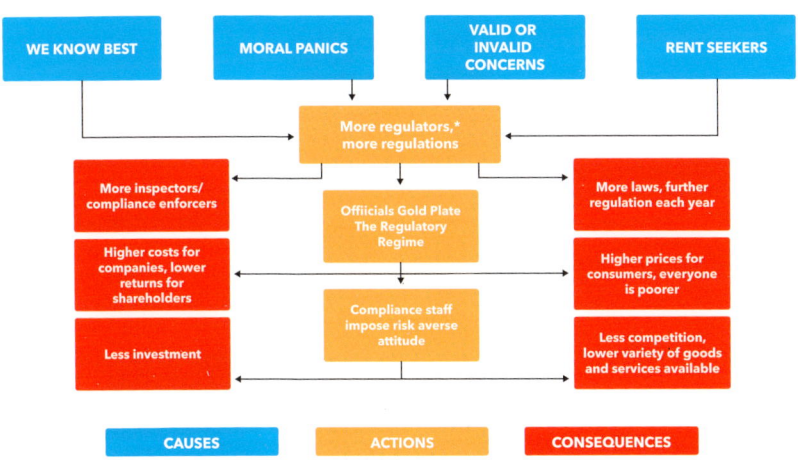

In the extreme, multiple regulators addressing the same issue [2]

How has this come about? What is its impact on economic growth? And what can we do about it?

In the following pages, we discuss the crisis of regulation and regulators that the UK currently faces:

1. Studies show that excessive regulation slams the door on growth.
2. In the UK, the regulatory mindset is now embedded.
3. Regulation has metastasised, often into ludicrous areas.
4. The costs of regulation in the UK, financial and otherwise, are vast.
5. Much of the time, regulation doesn't even succeed in its objectives.
6. Obtrusive regulation on top of high taxes is driving companies, rich people and young high achievers out of the country, thus further crimping future economic growth.
7. Loosening the grip of regulation will need an upheaval of the political and regulatory status quo.

STUDIES SHOW THAT EXCESSIVE REGULATION SLAMS THE DOOR ON GROWTH

Why do I devote an entire chapter to regulation? The reason is clear: excessive regulation inevitably leads to much slower growth in the modern western economy, and its effect is astonishingly large. This is true of almost all regulation, but in particular, it's the case for regulation aimed at business in any way.

Overregulation inevitably leads to less economic activity

In Palumbo and Iacono's review, they cite a key study by John Seater and John Dawson from the US, who performed an economic analysis of the growth in federal regulation and its impact on the US economy. The two are quoted as saying:

> Regulation's overall effect on output's growth rate is negative and substantial. Federal regulations added over the past fifty years have reduced real output growth by about two percentage points on average over the period 1949–2005. That reduction in the growth rate has led to an accumulated reduction in GDP of

Woelf et al.'s result, shown in Chart 2.62. (Note that on this one measure, the UK was found to have had, in 1998, a highly unregulated market. As the UK's data points in Chart 2.61 show, we are by now far more highly regulated.)

Chart 2.62: Anticompetitive Product Market Regulation (1998) Versus GDP Per Capita (2007)

The more the regulation that limits competition, the lower is the economic growth.

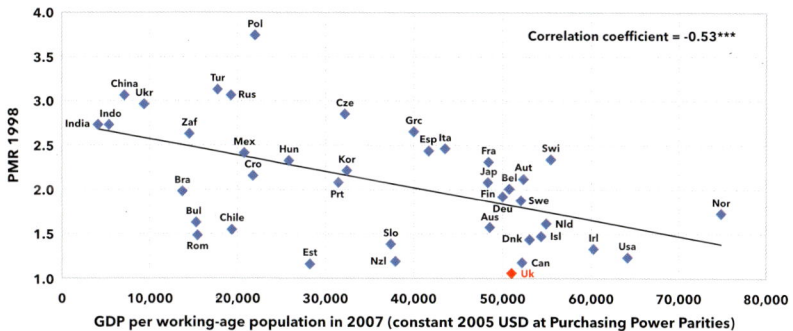

Note: The values on the vertical axis are based on a 'simplified' OECD product market regulation (PMR) indicator (see Woelf et al., 2010). PMR measured in 1998 for OECD countries; 2008 for Chile, Estonia, Israel, Slovenia, Brazil, Russia and China; 2007 for Croatia, Indonesia, South Africa and Ukraine; and 2006 for Bulgaria, India and Romania. *** denotes significance at the 1 per cent level.
Source: Woelf et al. (2010),[8] EIB Papers

Of course, some regulation is always necessary. The data shows, however, that any regulation, whether necessary or not, is likely to carry with it a heavy growth penalty. Much regulation offers far less benefit than the penalties it creates, often carrying little benefit at all. Thus, existing and suggested regulation needs to be carefully scrutinised and any potential impact on growth must be worried about. Using that lens, much regulation would, given the imperative to promote growth, be removed or softened.

Why should anticompetitive regulation have such a major impact? The answer lies in the way that free markets develop. Most new products represent an improvement or progression of some old product; the more the old product has its incumbency in the market cemented by tightly drawn product or service standards, or sweetheart deals or predatory pricing behaviour, the less impact a new competitor can have and the less likely it is therefore that an entrepreneur will risk their all to bring a competing product or service to market. When that's the case, the market stultifies and there is no economic growth.

THE REGULATORY MINDSET IS NOW EMBEDDED IN THE UK

The current over-regulated environment in the UK has been turbo-charged as a result of a three-stage public conversation now coming to be the default reaction to almost any newly discovered public issue. When a problem in society is – correctly or not – claimed to exist, it is then brought to the urgent attention of the British people via *The Guardian*, Sky News or, above all, the BBC's *Today* programme. At that point, the three-point line of public discussion almost universally predominates:

1. *'Something must be done'*: no perceived problem arises without a call straightaway going up for action, on television, from X, from other media, from the opposition – indeed, often from the government itself.

2. *'Money must be found'*: no problem uncovered in today's world can be solved, it seems, except by throwing public money at it.

3. *'There ought to be a law'*: beyond demands for more money, there

are then calls to legislate or regulate against the perceived problematic situation or behaviour – including, of course, creation of new regulatory powers and, if necessary, an entirely new regulator.

This three-phase default reaction is now embedded in our society. But the logical outcome of endlessly applying that approach is to squelch initiative, block off opportunity and deny aspiration. Problems that over time would be sorted out in a free market or through economic growth must instead be sorted out immediately, with money, laws and regulation. The process reached an early nadir during Theresa May's government, when she announced a Minister for Loneliness. The author is convinced that had May survived much longer as Prime Minister, a 'loneliness regulator' would have been appointed, with full powers to compel people not to be lonely. The Minister for Loneliness survives to this very day, accompanied by all the necessary trappings; for example, we now have a loneliness awareness week.[9] And the eagerness to regulate has plunged beyond that previous bottom, with Sunak's announcement that the innocent sport of the great British public, football, is now to have its own spanking new regulator – with the power to fine football clubs 10 per cent of their turnover.[10] Funny that – Starmer's government seamlessly adopted that policy.

The number of regulators has metastasised to an extraordinary degree. There is now the astonishing number of some ninety-two regulators, and their annual spend is about £4 billion – in addition to the approximately eighty professional associations in the UK.[11] In all, there were, as discussed earlier, 834 central quangos with a further 5,300 local quangos at the end of 2022.[12]

For both regulators and quangos, the same multifold problems arise as with the civil service, discussed in Chapter 6. This cannot be surprising because their personnel are drawn from the same pool; individuals can be tracked moving seamlessly from civil service department to regulator to other quango, and back again. Thus, you have precisely the same problems of excess pay, lackadaisical timekeeping, focus on process, snowflakery and a relaxed attitude to outcomes, timing imperatives or any other urgency.

It might be argued that this is a good thing: if we are to have regulators, it is best that they be incompetent ones. But no – for a start, believe it or not, most businesspeople are honest and have no desire to be thought of as flouting the law, so go to great lengths to stay within the regulations. And the cost of that means that much economic damage is done even before the regulator comes calling. But when they do come, it seems that regulators somewhat relish going after certain targets, and when they do, the often excruciatingly drawn-out process becomes the punishment, regardless of the eventual outcome – more value-destroying economic damage right there. The way has been opened for a seemingly endless march of regulation on society, on business, on entrepreneurship and on personal freedoms.

REGULATION HAS METASTASISED, OFTEN INTO LUDICROUS AREAS

The plethora of regulation stretching across the UK is way too extensive to cover in detail, even in a book as lengthy as this one; the discussion here can only lift up the rug for a brief peek.

Where are the regulations coming from? Let's look at some of the key natural habitats of the lesser-spotted regulation:

- retained EU law
- home-grown regulation
- regulation from moral panics

We discuss each of these in some detail.

Retained EU law

In the UK, the rapid growth of regulation over the past half century has been turbocharged by the UK's nearly fifty-year membership of the Common Market or EU. With the UK's increasing subservience over the years to innumerable force-of-law directives from Brussels, a roster of laws have increasingly come to prevail in British law and business governance, imposing more and more rigidity both on business and on life in general. Regulations and regulators have flourished and metastasised.

The impact of EU law in general on EU countries has been that economic growth there has, over the past three decades, been the slowest of all the major economic areas in the world, except for a very few obvious outliers (see Chart 2.63). The UK suffered the same fate because it accepted these regulations.

The UK had managed, from time to time (e.g. in the late 1990s), to grow a little faster overall than the core EU countries. It had done that by occasionally opting out from more egregious regulations where it could, and sticking to common law and common sense in those areas where EU directives had not yet replaced them. But after fifty years in the EU, the regulatory mindset has taken hold in our country. It will take an enormous effort to root it out if we wish to return our country to a level of economic growth that will bring levelled-up prosperity to all our people.

Chart 2.63: World: 2023 GDP Growth by Country

The EU's regulation approach seems inimical to growth.

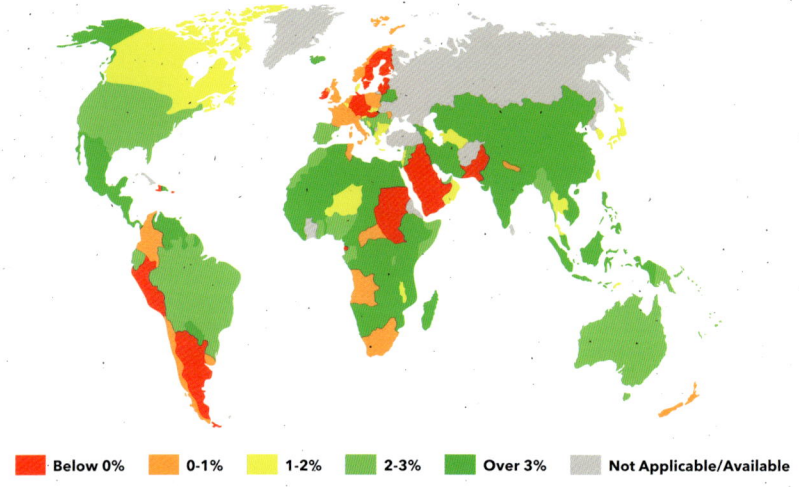

| Below 0% | 0-1% | 1-2% | 2-3% | Over 3% | Not Applicable/Available |

Source: International Monetary Fund[13]

Particularly over the past thirty years since Maastricht, we have had an enormous pile of anti-competitive directives forced upon us by Brussels. (These directives were then often foolishly gold-plated by our own civil service's kind hand.) The 2023 EU Retained Law Bill was intended to kibosh all that, yet when the matter came to the crunch, the government yielded to resistance in the civil service and bottled going through with the abolition of most of those laws.*

The belief that there's no problem that can't be solved with a bit more regulation goes deep. A classic example of this – the source of

---

* Some civil servants are making valiant attempts to continue with the deregulation initiative on retained EU law; they even have a website detailing progress on that. Actual abolition of the most egregious laws is not really happening: the reports we read mostly seem to discuss processes, rather than outcomes, in trying to get rid of these retained EU laws. See 'Retained EU Law – public dashboard', https://app.powerbi.com/view?r=eyJrIjoiMDY2MjAwZDMtMzcwOCooZjc4LTk3NDQtMzNkNDIyMTlhYTcwIiwidCI6ImNiYWM3MDAaLTAyYzEtNDNlNlYiriNDk3LWU2NDkyZDFiMmRkOCJ9&disablecdnExpiration=1715290751

much of our economy's ills – is the so-called precautionary principle. At its worst, for example in the EU's blanket ban of genetically
modified crops, it leads to appalling decisions such as the refusal
to allow cultivation and import of golden rice, a product which
is widely acknowledged to have the potential to reduce blindness
among hundreds of thousands of Vitamin A-starved citizens in underdeveloped countries.[14] Four hundred million poor people in the
world depend on rice. Half a million a year go blind; half of those
die within a year of their going blind.[15] All, as the critics of this ban
plausibly claim, because of the precautionary principle.* Regarding
this and many other examples, the Nuffield Council on Bioethics,
alluding to the EU's bans, stated, 'There is a compelling moral imperative to make genetically modified crops in developing countries
who want them, to help combat world hunger and poverty.'[16] The
green campaigner Mark Lynas has stated that 'children could die
because of Greenpeace's Golden Rice activism'.[17]

Application of the precautionary principle is not confined to the
EU: in particular, drug regulators around the world apply it. As just
one example, two decades ago the Food and Drug Administration
banned the effective and cheap antihistamine Seldane because heart
irregularities had been detected among a few elderly gentlemen who
had taken it. Now, in my view, the obvious sensible decision to take
would have been to provide warnings to elderly gentlemen (such as
myself) to beware of taking this drug, or at least to advise them to
be cautious as regards the potential impact on their hearts. Instead,
the FDA took the drug off the market instantly, banning all people,
not just elderly gents, from using it. It is not so much the several

---

* It has been alleged by some that the application of the precautionary principle in this case was part
of a cynical manoeuvre by the rice-selling companies who were in competition with golden rice. The
precautionary principle is, of course, applied in many other cases to hold back innovation.

billions of dollars of revenue that Seldane's manufacturer lost or the jobs lost thereby in that company that are the chief problems but what lay behind those losses: the disappearance of the huge amount of benefit and convenience that the over 100 million worldwide users of that antihistamine had enjoyed. Possibly not coincidentally, more expensive, *not* off-patent antihistamines saw their revenues soar as they took over much of Seldane's market share. (Remember what I wrote earlier about companies rent-seeking from government – or, in this case, seeking it from government agencies.)*

Home-grown regulations

Post-Brexit, we in the UK have added to and continue to grow our own list of homemade, growth-defeating regulations. There have also been many initiatives seeking to address that excessive regulation, notionally from, and directed by, the government. The most considerable of these was the TIGGR report, led by Sir Iain Duncan Smith MP reporting to then Prime Minister Boris Johnson.[18] This report contained a treasure trove of potential initiatives, across many sectors. And there are many other such reports on the opportunities for deregulation from individual industry bodies. There was very little response by government to any of these proposals apart from the work done in 2023 by the excellent government minister Andrew Griffith and subsequently followed up on by Minister for Business and Trade Dominic Johnson. Both of them had their remits clipped by the Sunak government.

Constraints on the individual reached florid levels during the

---

* To be fair, fear of brutal class-action suits in America, often based on entirely unscientific claims, may also have affected this and other withdrawals of drugs from the marketplace. But that speaks to the need for tort reform in the US; and the UK doesn't suffer from such suits so didn't need to follow the US.

Covid crisis and that is now, it seems, somewhat regretted given the lack of scientific justification behind some or even most of the actions taken during Covid, and the growing evidence of the damage caused by them. 'The pandemic's toll on schooling emerges in terrible exam results,' said *The Economist* – just one of many disastrous long-term outcomes from the way we treated young people during the pandemic.[19]

Regulation extends its tendrils everywhere. The Independent Business Network highlighted twenty-three areas where regulation is throttling growth, as seen in Chart 2.64.

Chart 2.64: IBN List of Growth Areas Throttled by Regulation

The Independent Business Network identified numerous areas where deregulation was needed.

• Health and safety at work regulation • Data protection regulation • Ports services regulation • Agriculture and fisheries regulation • Value Added Tax (VAT) regulation • Waste management regulation • Food information labelling regulation • Employment regulation • Artists' resale rights regulation • Energy efficiency regulation • Road transport regulation • Consumer product safety standards regulation	• Habitats licensing regulation • Boatmasters licensing regulation • Pensions governance regulation • Environmental impact regulation • Financial regulation • Agriculture-related regulation • Driver licensing regulation • Public procurement regulation • Sales of goods regulation • Network and information system security regulation • Recognition of professional qualifications regulation.

Source: Independent Business Network[20]

Clearly, there is a massive set of opportunities to amend or remove regulation across the economy. The following sections, not intended to be comprehensive, point the way to the more systematic, thoroughly supervised deregulatory process that would be needed to capture all the potential benefits from deregulation. Here, then, are some key problematic regulatory situations currently in the UK.

Healthcare: clinical trials

Since the turn of the century, the UK's share of the global market in clinical trials has been steadily declining. Many blame the EU's Clinical Trials Directive of 2001: an article commented that the UK had lost dramatic market share (over 5 per cent decline a year) because of 'the additional burden imposed by the directive deprived the UK of its former regulator simplicity'.[21] A massive blow to our economy. The directive was repealed in 2023, but too late for us. The MHRA traditionally oversaw clinical trials very well but seems to have lost the will to recover, now that we are free of the EU. We haven't yet capitalised on our Brexit freedoms – in the past four years, the number of clinical trials in the UK has actually *halved*.[22] We should task somebody of the stature and reputation of, say, Sir John Bell to work with the CEOs of the big pharma and contract research companies to find out what they need to make the UK a centre for their clinical trials again and for them to indicate a commitment to investing significantly in their UK locations. If we don't again become a world centre for clinical trials, our chances of developing as an advanced technological economy will be considerably slimmer.

The UK also used to be global leaders in the development of medical devices, yet now the majority of such development is done in the US, Germany and the Czech Republic. Much of this is down to the requirements of the CE marking process – the key, clearly, is to get our own UK Kitemark (UKCA) that avoids some of the more egregious CE roadblocks.[*] [23] The UK has really good scientists in this area, but the actual business of getting approval for EU devices

---

[*] An attempt was made to make this happen in 2023 and, of course, it was abandoned. A more determined government should make sure it happens.

is nowadays mostly done in Germany. The approval process for UK devices needs to be repatriated. While the UK has backslid on its plans to introduce its own UKCA mark by now, it still intends to do that by 2028 and is piloting the Innovative Devices Access Pathway to get good new products swiftly into the NHS. So, all is not lost there, but for now, it's just talk – not action.

Further, we should allow mutual recognition of devices and pharmaceutical products that have been approved for use in any other compliant country. This is a more general free trade point, which would, if accomplished, power up global sales of products as soon as they are approved by the MHRA.

Financial services

Regulation in the City has metastasised, sometimes to an astonishing degree. Rupert Lowe correlates this directly with the City's decline.[24] The number of regulators – the Bank of England, the Treasury, the Financial Conduct Authority, the Prudential Regulation Authority – expands and as each expands, so does their regulation. Together, they have a budget of £2 billion and 15,000 employees. Much of their regulation is self-invented, not created by legislation. There is, right now, a major opportunity for the City of London to recover its place as the world's leading financial services hub. The alternative is to see continued disastrous decline. Here I offer one overarching principle; one specific, badly needed reform; and a more detailed look at what needs to be done about the rolling catastrophe of the London Stock Exchange.

- Return to a principles-based, not the current rules-based, regulatory and compliance regime. This was how it used to be. The panic of the 2008 financial crisis led to massive, self-defeating stringency that entrenched incumbents and reduced both innovation and customer benefits.

- Dump or replace the Markets in Financial Instruments Directive 2014 (MiFID). Although it was intended to create a more transparent and competitive financial market, MiFID has failed to achieve its objectives and discourages the creation of new firms, primarily due to excessive (retained) EU regulation. Again, some steps have been taken here – but now we have a new government so all that will stop.

For both of these points, there are plenty of people in the City who are hugely qualified to help shape the needed regulatory reform. Note, however, that those wanting reform will in the main tend to be challengers or mid-size players. The incumbents love regulation because they can afford it, have in the main already implemented its requirements and have built systems to deal with it. It may lower their productivity, but they can live with that because, for now, the regulations keep their competitors out of the market as a function of the huge costs of building compliance from scratch. So, don't let incumbent institutions dominate the change process.

The London Stock Exchange

There is little public understanding of how ever-increasing regulation is coming closer and closer to destroying the UK's stock market. Apart from MiFID, a precautionary principle-type war on UK shares has been conducted by regulators since around 2000 and, in particular, through the Pensions Act 2004. For defined-benefit pension fund beneficiaries, they said all such funds should be mostly in government bonds. Great for UK governments over two decades, as their deficits were funded by these investments, but the requirement led directly to the leveraged LDI fund crisis of 2022 and the toppling of the Liz Truss government. And it may have cost you and me, dear reader, if public-sector entities with funded pension schemes lost money, which would then need to have been replenished by the taxpayer.

Above all, this mandate, having pushed these pension funds into government bonds, lowered the funds' overall investment in UK equities from a robust 53 per cent to a tiny 6 per cent, as shown in Chart 2.65.

Chart 2.65: Allocation of UK Pensions to Equities and Bonds 1997–2021

Regulation and legislation pushing the UK's pension funds into bonds have had a devastating impact on the equities market in the UK.

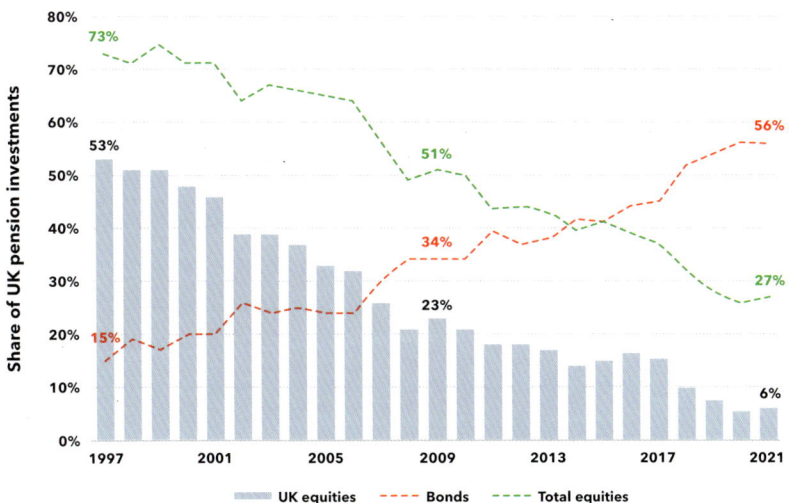

Source: moyniteam and New Financial analysis of data from the ONS, LGPS Advisory Board, PPF, Willis Towers Watson, UBS[25]

This, in essence, reduced the amount which these funds invested in the UK's stock market by some £1.4 trillion, as shown in Chart 2.66.

Chart 2.66: Allocation of UK Pensions to Equities 1997–2021

Had the UK's pension funds kept the same proportion of their money in UK equities, £1.4 trillion more than currently would by now have been invested there.

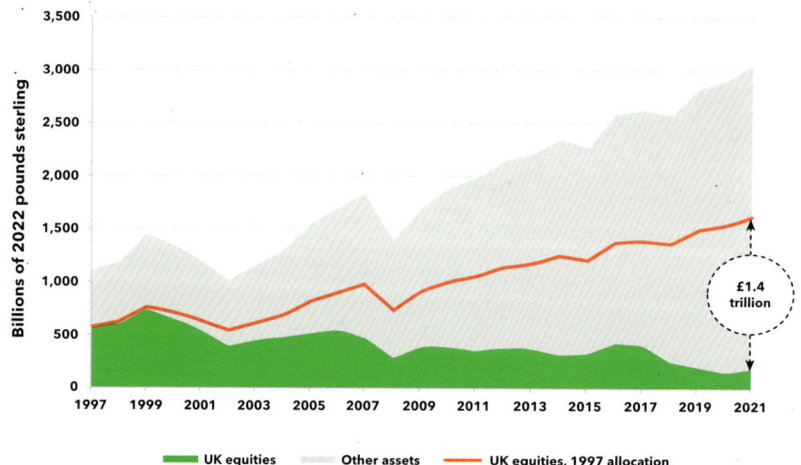

Source: *new moyniteam analysis of financial data from the ONS*[26]

A major stock exchange relies on many things, including a sensible regulatory environment, which London no longer really has.[27] But one thing is crucial if stocks on that exchange are to trade at reasonable prices: a deep pool of domestic liquidity. The UK no longer has that; the extraordinary sum of £1.4 trillion has been withdrawn from the liquidity pool. The total value of LSE shares is some £3.2 trillion, so almost half of the money that could be invested there has been removed because of this mandate. UK shares now trade at a 40 per cent discount to NYSE shares.[28] It's not surprising when companies list. with NYSE and NASDAQ, rather than LSE.

A final needed step to free up our financial markets is to remove all DEI/ESG constraints, currently imposed by both regulators and fiduciaries. Otherwise, sensible companies migrate to less woke exchanges.[29] We discuss this later in this chapter.

Employment

A major reason why many of our neighbours have such high unemployment levels is the view, urged on by unions and big corporates, that the more employment regulation there is, the better. The UK has avoided this trap, due to the reforms Lord (then Peter) Lilley put in during the 1990s, but that advantage has gradually been eroded as we since adopted more and more EU directives and added our own silly laws. (The new government's workers' rights bill will make things worse.) Professor J. R. Shackleton's paper 'How to Create New Jobs',[30] published in October 2020, outlined a swathe of already-needed deregulation:

- Occupational regulation and licensing: almost one in five UK employees (19 per cent) require a licence to work – a proportion that has doubled in the last fifteen years. Examples include taxi drivers, private security guards, heavy goods vehicle drivers, care workers and, most obscurely, farriers (someone who puts shoes on horses; you must undertake a four-year apprenticeship to get this licence). Recent further examples include childcare staff, security staff, private investigators, estate agents, social workers, plus the absurdly damaging requirements for graduate-only police and nurses. An IEA document titled 'Conspiracy against the public?' – which it is – pointed out that in the regulation-heavy EU, out of twenty-seven countries, only four (Slovenia, Austria, Poland and Czechia) have more regulated professions than we do.[31] We regulate 131 professions. Why? Estonia regulates fourteen, Germany and Italy both have eighty-six, France has ninety.
- Apprenticeship schemes: apprenticeships are good, but the apprenticeship levy is mostly an expensive farce, limiting employers' ability to use funds for appropriate retraining by tying them to

phony apprenticeship rules.[32] As I proposed earlier, in Chapter 7, the levy should be canned, but more than that, the whole scheme should be mostly shelved. (The new government seems to agree.) The levy and the complicated arrangements and requirements around it need to be dumped; they make companies less likely to succeed and less likely to grow organically.

- Pension auto-enrolment: pension reform should attempt to maximise the number of people who have a preference to save but because of inertia choose not to, whilst minimising the number of people who remain contributing due to inertia but for whom it is not rational to save. The following three reforms would move the scheme in that direction whilst reducing burdens on employers.

  - Increase the minimum earnings threshold that requires auto-enrolment to £15,000 a year and index it to inflation. This would roughly triple the minimum contribution and make it meaningful – i.e. avoid a costly bureaucracy of low contributions that would yield annual pensions of only £10–£15 from the age of sixty-five.
  - Increase the age at which individuals are auto-enrolled to twenty-five.
  - Reduce the employer's obligatory contribution to zero, however much the politically difficult taunts would fly.

- Agency worker rules: workers employed via agencies currently have the right to full employee status after twelve weeks working for a company. Agency working is important for employers trying to test the water in today's fragile economy, without committing to permanent contracts. Current law gives agency workers full employment rights too early and this raises costs and lowers employment. Flexibility is hugely important for giving a boost to the recovery. Recent laws treating some gig economy workers as full-time hit economic growth badly.

• Minimum wage and national living wage: regulations are created often from moral sentiments, but this, as so often happens with a scolding approach, can have the opposite effect of what was intended. The economist Douglas McWilliams was traditionally a supporter of the minimum wage but now thinks it has been too greatly increased by Chancellors wanting to be kind-hearted but not understanding the ramifications of having imposed these increases, which are now badly damaging economic growth.[33] The entrepreneur (now Prisons Minister) James Timpson, whose family business employs ex-offenders with criminal convictions among his 5,600 staff, stated that Britain is now in a new era of government-directed pay deals: 'The government is now in control of how much we pay people in this country.'[34] To pay his staff so much more, his prices have to be raised: his company will do less business and fewer people will be employed. Other business leaders echo Timpson's experience.

These are just a brief sample of the onward march of employment regulation in the UK; the new government has nebulous but ominous-sounding plans in this area. Even before that, journalist Matthew Lynn, noting in early 2024 that we had one of the highest minimum wages in the world, with new permissions requiring acceptance of 'flexible working arrangements' from day one of any new job and with financial incentives to move toward 'inactivity' even among younger workers, stated, 'Britain is squandering its last remaining competitive advantage.'[35]

Intrusive nanny state

Data protection

The GDPR regime is inherently protectionist: its prescriptive and complex requirements mean small companies find it expensive to ensure compliance. They lack the resources to monitor and record compliance with GDPR, which also obliges businesses to have a dedicated data protection officer. The Information Commissioner's Office (ICO) doesn't help; it investigates and fines private companies in an often-Orwellian process. Smaller firms might choose to risk sanction so as to avoid the substantial compliance costs, making GDPR self-defeating.

These things should be determined by freedom of contract. The whole thing is a huge drag on productivity, both for providers and users – if you add up the number of times millions of people are clicking 'I accept cookies' on webpages over and again every day, you can easily imagine the vast seething cauldron of irritation and resentment among its victims – a process that lowers productivity and economic growth with every click. Indeed, the whole GDPR regime is an enabler of fraud because no one ever bothers to read any of the verbiage – the whole nation would grind to a halt if people did.

Personal and lifestyle

Significant economic growth and development of world-beating capability in the UK could be created by developing products related to individual freedom and personal lifestyle; yet here, the full blast of the nanny state has been deployed. 'For our own good', both left- and right-wing governments have deployed Pigouvian taxes, government propaganda, outright bans and a growing array of nudge units, doing work to subtly persuade citizens into (often

unknowingly) embracing desired government policies.[36] Rishi's initiative to ban all smoking now becomes Keir's. This overregulation
is illuminatingly documented by Christopher Snowdon.[37]

We should, instead of reflexively banning stuff, repeal Article
20 of the Tobacco Products Directive, which created petty and
pointless regulations for the sale and promotion of e-cigarettes and
e-cigarette fluid; and repeal the ban on menthol cigarettes, which
is a legacy of EU membership and which currently fuels the UK's
already large black market for tobacco. Similarly, remove the ban on
retailers being able to recommend reduced-harm tobacco products
to customers. And, of course, abandon the outrageous upcoming
laws on banning cigarettes altogether.*

Childcare

Due to restrictive laws, many mothers can't afford childcare; the
cost is among the highest in the OECD. We should reduce the cost
by softening the regulation. For example, UK regulation only allows
one carer per four infants under the age of two. France has one per
eight or twelve infants, Ireland one per six or eleven (depending
on circumstance) and Denmark, Germany and Sweden have no
mandatory requirement.[38] This would allow more mothers to send
their children to more affordable childcare centres, thus liberating
mothers, giving joy to them and growth to the economy.

Hospitality

- Restaurants: keep an eye on whether employment restrictions
  in this area shouldn't be relaxed even more.[39] Consider allowing
  more hiring from abroad (without dependents and only if the

---

* The author does not (in the main) smoke. He believes in the liberty of individuals to make their own
choices on the matter.

employer provides private healthcare for the immigrant for the first five or seven years, so they are not a strain on the NHS).

- Pubs: help pubs get back on their feet by allowing designated smoking rooms if the owner desires. Christopher Snowdon has explored the issue and has also suggested we halve alcohol duty, to bring it closer to the European average and get rid of some smuggling.[40] This could help pubs bounce back, helping many from going bust, as so many are at the moment.

Energy
- Safe nuclear energy: despite having the science base to do well in this area, we are being outcompeted by (for example) the US and Canada, who are now racing ahead on new nuclear energy. We need to figure out what is stopping people in this country from doing better at developing fusion or molten salt reactors, when governments are already handing out contracts for the latter in Canada and the US.[*] The biggest obstacle to moving forward with safe nuclear energy is regulation that is unhelpful both to development and to safety. Jack Devanney, a campaigner on the issue, has laid out the issues in numerous blogs, showing how nuclear could be made both safe and very cheap if regulation was more sensible.[41]
- Hydrogen: some say it has a big future, others that it will always be too expensive. It shouldn't be for us to judge. One UK manufacturer, JCB, is pouring hundreds of millions into innovative new hydrogen-powered machines that, if they succeed, could be as successful as Tesla has been. We should not regulate to make it difficult for people to develop new hydrogen technology in this country.

---

[*] Declaration of interest: I have an investment in a molten salt nuclear power generator company.

- Fracking: as we all know, using fracked gas* has a far more beneficial impact on lowering our carbon emissions than most green approaches. The current ban on fracking in the UK is a perfect example of the irrationality of moral panic-driven regulation. Fracking would be a major geopolitical defence against Russia's, Iran's and Venezuela's encroaching gas hegemony. And it would slow the steady drain of jobs away from UK companies that are high consumers of energy, a drain that is sending our manufacturing bases off to China, Germany and the US. When these jobs go to China or Germany, global pollution increases, not decreases: those two countries rely so much on coal that global emissions rise when the production of UK factories is relocated there.

Food

- Fishing, processing and exporting: many expert commentators, such as Sir John Redwood, have written compellingly on the various ways in which our fisheries policies could be re-formulated, both to improve fishing stocks and to support our fishing industry.[42] I don't elaborate any further on this area here but refer to those many documents, with the overall suggestion that considerable benefit could be captured for the environment, for our fishermen and for our fish processing industry, were those more sensible policies to be adopted.
- Cultivated meat: even the most impeccably woke business initiatives can be regulated out of existence. Ross Tucker, co-founder of a company making real meat grown in petri dishes, complains that retained EU law is preventing him from building a world-beating business.[43] Singapore has had a new supportive

---

* Which of course we do: we import it from Texas.

regulatory regime on this since 2019. Meatly, the cultivated meat company, now has permissions from the half-dozen UK regulatory authorities – but only to grow 'meat' for pets! Others consider moving to the US.[44]

- Agriculture: even greater (and green) opportunities are being held back by retained EU law, which permits new crop strains produced by exposure to nuclear radiation yet forbids gene silencing and editing and other genetic modification technologies that can improve crop yields tremendously while massively reducing the need for pesticides.[45] This is an optimistic future for the world being ignorantly held back through doctrinaire ignorance; if we embraced it, we could create world-beating businesses that would save life *and* the environment.

Housing, building and planning

- Planning: relax size restrictions and minimise green regulation such as net neutrality, biodiversity, net gain, protection of bats and newts and so on. Require councils to decide planning within ninety days or automatic permission is granted. Remove planning restrictions on any building with one mile of a tube station in London. Sorting out the huge housing problems caused by our planning system would provide enormous benefits for our citizens. A lengthy report[46] by Kristian Niemietz, discussed in later pages, shows how.
- Categorisation: de-regulate to allow easier switching from retail to housing, work or living spaces – especially to save our high streets. Allow streets to vote by majority for zoning changes.
- Green belt: reform the green belt. It has grown significantly in recent years. We should allow construction on parts of it,

especially on brownfield sites and on parts close to train and tube stations and city centres.

- Labour says it will do a lot of the above. Let's see.
- Stamp duty: this is mostly a tax issue, already discussed. But it is also a policy/regulatory issue, because mobility of labour is a crucial requirement for economic growth, and stamp duty deters people from moving home – they would lose too much wealth if they did. It is not enough to say that increases in stamp duty lead to an overall increase in tax revenues; account needs to be taken of the very significant reductions in work mobility, economic growth and personal freedoms that these increases have led to. Radomir Tylecote and Sir Jacob Rees-Mogg explored these policies in their paper 'Raising the Roof', released in 2019.[47] A few of their proposed changes were put in train.

The pharmaceutical industry

Attacking pharma has led to AbbVie and Eli Lilly pulling out of their drugs agreement with the UK, with AbbVie declaring the government's policies are having 'a demonstrable impact on our ability to operate sustainably in the UK'.[48] In turn, Bayer has stated that it is now deprioritising Europe and the UK and that these countries are making 'big mistakes'; in particular, the UK expanding the medicines levy and other retrospective taxes and forcing Bayer into price cuts.[49] The pharma industry was, until recently, a jewel in the crown of the UK's economy, but over the past couple of decades, companies such as Pfizer have been pulling out of the UK and now others are following suit. An environment that is friendly to pharma, including the tax environment, needs urgently to be rebuilt.

Transport
- Deregulate public transport fares and end taxi licensing. A short brief on this topic can be found at the endnote.[50]
- E-scooters: Allow their ownership and widespread use. Possibly impose speed limits and certainly restrict their use on pavements, but in general, be as liberal as possible. These scooters are, of course, far better for the environment than cars.
- Please (a probably now in-vain plea) don't nationalise rail: the muddleheaded cry for rail nationalisation (and nationalisation of other utilities) that has gone up from people who are old enough to remember, and thus know better, shows how swiftly people forget how appalling the UK's nationalised services were prior to their privatisation.

Business in general

Just one of many potential examples here: the chief executive and leader of one of our key computer chip companies, Paragraf, says that red tape is throttling his company. It took them one full year and £1 million to install just one power cable. He notes he is constantly approached to move to the US – Arizona, Indiana, North Carolina.[51]

As can be seen from the far-from-complete list above, the opportunities for deregulation are enormous. The positive impact on growth that would be achieved by implementing even a portion of them would be substantial.

Regulation from moral panics

Looking objectively at events over the past decade or more, an astonishing new social, political, economic and regulatory front has been opened up by the 'we know best' crowd, and by less rational but strident elements of society, that now exerts a major negative force on economic growth. The phenomenon has now spread across western society but, for some reason, most of all in English-speaking countries such as the UK. It seeks to constrain people, organisations and companies in what they do through strictly defining what we might call goodthink versus badthink and by then sanctioning both organisations and individuals should they choose to step outside those strictly defined, allegedly moral, bounds. Many jokingly characterise this trend as political correctness or woke, but it's serious: the strictures have rapidly transferred themselves across into the regulatory sphere in a way that allows massively growth-destroying impositions across the entire economy. Combined with the general mushrooming of regulation over the past few decades, if this 'moral panic' trend continues to grip our institutions and businesses then the combined mass of regulatory blocks to growth could well doom our country to significant *negative* growth.

The trend to limit free speech – or even free thought – has morphed into a doctrinaire imposition of various quasi-religious obligations, presented as societal imperatives, on all persons and entities, with associated legal requirements and vast pressure to conform on these issues.[52] Chart 2.67 shows that just about every year now for the past decade or more, a new fanciful concept – mostly lacking in any kind of solid academic, scientific or even logical basis – is attempted to be imposed across society on both commercial and on non-commercial institutions. The latter includes schools, academia in general, our armed forces and police, the civil service and even the House of Lords.[53] The result is an increasingly indoctrinated society with regulations that clumsily seek a millennial nirvana, more and more divorced from reality and less and less likely to engender an entrepreneurial and growth-creating environment.

Chart 2.67: A Decade and a Half of Moral Panics, 2010–24

Almost every year now, society comes up with another quasi-religious imperative in a rolling series of moralistic campaigns, which collectively threaten to destroy the ability of organisations to pursue their core missions.

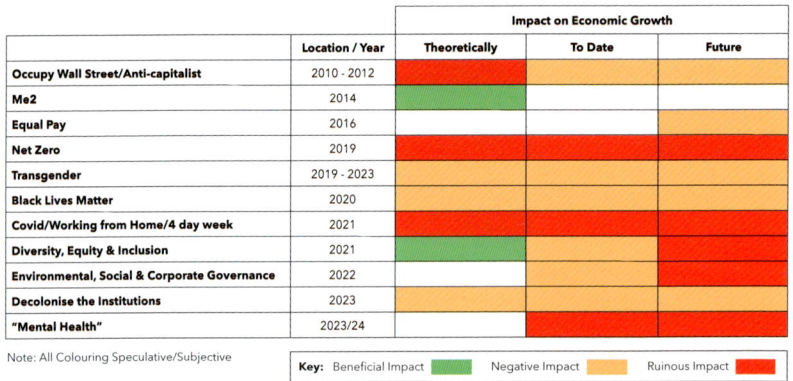

	Location / Year	Impact on Economic Growth		
		Theoretically	To Date	Future
Occupy Wall Street/Anti-capitalist	2010 - 2012			
Me2	2014			
Equal Pay	2016			
Net Zero	2019			
Transgender	2019 - 2023			
Black Lives Matter	2020			
Covid/Working from Home/4 day week	2021			
Diversity, Equity & Inclusion	2021			
Environmental, Social & Corporate Governance	2022			
Decolonise the Institutions	2023			
"Mental Health"	2023/24			

Note: All Colouring Speculative/Subjective

Key: Beneficial Impact ▇ Negative Impact ▇ Ruinous Impact ▇

A good number of the ideas shown here could, at first sight, merely be descriptions of issues being discussed by a society that is only seeking to improve itself through discussion and public debate. I give them the name 'moral panics', however, because in general, we have treated them as catastrophic problems that need doctrinaire and tightly defined regulatory or legal impositions on society. Belief in 'we know best' has come to be so implanted and dominant in the political space that laws and regulations for each or most of these 'moral panic' items are proliferating while, especially in the public sector, courses indoctrinating employees in the relevant goodthink are often mandatory and HR processes are put into place that result in ludicrous posturing and restrictions within the workplace. The result is a major stultification of the kind of risk-taking environment that an economy needs if it is to grow.

In the following pages, I review a sample of these moral panics and their malign impact on growth:

- net zero
- diversity, equity and inclusion
- environmental, social and corporate governance
- mental health

Net zero

Regulations deriving from moral panics are not likely to end well. Consider, for example, what could go wrong with what is perhaps the biggest (and most growth-destroying) regulatory programme in the UK: net zero. For the net zero programme to work, *not a single one* of the following problems must become the case:

- The climate models that forecast linear then exponential growth in global temperatures caused by increasing amounts of CO_2 in the atmosphere turn out to be incorrect, just as so many similar scientific models have recently done. (The scaremongering models promoted by most net zero warriors have so far failed to eventuate.)
- The mitigating actions taken don't work in reducing CO_2. The UK causes less than 1 per cent of emissions worldwide. The major polluters – China, India, increasingly Africa – show no sign of reducing their emissions. Indeed, they are increasing them rapidly. So, will the existing stock of CO_2 reduce? Unlikely.
- The proposed mitigating actions are so unpopular that they are abandoned or evaded. Electric cars, anyone? Heat pumps? Already, the Labour government is stepping back from these.
- The cost of the mitigations is eventually seen as prohibitive and they are abandoned. Even the Climate Change Committee estimates the cost at £1 trillion; Civitas says it will be 'only' £5 trillion.[54] Of course, neither of these numbers is affordable.

- China and African countries go full steam ahead on coal-fired generators, which is exactly what's happening so far. In the case of China, this is in part to power the industries we have handed over to them; in the case of African countries it is because they are *developing* and *need to grow*.
- Other countries are not as enthusiastic at implementing net zero as we are (that also is the case so far).
- Other countries don't do it in the same timeframe as we are saying we will (that also is the case so far).
- CO_2 in the atmosphere doesn't reduce. This is the likely scenario; carbon will most likely keep rising until a cheap new technology emerges, which is unlikely to happen for decades.
- The reduced CO_2 in the atmosphere – if the reduction actually happens – has no major impact on temperatures or weather (the jury's currently out on that one).

Not one of any of these must occur if net zero is to work. Yet already several *are* currently the case. Many large economies are in practice ignoring net zero (while paying lip service to it, of course). The Conservative government had started stepping away from multiple aspects of the plan – let us see what Labour decide, when faced with the reality in the next few years. The forecasted cost of the net zero plan is going up and up, the energy-intensive sectors of the economy are already suffering badly, the claims on the affordability of the renewables approach look more and more shaky and the climate models are more and more coming under attack.

As the net zero hysteria has gripped harder, regulation and legislation doubles down, with seemingly net zero understanding of the central role played by oil and hydrocarbons in our economy – 54 per cent of our oil goes into products other than fuel. Consequently, we will be using plenty of oil for many decades to come. It is therefore important to produce as much oil as we can ourselves.[55] An early entry into these counterproductive regulatory stakes was carbon regulation, with complicated carbon credit regimes and the measuring and reporting of carbon emissions. Companies started reporting their carbon footprint and what they were doing about it. What could possibly be wrong with that? Bit by bit, those at the top of leading business organisations started taking their eye off the ball. Instead of serving their customers with the excellent goods and services that they were supposed to be providing, they capered to the tune of the regulators and pressure groups who pushed the government and regulators toward their own particular goals.[*] Now, even the trade unions are raising the alarm about this reckless dash to decarbonise; the GMB union says cutting carbon emissions is 'decimating working class communities.[56]

The cost to our country of being wrong on net zero (which the net zero warriors almost certainly are) will be enormous; so far, green regulations make things far worse, not better. Despite Theresa May's fact-free insistence that we are 'falling behind', the OECD says that our economy will be £60 billion smaller because of our foolish net zero by 2050 pledge (where we are, depressingly, further along than any other developed country as the first economy to halve emissions since 1990).[57] Even Dale Vince, whose company Green Britain Group has been at the forefront of the movement to transition to green energy, advocates against heat pumps.[58] And yet, the Conservative government doubled down. Sorrowfully saying at their last budget that they had little room to ease pressure on the

---

[*] There are, of course, many winners from carbon taxes and carbon credits; the winners (banks, large landowners) enthusiastically promote the idea while the losers, hit over the head with the moral outrage of it all, glumly pay up. The economy suffers.

taxpayer, they nevertheless decided to increase energy bills by £1.4 billion, so as to further subsidise wind power.[59] Labour will be far worse.

This book is about growth. It would be double the size, and doubly contentious, if it attempted to make a philosophical or moral case for or against a societal imperative such as net zero. But that's not necessary: I only need to show that an approach like that won't actually work. Let's take one example of the impact a moral campaign like net zero, sanctioned by the vast majority of the world's and this country's institutions, has had: it has resulted in multiple laws and regulations being imposed in the UK, with vast swathes of the economy (housing, transport, energy, home heating etc.) now essentially run as a communist-like central economy that defines what products can be bought, what their price must be, what products are banned and imposes huge fines for non-compliance.

One part of that is the requirement for all UK car manufacturers to have 22 per cent of their annual car production in 2024 be electric vehicles (EVs).[60] By 2030, that number must be 80 per cent and by 2035, 100 per cent. One of the UK's major car producers, Vauxhall, is now saying it will have to shut down production at two plants if the requirements are maintained.[61] (These requirements ensure, of course, that no new car company can start up with any new petrol-based technology, even if it was a brilliant, low-carbon innovation.)

Now, China dominates both the cheaper end of the EV market *and* its supply chain.[62] Around half of an EV's carbon footprint is in its manufacture.[63] Transportation from China to the UK increases that carbon footprint even more. And car production is just one industry that our short-sighted policies are transferring from the UK to China.

Chart 2.68: Coal-Fired Power Units in China, Early 2024

China continues to develop and give new permits for scores of new coal-fired generating stations, in complete violation of its announced green commitments

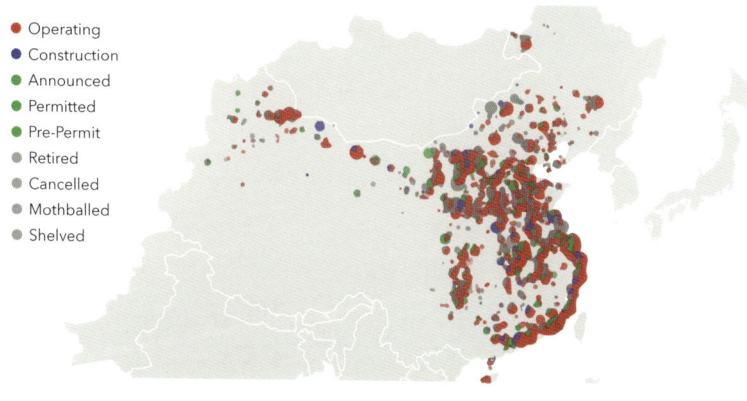

© *Global Energy Monitor*[64] *via Creative Commons*
Attribution 4.0 International Public License

China, whatever it *says* about meeting net zero targets by 2060, is *doing* the opposite, building two coal-fired power stations a week without restraint and using dirty coal (Chart 2.68).[65] Saying and doing are two different things, yet campaigners who are so passionate that the UK should immiserate itself with its dubious net zero programme seem indifferent to China's coal-fired expansion. As the *Wall Street Journal* put it, 'Last year, [China] reneged on its Net-Zero commitment with little public outcry'.[66]

The Global Energy Monitor and the Centre for Research on Energy and Clean Air (CERA) report that China is set to miss its 2025 climate targets. All the evidence, based on their actions, indicates the hollowness of what China has promised. CERA state that the building of new plants is 'accelerating further from the frantic pace of permitting two new coal power plants per week'.[67] Given China's continuing record of doing the opposite of what it has promised in so many areas, it is reasonable to claim that those who continue to praise or find credible China's intention to meet net zero targets are incredibly naïve and are handing large parts of our economy over to China, to the ultimate detriment of the climate that they claim they wish to protect.[68]

Thus, the effect of just this one net zero policy in the UK is to destroy one of our key industries, strengthen a totalitarian carbon-generating ideological opponent *and* increase the amount of carbon in the atmosphere. Bravo! Truly, a 'we know best' classic.

It is, of course, worth noting that any developing country that has much lower GDP than the UK would be insane to avoid building power stations, whether they use hydrocarbons, or coal. Indeed, most are going ahead with such power plants. The net zero approach of the UK amounts to a 'luxury belief', held by those in society who believe that such a policy will not significantly affect them personally. In that they are probably wrong, but for sure, the policies will massively affect the population overall, particularly those individuals and entire communities who lose their jobs.

Amid all the pious aspirations and wilful denial, the crucial issue of energy security has been lost. The world is now ideologically bifurcated, and unfortunately (almost inevitably), the hydrocarbons in the ground mostly belong to the bad guys. The major exception is the US, which has now both risen to be the world's largest hydrocarbon producer and seen the greatest reduction of its carbon emissions, *thanks to fracking*. But even there, Biden recently contemplated cutting off oil and gas exports to Europe. If that wasn't a wake-up call (and in the main it wasn't, however much we now strongly rely on fracked gas from Texas), then our level of fecklessness must be very high.

In 2022, our bill for importing electricity was some £120 billion.

Other countries are closing down their generator plants; what will happen if and when they choose to no longer sell electricity to us?* Some 40 per cent of our energy is said to come from renewables. What will happen on days that they fail, especially if we have closed down, or failed to build, standby gas generation plants? A leading French economist, Jean Pisani-Ferry, states, probably correctly, that economic growth will be negative in a world dominated by renewable energy before we get the supposed benefit of beating off climate change.[69] What will happen to our supply of hydrocarbons now that we have so comprehensively put off North Sea oil exploration and drilling companies and now that we have so foolishly banned fracking? Javier Milei, on the other hand, is bidding to create an economic boom in Argentina on the back of drilling and fracking.[70] And if New Zealand of all places decides that it's essential for its energy security to reverse its ban on drilling for oil, surely shouldn't we too?[71]

Instead of facing up to these undeniable and urgent issues, our politicians seem bent on ignoring them. Lord King, former governor of the Bank of England, states that the transition to net zero 'has turned into a quasi-religious debate'.[72] Car buyers are in retreat from EVs, yet the EV mandate will destroy the UK's car industry, and house owners will stay away from heat pumps.[73] Meanwhile, small manufacturers are required to fill in 300-question spreadsheets on their compliance with net zero.[74] The news of how unaffordable and unachievable net zero is finally beginning to leak out – even from the IMF.[75]

---

* A recent report in *The Times* stated that in February 2024, 25 per cent of the UK's electricity over one day came from overseas. It was not possible to identify the source of that electricity, and therefore also impossible to know whether it would be available in the future. See Tony Lodge, 'UK can't keep track of emissions with imported electricity', *The Times*, 6 May 2024, https://www.thetimes.com/comment/columnists/article/uk-cant-keep-track-of-emissions-with-imported-electricity-s9fqov6qf)

At certain times when writing this book, I have felt caught in a race against time when denouncing the more ridiculous of some of our public policies – nowhere so much as with net zero. It has always been inevitable that those governments round the world who actually believed in net zero would have to start pulling back as it was proved wrong, unachievable and unaffordable. If our government became, magically, one of those who quickly started to backpedal from much of the net zero stupidities, it would make all of my ranting in this book superfluous and outdated, possibly even before publication. I gritted my teeth, for example, when the government, having previously told us all that we were on course to get 100 per cent of our energy from renewable sources, suddenly (and, let me hasten to say, very much welcomed by me in the wider sense) announced in March 2024 that it was going to build a number of 'unabated' (that is to say, allowed to vent their emissions into the air) gas-powered generation stations.[76] An extraordinary outbreak of sanity. If stuff like this continued to happen, I thought, I'd have to start rewriting the book.

It looks, however, like I should not worry too much about all that: so long as I manage to get the book out sometime in the 2020s, the list of stupidities will be far too long for any UK government to get rid of them all before publication. For example, even if these gas power stations are built, we would still, in order to power them, have to purchase gas from Texas that had been fracked, piped to Houston, liquefied, shipped at great expense in special vessels across the Atlantic, brought ashore, regasified and then piped to that new-built UK power station. Brilliant.

The whole net zero crusade has inevitably become a festering mass of regulation, regulatory evasion, subsidy seeking and dodgy claims of success.[77] The green agenda is widespread and growing aggressively. For example, an organisation of the forty major cities around the world, C40, chaired by Mayor of London Sadiq Khan, has an aggressive, growth-destroying agenda ranging far and wide, with specific intent to tie down citizens of these cities across their entire way of life, from transport restrictions (ULEZ, 20 mph speed limits, take fewer holiday flights, own fewer cars) to consumption (purchase fewer clothes) to diet (eat less meat and dairy). The C40 mayors, recently benefiting from a £46 million donation from green hedge fund manager Sir Christopher Hohn, quite blatantly embrace the most extraordinary restrictions on personal actions and liberty.[78]

Quite certainly, the C40 programme, if implemented, will have a crushing effect on economic growth. See, for example, the C40 research report entitled 'The future of urban consumption in a 1.5°C world'.[79] The items in the report – aimed at enforcing fewer purchases of clothing, less meat and dairy consumption, fewer flights and reduction in car ownership – are not a wish list. They are firm intentions backed with developed action plans and planned legislation that will directly impact you and your personal consumption choices – plans that the mayors and their political operations are attempting to make compulsory through signing their country up to international treaties such as the Paris Agreement.[80] For reasons both of personal liberty and economic growth, you can be confident that such extreme constraints, planned to be coming in your lifetime, will have a strong negative impact on growth and significantly reduce the happiness of many humans – you, most probably, among them.

Net Zero Watch states that as far as employment levels go, planned energy policies from Labour's Ed Miliband will be a disaster for the working classes, bringing wholesale deindustrialisation and 'industrial closure on an unprecedented scale'.[81] With the closure of the Port Talbot steelworks and the many manufacturers that have already moved offshore, the direction of travel is clear; the question is whether we will be left with any industrial base by the time this foolishness ends, if it ever does. All these products will still be made, polluting as much as when they were made in the UK; the difference is that we will have created national economic ruin for the UK and enriched the other countries around the world, often our ideological enemies, that took up our manufacturing slack.

Diversity, equity and inclusion

Diversity

Diversity: the concept is based on the identitarian tropes of sex, gender, race and sexuality – not on diversity of thinking or of political viewpoint.

Diversity, when zealously pursued within an organisation, can play absolute havoc with an organisation's success and even its entire viability. Using language focusing on the – at first glance, praiseworthy and innocuous – objective of making sure that everyone gets a fair shot in an organisation, it quickly moves to an assertion, taken as gospel by SJWs, that a mix of types focusing on gender, race and sexual preference is crucial for success in an organisation. Lamentably, it is my old alma mater, McKinsey, who have provided spurious pseudo-scientific cover for this view, claiming that more diverse organisations have had more success. The findings have this year been reviewed extensively and thoroughly debunked by two scholars, Jeremiah Green and John R. M. Hand.[82] They state that the conclusions of the McKinsey work, a series of studies that are highly influential in the business world, cannot be replicated. They point out that the design of the analysis was, if anything, structured to show only that successful companies diversify their leadership, rather than that companies with diverse leadership become success-ful. Other papers by them and Chapel Hill's Sekou Bermiss find zero relation between diversity and the success of an organisation.[83]

The matter might, on the face of it, seem to be a storm in a teacup. If diversity doesn't make much difference either way, why not go for it anyway? But that's not the problem. What creates the havoc is what happens to any promotion process when you start insisting on quotas for and/or forced promotions of specific gender, race, sexuality. Let's take women as an example. Please excuse me, you many successful women who entirely deserve your places as entrepreneurs or your positions high in your organisations; I am not talking about you, although it must make you as cross as anybody else to see diversity hires casting an unfairly doubtful question on your own real achievements.

It is important to recognise, as I do, that women – the majority of whom will already be, or will become at some stage, mothers, with all the resulting potential complications to their work life – should be given every possible personal help, encouragement and support to remain in the workforce, to climb the promotion ladder and to be entrepreneurs. It is also important to ensure stringently that there is no pay discrimination against women in the organisation. Any other approach condemns talent to be sub-optimised.

Yet at the same time it is equally crucial to absolutely turn one's face away from any promotion of a woman *because* she is a woman, or from launching some initiative to 'find more women', or to seek to increase the number of women at any level in the organisation, or to require a given level of representation, at any level, by women. Why? Because doing that would mean prioritising ideology over common sense, putting weight on the individual's identity rather than only on their merit or capability, thus making hiring or promoting the wrong woman more likely, which would set up the organisation, and the individual woman, for failure. The same consequences can be likely for any hiring decision that focuses on one or another identity characteristics that the applicant holds, rather than on merit. The identity aspect should be ignored; it should not come into the hiring decision in any way.

The people who suffer the most from this are those of any particular identity who have been hired or promoted on pure merit and skill. Outsiders, looking at the decision, now wonder whether that person got the position because of their ability or as a diversity hire? Have they unfairly supplanted someone more talented who failed to tick the right identity boxes? If the promoted person in fact entirely deserves that promotion, will people know and understand that they are truly talented or will that person be unfairly tagged as a diversity hire who doesn't deserve their job? Should the leadership of that person be accepted, or subverted or worked around? If the organisation promotes on identity, then identity hustlers can work their way to levels that are astonishingly higher than their capabilities warrant and they will in turn promote more identity hustlers beneath them; the organisation can end up being led by scoundrels.

Equity
Equity moves us on from the praiseworthy objective of equality (usually taken to mean 'equality of opportunity') to equity, which, McKinsey proudly informs us, means 'equality of outcome'.[84] I would personally like to enter for the 100-metre sprint at the Olympics and insist on an equality of outcome, but were I to say that, people certainly should laugh at me and say I was being ludicrous. So why don't they say the same whenever equity, equality of outcome, is

advocated? This 'equity' in DEI is particularly pernicious, precisely because equality of outcome is unachievable. Outcomes differ among people for so many reasons: intelligence, charm, beauty, forcefulness, a roll of the dice, the serendipity of opportunity. If equality of outcome is promised, but not achieved, grievances will spring up and trust and harmonious working disappear. So, by promoting the 'E' of DEI, the woke warriors are guaranteeing to make their organisations dysfunctional.

But DEI is everywhere now many companies are signing up (incautiously, in my view) to be a B Corp. This includes the obligation, ultimately legally enforceable, to embrace DEI.[85] Case data from the Free Speech Union shows DEI policies are being invoked to penalise employees who voice unfashionable opinions on hot-button issues, with thousands losing their jobs for not going along with the DEI mantras.[86] We are told:

- Employees opining on gender, race, sexuality and religion risk being sacked.
- DEI policies are often compulsory for employees.
- One in twenty of the Free Speech Union's cases arise from DEI training, which is politicising the workplace.
- Organisations such as Coutts and the Church of England's investment bodies have signed up to the UN Principles for Responsible Investment – which encompasses DEI and net zero policies.
- Individuals are told that they will fail their DEI training if they don't pass with a 'sufficiently high score' (i.e. by parroting these untruths).
- DEI training materials present issues such as critical race theory, microaggressions or anti-racism as ideas not to be questioned.

- The organisation B Lab UK is seeking a change in the law to further embed these practices in British companies.
- The Better Business Act would see the Companies Act 2006 'amended to give chiefs a duty to consider "people and the planet", not just profit'.[87]

Nowhere are the woke DEI mantras being imposed more heavily, or causing more damage, than in the public sector. Take the NHS as an example. It has at least 800 DEI staff and spends over £100 million on DEI. Though, remember, that cost, large as it is, is not where the biggest damage is caused; the largest damage is done by the numerous ways in which DEI prevents people doing their job properly or well. Directors of DEI earn around £100,000 a year. Their job? To make sure hardworking NHS staff are put to work writing and filing numerous statements of various sorts to prove their compliance with DEI mandates.[88]

I could, but won't, continue over several more pages about the random yet highly important state bodies who've gone crazy over diversity, while neglecting their core tasks. It's a perfect storm: spending huge amounts of money to hire useless people who spend their time making sure the work of each of these enterprises is less effective. This happens right across the state and now is marching well on into the private sector. The problem will enter a deeper circle of hell with a Labour government who have promised a new Race Equality Act, which, as Daniel Hannan has pointed out, won't achieve anything.[89] UK companies everywhere are being assailed on environmental, social and governance (ESG), whether from regulators or from large B Corp-type companies who drive ESG (discussed more in a couple of pages) down into their supply chains.[90]

B Corps: A new, insidious approach

One of the most alarming new developments in the economy at this time is the mushrooming number of organisations that are electing to become 'certified B corporations' or B Corps. Those companies, according to parent company 'B Lab', are those who have been verified by B Lab to be meeting 'high standards of social and environmental performance, transparency, and accountability'.[91] Thousands of organisations around the world, a couple of thousand so far in the UK, are now signing up. To be certified, a company must have a verified high score on its 'impact assessment' and make legally binding amendments to its articles of association that no longer place its shareholders as paramount but consider employees, suppliers and customers as having equal standing.[92] This legally binding document will play havoc with economic growth. It will tie organisations into knots as politically-minded employees wrangle with management, opening these organisations up to legal suits, and it will have a chilling impact on discussions among the leadership (the document explicitly talks about 'leadership changes' as part of the signed-up-to legal requirement).

As this movement spreads, so will western economies further congeal. Our economic, and indeed ideological, opponents in places such as China and Russia must be splitting their sides with laughter.

Inclusion

Inclusion: making sure everyone is welcome (but not anyone who is repelled by the woke agenda, of course). This one's even more nebulous; it might formerly have been called 'manage people well, have a good EQ'. Nothing wrong with that, but when it gets in the way of managing the company towards proper outcomes for its customers or shareholders – as with the faddish and totally bonkers concept of 'reverse mentoring', say – it gets counterproductive.

A fightback of sorts is taking place: the founder and CEO of the highly regarded Scale AI (currently worth $14 billion) has announced their formal hiring approach, namely MEI.[93] The approach, endorsed by Elon Musk, emphasises merit, excellence and intelligence. The approach is a direct challenge to DEI. It will be interesting to see the survival rate and the investment performance of MEI versus DEI companies.

Environmental, social and corporate governance

These three magnificently nebulous terms allow any old politically correct nonsense to be imposed on companies; and thus is it happening. As moral panics proliferate, regulation proceeds to metastasise. The Financial Conduct Authority (FCA) now *requires*, via a 68-page ESG source book of 'rules and guidance', all 1,600 listed UK companies to report on and meet targets for their compliance with ESG.[94] This includes, for example, requirements for the percentage of board positions that must be held by women (40 per cent required) and ethnic minorities (1 member required), with details demanded on sex, gender identity and ethnicity of all board and senior management. These are not light regulations: read the report at the endnote and you will see there is a thicket of detailed requirements to comply with.[95] Many argue that the result of all of that has been numerous 'diversity appointments', with insufficiently qualified individuals being put in place because of their race or gender, leading to badly run, poorly led companies.

In the UK, we have now got to the stage of being in full tonto regulatory mode on such matters. We need hardly look any further than the FCA's ESG mandate to see why so very few companies are now listing in London. The three little words open the door to an infinity of accusations, regulatory actions and potential shareholder suits. They ensure that some companies, roiled by the need to comply, take their eye off the customer and do less well as a result, while others, rolling their eyes, go off to search other stock markets that don't enforce such cockamamie rules. As *Forbes* magazine recently headlined an article, 'Central banks and ESG investing: a fatal combination of incompetence and overreach.'[96]

The 'E' of ESG is leading to particularly damaging results. The impact of green policies on house building has been disastrous. 'Eco-fanatics are creating a new housing crisis,' said the chairman of the Growth Commission.[97] At least 500,000 houses need to be built in the UK every year, but we will be lucky to get 100,000 this year. Stringent neutrality rules mean a developer is fined £600,000 for destroying a home of a bat; habitat regulations mean 45,000 homes a year are not built, and the list goes on.[98]

Another ESG area, already discussed in the previous chapter on tax, is the Carbon Border Adjustment Mechanism (CBAM). It is reported that the UK plans to adopt it because the EU has adopted it.[99] Our pre-existing domestic carbon regulation has already sent the price of our homemade products shooting up, so they get made elsewhere in the world and our factories close down, but then we still need those products, so we import them back into the country (sorry about the lost jobs, growth and profit). So, now – the icing on the cake – we plan to charge those imported products with a CBAM tax, to increase costs to the consumer yet again. Pure, classic, EU-originated protectionism, disguised as environmentalism by using the EU's particular method of accounting for emissions.

Our decision to follow the EU's lead is yet another wasted Brexit opportunity.

The proliferation of regulation under the general guise of ESG doesn't stop, and each new regulation suppresses growth further. In 2023, we had 'nutrient neutrality' come to the fore – you can't build new houses unless they achieve nutrient neutrality, meaning that many homes have not been granted planning permission. In 2024, biodiversity net gain went live; mandatory for some buildings, voluntary (for now) for others.[100] This one means that essentially you won't be able to build housing developments unless there's a gain in biodiversity, so again, houses that are built will cost more to build and thus cost more to buy, making the housing crisis worse. Some house builders will give up, so fewer houses will be built.

So greatly has the ESG mindset invaded the HR function in commercial organisations that it – as with so many of these dubious moralistic campaigns – threatens to become firmly implanted into the mindset and behaviour of a large number of the UK's institutions and large companies. It is being imposed in the form of laws, legal rulings and regulations on the whole of society. It is society as a whole, but particularly smaller companies and lower-earning citizens, who will bear the brunt of the enormous losses in GDP that are already beginning to eventuate from these policies. My contention is that the economy is increasingly grinding to a halt as HR departments and woke-ised boards come to dominate more and more companies and other bodies, imposing more and more value-destroying requirements on these organisations, as the law is used to cement the cost of these panics on the whole of society.*

---

* Particularly human rights law, as imposed by the Equalities Act and the European Court of Human Rights.

Mental health

The latest moral panic, 'mental health', is at first glance relatively innocuous yet is potentially one of the more dangerous of these panics. The concept of the need to attend to, and cater for, the alleged psychological fragility of large swathes of society is spreading far and wide, adding enormous cost to the nation's welfare bill and creating a permanent class of 'kidults' in society who will further dent the economy's ability to become more productive.

The problem starts with ill-disciplined children, already suffering from two years of knowledge-destroying Covid lockdown, in schools that fail to have the proper disciplinary approach that creates order. This is bad enough because they grow up unable to interact properly and productively with society, but recent developments have made it even worse. In most ill-disciplined schools, children who find it difficult to settle down, instead of being required to stick to proper classroom behaviour, are now being given special educational need (SEN) status or being put on an Education, Health and Care (EHC) plan. The number of children with the latter rose to 576,00, an increase of 11.4 per cent, in 2024.[101] The focus of reports and discussion on SEN seems to be to medicalise behaviour problems, rather than (as 'warm-strict' schools do) insist on, and achieve, good behaviour from all.[102]

This problem, although exacerbated by Covid, has been growing for twenty years. These kids then move into the general workforce. As has been widely reported, the number of working-age adults off work with 'mental health' issues has ballooned, particularly post-Covid, and continues to grow.

Why this increase in mental fragility? Arguably, the answer is that the growing number of mental health conditions that we are seeing are, in the main, a state of mind within the normal healthy range of human experience. To a degree, this is possibly a lingering effect of the Covid era. But they are almost always not a medical condition. Better to ignore the complaint while advocating a more self-reliant approach to life. Having a job is better for depression or anxiety than sitting jobless at home. As discussed in Chapter 6, our social benefits system creates a significant financial incentive to claim a mental health disability instead. This comes at us in three ways.

First, the increasing medicalisation of stress. Stress has traditionally not been seen as a disability, but a court has now ruled that it can be if it is a long-term (twelve months) condition.[103] A very subjective matter, as you can see. This ruling will make employers liable for not dealing properly with the employee's problems – so now, all employers will have to jump to accommodate anyone who claims stress and who can show that the stress might last twelve months. This will require all sorts of accommodations or, very likely, the individual going on long-term disability and a PIP. Another condition analogous to stress is post-traumatic stress disorder (PTSD). The Borough of Hammersmith and Fulham were ordered this year to pay £4.6 million to a senior employee suffering from PTSD who they had fired.[104] The opportunities for compensation, and large amounts of it, seem to be growing rapidly.

Well-meaning over-concerns regarding mental health seem to have encouraged top-up payments for part-time workers moving out of unemployment. They instead incentivise individuals to move backwards from full-time work to part-time work, with the state topping up for the lost days. (Worse, individuals take a second job off the books and claim Universal Credit for the days they are supposedly not working.) Rules were recently changed to push people from part-time working to longer hours, but only up to fifteen hours.[105]

Has the decade of moral panics been good for the world?
All of the topics raised earlier in Chart 2.68 are important and deserving of consideration by any human being. Each of them, however, has been turned into a moral panic. In the end, almost all of them can be seen to be specious and indicative of a left-wing or identitarian view of the world, with demands that are extremist, absolutist and usually nonsensical. Wall Street and the City needed to be 'occupied'. Anyone remotely alleged (whether or not with evidence) to be a sexual harasser or predator has to be expelled from their industry and thus lose their livelihood. We must completely decarbonise by 2050. Shut down the entirety of society during Covid. Hire based on identity not talent. Make ESG compulsory for every listed company on the London Stock Exchange. And so on.
Now, for any one of the 'panics' listed in Chart 2.67, honest people can differ as to their importance and what society's response should be. It is not possible in this book to argue the toss on each panic – each deserves a full book to itself. But the chief issue is the likely efficacy of the actions and regulations proposed to address each supposed problem that has been stridently scaremongered about by the 'we know best' crowd, often with little scrutiny or debate as to the expected outcome, financial cost, or collateral damage.

Nobody arguing rationally can disagree with the proposition that if the management (or the employees) of any large organisation spend their time focused on these multifarious matters, their attention will be massively distracted from doing what the organisation has been set up to do. Many employees, particularly those who have only just joined the workforce, now believe that the primary purpose of their work for their company is to save the world – not to make and sell a product or provide a service.

In this discussion, I tried not to argue whether this or that item was right or wrong; rather, I tried to focus on the likely consequences of these approaches as they are being adopted. Are they feasible? What will they cost? Will they work? And above all, what will be the trade-off on the country's economic growth? The answer, for each, is almost universally negative. We need to snap out of our thraldom to moral panics.

Finally, whether looking at unemployment credit, universal credit or disability credit, there is now an insufficiently large financial gap between what you get from the state versus what you get from an employer from being fully employed.

The end result is proving catastrophic for the national finances. In early 2024, we were spending around £30 billion each year on various incapacity benefits and we are told that if the present trend of increase continues that will have risen to £48 billion – almost 5 per cent of our entire national budget – by the end of the decade.[106]

So, when deciding on payments to the unemployed and part-time employed, the belief that 'we know best', combined with the desire to 'be kind', has led to a situation where there is a catastrophically large and growing bill to pay, one that the economy cannot afford. This all has come about through a baffling and scientifically questionable moral panic labelled 'mental health'.

THE COSTS OF REGULATION, FINANCIAL AND OTHERWISE, ARE VAST

The chief negative repercussion of regulation, apart from the many demoralising constraints it lays upon the individual, is the way it distracts business from, and represses, economic activity. For people's standards of living to grow, the answer is not more regulatory jobs, more compliance jobs, more 'green' jobs – the answer is the liberation of individuals to be more innovative and better producers. Instead, we have regulation, whose costs are both direct (compliance costs) and indirect (loss of future growth). Michael Gove's war on landlords, for example, was said to risk 'billions for [the] economy and thousands of jobs', and, of course, it reduced the housing stock, as the put-upon landlords no longer bought and refurbished derelict properties.[107]

Regulation has semi-destroyed house building. In any country, much of its economic growth comes from the property sector, as citizens seek to house themselves and their families and as companies seek more or better premises. But it is now estimated that we have a shortfall of 5 million houses in this country. As the population grows and we still build at no more than a fraction of what's required, the gap increases. Strict planning regulations mean that not nearly as many houses as we need are being built. An entire generation is being failed as they grow to adulthood and find they cannot afford the few properties that *are* being built.

Governments like to ignore the basics of supply and demand. Demand continues to grow as our population expands (steadily and significantly, mostly because of liberal immigration policies). Supply, constrained by planning and green regulation, does not. Therefore, house prices just go up and up. Bizarrely, the government responds by punishing those who build or refurbish houses – developers, landlords, buy-to-let investors. How beating up these economic actors is supposed to increase our supply of housing is difficult to discern. But still more punishments come, both main parties agree: bans on no-fault evictions, confiscation of marriage value from freeholders, landlords blocked from letting if homes fail net-zero test.[108] A *Telegraph* article stated that 'the [former] government plans to force up to 2 million landlords to increase the Energy Performance Certificate rating of the properties', at a significant refurbishment cost per property. Isn't the new government likely to do the same?

Possibly the government thinks that landlords will then have to release some of their properties onto the market, with buyers snatching them up, but less than two thirds own. Renters need properties just as much as owner-buyers do. Landlords also do more than just buy and rent out houses; they improve and refurbish them too, using their capital to maintain and improve the housing stock. Developers, landlords and buy-to-let citizens inject capital and energy into the housing market and build houses themselves. Penalise them: you end up losing more housing. Change formerly rented premises into occupier-owned premises: the cost of rented accommodation (obedient to our old friend, the supply-demand law) shoots up. London, for example, has seen an almost 7 per cent annual increase in rental prices since 2006.[109]

A new requirement for holiday-let landlords to get planning permission before they can let their houses out led the *Telegraph* to comment, 'Gove's war on buy-to-lets will kill the holiday economy.'[110] And, as discussed, net nutrient and biodiversity regulations are preventing tens of thousands of homes from being built, and the end of no-fault evictions will take a lot of property off the market. Even the Competition and Markets Authority has now stated that the planning system is a cause of high prices and housing shortages.[111] Out of twelve large European economies, the UK is in eleventh place on housebuilding rates, better only than Sweden.[112]

A new report from the Adam Smith Institute shows the startlingly negative impact on wealth and growth in the UK from housing restrictions.[113] Construction of a new London house *costs* £300,000 on average, but shortages due to regulation and regulatory costs mean that the average *price* is £685,000. In other words, if regulation was eased sufficiently to allow an efficient market in house building, selling and letting, the price of a house in London could more than halve. According to the Adam Smith Institute (ASI), welfare per person would be boosted by around 12 per cent across the UK and real GDP would be increased annually by 3–6 per cent.[114]

And this is just in housing and building. Similar problems stretch across the economy and encourage an ever-increasing suspicion, and massive over-regulation, of both businesses and individuals. As Tom Hartley put it in the *Daily Mail*, 'From the local deli to Jeremy Clarkson's TV farm … Why can't meddling politicians stop stifling business?'[115] As another recent article put it before the election was announced, pointing to yet another growth-damaging regulatory own goal, 'The creeping criminalisation of business risks Hunt's plans for economic recovery.'[116]

The view of business as the problem, rather than the solution, is a socialistic, 'we know better' idea. The tendency of Conservative MPs and recent Conservative governments to adopt such a lefty outlook is odd; will Labour be better or worse than the Conservatives have been? Politicians, regulators and civil servants mostly don't have the experience of building or operating a business. In their ignorance, they blithely impose laws and regulations that shatter the potential for business to succeed. Low or no economic growth is the result.

MUCH OF THE TIME, REGULATION DOESN'T EVEN SUCCEED IN ITS OBJECTIVES

The classic example of how catastrophic 'we know best' regulation can turn out is the Lysenko story. The Russian agronomist Trofim Lysenko took a (then) semi-respectable, but later proven wrong, scientific theory called Lamarckism – the idea that the genes of organisms, such as plants and animals, are changed after their life has commenced and the changes are then transmitted from them to their offspring – and turned it into a nonsense dogmatism that became the prevailing and only agricultural method in Russia. From 1940 to 1953, Lysenko, as director of the Soviet Academy of Agricultural Sciences, was imposed ('The only correct theory' – Joe

Stalin) on all Russian crop-growing. The inevitable result: millions died of starvation in Russia. Amazingly – in 1958, when the theory had already been comprehensively discredited – the Chinese communists then picked these worthless ideas up and killed millions more.

Of course, nowadays, we superior beings smugly say that we would never fall for such pseudoscience as Lysenko's, particularly as we don't have Stalin's brooding presence to terrify us into agreeing any old stupidity. But we have a whole host of Al Gore-style prophets of the net zero era terrifying us into submission, with the threat of cancellation (get socially ostracised, lose your job and your livelihood, lose your friends and your marriage), with equally dubious and unproven assertions, not to mention the cringeworthy obsession that many senior politicians had with the short-on-facts Greta Thunberg. What makes us so sure that our society is any smarter, less prone to fall for scientific delusion, than the Lysenko-era Russians were? Particularly when we have so few STEM-trained politicians, so many politicians with a legal, history or PPE education – almost none of them with training in quantitative, logical thinking?

Every time the 'we know best' crowd seize control of the political discourse, the same thing happens. Ludicrous rules and regulations are imposed, all with the best of intentions, by people who can't possibly conceive that they might have got it wrong and who think that always 'there ought to be a law', despite Hayek's compelling proof that there's no way they can know best, that there oughtn't to be a law, that the best way to sort problems out is through free markets and democracy, not autocracy.

Reverting to China, the 'we know best' approach reached a zenith in the years after Mao came to power in 1949. The Chinese are among the smartest and most logical people in the world. But they were ruled by those who believed in communist collectivist approaches, where the guy at the centre would tell everyone what to do. Boy, did they manage to get it wrong, thrusting their ancient civilisation back into the stone age as a result of a series of quite idiotic promulgations:

- The Great Leap Forward 1958–62, primarily consisting of collectivisation, Lysenkoism and compulsory confiscations (as had happened twenty years before with the Holodomor). This is estimated to have resulted in somewhere between 15 and 55 million deaths.
- The steel component of the Great Leap Forward: household pots and pans and agricultural implements were ordered to be thrown into backyard furnaces across the entire country to make steel. Not an ingot of that steel was, it turned out, usable. With the near absence of basic utensils and implements, deaths rose to epic levels.
- The Cultural Revolution 1966–76: the violence against, torture, exile or murder of anyone who was seen as a dissident thinker or an intellectual. This encompassed ten years of violence, up to two million deaths and further economic decline.
- The one-child policy 1980–2016: China would solve its population problem by only allowing one child per couple. This was perhaps the biggest madness of them all.[*] As Chart 2.69 shows, it has ensured that by 2100, China will never be, as it had aspired one day to be, the greatest of the great powers. It will instead – now foreordained by the remorseless logic of the future ageing of China's existing population – be in catastrophic decline,

---

[*] Not least because it resulted in the murder of an estimated tens of millions of newborn Chinese baby girls.

burdened by an ever-more ageing population and with less than half the (more youthful) population of India.*

Chart 2.69: How the Demographics of China and India are Diverging
The impact of China's one-child policy

By the year 2000, the damaging impact of China's one-child policy could already be seen in the under-twenty cohorts. By 2100, China will be dominated by its elderly and its population will be half that of India's.

By 2000, an already-distorted pyramid in China leads to a catastrophic, collapsed, top-heavy pillar by 2100 and domination by India.

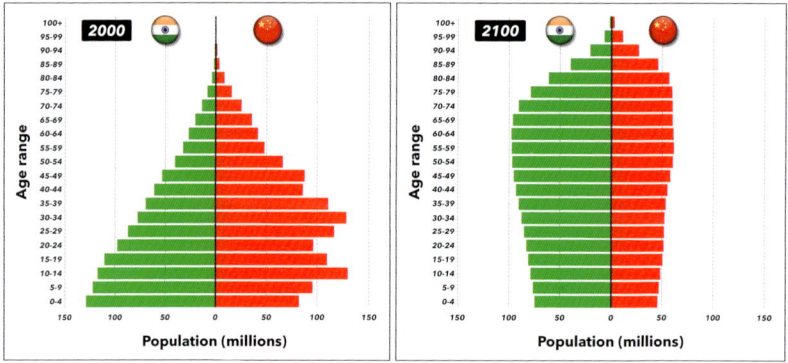

For an interesting animated version of how this plays out over the twenty-first century, see the link at the endnote.
Source: Visual Capitalist[117]

Dear reader, does this give you any kind of pause as you reflect on my list of moral panics in the earlier section? Remember, some really smart people in China thought all their own wheezes were very clever policies.

Like it or not, the Chinese have significantly higher IQs than

---

* India had attempted its own population control under Indira Ghandi, offering transistor radios to men who agreed to get the snip. Trouble is, the entire village then taunted any man walking round with a transistor radio and this led to the collapse of the policy. Ghandi's son Sanjay then tried compulsory sterilisation (11 million sterilised), but India was a democracy, hated the policy and its coercion, and inflicted electoral defeat on Indira. Sanjay died in a plane crash.

us Brits. Modelling the expected outcome of the one-child policy could not have been too difficult, had they wanted to. If they could, despite all that, screw up so colossally, is it possible that we ourselves might be on a path of emulating these past Chinese mistakes with our own 'we know better' foolishness?

• • •

So, even the smartest people can be totally, catastrophically wrong, if they rely on the view that the centre knows best, that decisions can't be left to the interaction of free markets and individual choice. The likelihood is, therefore, that bad outcomes will occur in the future because of existing regulation in the UK. Let's look at two practical examples in the UK right now: eco regulation and fraud prevention.

Eco: as we have seen, a lot of regulation these days comes into being as part of a belief that it is necessary to save the planet from hypothesised catastrophe. But as we also have seen, most of this eco regulation doesn't in the least have the effect that was intended; indeed, much of it makes the situation worse, not better. We have seen how, as we export our carbon emitting factories to places such as Germany and China, the overall amount of carbon and pollutants in the air increases. We see how a large number of expensive, impractical products, such as EVs and heat pumps, are forced on our citizens but rejected by them.

Fraud: a prime purpose of regulation is to prevent illegality and fraud. But they continue, regardless of regulation. Despite more and more anti-fraud laws and regulators, the amount of business fraud in the UK certainly has not diminished – it continues to hit the headlines.[118]

How to lower the amount of financial fraud in companies? Not by vague, box-ticking regulation. In the 2006 Companies Act, senior officers of the company became required to sign off the truthfulness of their company's accounts. What could go wrong with that? Financial fraud seems, since then, to have merrily continued and probably worsened (see later). It can accordingly be argued that the box-ticking mandate was a foolish piece of overregulation.

To this day, obeying regulations on financial certification takes up a great deal of every executive's time, requiring them to certify matters that it is pretty much impossible for them to know much about. It makes the job of being at the top of the company more perilous, since it exposes the senior individual to criminal prosecution for the criminal acts of others that, occurring at some lower level in the company, the executives don't have a hope of spotting. The entrepreneur Luke Johnson's travails with his company, Patisserie Valerie, spring to mind.[119] Criminal fraud is criminal fraud and should be dealt with robustly in the criminal courts – not with useless, counterproductive, time-consuming regulatory requirements. Mike Lynch's acquittal of fraud by a California jury again shows the superiority of courts over regulators.[120]

Worse, with the wave of additional regulation, the number of people working in 'compliance' within companies has risen exponentially.[121] Given these compliance bureaucrats' evident lack of impact on the occurrence of fraud, and in particular their lack of impact before, during, and after the financial crisis of 2008, it can be argued that their work was in the main nugatory (but amazingly costly).

This phenomenon of useless compliance people uselessly attempting to enforce useless regulation has to be at its worst in the financial services industry, which is still (but for how long?) the largest and most profitable industry within the UK, contributing over 10 per cent of government receipts from all taxes in the UK – £75.6 billion in 2020.[122] Since 2008, when the financial services industry around the world went into meltdown, any new problem in any *one* financial services company has led to further new regulations imposed on *all* financial services companies. For this reason, and others explored some pages back, the City of London may possibly be in terminal decline. Many financial centres around the world also have foolish regulation, which helps London keep its dominance, but not all. More sensitive and more thoughtfully regulated centres like Singapore are rapidly catching up with and overtaking the City. Advances in technology such as AI are leading to major stock exchanges exploring moving to 24/7 trading.[123] With (for example) the recent decision to create a new stock exchange in Texas, capitalising on Texas's favourable regulatory and tax environment, all this means that the City's dominance is even more threatened.[124]

The regulation-and-compliance regime on business is, of course, not at all limited to the financial services industry; it is imposed one way or another on all companies in every sector. Once started, the criminalisation of business proceeds continues without let-up.[125] Regulations made in the Companies Act 2006 were updated in the Bribery Act 2010, the Criminal Finances Act 2017, the Online Safety Bill and the Economic Crime and Transparency Act 2023. A huge amount of new compliance is required as a result.

And the imposition of those regimes was just the start! Stiff regulation and supervision over companies' financial reporting has helped a mindset develop among governments and regulators that there is no limitation to what might be thought of as being 'good' new regulation. Until a government comes to power in the UK that realises business is a good thing, and that the best way to let it flourish is to get out of the way and let the market decide, regulation will undoubtedly continue to metastasise.

It's important to understand how dubious the benefits are from anti-fraud overregulation. All over the world, regulators are failing in their basic duty to control fraud – a failure of the 'heavy regulation' approach, rather than an approach of having robust *caveat emptor* and criminal processes, with reliably severe punishments for convictions. The failure to prevent fraud is because the regulator is either just not spotting obvious frauds or is inevitably ten steps behind newly inventive fraudsters.

In Germany, regulators were totally fooled by the con men at the top of Wirecard. This company, the pride of Germany's private-sector economy, grew to have a market value of €24 billion, all based on fraudulent representations. The company's CEO, Markus Braun, has been in jail pending trial since 2020. The COO, Jan Marsalek, ended up in Moscow after going on the run – where in an interesting twist, details of which are still playing out, it now turns out that he was a long-time Russian agent.[*][126] Several billion dollars went, and remain, missing: the money trail went cold in the Philippines. All this came about despite the fact that most of the fraud, including the theft of the money, was of a common or garden accounting misrepresentation variety, which the relevant auditors and regulators totally failed to pick up on for years.

In the US, regulators have stumbled yards and years behind multiple frauds in the cryptocurrency sector. The poster child of this widespread fraud is FTX, whose market value rose at one point to $32 billion. Its chief executive, Sam Bankman-Fried, lived an openly

---

[*] An example of how fraud is metastasising to now include numerous state actors, not just individual crooks. Chinese cyber crime is another example of that – any useful innovation in the west is immediately snaffled by China (see, for example, their recently displayed fighting robot dog, a clear steal from Boston Dynamics).

bizarre, hedonistic lifestyle offshore in the Bahamas, in a $30 million penthouse. He paid no attention to regulatory requirements. He was courted by multiple figures such as Bill Clinton and was celebrated for (and perhaps gained temporary immunity because of) his alleged philanthropic intentions – despite those being mostly assertions as to what he *planned to* donate to save the world, rather than what he *did* donate. His immunity may also have been helped by one of the few donations that he *did*, apparently, make: £100 million in political donations. All of his wild claims were lapped up by credulous media and politicians. FTX is now bankrupt (as are numerous other crypto businesses) and at least $8 billion went missing. Bankman-Fried went to jail and was tried and found guilty in November 2023, now sentenced to twenty-five years. The senators on the Banking, Housing and Urban Affairs Committee, whose enormous quantity of finance sector regulation over the last twenty years completely failed to prevent the FTX fraud, are now threatening a *further* swathe of regulation that will, they seem to think, do a great job of shutting that particular stable door, now that this crypto horse has galloped off over the hills.[127]

The London Capital and Finance (LCF) fiasco shows how inept regulators can make things worse, not better. LCF found a loophole to sell high-risk product to gullible uninformed investors. They did this because the Financial Conduct Authority had authorised LCF. As the *Financial Times* put it, 'FCA authorisation … gave a false impression of security to customers who bought its unregulated minibonds.'[128] The official at the FCA responsible for the foolish authorisation was then promoted (but seems to have resigned soon after).

In the UK, it seems that our torrents of regulation have done little to protect consumers from fraud – so much so that London is now dubbed the world capital of banking fraud.[129] Fraud on consumers here is now at triple the rate that is found in the US. According to one commentator, 'The most sophisticated fraud tends to start in the UK, and then move two years later to the US and then around the world.'[130]

If some of these regulators, so singularly ineffective at what they are supposed to do, could be removed and the activities of others curtailed – without eliminating truly essential regulation but reducing the heavy weight of regulation from its inhibition of the growth economy – would this lead to significant problems or not? By how much would the cost of government be reduced? How much faster would the UK's economy grow? This chapter asserts that their removal would not increase fraud and the impact on economic growth would be significant.

The already too-great length of this book and the consequent high imposition on your patience require that we stop at these two important areas of unintended consequences: the case has already been made for removing multiple business regulations. Readers can see for themselves what a more humble, smarter, lighter, law-based and market-based, rather than regulation-based, approach would do for human happiness, let alone economic growth. How this is actually to happen is beyond the scope of this book.

OBTRUSIVE REGULATION IS DRIVING COMPANIES, RICH PEOPLE AND YOUNG HIGH ACHIEVERS OUT OF THE COUNTRY

We have already seen that high taxes drive companies, high earners and high performers to leave the country. A particularly depressing feature is that a large number of business owners who retire or sell off their business say they do so because they just can't stand the rules and regulations. When they depart, economic growth is thereby starved, opportunities are fewer and frustration is greater. The resultant outflow of capital and talent creates a further boost to the vicious cycle of high taxes, high regulation and low growth. As discussed in the previous chapter, a quite astonishing outflow of high-flyers from the UK is now taking place; it is a commonplace for observers to remark how many are leaving.

People worry that we have too-high net migration: 685,000 in the year ending December 2023.[131] But that net number obscures that over *1.2 million people* came into the UK in that period, while 532,000 left.[132] The majority of that 1.2 million are likely to end up within that 54 per cent of the population who get more state benefit than they pay in tax; since Brexit, the balance of immigration has tilted away from EU to non-EU migrants (almost 1 million out of the 1.2 million).[133] These make on average, according to Full Fact, 'a negative fiscal contribution overall', which 'cost the UK £624 billion between 2001 and 2011'.[134] Much more now. And, as the data on millionaires show, those 500,000 departers contain many in that top 10 per cent of earners who pay 60 per cent of income tax.[135] Regulation is driving those people out. Where is the sense in that?

LOOSENING THE GRIP OF OVERREGULATION WILL NEED AN UPHEAVAL OF THE POLITICAL AND REGULATORY STATUS QUO

The Brexit vote in 2016 was driven by the slogan 'take back control'. After the vote, it then took the government a full three and a half years to sign a Withdrawal Agreement with the EU – an entirely unsatisfactory, appallingly negotiated agreement from the viewpoint of sovereignty, and from many other viewpoints. Most of the problems and delays were thanks to the shenanigans of some die-hard EU-philes in our parliament and due to us having, for most of that time, a Remainer as Prime Minister – one who apparently did not understand what Brexit meant.

When the exit agreement was finally signed, the first cases of Covid were already springing up. We have been out of that Covid era for less than three years. Given this, it is understandable (though not in the least acceptable) that the social and economic landscape in the UK has changed only somewhat from 23 June 2016. Although benefits will continue to accrue from the freedoms of Brexit, the warning signs are there as the new Labour government promises closer ties with the EU. (Not that such is per se bad, except when it means adopting foolish EU regulation.) The electorate wanting to 'take back control' from Brussels was due to the desire of the majority of British voters to have sovereignty, to re-establish direct democratic control over our legislation, to have control of our borders. It was also driven by the fact that continental Europe looks at law and regulation from a completely different perspective. The Napoleonic Code – the ruling force across mainland Europe – is driven by the mantra 'Everything that is not explicitly allowed is forbidden'. We in the UK now have to give far greater play to 'Everything that is not explicitly forbidden is allowed'. Over the fifty years of Britain's membership of the EU, an ever-increasing and never-ceasing stream of directives came over from Brussels, all driven from the Napoleonic Code perspective, prescribing in detail how things should be – rather than allowing freedom-loving British citizens to lead their life as they wished. Only with some exceptions from our existing common law have we been able to limit the depredations of the Napoleonic Code on our traditional freedoms.

This book is about Britain's economy, not so much about personal freedoms – although we bear in mind that personal freedom, and the ability to experiment that comes with it, is a fundamental underpinning of a growing economy. But in any event, the greater part of Brussels's directives were to do with the economy. Over and again, pre-Brexit, ministers were told that particular directives were wrong for the UK economy but that we had to accept them anyway because of internal market rules and our signing of the Maastricht Treaty. Worse, and notoriously, British civil servants gold-plated many directives, thus crimping and constraining the economy even more than was necessary to obey the directive. We no longer belong to the single market and are no longer required to obey these directives. There is now an enormous opportunity, not yet taken up, to deregulate the economy and create more jobs, higher wages and a better future for the UK. We will discuss the practical steps towards that in Volume Two.*

SUMMARY: THE EXPECTED IMPACT OF MY PROPOSED CUTS TO SPEND, TAX AND REGULATION

At the end of the previous chapter, we showed the expected economic impact of the proposed programme of spending and tax cuts. In this, the last chapter of Volume One, I have discussed the additional further benefits that we can get from deregulation.

Achieving a goodly amount of deregulation can be expected to have a major positive impact on growth. However, the UK has over the past few decades extinguished its prospects for economic growth by imposing a suffocating web of overregulation. How big would be the improvement in economic growth if we could free ourselves from that vast cobweb? Our model indicates a further sharp improvement in the UK's economic fortunes from doing so, as shown in Chart 2.70.

---

* Some of the proposed solutions discussed in this chapter and elsewhere come up against the Human Rights Act 1998 and the ECHR; abandoning these (or not) is a flashpoint issue among UK politicians of various views. A detailed discussion of the pros and cons of leaving the ECHR and rewriting our Equalities Act is, as reviewed in Appendix B, beyond the scope of this book.

Chart 2.70: The UK Economy with Tax and Spend Cuts and Deregulation

Adding deregulation to lower spend and lower taxes fully turns the corner for the economy.

TAX, SPEND, REGULATION CUTS	-1 2023/24	0 2024/25	5 2029/30	10 2034/35	15 2039/40	20 2044/45
KEY INPUTS (ASSUMPTIONS)						
Government Spending as % GDP	44.5%	43.9%	42.2%	36.1%	34.3%	32.4%
Government Receipts as % GDP	40.4%	40.4%	40.4%	33.6%	33.1%	32.6%
Annual Productivity Growth	0.1%	0.1%	0.1%	0.5%	0.6%	0.6%
Gross fixed capital formation as % GDP	18.4%	16.8%	17.2%	20.2%	24.0%	24.4%
Human Capital Index annual growth rate	0.2%	0.2%	0.4%	0.9%	0.9%	0.9%
Total population, million	68.4	69.0	69.6	71.4	73.0	74.6
Working population, million	35.8	36.2	36.9	39.1	41.2	43.3
OUTPUTS (RESULTS)						
GDP Growth	0.2%	0.8%	1.8%	2.6%	3.0%	3.2%
Real GDP, £trillion	2.7	2.8	2.8	3.1	3.5	4.1
GDP per capita	39,963	39,889	40,265	42,973	48,377	55,358
National Debt as % GDP	100%	103%	103%	103%	97%	85%
Budget Deficit, £billion	114	97	51	76	44	(10)
Budget Deficit as %GDP	4.2%	3.5%	2.5%	2.5%	1.2%	-0.2%

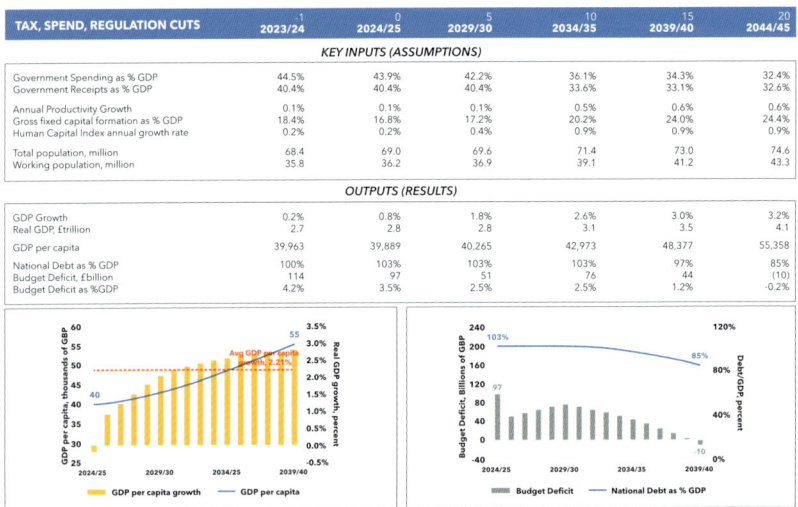

Source: moyniteam analysis

The additional impact of deregulation on the economy, beyond that already achieved through spend and tax cuts, is large:

- Despite major tax cuts, tax *revenues* increase by 21 per cent (£88 billion) in real terms over 2023/24, compared with only 13 per cent under our 'status quo' scenario. The debt-to-GDP ratio plummets.
- GDP per capita rises by 39 per cent (as opposed to 5 per cent under status quo).
- Working people are far richer. The median wage earner would see take-home pay (including taxes saved) increase over 50 per cent from £31,500 to some £48,000 a year.[*]

---

[*] Assumes wages rise in proportion to GDP per capita, plus expected savings from income tax and NIC reductions.

- With working people standing financially and happily on their own feet, far less welfare needs to be paid: more money available for other pressing needs.

CONCLUSION: RETURNING THE UK'S ECONOMY TO GROWTH

———

To sum up the arguments in this book, it is, above all, a moral imperative for any government to foster growth:

- Without growth, we won't be able to maintain, let alone improve, our position as the global scientific powerhouse that we have enjoyed in the past.
- Without growth, the improved services that the UK's citizens demand from their government, year after year, cannot be funded.
- Without growth, the people of the UK cannot rationally aspire to better themselves, to find new and better job opportunities, to earn a better real wage for their work or to support their families.
- Without growth – necessarily accomplished by a shrinkage of the overall share of our economy that government expenditure takes – we will have a series of increasingly serious debt and inflation crises, with the long-term outcome pointing toward national bankruptcy.
- Without growth, the possible expansionist future that we all hope for won't be discovered. Only a flat version of today, with all its obvious problems and issues, will remain.

This Volume One has shown that it is possible to steer the UK back to the desired path of higher economic growth. It has clearly laid out the requirements for that growth to be fostered and has indicated the particular steps that need to be taken in the UK to create those preconditions. A more detailed discussion of how we can accomplish this over a fifteen-year period, and a review of three other important preconditions for growth, will be laid out in Volume Two.

Of course, as I commit this book to print shortly after the July 2024 general election that returned a Labour government, the times make it entirely unlikely that even a start will be made on such a project. Politics, the media and even the money currently donated into the political arena are all dominated by hard-left or left-of-centre ideas that seek to take a larger and larger share of the economic pie into the ambit of government and distribute that extra slice of pie into areas that are unproductive of economic growth. In consequence, the lot of the average citizen in the UK will, inevitably, in the short to medium term get worse rather than better.

The prescriptions offered in this book – smaller government, lower taxes, less regulation – are thought of as right-wing ideas (ideas, moreover, that nowadays quite a few try albeit unconvincingly to claim as having been discredited). The one idea that seems to unite most of the political spectrum is the importance of growth, with dissent from that objective only from the far edges of the eco crowd and the absolutist no-growthers. Respectable and thoughtful left-wing politicians (the new Prime Minister, Keir Starmer and his Chancellor, Rachel Reeves) acknowledge the centrality of growth in procuring economic improvement for our citizens and even in ensuring we can afford our current expenditures. Yet once the urgency of finding a way to grow the economy has been acknowledged, it is difficult for commentators to duck the fact that without the three key prescriptions laid out in this volume – less government, less tax, less regulation – you won't get that growth.*

This book has been a plea, both to the electorate and to the elected, to take a fresh and different look at what's important for both our future and for the future of our descendants. If, going forward, we do not grow the economy at a high enough pace – significantly faster than the growth in our population – then more people will get sick, will not be cured in such numbers as would otherwise be the case, and will likely die earlier, at a greater rate and with greater distress than would have been the case had our economy grown faster. If we don't grow fast enough, our young people won't be educated well enough. We won't have sufficient housing to accommodate our growing population. The economy won't be creating decent jobs for them. Wage earners won't see a steadily rising standard of living and won't get salary increases that make them optimistic about the future and optimistic about being able to bring happiness and fulfilment to their families.

Growing the economy at a decent rate necessarily means our accepting that the state needs to have a smaller role than it does now. We need to accept that not all problems can or should be solved with state interference or state money; we should accept that calls for self-reliance must replace calls for 'something must be done' and 'there should be a law'. As the smaller state, lower-tax economy brings benefits to wage earners, the approach I and so many others recommend, of people standing on their own feet, will become self-reinforcing. Taxes must be lower, especially taxes on business.

---

* Three further valuable additions – free markets, free trade, sound money – are discussed in the forthcoming Volume Two.

We must cut state expenditure to what we can afford. We have to abandon our doctrinaire approach to the NHS and recognise that we have brought disease and death to many of our citizens, as well as unnecessary cost, by insisting on the absolutist socialist approach of the NHS. We have to recognise we need major reform in both *the way* we teach our children, and *what* we teach them. We have to grasp the nettle of abandoning the impossibly expensive defined-benefit pension schemes of the public sector and cease bribing our pensioners with the unsustainable triple lock.

Yes, all this means abandoning doctrinaire approaches that focus on equity, inclusion, 'privilege' and other such luxury concepts. And it will mean that rich people will continue to acquire Rolls-Royces and yachts.*

Taking such a fresh look at how the UK runs its economy will require an entirely different view of the role of business in our national life. Business, as I have shown, is the source of the vast majority of our taxes: it provides our jobs and our wealth. If we succeed as a nation in growing faster, thus in time being able to afford much that we can't afford now, it will be because of entrepreneurs who come up with wild and crazy ideas. As often as not, those entrepreneurs will fail and in doing so, sacrifice not only their own savings but also the savings of what their loving friends and family were coaxed into investing. These entrepreneurs and their investors risk all to turn their crazy ideas into products and services that, where they do succeed, grow the economy, create employment, and, in many cases, mightily benefit mankind.

Growth will often come prosaically, rather than with some

---

* Although, in truth, nobody has ever really begrudged the likes of Marcus Rashford, Lewis Hamilton, Adele, Ed Sheeran, Little Mix, Dua Lipa, Cara Delevingne, and so on, their riches and baubles – for some reason, it seems to be only successful, growth-creating businesspeople who have to suffer from the growth-destroying politics of envy.

world-beating invention. It will be because of that person in the community – multiplied by a couple of hundred thousand others across the UK – who started up a hairdressing salon, a coffee shop or a fashion boutique and now offers employment to half a dozen people. It will be because of that clothes manufacturing business in a former coalmining town in the Midlands, creating new and badly needed employment, supporting the local school, beating off – through excellent design and a deep understanding of their customer – the low-cost competition from other countries. It will be because of middle managers in a large corporation, working to maintain that company's success, developing new ideas and markets for their company. It will be, above all, from every business that is working in a free market to meet the needs of their customers, who are not spending half their time looking for government subsidies, or navel-gazing about their diversity, or self-sabotaging by worrying about other nebulous woke imperatives.

If we could have a nation that gets behind the ideas in this book, a nation that accepts the thesis that honour lies in private-sector entrepreneurialism and that kudos should be accorded to successful businesspeople, then we are halfway to achieving the kind of dynamic economy that the US, which has always embraced such ideas, continues to enjoy.

In the present economic environment, where the majority of politicians, media and academia seem to be strongly in support of the social democratic project, it is clearly a daunting challenge to seek support for the free-market view from the entire electorate, rather than from just the right wing of the Conservative Party. It is not, however, an impossible task. There is growing dismay at the dismal performance of the UK's economy over the past few decades; the continued worsening performance through government after government tells us that 'more of the same' is not going to work. Our new government has now entered into ownership of the economic outlook for the next five years, and it is not appealing. Over time, free-market ideas will return to prominence as the success gap between the free-market and the social-democrat economies continues to grow, giving further and further evidence that changes in the tax and regulatory regime can improve economic growth to the benefit of all citizens. Margaret Thatcher, inspired by various pathbreaking works, was able to reverse the UK's 1970s socialistic direction.[1] The common sense of the British electorate has saved the day in the past and can do so in the future. Getting there will, however, require a rebirth or renaissance of the free-market narrative, with the message reformed and reiterated over an extended period of time.

True, many in the UK who are unreconciled – one hopes not forever – to the result of the 2016 Brexit referendum do hanker for the UK to adopt the EU's social democratic model for our economy. But the more that the social-democracy model fails to deliver growth in the EU (with EU electorate after EU electorate now angrily searching for a better way) and the more that other countries around the globe manage to deliver better growth for their people by having a less welfarist approach, then the more the pressure will increase to understand why the EU and, currently, the UK fail to provide the growing and greater standards of living that other parts of the world increasingly enjoy – and why so many of our high-talent citizens choose to seek their fortune abroad. The underlying drivers of growth will become ever more difficult to ignore or belittle and the free-market, liberal economics argument will increasingly be looked to as the solution.

My hope is that this book will help in some way to contribute to and influence that ongoing debate, so that we can return to a sensibly structured economy more quickly and more successfully. Current and future British governments must plot a path to re-structure Britain as a small-government, low-tax, light-regulation, high-growth open economy, so that we can return to building a better future for all our people through economic growth. If, as an electorate, we can coalesce our polity around these ideas, we stand a chance of a return, after many decades, to growth.

AFTERWORD

———

2024 has, politically, been a turbulent year. This book was orig-inally intended to be published in the period leading up to an expected general election in around November 2024; those plans, however well laid, were foxed by the bemusing decision of Rishi Sunak and his hapless advisers to abandon governing and go to the country early. For now, as the weeks and months go by since the election, the revolutions of the political wheel seem to be speeding up, rather than settling down. The arrival of a Labour government makes it unlikely, at first sight, that a political regime will emerge that encourages faster economic growth. That conclusion is not so clear-cut, however, as might be initially thought: sometimes a left-wing government can take bolder economic steps than some puta-tively 'right-wing' ones have seen themselves as being a position to take (cf. the Conservatives for most of the previous fourteen years).

Let's look at each of the three areas this Volume One of *Return to Growth* has focused on and then try to sum up what the likely impact on growth will be from our new Labour government's an-nounced forthcoming policy steps.

1. Shrinking expenditures: While the new government has said little so far on this overall topic, Tony Blair and his omnipresent

Institute have come up with a report on the size of UK government[1] and its impact on growth (growth, they say, 'is rightly the
focus of the new government's proposals to cut the size/cost of
the UK'). The report seems in many ways to mimic what I have
written in this book, calling for a smaller government through
cuts which, however, are, unfortunately, of an order of magnitude
smaller than my own proposals (and perhaps rather too optimistically are said to be achievable through the savings potential of
AI); the report is nevertheless in the spirit of this book.[*] As another positive example: while not committing to cut costs in the
NHS, the new Health Secretary Wes Streeting seems commendably focused on efficiency improvements, rather than throwing
even more money at the problem.[2] In general, though, this new
government is going to find it difficult to not expand the size of
government even further. The promises are of bigger government
expenditure: nationalisations, 'Great British' Energy, a sovereign
wealth fund (aka subsidies to favoured industries – where does
the money come from for that?), more and larger green subsidies.

2. Lowering taxes: Despite the high hopes for Rachel Reeves and
   her reputed commonsensical approach to her Chancellor's job,
   and despite her strong pro-growth rhetoric, it is likely that her tax
   policies, at least in the first few years, will deviate little from those
   of her Conservative predecessor (apart from a few tax whacks on
   the likes of private schools and private equity managers). Taxes
   are, overall, likely to go up, not down – perhaps (at first) not by

---

[*] Even though the report has a healthy view on, for example, the importance of deregulation in the planning
area, and even though they interestingly call for 'Chief Productivity Officers' in each department, there
is still a flavour of the old 'We Know Best' conceit, calling for some central über-unit ('a new "Mission
Control" at the heart of government') to 'create and direct the AI revolution in government'. There is
little recognition of the formidable obstacles that the civil service would put in the path of any attempt to
transform the public sector in this way.

a lot, but nonetheless up. The impact on growth will continue to be negative.

3. Reducing regulation: Here, again, the new government is sending mixed messages: on the positive side, there have been strong statements on planning reform, which if followed through could lead to a mini-boom in the housing sector. In other areas, though, the focus seems very much on maintaining the status quo – or worse – that the various Conservative governments of the previous fourteen years (apart from the brief Truss period) stuck to. The new Labour government momentarily floated the idea of fully banning all North Sea drilling;[3] within a day, the swift upsurge in negative reactions (or because Ed Miliband's boss found out about it) led to a retraction of that story[4] – and yet, even later, a further reversal indicated that the ban would stay. And even were some North Sea drilling to be allowed, there are plenty of growth-destroying proposals to counterbalance that. Labour promise to introduce more 'We Know Best' regulation, including some of the most dismal ideas of the previous Conservative government – the attack on landlords, the ban on smoking for those born after 1 January 2009, the football regulator… Continuity of policy is a truly good indicator that the officials, not the politicians, are in charge. But as the new government sets forth, the workers' 'New Deal' will make it harder both to hire and to fire workers: another disincentive to start, or grow, a business. A darker cloud of regulation – workers' rights, green folly, more DEI and ESG – is coming our way.

4. The likely short- and longer-term prospects overall for economic growth: The beginning of the King's Speech stated: 'Securing economic growth will be a fundamental mission.' In theory, therefore, Truss abides. But apart from planning reform, and

the possibility of a Streeting-led assault on the moribund NHS, there are few signs of proper pro-growth policies. The triple lock is for now to be continued. The anti-'dynamic scoring' OBR is to be even more in charge. No assault on civil service numbers is actually expected. Schools policy will most likely move away from – not embrace – the Gove/Gibb reforms. And there will be plentiful anti-growth policies pursued (their counter-growth impact will be either not understood or ignored). Among a number of other green policies, three giant solar farms are to be built, which will lead to more subsidised increases in government expenditure, and continued high electricity bills.[5]

The prospect of wrenching the ratchet back to a pro-growth position is clearly some way off. If it is true that history repeats itself, let's hope we are in the late 1970s and will have a pro-growth government in place soon.

APPENDIX A

POLICY AREAS NOT DISCUSSED IN THESE VOLUMES

One of the major purposes of *Return to Growth* was to provide a far-reaching review of the state of the UK's economy and politics in the mid-2020s, trying to identify a series of practical policies that would get us out of the low-growth hole the UK has dug itself into.

As this first volume indicates, and Volume Two will confirm, the short-term chances of any of the needed, sweeping changes that I identify actually being implemented – including the short-term likelihood of gaining a parliamentary majority for my suggested programme, and a government that will successfully down the inevitable enraged backlash by incumbent office holders, gatekeepers and rent seekers – are low. It cannot be less than five years, and it could quite possibly be ten years, before a Javier Milei-style electoral success can come to pass – although it is not beyond possibility that over the next five years, the economy will get so significantly worse that the innate common sense of the British people will once more come to the fore and a parliamentary majority can be achieved for this book's proposed policies at the next general election. And anyway, even worse: as the calculations in this document have shown, it will take a number of years after that before the great turnaround starts to bear fruit.

Necessarily, there are policy areas so large and complex that to discuss them at the level of detail they deserve would have enlarged these volumes beyond any reasonable reader's patience. In particular, I have not gone into detail on four key areas: education, immigration, human rights and planning (though I have tried to indicate, within the text, how each would be dealt with within the context of a 'return to growth' programme).

To outline the importance of each being so addressed in the coming few years, I offer brief analysis in the following sections.

EDUCATION

Education was discussed in Chapter 6. There, I took the view that we could provide a great education to our children at or even below the current national level of spend. (I did not say this was easy, I just said it could be done.) I stated that the major problem with education at the moment is that the power of teachers' unions focus more on the needs of their members (the teachers) than on those of the children; the unions and many of their members fail to take note of and action the opportunities to do well by their pupils that are staring them in the face. This can be seen in the terrific success of various schools around the country that apply warm/strict and knowledge-rich policies. I'm not the only one saying this; how to persuade the educational establishment to adopt such policies, when they refuse to do so despite seeing how clearly those policies benefit children, is too complex to attempt to resolve in this more general book. A new Labour government, traditionally in thrall to public-sector unions, is unlikely to face them down; they will instead give them large rises with no work concessions.

IMMIGRATION

Immigration is a touchstone issue between the 'be kind' mob and the 'face the facts' crowd. The economists, the OBR, clearly got it wrong when they intimated that immigration was an unequivocal good, and have begun to admit that. In most people's views, immigration has been a disaster, not so much because it is a bad idea in general but because, for reasons that still baffle me and many others, the number of people allowed to immigrate into this country in the past couple of decades has been so many orders of magnitude greater than what we can comfortably assimilate. And in the media, the focus is on illegal immigration (mostly across the English Channel). It's not, in fact, the largest problem. 'Family' or 'chain' immigration into the UK, whether as relatives of existing immigrants or as family of incoming immigrants, including students, is much larger. Thanks to a dilatory response by officials, the workings of the Human Rights Act 1998 and the rulings of the European Court of Human Rights – which we should have pulled out of immediately after we voted to leave the EU – we now have a situation where the size of both legal and illegal immigration is astonishingly large, needing urgent attention.

Further, as discussed in these pages, the 'legal' immigration number that people discuss the most is the 2023/24 700,000-odd net migration figure. However, the gross number, 1.2 million, is far more important than the net, because 1.2 million incoming immigrants each year, a vast number of them dependents, will put a huge demand on social services and state benefits. The 500,000-odd who leave the UK each year will include all those wealthy, high-earning or high-talent individuals who are departing. One leaver does not necessarily balance out one immigrant; the gross incoming number is key, not the net.

In a small-welfare, free-market economy with minimal regulation, particularly in planning (so that enough housing can be built to accommodate both the indigenous and the incoming populations), immigration can be very much positive – as long as it is small enough to be assimilated into the general culture and economy, and so long as the majority of immigrants are not dependents, and include a healthy amount of high-skilled workers. Offering only a small level of welfare to immigrants would mean we only got immigrants who wanted to work. The high-welfare, high-immigration model that we have adopted has been disastrous for us – especially for GDP-per-capita growth. The problem with immigration is not just welfare costs but the costs of building additional housing, schools, hospitals and roads and having to employ more teachers, doctors, nurses, builders, police, judges and planning officers. Those who claim that immigration is an unmitigated positive must surely have failed to take these costs into account, and have certainly ignored the enormous pain and problems that our citizens have experienced when these new facilities are (inevitably) not delivered.

In this Volume One, our economic projections assume that we have managed to cut back immigration a great deal, in line with the most recent ONS forecast.[1] A change in approach to immigration could result in less immigrants ending up on welfare, and more qualified and entrepreneurial immigrants. The steps needed to accomplish that are, again, beyond the scope of these volumes, but it appears more or less certain that the needed actions will require removing ourselves from the jurisdiction of the ECHR, and completely revising the Human Rights Act 1998.

EUROPEAN COURT OF HUMAN RIGHTS

The ECHR is a super-national body whose rulings, by treaty, we are bound to obey. Many of the ECHR's recent rulings seem to be writing new law on the trot. The situation goes far beyond the issue of immigration: there are multiple areas of British law and government action that are subject to ECHR rulings, most of them resulting in the government having to spend more money on things that the electorate would, if asked, probably say less should be spent on. To reach a political environment where it was finally accepted that we must act as if we have only a certain amount of money to spend overall, rather than an environment that asserts we must spend wherever a need is identified, it would be essential to remove ourselves from the suzerainty of the ECHR.

To implement many of the policies suggested in Volume One, we make the assumption in our models that we have removed ourselves from the European Convention on Human Rights and have reversed or amended those parts of the Human Rights Act which bound us to the ECHR and its sovereignty. We also assume that we have been able to rewrite any other UK equalities legislation in a way that ensures governments can, and do, spend money only on what the electorate has told them to spend it on.

PLANNING

Over and again, one reads of the blockages to building houses, offices and infrastructure created by the UK's planning regime. It is not just the age-old war between NIMBYs and developers any more; there are the eco-regulators with their bat and frog protection, the extraordinary religious veneration of every inch of green belt, the building companies with their alleged market-distorting land banks, yet more retained EU law, ludicrous bans on both on- and off-shore drilling for oil and gas in both the UK and its overseas territories, the politicians with their obsessive focus on placating incumbents and the appalling war on landlords, freeholders and buy-to-lets.[2] The needed change is large.

I've discussed this problem in various parts of the text, but the subject needs much deeper discussion than there is space for here. A determined approach to across-the-board deregulation in these areas would unleash a boom in economic activity, lower house prices and impact a general improvement in human happiness.

• • •

I look forward to others more talented than I taking up the challenge to write the definitive volumes on these four policy areas.

APPENDIX B

THE GROWTH MODEL

———

Throughout this book, reference has been made to our growth model, which estimates, based on many academic studies, what the impact of implementing our proposed policies would be over a fifteen-year period – whenever those fifteen years might start. The model takes 2024's numbers as its starting point, since that is the only baseline available – although given recent events, the commencement of the fifteen-year period is in actuality likely to be 2029 at the earliest. The model analyses three alternative scenarios, which we refer to as 'status quo', 'expenditure and tax cuts', and 'expenditure, tax and regulation reductions'; these are explained in more detail below. The model itself is an extended version of the World Bank's long-term growth model (LTGM), which in turn is based on the well-known neoclassical Solow–Swan growth model.[*1]

THE SOLOW–SWAN MODEL

This well-known model, from which we derive our own, is based on an aggregated Cobb–Douglas production function with human capital:

---

[*]   Specifically, the modified version that includes human capital.

$$Y_t = A_t K_t^{1-\beta} (h_t L_t)^\beta$$

Where at any given time t:

Y_t = output (GDP)

A_t = total factor productivity (TFP)

K_t = capital stock

h_t = human capital per worker

L_t = number of workers in the economy[*]

β = labour share in output

The number of workers in the economy is $L_t = N_t \omega_t \rho_t$, where at any time t:

N_t = total population

ω_t = share of working-age population in total population

ρ_t = labour force participation rate (share of working-age population who are employed or actively seeking employment)

Capital stock evolves according to the following difference equation, which states that its current level is equal to its previous level, adjusted for depreciation δ and new investment I_t:

$$K_{t+1} = (1-\delta)K_t + I_t.$$

---

[*] A fair criticism of this model is that it assumes that any new member of the workforce has the same level of human capital and is as productive as the average current member. Thus, the model can significantly overestimate the positive impact of immigration on GDP growth, especially given the cost of the additional national infrastructure that is needed to support the additional numbers. Our own calculations assume much less immigration in the fifteen-year period than in the past few years, so reduce the size of any such overestimates.

The model is calibrated for the UK economy using the following parameters:

Variable	Value	Source
β	0.59	Penn World Table version 10.01 [2]
δ	0.0397	Penn World Table version 10.01
K_o/Y_o	3.5	IMF Investment and Capital Stock dataset [3] and Penn World Table version 10.01, average value for 2019

A conventional version of the Solow–Swan model has one important drawback: it assumes that the path of the key variable, Total Factor Productivity (TFP), is exogenous. As a central new feature of this approach, we extend the Solow–Swan model using our findings on the impact on TFP from four variables: the three key drivers discussed in Volume One (government expenditures as a percentage of GDP, tax revenues as a percentage of GDP and level of business regulations) and a fourth variable, trade freedom, which is discussed in Volume Two. (In our calculations for Volume One, we fix that fourth variable at a constant level.)

These four factors are defined as follows:

I_t^{exp} – index of government expenditures, scaled from 0 to 10

I_t^{tax} – index of tax revenues, scaled from 0 to 10

I_t^{reg} – index of business regulations, scaled from 0 to 10

I_t^{trade} – freedom of trade index, scaled from 0 to 10

The index of government expenditures is constructed as follows:

$$I_t^{exp} = 10 \; (G_{max} - G_t) \, / \, (G_{max} - G_{min})$$

G_t is government expenditures as a percentage of GDP, G_{max} and G_{min} are set at 70 per cent of GDP (the largest observed number for G_t since 1975 in our sample of countries, rounded up to the nearest whole percentage) and 11 per cent of GDP (the smallest observed amount value for G_t in our sample of countries, rounded down to the nearest whole percentage) respectively. A lower value of I_t^{exp} reflects a higher level of government expenditures G_t.

The index of tax revenues is similarly constructed as follows:

$$I_t^{tax} = 10 \ (T_{max} - T_t) \ / \ (T_{max} - T_{min})$$

Where T_t denotes tax receipts as a share of GDP, T_{max} and T_{min} are set at 51 per cent of GDP (the highest level of tax revenues rounded up to the nearest whole percentage) and 21 per cent of GDP (the lower level of tax revenues rounded down to the nearest whole percentage) respectively. A lower value of the index I_t^{tax} reflects a higher level of taxation T_t.

For the index of business regulations I_t^{reg} and the freedom of trade index I_t^{trade}, we use the business regulations component (5C) and tariffs component (4A) of the Fraser Institute's Economic Freedom of the World ranking. Both indices are originally scaled from 0 to 10. A lower value I_t^{reg} corresponds to a higher regulatory burden, whereas a lower value of I_t^{trade} corresponds to higher trade barriers.

We then construct a composite index I_t by averaging the data for each of the four variables and then rescaling from 1 to 100:

$$I_t = (I_t^{exp} + I_t^{tax} + I_t^{reg} + I_t^{trade})/4 \ \ 99/10 + 1,$$

TOTAL FACTOR PRODUCTIVITY AND THE COMPOSITE INDEX

To obtain a quantitative relationship between TFP growth and our composite index of the aggregation of the four variables, we constructed a regression model in which the TFP growth rate is a function of a contemporaneous value of the composite index:

$$g_t^{TFP} = \xi_0 + \xi_1 \ \ln I_t + \varepsilon_t,$$

where:

g_t^{TFP} = TFP growth rate in year t

I_t = composite index at t, scaled from 1 to 100

ε_t = residuals

The alert reader will have noticed an implicit assumption in our approach, which is to give equal weight to each of the four measures. It would, of course, be better if we could have concluded on the relative degree of impact on growth of changes in each separately. However, the high correlation between the variables, particularly the first two, makes problematic any stab at estimating the differing effects of individual variables. Assuming a similar level of impact for each variable should lead to calculated outcomes that could be a degree – but most likely only to a degree – inaccurate.[*]

Our regression analysis was conducted using, as a sample, the

---

[*]   We discover, to our pleasure, that the World Bank came to almost identical conclusions in its own use of this model. See p.77 of their long-term growth model paper, linked to in the text.

twenty-three developed countries that have been long-standing members of the OECD 2000–2019.[*]

The TFP growth-time series is derived from the Penn World Tables (PWT) version 10.01 database. The time series for government expenditures and revenues come from the IMF's Public Finances in Modern History database. The table below summarises the regression results.

As previously noted, the model assumes/implies one-to-one correspondence between TFP growth and GDP-per-capita growth.

Chart A.I: TFP Growth against Changes in Our Composite Index, 2000–2019

Regressing TFP growth versus our composite index confirms the positive relationship between those factors and TFP. The UK's position on the scatter plot shows how Britain's economic position has deteriorated in the past two decades.

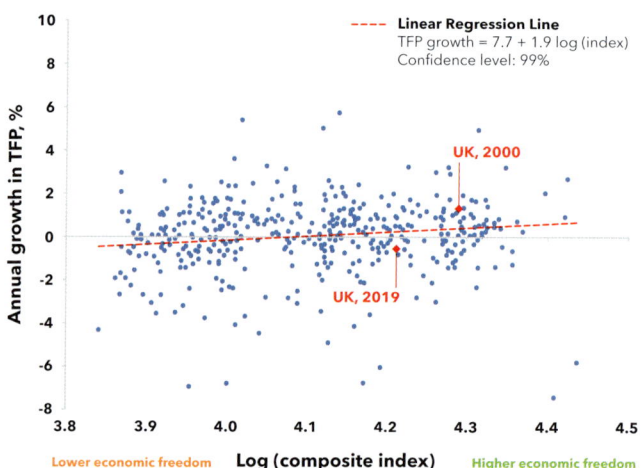

Source: Penn World Tables version 10.01, Fraser Institute, International Monetary Fund, OECD, moyniteam analysis[4]

---

[*] Australia, Austria, Belgium, Canada, Denmark, Finland, France, Germany, Greece, Iceland, Ireland, Italy, Japan, Luxembourg, Netherlands, New Zealand, Norway, Portugal, Spain, Sweden, Switzerland, United Kingdom and the United States.

Chart A.2: Four Composite Index Variables:
The UK's Position 2000 Versus 2019

We use four variables to make up the composite index that drive our model. Only the first three of these variables are used in the scenarios for Volume One (the fourth, tariffs, is discussed in Volume Two). Our position in all three has, as can be seen in Chart A.2, declined by 2021 and we can expect it to have become even worse by 2024.

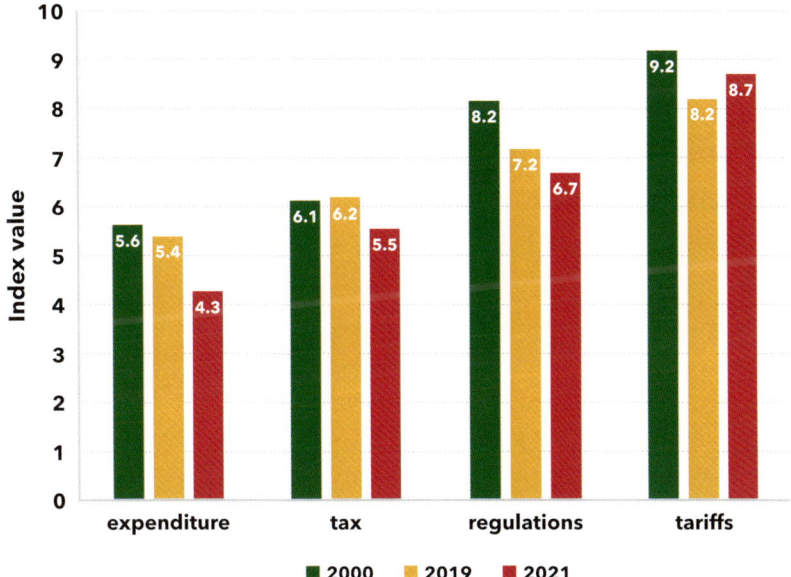

Source: Penn World Tables version 10.01, Fraser Institute,
International Monetary Fund, OECD, moyniteam analysis[5]

As can be seen in Chart A.1, the relationship posited in our model is confirmed (by the regression analysis) to exist. The model's outputs show that if the UK could just return to the levels in 2000, annual growth would increase by some one third of 1 per cent (5 per cent over fifteen years). Adopting our proposed actions would improve growth by far more than that.

The two red data points show that the UK's economy has

deteriorated significantly between 2000 and 2010.[*] Our TFP deterioration for each of the four factors is shown in chart A.2.

OUR SCENARIOS

As mentioned earlier, we created three different scenarios for the UK over a forthcoming fifteen-year period. First, the 'status quo' scenario, based on the assumption that the UK economy will continue pretty much as it is in 2024: in this scenario, tax revenues, government expenditures (excluding debt interest), regulation and tariff indices, labour participation and human capital growth all continue at their current level. The level of investment as a share of GDP evolves in line with the IMF forecast in the first five years and remains constant thereafter.

The second 'expenditure and tax reductions' scenario assumes that government expenditures and taxes will be cut over the first five years (the former starting in year one and the latter starting in year two) in accordance with the proposals put forward in Chapters 6 and 7. After those first five years, expenditures are permitted to grow each year according to a fiscal rule that expands spending by no more than 60 per cent of the previous years' growth in GDP, whereas taxes as a percentage of GDP continue to decline at one tenth of a percentage point annually. The outcome of that rule is that by year fifteen, expenditure as a percentage of GDP has fallen to an estimated 34.4 per cent and taxes have fallen to 28.9 per cent of GDP, with total government revenues, augmented by an assumed 4.3 per cent of 'other revenue', at 33.2 per cent. Regulation and tariff indices remain unchanged; the labour force participation

---

[*] The UK's 2019 TFP growth was, in fact, negative.

rate improves over fifteen years, hitting the current level of Switzerland in year fifteen; and human capital growth recovers in the first five years, reaching the average UK level of 2001–10. The investment level reaches the (present) level of the US in ten years.

The third scenario, 'expenditure, tax and regulation reductions', assumes that in addition to the changes assumed in scenario two, the deregulatory measures discussed in Chapter 8 are implemented over the first five years, so that the regulation index $I_t^{reg} = 10$ is optimised, starting from year six. The outcome of this scenario is that by year fifteen, because GDP has consequently grown faster, government expenditure as a percentage of GDP has fallen to an estimated 32.4 per cent and taxes are at 28.3 per cent of GDP (with total government revenues, augmented by the assumed 4.3 per cent of 'other revenue', at 32.6 per cent). In this scenario, labour force participation rate increases over fifteen years, achieving the (current) level in Sweden in year fifteen, and human capital growth recovers in the first five years, reaching the average UK level that we saw in 1991–2000. The investment level reaches the (current) level of Switzerland after ten years.

In all three scenarios, the total population N_t and working population ω_t in the UK are hypothesised to evolve in line with the ONS principal projection of 30 January 2024.[6] Non-tax receipts are assumed to remain at a constant 4.3 per cent of GDP, based on the OBR Economic and Fiscal Outlook March 2024 figures.[7] Real GDP is expected to grow by 0.8 per cent in 2024/25, in line with the IMF forecast.[8]

APPENDIX C

WELFARE SPENDING

The following table breaks down welfare spending for the financial years 2022/2023 and 2023/24.

Category/Benefit	Cost in 2022/23, £ billion	Cost in 2023/24, £ billion	% of Total Welfare, 2023/24
Pensioner Spending	**123.3**	**137.6**	**46.5%**
State Pension	110.5	124.1	41.9%
Pensioner Housing Benefit	5.9	6.1	2.1%
Pension Credit	4.9	5.4	1.8%
Winter Fuel Payments	2.0	2.0	0.7%
State Pension Transfers	0.0	0.0	0.0%
Universal Credit and Legacy Equivalents	**73.8**	**82.3**	**27.8%**
Universal Credit	41.9	51.9	17.5%
Employment and Support Allowance	12.1	12.7	4.3%
Housing Benefits (non pensioner)	9.7	9.3	3.2%
Personal Tax Credits	8.9	7.3	2.5%
Income Support	0.9	0.6	0.2%
Jobseeker's Allowance	0.3	0.3	0.1%
Disability Benefits	**33.3**	**39.6**	**13.4%**
Personal Independence Payment	17.6	21.6	7.3%
Disability Living Allowance	6.0	6.8	2.3%
Attendance Allowance	5.7	6.7	2.3%
Carer's Allowance	3.2	3.7	1.3%
Industrial Injuries Benefits Scheme	0.7	0.7	0.2%
Armed Forces Independence Payment	0.0	0.0	0.0%
Severe Disablement Allowance	0.1	0.1	0.0%
Incapacity Benefit	0.0	0.0	0.0%
Child Benefits	**15.3**	**16.5**	**5.6%**
Child Benefit	11.6	12.5	4.2%
Statutory Maternity Pay	2.7	2.8	1.0%
Tax Free Childcare	0.5	0.6	0.2%
Maternity Allowance	0.4	0.4	0.1%
Paternity, Parental and Adoption Pay	0.1	0.1	0.0%
Sure Start Maternity Grant	0.0	0.0	0.0%
Cost of Living Payments	**8.2**	**10.2**	**3.5%**
Other Spending	**8.9**	**9.7**	**3.3%**
Nothern Ireland Social Security	7.704	8.872	3.0%
Cold Weather Payments	0.139	0.038	0.0%
Bereavement Benefits	0.399	0.257	0.1%
Financial Assistance Scheme	0.241	0.246	0.1%
Christmas Bonus	0.167	0.170	0.1%
Discretionary Housing Payments	0.111	0.000	0.00%
Funeral Expenses Payments	0.046	0.048	0.02%
Mesothelioma 2008 & 2014	0.042	0.043	0.01%
Pneumoconiosis 1979	0.036	0.028	0.01%
New Enterprise Allowance	0.005	0.000	0.000%
Support for Mortgae Interest	0.004	0.003	0.001%
Total UK welfare bill	**262.9**	**296.0**	**100%**

Source: Department for Work and Pensions[1]

APPENDIX D

THINKERS VERSUS FEELERS

————

In Chapter 6, while discussing the civil service, I go off at a slight tangent regarding the 'feeler' characteristics that are frequently found in the private sector. The concept of 'thinkers' versus 'feelers' is not hard to grasp; most recognise the idea and agree as to its importance. Take any random group of people and ask each individual in it to self-identify either as a 'justice' person (thinker) or as a 'mercy' person (feeler). When, after the self-identification, you separate the group into 'justice' and 'mercy' teams, each team will have pronounced and instant views on what the categorisation implies for those who have potted themselves into the opposite category. The justice team usually think the mercy gang are nice but muddled; the mercy team tend, regrettably, to think the justice bunch are terrible, fascistic people. The distinction of thinker versus feeler has been validated in millions of tests worldwide, and how a person categorises themselves is usually (not always) invariant for life. The distinction is quite key and should be a major factor in all discussions about the need for 'neurodiversity' in organisations.

Some may find all this tiresome, but others may want to know more, so here is an appendix that discusses the topic's importance in a little more detail, showing how we are creating problems for ourselves if we have now created a public sector that, in both its leadership and its overall staff composition, is predominantly feeler in type.

LEADERS

In the main text, I discuss the different impacts of feeler and thinker leaders. As I imply there, a 'feeler' leader would likely have sympathy with those who assert that their life is being made miserable by microaggressions or the like. The feeler leader would be unlikely to want to put an end to nonsense such as diversity training days. A good thinker leader, on the other hand, would be incensed that time and money were being wasted on such things, and would, once support from the legal framework could be found, briskly find a way to shut those initiatives down, so as to get departmental staff back to doing what they were supposed to do. The fact that the civil service at this time is failing so dismally in its proper tasks and that woke is spreading so thoroughly through the public sector implies that we have many feeler and few thinker leaders in the civil service today.

STAFF

In its general population, the UK has 50 per cent thinkers and 50 per cent feelers. This in itself is interesting, especially when we compare ourselves with other countries, which I do in chart A.4.

In the chart, we see that the Anglosphere tends to balance near to fifty-fifty in the same way as the UK. France shows a uniquely low number of thinkers, with a few other countries leaning upwards toward the fifty-fifty mark.* Other countries, several of them our

---

* Interesting, therefore, that alone among nations, France decided in the 1950s and 1960s to go full-tilt into nuclear power, thus creating an enormous economic advantage for itself for the subsequent decades.

ideological opponents, show a strong preponderance of thinkers in their national composition. These are countries that will, given that makeup, put sentiment (moral or otherwise) aside to remorselessly and logically pursue their goals, often very much against our interests.*

Chart A.4: Split of Thinkers Versus Feelers, Selected Nations

The UK overall is fifty-fifty feelers versus thinkers, which seems a good thing – but is the UK's public sector the same fifty-fifty split?

High feelers			Balanced thinkers			High thinkers		
Country	T%	F%	Country	T%	F%	Country	T%	F%
France	41	59	UK	50	50	Turkey	81	19
Japan	45	55	Canada	51	49	India	80	20
Ireland	46	54	US	52	48	Brazil	76	24
S. Korea	47	53	Denmark	53	47	Russia	76	24
Netherlands	48	52	Australia	53	47	China	65	35

Source: Typology Triad, moyniteam analysis[1]

It would probably be possible for an insider to uncover the actual facts about how prevalent feelers versus thinkers are in the civil service, since over the years it is likely that hundreds of thousands of civil servants at different levels have taken the Myers–Briggs test. It is, however, less likely in practice that those numbers will be divulged – even though that could be done in carefully anonymised fashion. We only have, at this stage, the facts laid out in the body of this book, plus my assertion and intuition (and, of course, yours, dear reader) to go on when evaluating my belief as to the predominance of feelers among the civil service's leaders and staff. Many are

---

* Also interestingly, and as the chart shows, other non-aligned countries such as Brazil have a very high proportion of thinkers.

likely to concur with my view that feelers massively predominate; others maybe not.

If the UK's overall population is fifty-fifty feelers versus thinkers, then a tilt towards feelers among our public servants would imply a France-type level, or likely quite a bit worse, influence from feelers. I would argue that France – with a current fiscal deficit of 5.5 per cent of GDP, a public sector becoming actually larger than the private sector and a looming debt crisis that is probably only contained at the moment through the good offices of the French Christine Lagarde at the European Central Bank – is not a good model for us. It is precisely what, as I argue throughout this book, we need to be avoiding.

What was the composition of the civil service, particularly among its leaders, in its heyday of 100 or 150 years ago? From what we can read of those times, it contained a far greater proportion of thinkers – perhaps not as high as, we find in Chart A.4, in India or Brazil. (Developing countries face very different, much tougher challenges than we do.) To a thinker like me, the prevalence of thinkers in some of those countries is a comfort – so long, of course, as they have not embraced (and so many have, unfortunately) bonkers or barbaric ideologies. Similarly, the Treasury has always been seen as the stern citadel of thinker-style prudence. The failure in recent years to control the number of civil servants, and the generally outrageous level of expenditure both during and after the Covid era, imply that is no longer likely to be the case.

Our fifty-fifty split of thinkers versus feelers in the UK seems to have worked well for us in the past; clearly, having citizens with both characteristics helps in the progression of civilisation. It would be lamentable if, for whatever reason, we have allowed our government workers to no longer reflect the makeup of overall society.

In a feeler world, rules tend to be important – to be followed as closely as possible. Overseers and regulators are crucial. Processes are key and must be followed in every detail. Upsetting people is out. Fairness is everything and outcomes are less important. This is all wonderful, but how will we fare, if that is how we are to be governed, in a world where some much more ruthless, logical, outcome-orientated countries are out to eat our lunch?

NOTES

OVERVIEW

1   UK real GDP grew at an average (geometric mean) annual growth rate of 2.52 per cent in 1960–2000 compared to 1.38 per cent in 2001–2023, thus implying a 29 per cent difference: $(1.0252/1.0138)^{23}$ - 1 = 0.2933. Based on International Monetary Fund 'Public Finances in Modern History' and 'World Economic Outlook (April 2024)' datasets, https://www.imf.org/external/datamapper/datasets

2   Average weekly earnings for total pay in June 2023 were £670, implying annual earnings of £34,840 (assuming fifty-two weeks in a calendar year). We take the mid-year earnings as an approximation for the annual average figure. Data from Office for National Statistics, 'Average weekly earnings in Great Britain: June 2024', https://www.ons.gov.uk/employmentandlabourmarket/peopleinwork/employmentandemployeetypes/bulletins/averageweeklyearningsingreatbritain/june2024. The average annual growth rate in real earnings 1960–2000 was 2.56 per cent, compared to 0.75 per cent in 2001–2023. This implies that current earnings would be c. 51 per cent higher if the growth in real earnings had continued for the last twenty-three years at the previous average level of 2.56 per cent: $(1.0256/1.0075)^{23}$ - 1= 0.506. Growth rate for the period 1960–2000 derived from the Bank of England's, 'A millennium of macroeconomic data' database, https://www.bankofengland.co.uk/-/media/boe/files/statistics/research-datasets/a-millennium-of-macroeconomic-data-for-the-uk.xlsx. The rate of growth for 2001–2023 derived from Office for National Statistics, 'X09: Real average weekly earnings using consumer price inflation (seasonally adjusted)' dataset (June 2024 edition), https://www.ons.gov.uk/employmentandlabourmarket/peopleinwork/earningsandworkinghours/datasets/x09realaverageweeklyearningsusingconsumerpriceinflationseasonallyadjusted

3   As of 2024/25 tax year, gross salary of £52,546 implies net pay of £41,034, whereas gross salary of £34,840 leaves £28,604 after subtracting income tax and national insurance. The difference between the two is £12,430.

4   International Monetary Fund, 'World Economic Outlook (April 2024)', https://www.imf.org/external/datamapper/datasets/WEO

5   International Monetary Fund, 'Public Finances in Modern History', https://www.imf.org/external/datamapper/datasets/FPP

6   International Monetary Fund, 'General Government Debt', https://www.imf.org/external/datamapper/GG_DEBT_GDP@GDD/AUS/BEL/DEU/FRA/ISR/ITA/NLD/PRT/ESP/SWE/GBR/USA/CZE/JPN/CAN/GRC

7   International Monetary Fund, 'World Economic Outlook (April 2024)', https://www.imf.org/external/datamapper/GGXWDG_NGDP@WEO/OEMDC/ADVEC/WEOWORLD

8   International Monetary Fund, 'Public Finances in Modern History', https://www.imf.org/external/datamapper/datasets/FPP

PROLOGUE

1   Office for National Statistics, 'X09: Real average weekly earnings using consumer price inflation (seasonally adjusted)', https://www.ons.gov.uk/employmentandlabourmarket/peopleinwork/earningsandworkinghours/datasets/x09realaverageweeklyearningsusingconsumerpriceinflationseasonallyadjusted

2   Office for Budget Responsibility, 'Data', https://obr.uk/data/

3   'How the West fell out of love with economic growth', The Economist, 11 December 2022, https://www.economist.com/finance-and-economics/2022/12/11/how-the-west-fell-out-of-love-with-economic-growth

4   Thomas Hobbes, Leviathan (Penguin Classics, 1651)

5   The National Archives, 'Great Domesday Book', https://beta.nationalarchives.gov.uk/explore-the-collection/explore-by-time-period/medieval/domesday/

6 Bank of England, 'A millennium of economic data', https://www.bankofengland.co.uk/-/media/boe/files/statistics/research-datasets/a-millennium-of-macroeconomic-data-for-the-uk.xlsx

7 Bank of England, 'A millennium of economic data', https://www.bankofengland.co.uk/-/media/boe/files/statistics/research-datasets/a-millennium-of-macroeconomic-data-for-the-uk.xlsx; Office for National Statistics, 'Number of People in Employment (aged 16 and over, seasonally adjusted):000s', https://www.ons.gov.uk/employmentandlabourmarket/peopleinwork/employmentandemployeetypes/timeseries/mgrz/lms

8 International Monetary Fund, 'Real GDP Growth Rate, percent', https://www.imf.org/external/datamapper/rgc@FPP/DEU/GBR/SWE/CZE/BEL/GRC/FRA/ITA/PRT/NLD/CHE/ESP. Major western European economies are considered those included into the IMF advanced economies list, with an annual GDP over $1 trillion. A 2019 cutoff is used to exclude the effects of the Covid-19 pandemic.

9 University of Groningen, 'Maddison Project Database 2020', https://www.rug.nl/ggdc/historicaldevelopment/maddison/data/mpd2020.xlsx; International Monetary Fund, 'World Economic Outlook (April 2024)', https://www.imf.org/en/Publications/WEO/weo-database/2024/April

10 International Monetary Fund, 'Public Finances in Modern History', https://www.imf.org/external/datamapper/rgc@FPP/FRA/DEU/ITA/NLD/ESP/GBR

11 University of Groningen, 'Maddison Project Database 2023', https://www.rug.nl/ggdc/historicaldevelopment/maddison/data/mpd2020.xlsx

12 Thomas Piketty and Arthur Goldhammer, *Capital in the Twenty First Century* (Harvard University Press, 2014), https://www.amazon.co.uk/Capital-Twenty-First-Century-Thomas-Piketty/dp/067443000X

13 Daron Acemoglu and James A. Robinson, 'The Rise and Decline of General Laws of Capitalism', *Journal of Economic Perspectives*, vol. 29, no. 1, winter 2015, pp. 3–28, https://www.aeaweb.org/articles?id=10.1257/jep.29.1.3

14 Douglas McWilliams, *The Inequality Paradox: How Capitalism Can Work for Everyone* (Abrams Press, 2019), https://www.amazon.co.uk/Inequality-Paradox-Capitalism-Work-Everyone/dp/146831498X#:~:text=In%20his%20illuminating%20new%20book,even%20as%20worldwide%20poverty%20drops

15 International Monetary Fund, 'Population', https://www.imf.org/external/datamapper/LP@WEO/GBR

16 International Monetary Fund, 'Public Finances in Modern History', https://www.imf.org/external/datamapper/datasets/FPP; University of Groningen, 'Maddison Project Database 2023', https://www.rug.nl/ggdc/historicaldevelopment/maddison/releases/maddison-project-database-2023; International Monetary Fund, 'Public Finance in Modern History', https://www.imf.org/external/datamapper/datasets/FPP

17 'Britain's economic record since 2007 ranks near the bottom among peer countries', *The Economist*, 15 December 2022, https://www.economist.com/britain/2022/12/15/britains-economic-record-since-2007-ranks-near-the-bottom-among-peer-countries

18 The World Bank, 'Data Bank: Population estimates and projections', https://databank.worldbank.org/source/population-estimates-and-projections

19 Georgina Sturge, 'Migration Statistics', *House of Commons Library*, 24 May 2024, https://commonslibrary.parliament.uk/research-briefings/sn06077/

20 The World Bank, 'Data Bank: Population estimates and projections', https://databank.worldbank.org/source/population-estimates-and-projections

21 Peter Walker, 'Liz Truss blames "groupthink" for economic damage under her watch', *The Guardian*, 18 September 2023, https://www.theguardian.com/politics/2023/sep/18/liz-truss-denies-crashing-economy-and-attacks-media-and-bank-groupthink

22 Will Hazell, 'Migrants' boost to economy overestimated, claims think tank', *Daily Telegraph*, 23 March 2024, https://www.telegraph.co.uk/news/2024/03/23/migrants-boost-to-economy-overestimated-claims-think-tank/

23 OECD Library, 'Demography', https://www.oecd-ilibrary.org/social-issues-migration-health/demography/indicator-group/english_5f958f71-en

24 The World Bank, 'GDP per capita, PPP (current international $) – OECD Members', https://data.worldbank.org/indicator/NY.GDP.PCAP.PP.CD?end=2022&locations=OE-AU-AT-BE-CA-CL-CO-CR-CZ-DK-EE-FI-FR-DE-GR-HU-IS-IE-IL-IT-JP-KR-LV-LT-LU-MX-NL-NZ-NO-PL-PT-SK-SI-ES-SE-CH-TR-GB-US&start=2022&view=bar

25 International Monetary Fund, 'World Economic Outlook (April 2024)', https://www.imf.org/external/datamapper/datasets/WEO

26 Muzaffar Chishti, Kathleen Bush-Joseph and Colleen Putzel-Kavanaugh, 'Biden at the three-year mark: the most active immigration presidency yet is mired in border crisis narrative', *Migration Policy Institute*, 19 January 2024, https://www.migrationpolicy.org/article/biden-three-immigration-record

27 Robert Colvile, 'The morality of growth', *CAPX*, 13 January 2023, https://capx.co/the-morality-of-growth/

28 Benjamin M. Friedman, 'The Moral Consequences of Economic Growth', https://scholar.harvard.edu/files/bfriedman/files/the_moral_consequences_of_economic_growth.pdf; Tyler Cowen, *Stubborn Attachments*

(Stripe Press, 2018), https://tylercowen.com/dd-product/stubborn-attachments-vision-society-free-prosperous-responsible-individuals/

CHAPTER 1

1   Rikard Warlenius, 'Decolonizing the Atmosphere: The Climate Justice Movement on Climate Debt', *The Journal of Environment & Development*, vol. 27, no. 2, 9 December 2017, https://journals.sagepub.com/doi/abs/10.1177/1070496517744593?journalCode=jeda

CHAPTER 2

1   John Burn-Murdoch, 'Are we destined for a zero-sum future?', *Financial Times*, 22 September 2023, https://www.ft.com/content/980cbbe2-0f5d-4330-872d-c7a9d6a97bf6

2   Eir Nolsøe, 'Why the United States keeps getting richer – with Britian lagging ever further behind', *Daily Telegraph*, 23 April 2023, https://www.telegraph.co.uk/business/2023/04/23/us-richer-than-uk-finance-inflation-taxes/

3   University of Groningen, 'Maddison Project Database 2020', https://www.rug.nl/ggdc/historicaldevelopment/maddison/data/mpd2020.xlsx; International Monetary Fund, 'World Economic Outlook (April 2024)', https://www.imf.org/en/Publications/WEO/weo-database/2024/April

CHAPTER 3

1   Life expectancy at birth was 68.63 years in 1950; the figure for 2023 is 82.31 years according to United Nations, 'World Population Prospects 2022', https://population.un.org/wpp/

2   Office for National Statistics, 'Family Spending workbook 4: expenditure by household characteristic', FYE 2022 edition, https://www.ons.gov.uk/file?uri=/peoplepopulationandcommunity/personalandhousehold finances/expenditure/datasets/familyspendingworkbook4expenditurebyhouseholdcharacteristic/fye2022/workbook4expenditurebyhouseholdcharacteristics.xlsx

3   Office for National Statistics, 'Child and infant mortality in England and Wales: 2021', Figure 1 – Infant mortality rate, England and Wales, 1980 to 2021, https://www.ons.gov.uk/peoplepopulationandcommunity/birthsdeathsandmarriages/deaths/bulletins/childhoodinfantandperinatalmortalityinenglandandwales/2021

4   Matt Ridley and David Hill, 'The effect of innovation in agriculture on the environment', *Institute of Economic Affairs*, November 2018, https://iea.org.uk/wp-content/uploads/2018/11/Effect-of-Innovation-in-agriculture_web.pdf

5   Office for National Statistics, 'Travel Trends: 2022', Figure 9 – UK residents' visits abroad by purpose, 2001 to 2022, https://www.ons.gov.uk/peoplepopulationandcommunity/leisureandtourism/articles/traveltrends/2022

6   Rob Henderson, 'Luxury beliefs are status symbols', Rob Henderson's Newsletter, 12 June 2022, https://www.robkhenderson.com/p/status-symbols-and-the-struggle-for

7   The Growth Commission, 'The Growth Challenge: The decline in GDP per capita growth in advanced economies', July 2023, https://www.growth-commission.com/wp-content/uploads/2023/07/64ae4fd40046a0fodbd8f7f8_The-Growth-Challenge-1.pdf

8   The classic research on this topic is William J. Baumol, 'Entrepreneurship: Productive, unproductive, and destructive', *Journal of Business Venturing*, vol. 11, no. 1, January 1996, pp. 3–22, https://www.sciencedirect.com/science/article/abs/pii/088390269400014X

9   Tim Stickings, 'The UK's brain drain – and the countries trying to tempt away the talent', 6 January 2023, *National News*, https://www.thenationalnews.com/weekend/2023/01/06/the-uks-brain-drain-and-the-countries-trying-to-tempt-away-the-talent/

10 Hannah Ritchie and Pablos Rosado, 'Natural Disasters', Our World in Data, https://ourworldindata.org/natural-disasters

11 'Wagner's Law', Wikipedia, https://en.wikipedia.org/wiki/Wagner%27s_law

12 International Monetary Fund, International Financial Statistics, https://data.imf.org/regular.aspx?key=63122827; Office for Budget Responsibility, 'Economic and fiscal outlook – March 2024', https://obr.uk/efo/economic-and-fiscal-outlook-march-2024/; Giorgos Kallis, *In Defense of Degrowth* (Uneven Earth Press, 2018), https://indefenseofdegrowth.com/

13 Janet Daley, 'Climate hysteria is a serious threat to mankind's survival', *Daily Telegraph*, 29 July 2023, https://www.telegraph.co.uk/news/2023/07/29/climate-hysteria-is-greatest-threat-to-mankinds-survival/; Jenny Hjul, 'Take the heat out of climate change hysteria', *Reaction*, 9 September 2023, https://reaction.life/take-the-heat-out-of-climate-change-hysteria/; Mark Higgie, 'Europe's summer of climate hysteria', *Spectator Australia*, 12 August 2023, https://www.spectator.com.au/2023/08/europes-summer-of-climate-hysteria/

14 Jodie Keane, 'New EU trade rules could put poor countries in a billion dollar "green squeeze"', The Conversation, 24 April 2024, https://theconversation.com/new-eu-trade-rules-could-put-poor-countries-in-a-billion-dollar-

green-squeeze-228537; John Cassidy, 'Can we have prosperity without growth?', *New Yorker*, 3 February 2020, https://www.newyorker.com/magazine/2020/02/10/can-we-have-prosperity-without-growth

15 Matthew Palumbo and Corey Iacono, *In Defense of Classical Liberalism: An Economic Analysis* (Create Space Independent Publishing Platform, 2014), https://books.google.co.uk/books/about/In_Defense_of_Classical_Liberalism.html?id=Xx7grQEACAAJ&redir_esc=y

CHAPTER 5

1 International Monetary Fund, 'General Government Debt', https://www.imf.org/external/datamapper/GG_DEBT_GDP@GDD/AUS/BEL/DEU/FRA/ISR/ITA/NLD/PRT/ESP/SWE/GBR/USA/CZE/JPN/CAN/GRC

2 International Monetary Fund, 'Public Finances in Modern History', https://www.imf.org/external/datamapper/datasets/FPP

3 International Monetary Fund, 'General Government Debt', https://www.imf.org/external/datamapper/GG_DEBT_GDP@GDD/AUS/BEL/DEU/FRA/ISR/ITA/NLD/PRT/ESP/SWE/GBR/USA/CZE/JPN/CAN/GRC

4 International Monetary Fund, 'World Economic Outlook (April 2024)', https://www.imf.org/external/datamapper/datasets/WEO

5 International Monetary Fund, 'Fiscal Monitor (April 2024)', https://www.imf.org/external/datamapper/datasets/FM

6 International Monetary Fund, 'General government net lending/borrowing', https://www.imf.org/external/datamapper/GGXCNL_NGDP@WEO/OEMDC/ADVEC/WEOWORLD

7 International Monetary Fund, 'World Economic Outlook (April 2024)', https://www.imf.org/external/datamapper/datasets/WEO

8 UK Public Spending, 'UK Revenue and Deficit Forecast', https://www.ukpublicspending.co.uk/download_multi_year#copypaste

9 International Monetary Fund, 'World Economic Outlook (April 2024)', https://www.imf.org/external/datamapper/GGXWDG_NGDP@WEO/OEMDC/ADVEC/WEOWORLD

10 Neil O'Brien, 'Welfare spending and mental health', Neil's Substack, https://www.neilobrien.co.uk/p/welfare-spending-and-mental-health; Department for Work and Pensions, 'Modernising support for independent living: the health and green disability paper', GOV.UK, https://www.gov.uk/government/consultations/modernising-support-for-independent-living-the-health-and-disability-green-paper

11 HM Treasury, 'Whole of Government Accounts: year ended 31 March 2021', https://assets.publishing.service.gov.uk/government/uploads/system/uploads/attachment_data/file/1171941/Whole_of_Government_Accounts_2020-21_Final_Version_for_laying_and_publishing.pdf

12 'Pensions in the national accounts, a fuller picture of the UK's funded and unfunded pension obligations: 2018', Office for National Statistics, https://www.ons.gov.uk/economy/nationalaccounts/uksectoraccounts/articles/pensionsinthenationalaccountsafullerpictureoftheuksfundedandunfundedpensionobligations/2018

13 'Public finances databank 2022–23', Office for Budget Responsibility, https://obr.uk/public-finances-databank-2022-23/

14 International Monetary Fund, 'World Economic Outlook, April 2024', https://www.imf.org/en/Publications/WEO/Issues/2024/04/16/world-economic-outlook-april-2024

15 Office for National Statistics, 'UK Government debt and deficit: September 2023', https://www.ons.gov.uk/economy/governmentpublicsectorandtaxes/publicspending/bulletins/ukgovernmentdebtanddeficitforeurostatmaast/september2023

16 International Monetary Fund, 'General Government Debt', https://www.imf.org/external/datamapper/GG_DEBT_GDP@GDD/AUS/BEL/DEU/FRA/ISR/ITA/NLD/PRT/ESP/SWE/GBR/USA/CZE/JPN/CAN/GRC?year=2021

INTRODUCTION TO PART II

1 Daron Acemoglu and James A. Robinson, *Why Nations Fail: The Origins of Power, Prosperity, and Poverty* (Crown Business, 2012), https://wcfia.harvard.edu/publications/why-nations-fail-origins-power-prosperity-and-poverty

2 OECD, 'Tax revenue', https://data.oecd.org/tax/tax-revenue.htm

3 International Monetary Fund, 'World Economic Outlook (April 2024)', https://www.imf.org/external/datamapper/datasets/WEO

4 Robert J. Barro, 'Determinants of Economic Growth: A Cross-Country Empirical Study', *National Bureau of Economic Research*, working paper 5698, August 1996, https://www.nber.org/papers/w5698

5 World Bank, 'Life expectancy at birth, total (years)', for the selected economies, https://data.worldbank.

org/indicator/SP.DYN.LE00.IN?ncid=txtlnkusaolp000000618; Matthew Palumbo and Corey Iacono, *In Defense of Classical Liberalism: An Economic Analysis* (Create Space Independent Publishing Platform, 2014), https://books.google.co.uk/books/about/In_Defense_of_Classical_Liberalism.html?id=Xx7grQEACAAJ &redir_esc=y

6   Eir Nolsøe, 'Why the United States keeps getting richer – with Britain lagging even further behind', *Daily Telegraph*, 23 April 2023, https://www.telegraph.co.uk/business/2023/04/23/us-richer-than-uk-finance-inflation-taxes/

7   International Monetary Fund, 'GDP per capita, current prices', April 2024, https://www.imf.org/external/datamapper/PPPPC@WEO/USA/GBR

8   'Politicians must send the right signals on "green" jobs', *Financial Times*, 19 June 2023, https://www.ft.com/content/05f19822-6550-405c-9743-749ea56f810f

9   Molly Broome, Stefano Cellini, Kathleen Henehan, Charlie McCurdy, Capucine Riom, Anna Valero and Guglielmo Ventura, 'Net Zero Jobs: The impact of the transition to net zero on the UK labour market', The Resolution Foundation, June 2022, https://economy2030.resolutionfoundation.org/wp-content/uploads/2022/06/Net-zero-jobs.pdf

10 Office for National Statistics, 'The challenges of defining a "green job"', 7 April 2021, https://www.ons.gov.uk/economy/environmentalaccounts/methodologies/thechallengesofdefininggagreenjob

11 Andrew P. Morriss, William T. Bogart, Andrew Dorchak, Roger Meiners, 'Green Job Myths', U Illinois Law & Economics Research Paper No. LE09-001, 12 March 2009, https://papers.ssrn.com/sol3/papers.cfm?abstract_id=1358423; Gordon Hughes, 'The Myth of Green Jobs', Global Warming Policy Foundation, 2011, https://www.thegwpf.org/content/uploads/2012/08/Hughes-Greenjobs2.pdf; Andy Mayer, 'The "Green Jobs" Fallacy', Institute for Economic Affairs, 28 September 2018, https://iea.org.uk/the-green-jobs-fallacy/

12 OECD, 'OECD Data Explorer: Average annual wages', https://data-explorer.oecd.org/vis?tm=average%20annual%20wages&pg=0&hc[Measure]=Wages&hc[Pay%20period]=Annual&snb=2&vw=tb&df[ds]=dsDisseminateFinalDMZ&df[id]=DSD_EARNINGS%40AV_AN_WAGE&df[ag]=OECD.ELS.SAE&df[vs]=1.0&pd=2020%2C2022&dq=USA%2BCHE%2BGBR....V%2BQ..&to[TIME_PERIOD]=false&ly[rw]=REF_AREA%2CPRICE_BASE%2CUNIT_MEASURE&ly[cl]=TIME_PERIOD; 'Summary Table: Income', Singapore Ministry of Manpower, https://stats.mom.gov.sg/Pages/Income-Summary-Table.aspx

13 Legatum Institute, *The 2023 Legatum Prosperity Index*, 16th edition, https://www.prosperity.com/download_file/view_inline/4789

14 Wei Tien Sng, 'Nation building 101: lessons from Singapore', CapX, 23 February 2016, https://capx.co/nation-building-101-lessons-from-singapore/

15 'Life Expectancy of the World Population', Worldometer, https://www.worldometers.info/demographics/life-expectancy/

16 Office for National Statistics, 'Gross Domestic Product at market prices: current price: seasonally adjusted £m', https://www.ons.gov.uk/economy/grossdomesticproductgdp/timeseries/ybha/pn2

17 The World Bank, 'GDP per capita, PPP (current international $) – United Kingdom, United States', https://data.worldbank.org/indicator/NY.GDP.PCAP.PP.CD?end=2022&locations=GB-US&start=2022&view=bar

18 Robert J. Barro, 'Determinants of Economic Growth: A Cross-Country Empirical Study', *National Bureau of Economic Research*, working paper 5698, August 1996, https://www.nber.org/papers/w5698

19 Children's Commissioner, 'Almost one in five children left education at 18 last year without basic qualifications', 20 September 2019, https://www.childrenscommissioner.gov.uk/news/almost-one-in-five-children-left-education-at-18-last-year-without-basic-qualifications/

CHAPTER 6

1   Robert J. Barro, *Determinants of Economic Growth: A Cross-Country Empirical Study* (MIT Press, 1997), https://scholar.harvard.edu/barro/publications/determinants-economic-growth-cross-country-empirical-study

2   James Gwartney, Randall Holcombe and Robert Lawson, 'The Scope of Government and the Wealth of Nations', *Cato Journal*, vol. 18, no. 2, October 2011, https://www.researchgate.net/publication/247996807_The_Scope_of_Government_and_the_Wealth_of_Nations

3   Joseph Connors and Seth Norton, 'The Scope of Government and the Wealth of Nations Revisited', Hastert Center Public Policy Series, August 2012, https://faktasiden.com/dokumenter/gdp.pdf

4   International Monetary Fund, 'Public Finances in Modern History', https://www.imf.org/external/datamapper/datasets/FPP

NOTES

5   James Gwartney, Robert Lawson and Randall Holcombe, 'The size and functions of government and economic growth', Joint Economic Committee, April 1998, https://ohu.people.ysu.edu/articles/govt_size_economic_growth.pdf; Richard W. Rahn, 'The Optimum Government', Cato Institute, 29 January 2009, https://www.cato.org/commentary/optimum-government; Dimitar Chobanov and Adriana Mladenova, 'What is the optimum size of government', Institute for Market Economics, Bulgaria, August 2009, https://ime.bg/uploads/335309_OptimalSizeOfGovernment.pdf

6   International Monetary Fund, 'Public Finances in Modern History', https://www.imf.org/external/datamapper/datasets/FPP

7   Matt Palumbo and Corey Iacono, *In Defense of Classical Liberalism: An Economic Analysis*, (Create Space Independent Publishing Platform, 2014) https://www.abebooks.co.uk/9781503247499/Defense-Classical-Liberalism-Economic-Analysis-150324749X/plp

8   Andreas Bergh and Magnus Henrekson, 'Government Size and Growth: A Survey and Interpretation of the Evidence', IFN working paper 858, 23 January 2011, https://papers.ssrn.com/sol3/papers.cfm?abstract_id=1734206

9   Paul Krugman, 'The Conscience of a Liberal – Reinhardt-Rogoff, Continued', *New York Times*, 16 April 2013, https://archive.nytimes.com/krugman.blogs.nytimes.com/2013/04/16/reinhart-rogoff-continued/?

10 Livio Di Matteo, 'Measuring Government in the Twenty-First Century: An international overview of the size and efficiency of public spending', Fraser Institute, 2013, https://www.fraserinstitute.org/sites/default/files/measuring-government-in-the-21st-century.pdf; Dimitar Chobanov and Adriana Mladenova, 'What is the optimum size of government', Institute for Market Economics, Bulgaria, August 2009, https://ime.bg/uploads/335309_OptimalSizeOfGovernment.pdf; Ryan Bourne and Thomas Oechsle, 'Small is Best, Lessons from Advanced Economies', Centre for Policy Studies, May 2012, https://cps.org.uk/wp-content/uploads/2021/07/120522105633-smallisbest.pdf; Anthony Davies, 'Human Development and the Optimal Size of Government', *Journal of Socio-Economics*, vol. 38, no. 2, March 2009, pp. 326–30, https://www.sciencedirect.com/science/article/abs/pii/S1053535708001236

11 Ryan Bourne & Thomas Oechsle, *Small is Best: Lessons from Advanced Economies*', May 2012, Institute for Policy Research, https://cps.org.uk/wp-content/uploads/2021/07/120522105633-smallisbest.pdf

12 Helena Cenc, 'Government Expenditure and Economic Growth in Euro Area Countries', *Naše gospodarstvo*, vol. 68, no. 2, June 2022, pp. 19–27, https://www.researchgate.net/publication/361921645_Government_Expenditure_and_Economic_Growth_in_Euro_Area_Countries

13 Horst Feldmann, 'Government Size and Unemployment: Evidence from Developing Countries', *Journal of Developing Areas*, vol. 43, no. 1, Fall 2009, pp. 315–30, https://www.jstor.org/stable/40376286

14 Bee Boileau, Laurence O'Brien and Ben Zaranko, 'Public spending, pay and pensions: Green Budget 2022 – Chapter 4', IFS, 8 October 2022, https://ifs.org.uk/publications/public-spending-pay-and-pensions#:~:text=In%20July%202022%2C%20average%20annual,public%20sector%20(%C2%A330%2C657)

15 Office for Budget Responsibility, 'Economic and Fiscal Outlook – March 2024', https://obr.uk/efo/economic-and-fiscal-outlook-march-2024/

16 International Monetary Fund, 'World Economic Outlook (April 2024)', https://www.imf.org/external/datamapper/datasets/WEO

17 Office for Budget Responsibility, 'Economic and Fiscal Outlook (March 2024)', https://obr.uk/efo/economic-and-fiscal-outlook-march-2024/

18 Joseph Connors and Seth Norton, 'The Scope of Government and the Wealth of Nations Revisited', Hastert Center for Public Policy Series, August 2012, https://www.wheaton.edu/media/migrated-images-amp-files/media/files/centers-and-institutes/fpe/publicpolicyseries/ScopeofGovernmentFinal08282012.pdf

19 Norman Gemmell, Richard Kneller and Ismael Sanz, 'Does the Composition of Government Expenditure Matter for Long-Run GDP Levels?', *Oxford Bulletin of Economics and Statistics*, vol. 78, no. 4, 15 December 2015, https://onlinelibrary.wiley.com/doi/abs/10.1111/obes.12121

20 Gábor Kutasi and Ádám Marton, 'The long-term impact of public expenditures on GDP-growth', *Society and Economy*, vol. 42, no. 4, September 2020, https://www.researchgate.net/publication/347573966_The_long_term_impact_of_public_expenditures_on_GDP-growth

21 HM Treasury, 'Public Expenditure Statistical Analyses 2023', 19 July 2023, https://www.gov.uk/government/statistics/public-expenditure-statistical-analyses-2023

22 HM Treasury, 'Public Spending Statistics release: November 2023', https://www.gov.uk/government/statistics/public-spending-statistics-release-november-2023

23 Robert Colville, 'The Morality of Growth', Centre for Policy Studies, 13 January 2023, https://cps.org.uk/wp-content/uploads/2023/01/The-Morality-of-Growth-1.pdf

24 Reemul Ball, 'Record number of Britons receiving benefits that amount to more than they pay in tax, study finds', Sky News, 23 January 2023, https://news.sky.com/story/record-number-of-britons-receiving-benefits-that-amount-to-more-than-they-pay-in-tax-study-finds-12793349

25 Tim Knox, 'The once great British middle class is now riddled with entitlement and dependency', *Daily Telegraph*, 28 July 2023, https://www.telegraph.co.uk/business/2023/07/28/the-once-great-british-middle-class-ridded-with-entitlement/

26 Tim Knox, 'The once great British middle class is now riddled with entitlement and dependency', *Daily Telegraph*, 28 July 2023, https://www.telegraph.co.uk/business/2023/07/28/the-once-great-british-middle-class-ridded-with-entitlement/

27 Department for Work and Pensions, 'Benefit expenditure and caseload tables for 2024', 19 April 2024, https://www.gov.uk/government/publications/benefit-expenditure-and-caseload-tables-2024

28 Department for Work and Pensions, 'Benefit expenditure and caseload tables 2023', 25 April 2023, https://www.gov.uk/government/publications/benefit-expenditure-and-caseload-tables-2023

29 Daniel Hannan, 'Moral arguments over the state pension are irrelevant. There is no money', *Daily Telegraph*, 23 March 2024, https://www.telegraph.co.uk/news/2024/03/23/moral-arguments-state-pension-irrelevant-there-is-no-money/

30 Ben Riley-Smith, 'Triple lock will stay for the rest of decade if Tories win election, says Sunak', *Daily Telegraph*, 26 March 2024, https://www.telegraph.co.uk/politics/2024/03/26/rishi-sunak-keep-triple-lock-parliament-affordable-pensions/

31 Jessica Beard, 'State pension age "should be raised to 70" to save Government from funding crisis', *Daily Telegraph*, 18 January 2022, https://www.telegraph.co.uk/money/pensions/news/state-pension-age-should-raised-70-save-government-funding-crisis/; International Longevity Centre UK, 'The UK and other ageing populations will have to increase their state pension age to 71 by 2050 to maintain the number of workers per retiree', 5 February 2024, https://ilcuk.org.uk/ageing-populations-forced-to-increase-state-pension-age-to-71-by-2050-to-maintain-dependency-ratio/

32 Ros Altmann, 'State pension age hike to 71 would be a brutal blow to poor and ill people', This is Money, 6 February 2024, https://www.thisismoney.co.uk/money/pensions/article-13048025/State-pension-age-71-poor-ill-ROS-ALTMANN.html

33 Frank Hobson, Rachael Harker, Esme Kirk-Wade, 'State Pension Triple Lock', House of Commons Library, 6 November 2023, https://researchbriefings.files.parliament.uk/documents/CBP-7812/CBP-7812.pdf

34 Jonathan Cribb, Carl Emmerson, Paul Johnson and Heidi Karjalainen, 'The future of the state pension', Institute for Fiscal Studies, 13 December 2023, https://ifs.org.uk/publications/future-state-pension

35 Mattie Brignal, 'The year the state pension will start to collapse – whoever wins the election', *Daily Telegraph*, 26 May 2024, https://www.telegraph.co.uk/money/pensions/state-pensions/state-pension-triple-lock-retirement-age-general-election/

36 Ashley Kirk, 'Aging Britain: one in 12 will be aged over 80 by 2039', *Daily Telegraph*, 29 October 2015, https://www.telegraph.co.uk/news/uknews/11962587/Aging-Britain-One-in-12-will-be-aged-over-80-by-2039.html

37 The Health Foundation, 'Health in 2040: interactive chart projections', 25 July 2023, https://www.health.org.uk/news-and-comment/charts-and-infographics/health_in_2040

38 James Robards, 'National Population projections: 2021-based interim', Office for National Statistics, 30 January 2024, https://www.ons.gov.uk/peoplepopulationandcommunity/populationandmigration/populationprojections/bulletins/nationalpopulationprojections/2021basedinterim

39 Department for Work and Pensions, 'Benefit Expenditure and caseload tables 2024', https://www.gov.uk/government/publications/benefit-expenditure-and-caseload-tables-2024

40 Sam Ashworth-Hayes, 'Families on benefits can be better off than those earning £70k', *Daily Telegraph*, 31 January 2024, https://www.telegraph.co.uk/money/tax/income/families-benefits-better-off-earning-70k-london/

41 Department for Work and Pensions, 'Benefit expenditure and caseload tables 2024', 19 April 2024, https://www.gov.uk/government/publications/benefit-expenditure-and-caseload-tables-2024; Department for Work and Pensions, 'Benefit expenditure and caseload tables', 20 September 2013, https://www.gov.uk/government/collections/benefit-expenditure-tables

42 Department for Work and Pensions, 'Benefit expenditure and caseload tables 2024', 19 April 2024, https://www.gov.uk/government/publications/benefit-expenditure-and-caseload-tables-2024; 'Millions paid benefits without ever having to find a job', *Daily Telegraph*, 24 May 2023, https://www.telegraph.co.uk/business/2023/05/24/millions-paid-benefits-without-ever-having-to-find-a-job/

43 Szu Ping Chan and Melizza Lawford, 'Four million at risk of abandoning work permanently as benefits surge', *Daily Telegraph*, 11 March 2024, https://www.telegraph.co.uk/business/2024/03/11/four-million-abandoning-work-permanently-benefits-surge/

44 Alana Semuels, 'The end of welfare as we know it', *The Atlantic*, 1 April 2016, https://www.theatlantic.com/business/archive/2016/04/the-end-of-welfare-as-we-know-it/476322/

45 Jennifer Scott, 'Rishi Sunak pledges to remove benefits for people not taking jobs after 12 months', Sky News, 19 April 2024, https://news.sky.com/story/rishi-sunak-pledges-to-remove-benefits-for-people-not-taking-jobs-after-12-months-13118419

46 Department for Work and Pensions, 'Benefit expenditure and caseload tables 2024', 19 April 2024, https://www.gov.uk/government/publications/benefit-expenditure-and-caseload-tables-2024

47 Robert Booth, 'Priced-out UK house-hunters turn to lorry-sized tiny homes', *The Guardian*, 15 January 2023, https://www.theguardian.com/society/2023/jan/15/priced-out-uk-house-hunters-turn-to-lorry-sized-tiny-homes

48 Victoria Purcell, 'Why tiny homes are on the up', *Grand Designs Magazine*, 6 January 2023, https://www.granddesignsmagazine.com/self-build/tiny-homes-uk/#:~:text=There%27s%20just%20one%20rule%20uniting,requirements%20for%20a%20London%20flat

49 Noah Eastwood, 'Benefits system left open to fraud after pandemic, says architect of Universal Credit', *Daily Telegraph*, 27 April 2024, https://www.telegraph.co.uk/money/consumer-affairs/benefits-system-fraud-pandemic-architect-universal-credit/

50 Department for Work and Pensions, 'Fraud and error in the benefit system, Financial Year Ending (FYE) 2024', 16 May 2024, https://www.gov.uk/government/statistics/fraud-and-error-in-the-benefit-system-financial-year-2019-to-2020-estimates/fraud-and-error-in-the-benefit-system-2019-to-2020

51 Department for Work and Pensions, 'Fraud and error in the benefit system 2019 to 2020', 29 May 2020, https://www.gov.uk/government/statistics/fraud-and-error-in-the-benefit-system-financial-year-2019-to-2020-estimates/fraud-and-error-in-the-benefit-system-2019-to-2020

52 Telegraph Reporters, 'Bulgarians pocket £50m from taxpayer in Britian's biggest benefits fraud', 10 April 2024, https://www.telegraph.co.uk/news/2024/04/10/bulgarian-gang-benefit-fraud-biggest-britain-50-million/

53 Department for Work and Pensions, 'Fraud and error in the benefit system, Financial Year Ending (FYE) 2024', 16 May 2024, https://www.gov.uk/government/statistics/fraud-and-error-in-the-benefit-system-financial-year-2023-to-2024-estimates/fraud-and-error-in-the-benefit-system-financial-year-ending-fye-2024

54 'How to stop over-medicalising mental health', *The Economist*, 7 December 2023, https://www.economist.com/leaders/2023/12/07/how-to-stop-over-medicalising-mental-health

55 Jonathan Cribb, Heidi Karjalainen and Tom Waters, 'Big rise in claims means disability benefits bill 70% higher than expected – and claimants on average waiting five months to receive', IFS, 6 July 2022, https://ifs.org.uk/news/big-rise-claims-means-disability-benefits-bill-70-higher-expected-and-claimants-average

56 Department for Work and Pensions, 'Personal Independence Payment statistics to January 2024', 19 March 2024, https://www.gov.uk/government/statistics/personal-independence-payment-statistics-to-january-2024

57 Department for Work and Pensions, 'Benefit expenditure and caseload tables 2024', 19 April 2024, https://www.gov.uk/government/publications/benefit-expenditure-and-caseload-tables-2024

58 Szu Ping Chan and Melissa Lawford, 'Welcome to the disability benefits capital of Britain', *Daily Telegraph*, 28 April 2024, https://www.telegraph.co.uk/business/2024/04/28/welcome-to-the-disability-benefits-capital-of-britain/

59 Jonathan Cribb, Heidi Karjalainen and Tom Waters, 'Big rise in claims means disability benefits bill 70% higher than expected – and claimants on average waiting five months to receive', IFS, 6 July 2022, https://ifs.org.uk/news/big-rise-claims-means-disability-benefits-bill-70-higher-expected-and-claimants-average

60 Department for Work and Pensions, 'Benefit expenditure and caseload tables 2024', 19 April 2024, https://www.gov.uk/government/publications/benefit-expenditure-and-caseload-tables-2024

61 Office for National Statistics, 'INAC01 SA: Economic inactivity by reason (seasonally adjusted)', https://www.ons.gov.uk/employmentandlabourmarket/peoplenotinwork/economicinactivity/datasets/economicinactivitybyreasonseasonallyadjustedinac01sa

62 'Is stress a disability?', TUC, 15 December 2006, https://www.tuc.org.uk/research-analysis/reports/stress-disability

63 Ruchi Gandhi, 'Walker v Northumberland County Council [1995] 1 All ER 737', Case Judgements, https://casejudgments.com/walker-v-northumberland-county-council-1995/

64 Kate Andrews, 'Why Britain stopped working', *The Spectator*, 24 February 2024, https://www.spectator.co.uk/article/why-britain-stopped-working/

65 'A growing number of Britons are on disability payments', *The Economist*, 2 May 2024, https://www.economist.com/britain/2024/05/02/a-growing-number-of-britons-are-on-disability-benefits

66 Theodore Dalrymple, 'It's time to eliminate the concept of "mental health"', *The Spectator*, 2 March 2024, https://www.spectator.co.uk/article/its-time-to-eliminate-the-concept-of-mental-health/

67 Matthew Parris, 'How to claim mental illness benefits', *The Spectator*, 16 March 2024, https://www.spectator.co.uk/article/how-to-claim-mental-illness-benefits/

68 Charlotte Anderson, 'YouTuber shares how she makes a fortune filing out disability applications for £650 a pop – as she boasts she has "only ever lost one claim in six years"', *Mail on Sunday*, 13 April 2024, https://www.dailymail.co.uk/news/article-13305479/YouTuber-shares-makes-fortune-filling-disability-applications-650-pop-boasts-lost-one-claim-six-years.html

69 'Author Discussion on the Crisis of Masculinity', C-SPAN, 31 October 2023, https://www.c-span.org/video/?531508-1/author-discussion-crisis-masculinity

70 Melissa Lawford and Ben Butcher, 'The English town where children grow up doomed to worklessness', *Daily Telegraph*, 24 March 2024, https://www.telegraph.co.uk/business/2024/03/24/middlesbrough-children-grow-up-doomed-worklessness/

71 Szu Ping Chan and Charles Hymas, 'Cut benefits bill instead of relying on migration to bring down debt, says OBR chief', *Daily Telegraph*, 7 February 2024, https://www.telegraph.co.uk/business/2024/02/07/cut-benefits-instead-relying-migration-bring-down-debt-obr/

72 Department for Work and Pensions, 'Benefit expenditure and caseload tables 2024', 19 April 2024, https://www.gov.uk/government/publications/benefit-expenditure-and-caseload-tables-2024

73 OECD, 'OECD Data Explorer', https://data-explorer.oecd.org/vis?tm=Health%20expenditure%20and%20financing&pg=0&snb=17&vw=tb&df[ds]=dsDisseminateFinalDMZ&df[id]=DSD_SHA%40DF_SHA&df[ag]=OECD.ELS.HD&df[vs]=1.0&pd=2021%2C2022&dq=GBR.A.EXP_HEALTH.XDC.HF23%2BHF22%2BHF21%2BHF12HF13%2BHF2HF3%2BHF32%2BHF3%2BHF31%2BHF122%2BHF121%2BHF11%2BHF2%2BHF1%2B_T.._T.._T...&ly[cl]=TIME_PERIOD&ly[rs]=PRICE_BASE&to[TIME_PERIOD]=false

74 OECD, 'OECD Data Explorer', https://data-explorer.oecd.org/

75 Macrotrends, 'UK population 1950–2024', https://www.macrotrends.net/global-metrics/countries/GBR/united-kingdom/population

76 Ross Clark, 'How this "Great Fat Lie" has become a Big Fat Truth: Remainers scorned the claim Brexit would give an extra £350m a week to the NHS. In fact, it's now getting an extra £710m', *Daily Mail*, 13 April 2024, https://www.dailymail.co.uk/debate/article-13304953/remainers-brexit-extra-350-nhs-ross-clark.html; Jonathan Barron, 'Budget 2024: what you need to know', NHS Confederation, 6 March 2024, https://www.nhsconfed.org/publications/budget-2024

77 Henry Oliver, 'Truss was right: The British economy can't afford low growth', The Critic, 21 December 2022, https://thecritic.co.uk/truss-was-right/

78 Office for National Statistics, 'The healthcare workforce across the UK: 2024', https://www.ons.gov.uk/peoplepopulationandcommunity/healthandsocialcare/healthcaresystem/articles/thehealthcareworkforceacrosstheuk/2024

79 Nuffield Trust, 'Elective (planned) treatment waiting times', 25 April 2024, https://www.nuffieldtrust.org.uk/resource/treatment-waiting-times

80 NHS England, 'Cancer Waiting Times', October 2023, https://www.england.nhs.uk/statistics/statistical-work-areas/cancer-waiting-times/#cwt-statistics-up-to-september-2023

81 Melina Arnold, Mark J. Rutherford, Aude Bardot, Jacques Ferlay, Therese M-L Andersson, Tor Åge Myklebust, 'Progress in cancer survival, mortality, and incidence in seven high-income countries 1995–2014 (ICBP SURVMARK-2): a population based study', *The Lancet*, vol. 20, no. 11, 11 September 2019, pp. 1493–1505, https://www.thelancet.com/journals/lanonc/article/PIIS1470-2045(19)30456-5/fulltext#tables

82 The World Bank, 'Health Nutrition and Population Statistics', https://databank.worldbank.org/source/health-nutrition-and-population-statistics

83 'Are young children in Britain getting smaller?', *The Economist*, 29 June 2023, https://www.economist.com/britain/2023/06/29/are-young-children-in-britain-getting-smaller

84 Eleanor Hayward and Chris Smyth, 'Satisfaction with the NHS falls to record low', *The Times*, 27 March 2024, https://www.thetimes.co.uk/article/nhs-uk-satisfaction-record-low-z2wpc2d05

85 Legatum Institute, 'The Legatum Prosperity Index 2023, Advancing the understanding of what drives success in nations', https://www.prosperity.com/rankings

86 Jacqueline Howard, 'US spends most on health care but has worst health outcomes among high-income countries, new report finds', CNN, 31 January 2023, https://edition.cnn.com/2023/01/31/health/us-health-care-spending-global-perspective/index.html

87 Full Fact, 'NHS England: £394 million more a week?', 26 November 2018, https://fullfact.org/health/nhs-england-394-million-more/

88 Kate Andrews, 'What junior doctors really earn', *The Spectator*, 15 April 2023, https://www.spectator.co.uk/article/what-junior-doctors-really-earn/

89 Sam Freedman and Rachel Wolf, 'The NHS productivity puzzle', Institute for Government, https://www.instituteforgovernment.org.uk/sites/default/files/2023-06/nhs-productivity-puzzle_o.pdf

90 Sophia Sleigh, 'How much? Four GPs were paid more than £1 million in year – SIX times more than PM, shock report reveals', *The Sun*, 7 April 2024, https://www.thesun.co.uk/health/27165669/four-doctors-paid-1million-report/

91 Georgie Frost, 'Highest-paying jobs in the UK', Times Money Mentor, 19 April 2024, https://www.thetimes.co.uk/money-mentor/income-budgeting/highest-paid-jobs-uk#What-are-the-highest-paying-jobs-in-the-UK?

92 James Bartholomew, 'The NHS is our national shame. It's time to abolish it', *Daily Telegraph*, 6 March 2024, https://www.telegraph.co.uk/news/2024/03/06/jeremy-hunt-budget-nhs-proud/

93 Sarah Knapton, '"BA don't ground planes at weekends" says Lord Darzi as he calls for seven-day NHS surgery', *Daily Telegraph*, 5 February 2024, https://www.telegraph.co.uk/news/2024/02/05/lord-darzi-seven-day-nhs-surgery-times-health-commission/

94 Wall-Y, 'Hospital cuts waiting lists with Formula 1 pitstop method', Warp News, 26 December 2023, https://www.warpnews.org/innovation/hospital-cuts-waiting-lists-with-formula-one-pitstop-method/; Emily Craig, 'Groundbreaking F1-inspired initiative which could help ailing NHS hospitals clear record waiting lists this winter', *Daily Mail*, 11 December 2023, https://www.dailymail.co.uk/health/article-12849435/Groundbreaking-F1-inspired-initiative-help-ailing-NHS-hospitals-clear-record-waiting-lists-winter.html

95 Rt Hon Steve Barclay, 'Over 50 new surgical hubs set to open across England to help bust the Covid-19 backlogs', Department of Health and Social Care, 26 August 2022, https://www.gov.uk/government/news/over-50-new-surgical-hubs-set-to-open-across-england-to-help-bust-the-covid-backlogs

96 Anna Fleck, 'Overburdened NHS pushes more Brits to go private', Statista, 8 February 2023, https://www.statista.com/chart/29261/share-of-uk-paying-for-private-health-insurance/

97 Jennifer Rudden, 'Total number of healthcare insurance corporations in Germany from 1980 to 2022', Statista, 6 December 2023, https://www.statista.com/statistics/729393/total-number-of-health-insurance-companies-germany-europe/

98 'How many UK residents have turned to private health insurance?', Expatriate Group, 27 April 2023, https://www.expatriatehealthcare.com/how-many-uk-residents-have-turned-to-private-health-insurance/

99 Katherine Keisler-Starkey, Lisa N. Bunch and Rachel A. Lindstrom, 'Health Insurance Coverage in the United States: 2022', United States Census Bureau, 12 September 2023, https://www.census.gov/library/publications/2023/demo/p60-281.html

100 'It does not cost the public £500,000 to train a doctor', Full Fact, 17 July 2023, https://fullfact.org/health/nadine-dorries-doctor-training-cost-australia-new-zealand/

101 Sam Ashworth-Hayes, 'Let Amazon run the NHS. That would cut the waiting lists', *Daily Telegraph*, 15 January 2024, https://www.telegraph.co.uk/news/2024/01/15/let-amazon-run-the-nhs-then-there-would-be-no-waiting-lists/

102 'Letters', *Daily Telegraph*, 18 August 2023, https://www.telegraph.co.uk/opinion/2023/08/18/letters-a-level-students-have-been-let-down-at-every-turn/

103 Miriam Blümel and Reinhard Busse, 'Germany: International Health Care Systems Profiles', Commonwealth Fund, https://www.commonwealthfund.org/international-health-policy-center/countries/germany

104 Martin Vlachynský and Matej Bárta, 'Why Singapore's Healthcare System is Unique', EPICENTER, 5 September 2023, https://www.epicenternetwork.eu/blog/why-singapores-healthcare-system-is-unique-3263/

105 'Wes Streeting, a Labour frontbencher, visits Singapore', *The Economist*, 14 December 2023, https://www.economist.com/britain/2023/12/14/wes-streeting-a-labour-frontbencher-visits-singapore

106 Caroline Hanson, Claire Hou, Allison Percy, Emily Vreeland and Alexandra Minicozzi, 'Health Insurance for people younger than age 65: Expiration of temporary policies projected to reshuffle coverage, 2023-33', *Health Affairs*, vol. 24, no. 6, 24 May 2023, https://www.healthaffairs.org/doi/10.1377/hlthaff.2023.00325

107 National Research Council (US), Institute of Medicine, Steven H. Woolf and Laudan Aron, 'US Health in International Perspective: Shorter Lives, Poorer Health', *National Library of Medicine*, 2013, https://www.ncbi.nlm.nih.gov/books/NBK115854/

108 House of Commons Health and Social Care Committee, 'NHS Litigation Reform', 20 April 2022, https://committees.parliament.uk/publications/22039/documents/163739/default/

109 Office for Budget Responsibility, 'Economic and Fiscal Outlook', March 2024, https://obr.uk/economic-and-fiscal-outlooks/

110 Office for Budget Responsibility, 'A brief guide to the UK public finances', https://obr.uk/docs/dlm_uploads/BriefGuide-M23.pdf

111 Office for National Statistics, 'Main figures from our time series explorer', https://www.ons.gov.uk/

112 Office for Budget Responsibility, 'The sensitivity of the Asset Purchase Facility to market conditions', March 2024, https://obr.uk/box/the-sensitivity-of-the-asset-purchase-facility-to-market-conditions/#:~:text=Our%20latest%20estimate%20of%20the,2024-25%20onwards%2C%20 respectively

113 Michael Simmons, 'When it comes to education, Scotland is an example of what not to do', *The Spectator*, 9 December 2023, https://www.spectator.co.uk/article/when-it-comes-to-education-scotland-is-an-example-of-what-not-to-do/

114 OECD, 'PISA 2018 results', https://www.oecd.org/pisa/publications/pisa-2018-results.htm

115 Sean Coughlan, 'PISA tests: UK rises in international school rankings', BBC News, 3 December 2019, https://www.bbc.co.uk/news/education-50563833

116 *'What is PISA'*, OECD https://www.oecd.org/pisa/

117 National Statistics, 'Level 2 and 3 attainment age 16 to 25', 25 April 2024, https://explore-education-statistics.service.gov.uk/find-statistics/level-2-and-3-attainment-by-young-people-aged-19#releaseHeadlines-charts

118 Sally Weale, 'English schools could lose £1bn by 2030 as pupil numbers fall', *The Guardian*, 11 April 2024, https://www.theguardian.com/education/2024/apr/11/english-schools-could-lose-1bn-by-2030-as-pupil-numbers-fall

119 Pete Henshaw, 'School buildings: Survey reveals poor condition of many classrooms', Headteacher Update, 11 March 2024, https://www.headteacher-update.com/content/news/school-buildings-survey-reveals-poor-condition-of-many-classrooms/; Arj Singh, 'Nearly 100 school playing fields sold off in seven years "putting Lionesses legacy at risk"', *The i*, 5 August 2022, https://inews.co.uk/news/politics/nearly-100-school-playing-fields-sold-off-in-seven-years-putting-lionesses-legacy-at-risk-1782214; Jack Kellam, 'Here's why UK teachers need a four-day week', Thomas Reuters Foundation, 20 January 2022, https://news.trust.org/item/20220120114450-ilozw/; Social Mobility Commission, 'Extra-curricular activities, soft skills and social mobility', Gov.uk, 19 July 2019, https://www.gov.uk/government/news/extra-curricular-activities-soft-skills-and-social-mobility

120 'Where did it go right for Blair and Brown?', *Financial Times*, 11 April 2010, https://www.ft.com/content/c43e3a7a-459a-11df-9e46-00144feab49a?accessToken=zwAGEYSc54nYkdPEPjp6RZoR39OeRgAUT-qomg.MEQCIHaIoT-pmELYQ8xK3O7McwbmWaxsgsFuz_EObBrQpowgAiAtKg3sZcAUs56DsJc74I837rdOLg7wjjpONdtuLOXlkg&sharetype=gift&token=df3360ef-144e-4858-8287-655a444805d8

121 Judy Friedberg, 'Teaching Assistants don't boost pupils' progress, report finds', *The Guardian*, 4 September 2009, https://www.theguardian.com/education/2009/sep/04/teaching-assistants-classroom-improvements

122 'School workforce in England (Reporting year 2023)', Gov.uk, 6 June 2024, https://explore-education-statistics.service.gov.uk/find-statistics/school-workforce-in-england

123 'Classroom Assistants', volume 463: debated on Tuesday 24 July 2007, UK Parliament, Hansard, https://hansard.parliament.uk/commons/2007-07-24/debates/07072486000069/ClassroomAssistants

124 'School Workforce in England (Reporting year 2023)', Gov.uk, 8 June 2023, https://explore-education-statistics.service.gov.uk/find-statistics/school-workforce-in-england

125 'Teaching Assistant average salary in United Kingdom, 2024', Talent.com, https://uk.talent.com/salary?job=teaching+assistant; 'True cost of an employee calculator', Accounting Services for Business (ASFB), https://accountingservicesforbusiness.co.uk/true-cost-of-an-employee-calculator/

126 Joanne E. Taberner, 'There are too many kids with special educational needs', Frontiers, 12 April 2023, https://www.frontiersin.org/articles/10.3389/feduc.2023.1125091/full

127 Maddy Shaw Roberts, 'Andrew Lloyd Webber slams education disparity: 'Only 12 percent of state schools have an orchestra', Classic FM, 28 June 2023, https://www.classicfm.com/composers/lloyd-webber/adopt-music-schools-scheme-children/

128 Astha Saxena, 'England's teachers among the best paid for fewest hours in Europe, latest survey finds', *The Express*, 1 February 2023, https://www.express.co.uk/news/uk/1729009/england-teachers-pay-oecd-survey-ont

129 Louisa Clarence-Smith and Ben Butcher, 'England's teachers among the best paid for fewest hours in Europe', *Daily Telegraph*, 31 January 2023, https://www.telegraph.co.uk/news/2023/01/31/teachers-strike-england-high-pay-fewest-hours-europe/

130 Parents and Teachers for Excellence, 'Warm, Rich, High, Wide: PTE's Philosophy for giving Britain's children an outstanding education', 23 September 2022, https://parentsandteachers.org.uk/pte-philosophy/

131 Philip Nye and Nick Davies, 'Performance Tracker 2023: Schools', Institute for Government, 30 October 2023, https://www.instituteforgovernment.org.uk/publication/performance-tracker-2023/schools

132 All metrics used in this section come from the 2021 CPS report 'The Cost of University' or from the

IFS report 'The Impact of undergraduate degrees on lifetime earnings'. See Conor Walsh, 'The Value of University', Centre for Policy Studies, September 2021, https://cps.org.uk/wp-content/uploads/2021/11/CPS_VALUE_OF_UNIVERSITY-1.pdf

133 Conor Walsh, 'The Value of University', Centre for Policy Studies, September 2021, https://cps.org.uk/wp-content/uploads/2021/11/CPS_VALUE_OF_UNIVERSITY-1.pdf

134 Jack Britton, Lorrain Dearden, Ben Waltmann and Laura van der Erve, 'The impact of undergraduate degrees on lifetime earnings', Institute for Fiscal Studies, 29 February 2020, https://ifs.org.uk/publications/impact-undergraduate-degrees-lifetime-earnings

135 Conor Walsh, 'The Value of University', Centre for Policy Studies, September 2021, https://cps.org.uk/wp-content/uploads/2021/11/CPS_VALUE_OF_UNIVERSITY-1.pdf

136 Chris Stickney, 'Visa Journeys and student outcomes', Office for National Statistics, 29 November 2021, https://www.ons.gov.uk/peoplepopulationandcommunity/populationandmigration/internationalmigration/articles/visajourneysandstudentoutcomes/2021-11-29

137 Conor Walsh, 'The Value of University', Centre for Policy Studies, September 2021, https://cps.org.uk/wp-content/uploads/2021/11/CPS_VALUE_OF_UNIVERSITY-1.pdf

138 Nicola Woolcock and Oliver Wright, 'Rishi Sunak to cut "Mickey Mouse" degrees to boost apprenticeships', The Times, 28 May 2024, https://www.thetimes.com/article/7056bda2-b240-461f-a635-c7a6fb373395?shareToken=f8e99a1d90649f252a7fa53a0dcf234c

139 John Dickie, 'The Elizabeth Line anniversary is a reminder of what London and other cities can achieve with the right kind of investment', City AM, 24 May 2023, https://www.cityam.com/the-elizabeth-line-anniversary-is-a-reminder-of-what-london-and-other-cities-can-achieve-with-the-right-kind-of-investment/

140 Molly Russell, 'London Heathrow Airport is set to revive 3rd runway plans next year', Simple Flying, 27 October 2023, https://simpleflying.com/london-heathrow-airport-revive-3rd-runway-plans-2024/

141 Ben Hopkinson, 'Building transport in Britain doesn't have to be this hard', Britain Remade, 25 August 2023, https://www.britainremade.co.uk/building_transport_in_britain_doesn_t_have_to_be_this_hard

142 'Natural England's ban on new homes began in June 2019, leaving builders in limbo', Housebuilders Federation, https://www.hbf.co.uk/nutrient-neutrality-4-years-on/

143 International Transport Forum 'Infrastructure investment data reveals contrasts between countries', https://www.itf-oecd.org/infrastructure-investment-data-reveal-contrasts-between-countries

144 Nishant Makhija, 'Lost decades of Japan', San Jose State University, Spring 2012, https://scholarworks.sjsu.edu/cgi/viewcontent.cgi?article=1308&context=etd_projects#:~:text=According%20to%20the%20Japanese%20Cabinet,high%20until%20the%20early%202000s

145 'HS2 cost projections and controversies still raise questions', Railtech.com, 21 November 2023, https://www.railtech.com/all/2023/11/21/hs2-cost-projections-and-controversies-still-raise-questions/?gdpr=accept&gdpr=accept; Melissa Lawford, 'Why high-speed rail projects like HS2 cost 10 times more in Britain than in France', Daily Telegraph, 4 October 2023, https://www.telegraph.co.uk/business/2023/10/04/why-high-speed-rail-projects-cost-more-britain-france/

146 Sean McPolin, 'Lower Thames Crossing planning costs reach £300m as pop-in event planned for Bluewater', KentOnline, 7 February 2024, https://www.kentonline.co.uk/gravesend/news/lower-thames-crossing-planning-costs-reach-300m-301419/

147 'The horror story of HS2: How a flagship project became a parable of Britain's problems', The Economist, 17 February 2024, https://www.economist.com/britain/2024/02/15/the-horror-story-of-hs2

148 'UK Government spending over time', IFS Composition Sheet, IFS Tax Lab, https://ifs.org.uk/taxlab/taxlab-data-item/ifs-spending-composition-sheet

149 Darya Korsunskaya and Alexander Marrow, 'Everything for the front: Russia allots a third of 2024 spending to defence', Reuters, 2 October 2023, https://www.reuters.com/world/europe/everything-front-russia-allots-third-2024-spending-defence-2023-10-02/

150 'SIPRI Military Expenditure Database' Stockholm International Peace Research Institute, https://www.sipri.org/sites/default/files/SIPRI-Milex-data-1948-2023.xlsx

151 'SIPRI Military Expenditure Database' Stockholm International Peace Research Institute, https://www.sipri.org/databases/milex

152 'UK Armed forces face nearly $22 bln equipment-funding shortfall over next decade – watchdog', Reuters, 4 December 2023, https://finance.yahoo.com/news/uk-armed-forces-face-nearly-085550375.html

153 'RAF recruitment drive boss "resigned over 160 cases of positive discrimination"', Forces Net, 2 February 2023, https://www.forces.net/services/raf/raf-will-learn-lessons-after-recruitment-drive-boss-resigned-over-160-cases-positive; Deborah Haynes, 'Applicants seeking to join RAF described as "useless white male pilots" in bid to hit "impossible" diversity targets', Sky News, 1 June 2023, https://news.sky.com/

story/raf-recruiters-were-advised-against-selecting-useless-white-male-pilots-to-hit-diversity-targets-12893684; Steven Edginton, 'Navy personnel told to introduce themselves with pronouns in trans guidance', *Daily Telegraph*, 30 September 2023, https://www.telegraph.co.uk/news/2023/09/30/royal-navy-inclusion-lgbtq-transgender-white-privilege/; Steven Edginton, 'Army to relax security checks for recruits in diversity drive', *Daily Telegraph*, 10 February 2024, https://www.telegraph.co.uk/news/2024/02/10/army-challenge-overseas-recruits-security-checks/

154 Robert Mendick, 'Military prepares for new push on diversity', *Daily Telegraph*, 17 August 2022, https://www.telegraph.co.uk/news/2022/08/17/military-prepares-new-push-diversity/

155 'Britain's armed forces are stretched perilously thin', *The Economist*, 29 January 2024, https://www.economist.com/britain/2024/01/29/britains-armed-forces-are-stretched-perilously-thin

156 Andrew Neil, 'At over £50bn a year, Britain is the world's 6th biggest defence spender. So why are our forces so badly equipped and humiliatingly hollowed out? The answer is that MoD bureaucrats are guilty of incompetence, stupidity and reckless squandering', *Daily Mail*, 10 February 2024, https://www.dailymail.co.uk/debate/article-13066863/Andrew-Neil-Britain-biggest-defence-spender-Armed-Forces-badly-equipped-incompetence.html

157 D. Clark, 'Number of public sector employees UK 2023, by industry', Statista, 23 February 2024, https://www.statista.com/statistics/284104/public-sector-employment-uk-by-industry/

158 National Institute of Economic and Social Research, 'National Institute UK Economic Outlook', Series A., No. 10, Spring 2023, https://www.niesr.ac.uk/wp-content/uploads/2023/05/Spring-2023-UK-Economic-Outlook.pdf

159 Office for National Statistics, 'EMP13: Employment by Industry', 13 February 2024, https://www.ons.gov.uk/employmentandlabourmarket/peopleinwork/employmentandemployeetypes/datasets/employmentbyindustryemp13

160 'UK Automotive', SMMT, https://www.smmt.co.uk/industry-topics/uk-automotive/

161 Alexandra Leonards, 'Employee numbers at largest UK banks see "highest increase in 10 years"', FS Tech, 6 July 2023, https://www.fstech.co.uk/fst/Employee_Numbers_At_Largest_UK_Banks_See_Highest_Increase_In_10_Years.php

162 Office for National Statistics, 'Public service productivity, quarterly, UK: January to March 2023', https://www.ons.gov.uk/economy/economicoutputandproductivity/publicservicesproductivity/bulletins/publicserviceproductivityquarterlyuk/januarytomarch2023

163 Committee of Public Accounts, 'Civil service workforce: recruitment, pay and performance management', UK Parliament, 22 March 2024, https://publications.parliament.uk/pa/cm5804/cmselect/cmpubacc/452/report.html

164 NHS England, 'Record recruitment and reform to boost patient care under first NHS long term workforce plan', 30 June 2023, https://www.england.nhs.uk/2023/06/record-recruitment-and-reform-to-boost-patient-care-under-first-nhs-long-term-workforce-plan/

165 Szu Ping Chan and James Warrington, 'Public sector to cost UK "tens of billions" as Jacob Rees-Mogg blames working from home', *Daily Telegraph*, 26 January 2023, https://www.telegraph.co.uk/business/2023/01/26/public-sector-cost-uk-tens-billions-productivity-slumps/

166 'Local Government structure and elections', Gov.uk, 11 January 2016, https://www.gov.uk/guidance/local-government-structure-and-elections; 'Departments, agencies and public bodies', Gov.uk, https://www.gov.uk/government/organisations

167 Cabinet Office, 'Guidance on the undertaking of Reviews of Public Bodies', 25 April 2024, https://www.gov.uk/government/publications/public-bodies-review-programme/guidance-on-the-undertaking-of-reviews-of-public-bodies

168 Christopher Snowdon, 'Sock Puppets: How the government lobbies itself and why', Institute for Economic Affairs, IEA Discussion Paper No. 39, June 2012, https://iea.org.uk/wp-content/uploads/2016/07/DP_Sock%20Puppets_redesigned.pdf

169 Simon Macdonald, *Leadership: Lessons from a life in diplomacy*, (Haus Publishing, 2022), https://www.jstor.org/stable/jj.1380403; Martin Stanley, *How to Be a Civil Servant*, (Politicos, 2000), https://www.abebooks.com/9781902301082/Civil-Servant-Stanley-Martin-1902301080/plp

170 Asset Publishing Service, 'Departmental Boards', https://assets.publishing.service.gov.uk/government/uploads/system/uploads/attachment_data/file/519772/Departmental_Boards.pdf; Assets Publishing Service, 'The Government Lead Non-Executive Annual Report 2020-21', https://assets.publishing.service.gov.uk/government/uploads/system/uploads/attachment_data/file/1064004/government-lead-ned-report-2021.pdf

171 Martin Stanley, 'Dismissal – Permanent Secretaries', Understanding the Civil Service, https://www.civilservant.org.uk/information-dismissal-permanent_secretaries.html

172 'Times letters: Labour leadership and credible opposition', *The Times*, 9 January 2020, https://www.thetimes.co.uk/article/times-letters-labour-leadership-and-credible-opposition-shcjp3t5c

173 'Principal–agent problem', Wikipedia, https://en.wikipedia.org/wiki/Principal%E2%80%93agent_problem

174 Helen Brown, 'The "laid back" life of a £67k train driver – and how it compares to other jobs', *Daily Telegraph*, 1 November 2023, https://www.telegraph.co.uk/news/2023/11/01/train-driver-salary-67k-easy-life-how-compares/

175 Tim Sigsworth, 'The absence epidemic has struck – welcome to sick day Britain', *Daily Telegraph*, 1 November 2023, https://www.telegraph.co.uk/news/2023/11/01/sick-leave-absence-human-resources-britain-working/

176 'The fight over working from home goes global', *The Economist*, 10 July 2023, https://www.economist.com/business/2023/07/10/the-fight-over-working-from-home-goes-global

177 Hugh Osmond, 'Endemic inefficiency, shirking from home… the sclerotic public sector has become a ball and chain holding Britain back', *Daily Mail*, 13 June 2023, https://www.dailymail.co.uk/debate/article-12191581/Sclerotic-public-sector-ball-chain-holding-Britain-writes-HUGH-OSMOND.html

178 Baringa, 'Solving the public sector productivity puzzle', Civil Service World, 16 November 2023, https://www.civilserviceworld.com/news/article/solving-the-public-sector-productivity-puzzle

179 Office for National Statistics, 'Labour Productivity', https://www.ons.gov.uk/employmentandlabourmarket/peopleinwork/labourproductivity

180 Emily White, 'HMRC to close self-assessment helpline from April to October each year – here's how to get help when you need it', MoneySavingExpert, 20 March 2024, https://www.moneysavingexpert.com/news/2024/03/hmrc-self-assessment-phonelines/

181 TaxPayers' Alliance, 'The civil service: a growing problem', 9 August 2023, https://www.taxpayersalliance.com/the_civil_service_a_growing_problem

182 Office for National Statistics, 'Public Sector Employment by Sector; Civil Service; GB; FTE; SA; Thousands', 12 March 2024, https://www.ons.gov.uk/employmentandlabourmarket/peopleinwork/publicsectorpersonnel/timeseries/g7g6/pse

183 Will Hazell, 'Crackdown on "activists" in the civil service', *Daily Telegraph*, 20 January 2024, https://www.telegraph.co.uk/politics/2024/01/20/crackdown-on-activists-in-the-civil-service/

184 Joshua Nevett, 'Rishi Sunak: No 91,000 target for civil service job cuts', BBC News, 1 November 2022, https://www.bbc.co.uk/news/uk-politics-63477209

185 Annabel Denham, 'It's time to take a chainsaw to the British civil service', *The Spectator*, 4 March 2024, https://www.spectator.co.uk/article/its-time-to-take-the-chainsaw-to-the-british-civil-service/

186 Office for National Statistics, 'Public Sector Employment by Sector; Civil Service; GB; FTE; SA; Thousands', 12 March 2024, https://www.ons.gov.uk/employmentandlabourmarket/peopleinwork/publicsectorpersonnel/timeseries/g7g6/pse

187 Martin Stanley, 'Civil Service Pay', Understanding the Civil Service, https://www.civilservant.org.uk/information-pay-general.html#:~:text=The%20Office%20for%20National%20Statistics,case%20of%20more%20qualified%20employees

188 Patrick Brione and Brigid Francis-Devine, 'Public sector Pay', House of Commons Library, 15 January 2024, https://commonslibrary.parliament.uk/research-briefings/cbp-8037/

189 Cabinet Office, 'Statistical bulletin – Civil Service Statistics: 2022', 2 March 2023, https://www.gov.uk/government/statistics/civil-service-statistics-2022/statistical-bulletin-civil-service-statistics-2022

190 Nick Gutteridge, 'Number of civil servants earning £100,000 salary almost doubles – despite pay freeze', *Daily Telegraph*, 9 August 2023, https://www.telegraph.co.uk/politics/2023/08/09/rise-in-senior-civil-service-whitehall-pay-freeze/

191 Guido Fawkes, 'Blob's wage bill balloons by billions', 9 August 2023, https://order-order.com/2023/08/09/civil-service-salaries-skyrocket-by-60-as-headcount-grows-by-100000/

192 Neil Record, 'Public sector pensions are pushing Britain into bankruptcy', *Daily Telegraph*, 11 August 2023, https://www.telegraph.co.uk/news/2023/08/11/public-sector-pensions-are-pushing-britain-into-bankruptcy/

193 'The Great British Rake-Off', Institute for Economic Affairs, 26 October 2021, https://iea.org.uk/media/public-sector-pensions-cost-57bn-per-year-more-than-is-declared-finds-new-iea-research/

194 Sophie Smith, 'Public sector pension bill surpasses size of UK economy for the first time', Pensions Age, 24 July 2023, https://www.pensionsage.com/pa/Public-sector-pension-bill-passes-size-of-the-economy-for-the-first-time.php

195 Charlotte Gifford, 'Why HMRC is everything wrong with the civil service', *Daily Telegraph*, 5 May 2023, https://www.telegraph.co.uk/money/tax/news/why-hmrc-is-everything-wrong-with-the-civil-service/

196 Cabinet Office, 'Cabinet Office: Civil Superannuation Annual Report and Accounts 2022–23', https://assets.publishing.service.gov.uk/media/6581c2a123b70a000d234c63/CSPS-accounts-2022-23-for-laying.pdf

197 NHS Business Services Authority, 'NHS Pension Scheme, Annual Report and Accounts 2022–2023',

https://www.nhsbsa.nhs.uk/sites/default/files/2023-09/NHS%20Pensions%20Annual%20Report%20 and%20Accounts%202022-2023.pdf

198 Ministry of Defence, 'Armed Forces Pension Scheme, Annual Report and Accounts 2022–23', https:// assets.publishing.service.gov.uk/media/64b79e0971749c001389ee43/Armed_Forces_Pensions_Scheme_ ARAC_22-23_Accessible.pdf

199 Department for Education, 'Teachers' Pension Scheme (England and Wales) Annual Report and Account 2022–2023', https://assets.publishing.service.gov.uk/media/6508172522a783000d43e734/2022-2023_TPS_ Annual_Report_and_Accounts.pdf

200 Neil Record, 'The £600 billion Question: How public sector pension liabilities are being undervalued at the expense of future generations', Intergenerational Foundation, May 2014, https://www.if.org.uk/research-posts/ the-600-billion-question-how-public-sector-pension-liabilities-are-being-undervalued-at-the-expense-of- future-generations/; Szu Ping Chan, 'Public sector pensions bill hits record £2.6 trillion', Daily Telegraph, 29 March 2024, https://www.telegraph.co.uk/business/2024/03/29/public-sector-pensions-bill-hits-record-26-trillion/

201 Ruby Hinchcliffe, '"I took a pay cut to get a public sector pension"', Daily Telegraph, 1 May 2023, https://www.telegraph.co.uk/money/money-makeover/money-makeover-i-took-pay-cut-to-get-public- sector-pension/

202 Neil Record, 'Sir Humphrey's Legacy: facing up to the cost of public sector pensions', Institute for Economic Affairs, September 2006, https://iea.org.uk/publications/research/sir-humphreys-legacy-facing- to-the-cost-of-public-sector-pensions

203 'Public Expenditure Statistical Analyses 2023', HM Treasury, 19 July 2023, https://www.gov.uk/government/ statistics/public-expenditure-statistical-analyses-2023

204 Agence France-Presse, 'Macron signs controversial pension changes into law after months of protests', The Observer, 15 April 2023, https://www.theguardian.com/world/2023/apr/15/macron-signs-controversial- pension-changes-into-law-after-months-of-protests

205 Tim Morgan, 'Oil, Finance and Pensions, Why Scots should say no', Centre for Policy Studies, September 2014, https://cps.org.uk/wp-content/uploads/2021/07/140915094337-OilFinanceandPensions.pdf

206 'Work from home: Whitehall's productivity crisis', Guido Fawkes, 7 July 2023, https://order-order. com/2023/07/07/40-of-civil-servants-still-working-from-home-significantly-less-productive/

207 Cabinet Office, 'Civil service headquarters occupancy data', Gov.uk, 30 June 2022, https://www.gov.uk/ government/publications/civil-service-headquarters-occupancy-data

208 'Taxpayers fund two millennia of self-care skiving', Guido Fawkes, 11 April 2023, https://order-order. com/2023/04/11/whitehall-wonks-take-2100-years-worth-of-stress-related-sick-days-in-one-year/

209 'Jeremy Hunt wants to improve Britain's public-sector productivity', The Economist, 20 November 2023, https://www.economist.com/britain/2023/11/20/jeremy-hunt-wants-to-improve-britains-public-sector- productivity

210 South Cambridgeshire District Council, 'Four-day working week', https://www.scambs.gov.uk/your-council- and-democracy/four-day-working-week-trial

211 Letter from Max Soule, Department of Levelling Up, Housing and Communities, to Liz Watts, Chief Executive, South Cambridgeshire District Council, 3 November 2023, https://www.scambs.gov.uk/media/ ngscs5jj/letter-03112023.pdf

212 Richard Littlejohn, 'Working from home – Money for nothing and your gas bills for FREE!', Daily Mail, 27 November 2023, https://www.dailymail.co.uk/debate/article-12797373/RICHARD-LITTLEJOHN- Working-home-Money-gas-bills-FREE.html

213 Martin Beckford, 'Michael Gove's Department for Levelling Up, Housing and Communities agrees to spend £160,000 to provide furniture to civil servants so they can work from home in comfort', Daily Mail, 22 May 2023, https://www.dailymail.co.uk/news/article-12109141/Michael-Goves-Department-agrees- spend-160-000-civil-servants-work-home-comfortably.html

214 Jonathan Leake, Lucy Burton and Dominic Penna, 'Civil servants given go ahead to work from the beach', Daily Telegraph, 18 November 2023, https://www.telegraph.co.uk/business/2023/11/18/civil-service-wfh- beach-overseas-working-staff-flexibility/

215 Steven Edginton, 'Healthcare workers invited to three-day diversity conference featuring pronouns and gender', Daily Telegraph, 24 September 2023, https://www.telegraph.co.uk/news/2023/09/24/healthcare-workers- diversity-conference-pronouns-gender/

216 'Sex Change Days Off – 91, Disability days off – 5', Guido Fawkes, 12 April 2023, https://order-order. com/2023/04/12/gender-bending-civil-servants-get-3-months-of-paid-leave-per-year/

217 Daniel Martin, 'Rolling your eyes is racist – nod your head instead, civil servants told', Daily Telegraph, 31 January 2024, https://www.telegraph.co.uk/news/2024/01/31/sexism-racism-civil-servants-diversity-training- controversy/

218 Amana Mohdin, 'Unconscious bias training is "nonsense", says outgoing race relations chair', *The Guardian*, 18 February 2023, https://www.theguardian.com/world/2023/feb/18/unconscious-bias-training-is-nonsense-says-outgoing-race-relations-chair; Jawad Iqbal, '"Unconscious bias" industry does more harm than good', *The Times*, https://www.thetimes.co.uk/article/unconscious-bias-industry-does-more-harm-than-good-nzftq3j9l

219 Mary Wakefield, 'The real reason the civil service needs reform', *The Spectator*, 25 November 2023, https://www.spectator.co.uk/article/whats-in-a-name/

220 'Create a culture of inclusivity with name pronunciation in email signatures', Rocketseed, https://www.rocketseed.com/blog/culture-of-inclusivity-with-name-pronunciation-in-email-signatures/

221 'Social Value – achieving community benefits', Local Government Association, https://www.local.gov.uk/our-support/financial-resilience-and-economic-growth/procurement/social-value-achieving-community

222 'Defunding politically motivated campaigns', Conservative Way Forward, https://www.conservativewayforward.com/_files/ugd/acef4a_5b5ec1d9017f40b987a68110f70d276c.pdf

223 Steven Edginton, 'Army to relax security checks for recruits in diversity drive', *Daily Telegraph*, 10 February 2024, https://www.telegraph.co.uk/news/2024/02/10/army-challenge-overseas-recruits-security-checks/; The Rt Hon Dominic Grieve QC MP, 'Diversity and Inclusion in the UK Intelligence Community', The Intelligence and Security Committee of Parliament, House of Commons, 18 July 2018, https://assets.publishing.service.gov.uk/government/uploads/system/uploads/attachment_data/file/740654/20180718_Report_Diversity_and_Inclusion.pdf

224 Steven Edginton and Gordon Rayner, 'Civil servant revolt at "woke takeover of Whitehall"', *Daily Telegraph*, 22 September 2023, https://www.telegraph.co.uk/politics/2023/09/22/woke-takeover-whitehall-risks-government-policy-simon-case/

225 Rory Stewart, *Politics on the Edge: A Memoir from Within* (Penguin Press, 2023), https://www.goodreads.com/book/show/96177657-politics-on-the-edge

226 Asher McShane, 'Tory fury as civil servants threaten strike as they "fear being forced to break the law" over Rwanda policy', LBC, 31 May 2023, https://www.lbc.co.uk/news/civil-servants-threaten-strike-forced-rwanda-policy/

227 Nick Gutteridge, 'Trussonomics was abandoned after Simon Case told PM it was causing market chaos', *Daily Telegraph*, 1 June 2023, https://www.telegraph.co.uk/politics/2023/06/01/liz-truss-abandoned-plan-simon-case-led-civil-service/

228 Rory Stewart, *Politics on the Edge* (Vintage, 2023), https://www.penguin.co.uk/books/442034/politics-on-the-edge-by-stewart-rory/9781529922868

229 Charlotte Pickles and James Sweetland, 'Breaking down the barriers: Why Whitehall is so hard to reform', Reform, August 2023, https://reform.uk/wp-content/uploads/2023/08/Barriers_Final.pdf

230 Liam Fox, 'Britain's civil service chiefs are sabotaging elected ministers, says Liam Fox', *The Express*, 2 September 2023, https://www.express.co.uk/comment/expresscomment/1808706/civil-service-elected-ministers-sue-gray-liam-fox

231 Chris Cook, '*The most powerful person you've never heard of*', BBC News, 10 July 2015, https://www.bbc.co.uk/news/uk-politics-33431580

232 'Priti Patel: Bullying inquiry head quits as PM backs home secretary', BBC News, 20 November 2020, https://www.bbc.co.uk/news/uk-politics-55016076

233 Pippa Crerar, 'Dominic Raab: how the Guardian revealed bullying allegations', *The Guardian*, 21 April 2023, https://www.theguardian.com/politics/2023/apr/21/dominic-raab-timeline-bullying-allegations-revealed-guardian

234 Adam Tolley KC, 'Formal complaints about the conduct of the Right Honourable Dominic Raab MP, Deputy Prime Minister, Lord Chancellor and Secretary of State for Justice, Investigation Report to the Prime Minister', 20 April 2023, https://assets.publishing.service.gov.uk/media/6442539622ef3b000f66f65f/2023.04.20_Investigation_Report_to_the_Prime_Minister.pdf

235 Michelle Donelan, Chloe Smith, Jonathan Reynolds, Alastair Campbell, 'Party Policy Special: Pathways to power', *New Statesman Spotlight*, https://www.newstatesman.com/wp-content/uploads/sites/2/2023/06/23/NS-Spotlight-Party-Policy-Special-Supplement-June-2023.pdf

236 Martin Stanley, 'Dismissal – Permanent Secretaries', Understanding the Civil Service, https://www.civilservant.org.uk/information-dismissal-permanent_secretaries.html

237 Cabinet Office, 'Government Lead Non-Executive's annual report 2021 to 2022', 24 May 2023, https://www.gov.uk/government/publications/government-lead-non-executives-annual-report-2021-to-2022/government-lead-non-executives-annual-report-2021-to-2022-html

238 Stan Tilton, 'Is it true that 95.4% of Executives are Thinkers (T) in the language of Myers-Briggs Personality Type?', 4 August 2016, https://www.linkedin.com/pulse/true-954-executives-thinkers-language-myers-briggs-type-stan-tilton

239 Kevin Rawlinson and agency, 'Former Foreign Office chief admits to telling colleagues he voted to stay in the EU', *The Guardian*, 11 September 2023, https://www.theguardian.com/politics/2023/sep/11/former-foreign-office-chief-simon-mcdonald-told-colleagues-he-voted-to-stay-in-eu

240 David Pegg, Felicity Lawrene and Rob Evans, 'Right-wing thinktank breached charity law by campaigning for hard Brexit', *The Guardian*, 5 February 2019, https://www.theguardian.com/politics/2019/feb/05/rightwing-thinktank-breached-charity-law-by-campaigning-for-hard-brexit; Clive Thorne, 'Biased BBC – A more rigorous, impartial regulator needed', Politeia, 20 April 2024, https://www.politeia.co.uk/biased-bbc-more-rigorous-regulation-needed/?mc_cid=a16f90f89f&mc_eid=78a29faaa3; James Beal, 'People of any gender can be pregnant, Bank of England states', *The Times*, 3 July 2023, https://www.thetimes.co.uk/article/people-of-any-gender-can-be-pregnant-bank-of-england-states-kv60dpdrr

241 Sarah Butler, 'Was John Lewis boss Sharon White too clever for the cruel retail world?', *The Guardian*, 7 October 2023, https://www.theguardian.com/business/2023/oct/07/was-john-lewis-boss-sharon-white-too-clever-for-the-cruel-retail-world

242 HM Treasury, 'HMT Public Expenditure Statistical Analyses (PESA)', 17 July 2013 (updated 19 July 2023), https://www.gov.uk/government/collections/public-expenditure-statistical-analyses-pesa

243 Neil Hedges, 'Public Sector Employment by Sector; Local Gov; UK; HC; SA; Thousands', Office for National Statistics, 12 December 2023, https://www.ons.gov.uk/employmentandlabourmarket/peopleinwork/publicsectorpersonnel/timeseries/g6nt/pse/previous/v33

244 HM Treasury, 'HMT Public Expenditure Statistical Analyses (PESA)', 17 July 2013 (updated 19 July 2023), https://www.gov.uk/government/collections/public-expenditure-statistical-analyses-pesa

245 TaxPayers' Alliance, 'Local authority productivity', 13 July 2023, https://www.taxpayersalliance.com/local_authority_productivity

246 Richard Norrie, 'The failing quango state', Civitas, April 2023, https://www.civitas.org.uk/publications/the-failing-quango-state/

247 This section uses a great deal of its material and commentary from the excellent Richard Norrie, 'The failing quango state', Civitas, April 2023, https://www.civitas.org.uk/publications/the-failing-quango-state/

248 'The Arms Length Body landscape at a glance', Gov.uk, https://assets.publishing.service.gov.uk/media/60eddaaad3bf7f5688e5d966/Public_Bodies_2020.pdf

249 Laura Alfaro, Saleem Bahaj, Robert Czech, Jonathan Hazell and Ioana Neamtu, 'LAH risk and interest rates', Staff Working Paper No. 1073, Bank of England, May 2024, https://www.bankofengland.co.uk/-/media/boe/files/working-paper/2024/lash-risk-and-interest-rates.pdf

250 'Nolan Investigates: Stonewall', *Nolan Investigates*, BBC Sounds, https://www.bbc.co.uk/sounds/play/p09yjpod

251 James Beal, 'People of any gender can be pregnant, Bank of England states', *Sunday Times*, 3 July 2023, https://www.thetimes.co.uk/business-money/economics/article/people-of-any-gender-can-be-pregnant-bank-of-england-states-kv60dpdrr

252 Simon Foy, 'Bank of England says people of any gender identity can be pregnant', *Daily Telegraph*, 3 July 2023, https://www.telegraph.co.uk/business/2023/07/03/bank-of-england-men-pregnant/

253 Tim Wallace, 'Andrew Bailey to install heat pumps at Bank of England in net zero drive', *Daily Telegraph*, 6 July 2023, https://www.telegraph.co.uk/business/2023/07/06/andrew-bailey-install-heat-pumps-bank-of-england-net-zero/

254 Conservative Way Forward, 'Defunding Politically Motivated Campaigns', https://www.conservativewayforward.com/_files/ugd/acef4a_5b5ec1d9017f40b987a68110f70d276c.pdf

255 Steven Edginton, 'Charities lobbying against Rwanda Bill given £209m of taxpayer money', *Daily Telegraph*, 1 February 2024, https://www.telegraph.co.uk/news/2024/02/01/rwanda-asylum-bill-lobby-charities-taxpayer-money/

256 Christopher Snowdon, 'Sock Puppets: How the government lobbies itself and why', IEA Discussion Paper no. 39, https://iea.org.uk/wp-content/uploads/2016/07/DP_Sock%20Puppets_redesigned.pdf

257 Nayyara Tabassum, 'UK Civil Society Almanac 2023', NCVO, 13 October 2023, https://www.ncvo.org.uk/news-and-insights/news-index/uk-civil-society-almanac-2023/

258 Home Office, 'Home Office annual report and accounts 2022 to 2023', 11 October 2023, https://www.gov.uk/government/publications/home-office-annual-report-and-accounts-2022-to-2023/home-office-annual-report-and-accounts-2022-to-2023-accessible

259 David Turver, 'Debunking the cheap renewables myth', Daily Sceptic, 16 May 2024, https://dailysceptic.org/2024/05/16/debunking-the-cheap-renewables-myth/?utm_source=ground.news&utm_medium=referral

CHAPTER 7

1 Alex Mengden, 'International Tax Competitiveness Index 2023', Tax Foundation, 18 October 2023, https://taxfoundation.org/research/all/global/2023-international-tax-competitiveness-index/

2   Caroline Turnbull-Hall and Richard Thomas, 'Length of tax legislation as a measure of complexity', Office of Tax Simplification, April 2012, https://assets.publishing.service.gov.uk/media/5a81daffe5274a2e87dbfd6b/OTS_length_of_legislation_paper_published_Apr12.pdf

3   Jack Barnett, 'Huge relative increase in taxes coming under Conservatives', *Sunday Times*, 18 April 2024, https://www.thetimes.co.uk/article/huge-relative-increase-in-taxes-coming-under-conservatives-mlbcb9lj7

4   International Monetary Fund, 'Public Finances in Modern History', https://www.imf.org/external/datamapper/datasets/FPP

5   Patrick Minford, Yue Gai and David Meenagh, 'North and South: A regional model of the UK', Open Economy Review, 28 October 2021, https://link.springer.com/article/10.1007/s11079-021-09633-7#citeas

6   Christina D. Romer and David H. Romer, 'The Macroeconomic Effects of Tax Changes: Estimates Based on a New Measure of Fiscal Shocks', *American Economic Review*, vol. 100, no. 3, June 2010, pp. 763–801.

7   Corey Iacono and Matt Palumbo, *In Defense of Classical Liberalism: An Economic Analysis* (CreateSpace Independent Publishing Platform, 2014), https://www.amazon.co.uk/Defense-Classical-Liberalism-Economic-Analysis/dp/1500963933

8   Martin Wolf, 'The economic consequences of Liz Truss', *Financial Times*, 20 September 2022, https://www.ft.com/content/a9be9db6-a91e-48e4-8d69-4bbfff7e0f5f?accessToken=zwAAAYZPmBzYkdOpvp22qR5I5NONaUu__34PXw.MEYCIQDehEDRNQIVswzlyzI6mcfcHxIPVQUpbGHAHe-1sNmKIQIhANoGURGfzC4zWwwZe3dIZSPMXT1HY5K_zDqHOEZXjN-K&sharetype=gift&token=4d3a216c-a1e9-4359-b596-d5e330e7e740

9   Szu Ping Chan, 'Britain will stagnate on world stage after Jeremey Hunt tax raid, warns CEBR', *Daily Telegraph*, 26 December 2022, https://www.telegraph.co.uk/business/2022/12/26/britain-will-stagnate-world-stage-jeremy-hunt-tax-raid-warns/

10 Office for National Statistics, 'Public sector current receipts: Appendix D', 23 April 2024, https://www.ons.gov.uk/economy/governmentpublicsectorandtaxes/publicsectorfinance/datasets/appendixdpublicsectorcurrentreceipts

11 Corey Iacono and Matt Palumbo, *In Defense of Classical Liberalism: An Economic Analysis* (CreateSpace Independent Publishing Platform, 2014), https://www.amazon.co.uk/Defense-Classical-Liberalism-Economic-Analysis/dp/1500963933

12 Simon Djankov, Tim Ganser, Caralee McLiesh and Andrei Shleifer, 'The Effect of Corporate Taxes on Investment and Entrepreneurship', *American Economic Journal: Macroeconomics*, vol. 2, no. 3, July 2010, pp. 31–64.

13 Isabel Díaz Ayuso, 'Tax cutting Madrid proves that freedom works', *Daily Telegraph*, 12 May 2023, https://www.telegraph.co.uk/news/2023/05/12/tax-cutting-madrid-proves-that-freedom-works1/

14 Davide Ghilotti, 'Windfall tax has "severely dampened" investment in UK North Sea, says oil and gas operator Ithaca', upstream, 25 August 2023, https://www.upstreamonline.com/finance/windfall-tax-has-severely-dampened-investment-in-uk-north-sea-says-oil-and-gas-operator-ithaca/2-1-1505124

15 Simeon Djankov, Tim Ganser, Caralee McLeish, Rita Ramalho & Andrei Shleifer, '*The effect of corporate taxes on investment and entrepreneurship*', NBER, Working Paper 13756, January 2008 https://www.nber.org/papers/w13756

16 'AstraZeneca Boss says company chose Ireland over Britain based on tax rate', *Irish Examiner*, 9 February 2023, https://www.irishexaminer.com/business/companies/arid-41068010.html

17 Szu Ping Chan and Oliver Gill, 'Dozens of US companies shun Britain over high taxes and no growth plan', *Daily Telegraph*, 4 March 2023, https://www.telegraph.co.uk/business/2023/03/04/dozens-us-companies-shun-britain-high-taxes-no-growth-plan/

18 Simon Jack, 'Shell reconsiders its exit from oil field off Shetland', BBC News, 22 March 2022, https://www.bbc.co.uk/news/business-60825744

19 'World's third largest oil company quits North Sea as Hunt doubles down on EPL', Aberdeen Business News, 17 May 2024, https://aberdeenbusinessnews.co.uk/worlds-third-largest-oil-company-quits-north-sea-as-hunt-doubles-down-on-epl/

20 'What is the windfall tax on oil and gas companies and how much do they pay?', BBC News, 6 March 2024, https://www.bbc.co.uk/news/business-60295177

21 Matthew Lynn, 'If Joe Biden can open massive new oil fields, then so can Britain', *Daily Telegraph*, 5 March 2023, https://www.telegraph.co.uk/business/2023/03/05/joe-biden-can-open-massive-new-oil-fields-can-britain/

22 Rachel Millard, Oliver Gill and Matt Oliver, 'Victory for Nicola Sturgeon as Shell walks away from North Sea oil project', *Daily Telegraph*, 2 December 2021, https://www.telegraph.co.uk/business/2021/12/02/abandons-major-north-sea-oil-project/; Ben Riley-Smith, 'Oil and gas licences to be sold every year under Rishi Sunak's new law', *Daily Telegraph*, 5 November 2023, https://www.telegraph.co.uk/politics/2023/11/05/oil-gas-licences-every-year-rishi-sunak-new-law/

23 Reemul Balla, 'Record number of Britons receiving benefits that amount to more than they pay in tax, study finds', *Sky News*, 23 January 2023, https://news.sky.com/story/record-number-of-britons-receiving-benefits-that-amount-to-more-than-they-pay-in-tax-study-finds-12793349

24 Matthew Keep, 'Tax statistics: an overview', House of Commons Library, 28 March 2024, https://commonslibrary.parliament.uk/research-briefings/cbp-8513/

25 Charlotte Gifford, 'How the government waged war on the self-employed', *Daily Telegraph*, 28 December 2022, https://www.telegraph.co.uk/money/tax/self-employed/how-government-waged-war-self-employed/

26 Office for National Statistics, 'Most of the fall in self-employment was seen in those "working for themselves"', https://www.ons.gov.uk/employmentandlabourmarket/peopleinwork/employmentandemployeetypes/articles/understandingchangesinselfemploymentintheuk/january2019tomarch2022#:~:text=Between%20January%20to%20March%202020,3.5%20million%20to%202.9%20million

27 Simon Lambert, 'Will a Chancellor ever be brave enough to fix Britain's tax mess?', This is Money, 30 March 2023, https://www.thisismoney.co.uk/money/bills/article-11919191/Will-Chancellor-brave-fix-UKs-tax-trap-mess.html

28 Carmen Ang, 'Mapping the Migration of the World's Millionaires', Visual Capitalist, 15 June 2022, https://www.visualcapitalist.com/migration-of-millionaires-worldwide-2022/

29 James Reinl, 'California grieving: two thirds of Golden State residents say its economy is tanking, with low wages and high rents driving millions to consider joining Joe Rogan and Mark Wahlberg and leaving', *Daily Mail*, 9 November 2023, https://www.dailymail.co.uk/news/article-12730163/California-residents-economy-tanking-wages-rents-Joe-Rogan-Mark-Wahlberg.html; Kurtis Lee, 'California's economy has been pinched by unemployment', *New York Times*, 11 March 2024 https://www.nytimes.com/2024/03/11/us/california-economy-unemployment.html?smid=nytcore-ios-share&referringSource=articleShare

30 TaxPayers' Alliance, 'Number of people paying income tax has surged since 2010, finds TaxPayers' Alliance', 9 February 2024, https://www.taxpayersalliance.com/number_of_people_paying_income_tax_has_surged_since_2010_finds_taxpayers_alliance

31 Isabella Fish, 'Huge fall in apprenticeships under "broken' levy"', *The Times*, 20 May 2024, https://www.thetimes.co.uk/article/huge-fall-in-apprenticeships-under-broken-levy-cm27db8qd

32 Jonathan Leake, 'How the energy industry turned against net zero levies on bills', *Daily Telegraph*, 8 October 2023, https://www.telegraph.co.uk/business/2023/10/08/energy-industry-turned-against-net-zero-levies-bills/; Edward Malnick, 'Net zero "grocery tax" will push shopping bills up by £4bn, Tories warned', *Daily Telegraph*, 3 June 2023, https://www.telegraph.co.uk/politics/2023/06/03/governments-grocery-tax-push-up-food-prices-supermarkets/

33 Aimee Stanton, 'Energy prices UK: why Britian has highest electricity costs in Europe – how other countries compare', National World, 29 September 2022, https://www.nationalworld.com/news/politics/energy-prices-uk-britain-highest-electricity-costs-europe-other-countries-compare-3861624

34 Greg Rosalsky, 'If a wealth tax is such a good idea, why did Europe kill theirs?', Planet Money, 26 February 2019, https://www.npr.org/sections/money/2019/02/26/698057356/if-a-wealth-tax-is-such-a-good-idea-why-did-europe-kill-theirs

35 Ed Magnus, 'Inheritance tax is named Britain's most hated levy because of "ideological resentment" and that's despite only 4% of people paying it', This is Money, 26 October 2021, https://www.thisismoney.co.uk/money/saving/article-10120521/Inheritance-tax-named-UKs-hated-levy-heres-why.html

36 Emma Revell, 'Stamping out tax on share purchases is a no-brainer', City AM, 4 March 2024, https://www.cityam.com/stamping-out-tax-on-share-purchases-is-a-no-brainer/

37 'Annual turnover concessions for VAT/GST registration and collection (domestic businesses)', OECD, https://www.oecd.org/tax/consumption/vat-gst-annual-turnover-concessions-ctt-trends.xlsx

38 HMRC, 'VAT rates on different goods and services', Gov.uk, 4 February 2014 (last updated 11 July 2022), https://www.gov.uk/guidance/rates-of-vat-on-different-goods-and-services

39 Keith Miller, 'The UK VAT system isn't like everyone else's', etc TAX, 5 May 2023, https://etctax.co.uk/blog-news/uk-vat-system/

40 'How to fix Britain's barmy VAT regime', *The Economist*, 22 April 2024, https://www.economist.com/britain/2024/04/22/how-to-fix-britains-barmy-vat-regime

41 Noah Eastwood and Ollie Corfe, 'Motorists to be taxed more than smokers as war on drivers revs up', *Daily Telegraph*, 19 April 2024, https://www.telegraph.co.uk/money/tax/motorists-taxed-more-than-smokers/

42 Nicholas Thomas, '20mph speed limits could increase pollution at city hotspots – new modelling', Nation Cymru, 27 October 2023, https://nation.cymru/news/20mph-speed-limits-could-increase-pollution-at-city-hotspots-new-modelling/

43 Transport for London, 'FOI request detail: ULEZ Income', 20 September 2023, https://tfl.gov.uk/corporate/transparency/freedom-of-information/foi-request-detail?referenceId=FOI-1691-2324#:~:text=TfL%20estimates%20that%20the%20London,of%20compliant%20vehicles%20increases%20and

44 HM Treasury, 'New UK levy to level carbon pricing', 18 December 2023, https://www.gov.uk/government/news/new-uk-levy-to-level-carbon-pricing

45 Julia Kagan, reviewed by Lea D. Uradu, 'Consumption Tax: Definition, Types, vs Income Tax', Investopedia, 19 October 2023, https://www.investopedia.com/terms/c/consumption-tax.asp

46 Erica York, Garrett Watson, Alex Duante and Huaqun Li, 'How taxing consumption would improve long-term opportunity and well-being for families and children', Tax Foundation, 12 October 2023, https://taxfoundation.org/research/all/federal/us-consumption-tax-vs-income-tax/

47 Simoney Kyriakou, 'Sunak must simplify Britain's "burdensome" tax code', FT Adviser, 2 March 2021, https://www.ftadviser.com/investments/2021/03/02/sunak-must-simplify-britain-s-burdensome-tax-code/

48 Madeleine Ross, 'How Macron stole Britain's millionaires', Daily Telegraph, 13 October 2023, https://www.telegraph.co.uk/money/consumer-affairs/france-macron-tax-breaks-stole-britains-millionaires/

49 Szu Ping Chang and Oliver Gill, 'Dozens of US companies shun Britain over high taxes and no growth plan', Daily Telegraph, 4 March 2023, https://www.telegraph.co.uk/business/2023/03/04/dozens-us-companies-shun-britain-high-taxes-no-growth-plan/

50 James Badger, 'Tax gap on alcohol and tobacco rises 9% to an estimated 3.7 billion in 2021', The Grocer, 25 July 2022, https://www.thegrocer.co.uk/convenience/tax-gap-on-alcohol-and-tobacco-rises-to-an-estimated-37-billion-in-2021/669790.article

51 Harry Wilson, 'Black Market is 10pc of UK economy, says IEA', Daily Telegraph, 4 June 2013, https://www.telegraph.co.uk/finance/economics/10097303/Black-market-is-10pc-of-UK-economy-says-IEA.html

52 Eleanor Dye, 'Nine out of 10 ULEZ cameras have been vandalised in southeast London – with just 29 out of 185 still operational in Sydenham, four intact in Bromley and just ONE working on the A225', Daily Mail, 24 August 2023, https://www.dailymail.co.uk/news/article-12439979/Nine-10-ULEZ-cameras-vandalised-southeast-London.html

53 Andy Summers and Arun Advani, 'How much tax do the rich really pay?', London School of Economics and Political Science, 14 January 2021, https://www.lse.ac.uk/research/research-for-the-world/economics/how-much-tax-do-the-rich-really-pay#:~:text=In%20one%20respect%2C%20the%20UK,by%20just%20over%20300%2C000%20individuals

54 Dr Hannah White, 'UK Projected to See Highest Millionaire Loss on Record', Henley Partners, https://www.henleyglobal.com/publications/henley-private-wealth-migration-report-2024/uk-projected-see-highest-millionaire-loss-record

55 Robert Watts, 'The Sunday Times Rich List 2024 revealed', Sunday Times, 20 May 2024, https://www.thetimes.co.uk/article/sunday-times-rich-list-2024-revealed-plt3t2xrt

56 Charlotte Gifford, 'The young high-earners deserting Britain – and never coming back', Daily Telegraph, 14 June 2023, https://www.telegraph.co.uk/money/tax/news/young-high-earners-emigration-uk-cost-living-income-tax/

57 Robert Colvile, 'Sunak's corporation tax raid will drive business over a cliff – but there is a way to defy gravity', The Times, 5 March 2023, https://www.thetimes.co.uk/article/sunaks-corporation-tax-raid-will-drive-business-over-a-cliff-but-there-is-a-way-to-defy-gravity-wrcmoxht7

58 Simon Calder, 'London, capital of the world', The Independent, 22 December 2007, https://www.independent.co.uk/travel/news-and-advice/london-capital-of-the-world-766661.html

59 Ford Rojas, 'Premier League footballers "will leave the UK" if the non-dom tax status is scrapped, analysis warns', Daily Mail, 4 March 2024, https://www.msn.com/en-gb/money/other/premier-league-footballers-will-leave-the-uk-if-the-non-dom-tax-status-is-scrapped-analysis-warns/ar-BB1jgOdh

60 Andy Summers, 'One in five bankers claims non-dom tax status', LSE, 7 April 2022, https://www.lse.ac.uk/News/Latest-news-from-LSE/2022/d-Apr-22/Non-doms; Arun Advani, David Burgherr, Mike Savage and Andy Summers, 'The UK's "non-doms": who are they, what do they do, and where do they live?', Warwick CAGE Research Centre, https://warwick.ac.uk/fac/soc/economics/research/centres/cage/publications/policybriefings/2022/the_uks_non_doms_who_are_they_what_do_they_do_and_where_do_they_live/

61 Alexi Mostrous, 'Non doms' tax loophole will close', The Times, 9 July 2015, https://www.thetimes.com/article/non-doms-tax-loophole-will-close-dh9zg6roptx

62 Bagehot, 'The myth of the "hedge fund boss boasting about paying less tax than his cleaner"', The Economist, 22 March 2012, https://www.economist.com/bagehots-notebook/2012/03/22/the-myth-of-the-hedge-fund-boss-boasting-about-paying-less-tax-than-his-cleaner

63 Michael Bow, 'How Italy shook off its "basket case" brand – and stole Britain's millionaires', *Daily Telegraph*, 3 July 2024, https://www.telegraph.co.uk/business/2024/07/03/how-meloni-lured-europes-super-rich-to-debt-ridden-italy/

64 HMRC, 'Statistical commentary on non-domiciled taxpayers in the UK', 6 July 2023, https://www.gov.uk/government/statistics/statistics-on-non-domiciled-taxpayers-in-the-uk/statistical-commentary-on-non-domiciled-taxpayers-in-the-uk--2

65 'Why Britain should scrap non-dom tax status', *The Economist*, 8 April 2022, https://www.economist.com/leaders/why-britain-should-scrap-non-dom-tax-status/21808704

66 'Abolishing tax perks for non-doms could significantly boost UK tax revenue without risking an exodus of the super-rich', Warwick CAGE Research Centre, 9 March 2023, https://warwick.ac.uk/fac/soc/economics/research/centres/cage/news/09-03-23-abolishing_tax_perks_for_non_doms_could_significantly_boost_uk_tax_revenue_without_risking_an_exodus_of_the_super_rich/

67 Nels Abbey, 'Britain's millionaires are fleeing. Good night and good luck, I say', *The Guardian*, 21 June 2024, https://www.theguardian.com/commentisfree/article/2024/jun/21/britain-millionaires-leave-tax-havens-uk

68 Daniel Woolfson, 'Tourist tax forcing US shoppers to abandon London', *Daily Telegraph*, 14 August 2023, https://www.telegraph.co.uk/business/2023/08/14/us-shoppers-abandon-london-luxury-tourist-tax-rishi-sunak/

69 Harriet Line, 'Scrapping tourist tax "would boost the economy by £10 billion, support jobs and provide net gain to the Treasury"', *Daily Mail*, 30 July 2023, https://www.dailymail.co.uk/news/article-12354523/Scrapping-tourist-tax-boost-economy-10BILLION-support-jobs-provide-net-gain-Treasury.html

70 Doug McWilliams, 'Call for an inquiry into Tourist Tax Fiasco', Reaction, 27 April 2023, https://reaction.life/call-for-an-inquiry-into-tourist-tax-fiasco/#r3z-addoor

71 Jim Pickard, 'Jeremy Hunt authorises OBR review of "tourist tax"', *Financial Times*, 4 February 2024, https://www.ft.com/content/30982b16-6d3b-48b8-aaea-f71a912a01c9

72 Martin Vander Weyer, 'Will Rachel Reeves scrap the private equity tax break?', *The Spectator*, 10 February 2024, https://www.spectator.co.uk/article/will-rachel-reeves-scrap-the-private-equity-tax-break/#:~:text=Back%20in%202021%2C%20Reeves%20pledged%20to%20close%20a,rather%20than%2045%20per%20cent%20top-rate%20income%20tax.

73 Henley & Partners, 'The Henley Private Wealth Migration Dashboard', https://www.henleyglobal.com/publications/henley-private-wealth-migration-dashboard/inflows-outflows

74 Office for Budget Responsibility, 'Economic and fiscal outlook – March 2024', https://obr.uk/efo/economic-and-fiscal-outlook-march-2024/

75 Office for Budget Responsibility, 'Economic and fiscal outlook – March 2024', https://obr.uk/efo/economic-and-fiscal-outlook-march-2024/

76 Jon Moynihan, 'It's unlikely that Miliband and Balls will get more tax out of us Brits, however hard they try', CapX, 13 April 2015, https://capx.co/its-unlikely-that-miliband-and-balls-will-get-more-tax-out-of-us-brits-however-hard-they-try/

77 Office for Budget Responsibility, 'The UK's tax burden in historical and international context', November 2022, https://obr.uk/box/the-uks-tax-burden-in-historical-and-international-context/

78 OECD, 'Tax revenue', 2023, https://data.oecd.org/tax/tax-revenue.htm

79 The Culture Factor Group, 'Intercultural management', https://www.hofstede-insights.com/intercultural-management

80 International Monetary Fund, 'Fiscal Monitor (April 2024)', https://www.imf.org/external/datamapper/datasets/FM

81 The Culture Factor Group, 'Intercultural management', https://www.hofstede-insights.com/intercultural-management

82 Jon Moynihan, 'Rishi Sunak's tax hikes have a fundamental flaw', *Daily Telegraph*, 11 February 2023, https://www.telegraph.co.uk/news/2023/02/11/rishi-sunaks-tax-hikes-have-fundamental-flaw/

83 Tim Stickings, 'The UK's brain drain – and the countries trying to tempt away the talent', National News, 6 January 2023, https://www.thenationalnews.com/weekend/2023/01/06/the-uks-brain-drain-and-the-countries-trying-to-tempt-away-the-talent/

84 Andy Bruce, 'UK becoming less attractive for investment, manufacturers warn', Reuters, 9 January 2023, https://www.reuters.com/world/uk/uk-becoming-less-attractive-investment-manufacturers-warn-2023-01-09/; Matthew Lodge, '"Britain is not firing on all cylinders": US multinational companies shun UK due to high taxes and no plan for growth, warns KPMG', *Daily Mail*, 5 March 2023, https://www.dailymail.co.uk/news/article-11823001/US-multinational-companies-shun-UK-high-taxes-no-plan-growth-warns-KPMG.html

85 'Are tax increases starting to suffer from the law of diminishing returns?', CEBR, 22 January 2024, https://cebr.com/reports/are-tax-increases-starting-to-suffer-from-the-law-of-diminishing-returns/

86 International Monetary Fund, 'Public finances in modern history', https://www.imf.org/external/datamapper/datasets/FPP

87 Office for Budget Responsibility, 'Public Finances databank 2022-23', https://obr.uk/public-finances-databank-2022-23/

CHAPTER 8

1 Edward Malnick, 'Climate chiefs admitted net zero plan based on insufficient data, leading physicist says', *Daily Telegraph*, 20 January 2024, https://www.telegraph.co.uk/news/2024/01/20/climate-change-wind-farms-royal-society-green-energy/

2 Robert Armstrong, 'We should stop duplicating regulators', Conservativehome, 7 December 2023, https://conservativehome.com/2023/12/07/robert-armstrong-the-uk-should-stop-duplicating-regulators/

3 John W. Dawson and John J. Seater, 'Federal Regulation and Aggregate Economic Growth', *Journal of Economic Growth*, February 2013, https://papers.ssrn.com/sol3/papers.cfm?abstract_id=2223315

4 Christen Hemingway Jaynes, 'Scientists create biodegradable plastics made from spirulina', EcoWatch, 11 July 2023, https://www.ecowatch.com/biodegradable-plastics-spirulina.html

5 John Hood, 'Lower taxes, higher growth: Scholarly research reveals economic benefits of fiscal restraint', Locke, 14 April 2014, https://www.johnlocke.org/research/lower-taxes-higher-growth-scholarly-research-reveals-economic-benefits-of-fiscal-restraint/

6 International Monetary Fund, 'Datasets', https://www.imf.org/external/datamapper/datasets; Fraser Institute, 'Economic Freedom', https://www.fraserinstitute.org/economic-freedom/dataset?geozone=world&year=2021&page=dataset&min-year=2&max-year=0&filter=0

7 Jens Matthias Arnold, Giuseppe Nicoletti and Stefano Scarpetta, 'Regulation, resource reallocation and productivity growth', *European Investment Bank Papers*, vol. 16, no. 1, 2011, pp. 90–115, https://papers.ssrn.com/sol3/papers.cfm?abstract_id=1983971

8 'Productivity and growth in Europe', European Investment Bank, vol. 16, no. 1, 2011, https://www.eib.org/attachments/efs/eibpapers/eibpapers_2011_v16_no1_en.pdf#page=92

9 Baroness Barran MBE, 'Loneliness minister: "It's more important than ever to take action"', Department for Digital, Culture, Media & Sport, 17 June 2021, https://www.gov.uk/government/news/loneliness-minister-its-more-important-than-ever-to-take-action

10 'UK's government to introduce independent football regulator', Al Jazeera, 19 March 2024, https://www.aljazeera.com/sports/2024/3/19/british-government-to-introduce-independent-football-regulator

11 Department for Business and Trade, 'UK regulated professions and their regulators', 14 February 2024, https://www.gov.uk/government/publications/professions-regulated-by-law-in-the-uk-and-their-regulators/uk-regulated-professions-and-their-regulators

12 'Quangos and quangocrats', Democratic Audit, https://www.democraticaudit.com/our-work/quangos/quangos-and-quangocrats/

13 International Monetary Fund, 'World Economic Outlook (April 2024)', https://www.imf.org/external/datamapper/datasets/WEO

14 Matt Ridley, 'Genome-edited crops help farmers and environment', 10 June 2020, https://www.mattridley.co.uk/blog/genome-editing-helps-farmers/

15 'The Golden Rice Project', Golden Rice Humanitarian Board, https://www.goldenrice.org/Content4-Info/info.php

16 'Moral imperative to make GM crops available to developing countries', Nuffield Council on Bioethics, 27 May 1999, https://www.nuffieldbioethics.org/news/moral-imperative-to-make-gm-crops-available-to

17 Mark Lynas, 'Children could die because of Greenpeace's Golden Rice activism', *The Spectator*, 25 April 2024, https://www.spectator.co.uk/article/children-could-die-because-of-greenpeaces-golden-rice-activism/

18 'Taskforce on innovation, growth and regulatory reform independent report', Prime Minister's Office, 10 Downing Street, 16 June 2021, https://www.gov.uk/government/publications/taskforce-on-innovation-growth-and-regulatory-reform-independent-report

19 'The pandemic's toll on schooling emerges in awful new exam results', *The Economist*, 5 December 2023, https://www.economist.com/international/2023/12/05/the-pandemics-toll-on-schooling-emerges-in-awful-new-exam-results

20 Independent Business Network, 'Brexit Dividend: Deregulation and Economic Growth', https://the-ibn.com/application/files/1916/8712/3636/IBN-_Deregulation.pdf

21 Markus Hartmann, 'Impact assessment of the European Clinical Trials Directive: a longitudinal, prospective, observational study analyzing patterns and trends in clinical drug trial applications submitted since 2001 to regulatory agencies in six EU countries', BMC, 29 April 2012, https://trialsjournal.biomedcentral.com/articles/10.1186/1745-6215-13-53

22 Michael Searles, 'UK "wasting Brexit freedoms" as drug trials held back by red tape', *Daily Telegraph*, 13 April 2024, https://www.telegraph.co.uk/news/2024/04/13/uk-brexit-freedoms-drug-trials-red-tape-nhs/

23 Nick Gutteridge, 'UK businesses to keep using Brussels' 'CE' safety mark', *Daily Telegraph*, 2 August 2023 https://www.telegraph.co.uk/news/2023/08/02/rishi-sunak-brexit-eu-rules-ce-mark/

24 Rupert Lowe, 'Regulatory power grab is endangering the City', *Daily Telegraph*, 15 May 2024, https://www.telegraph.co.uk/business/2024/05/15/regulatory-power-grab-is-endangering-the-city/

25 William Wright, 'Rebooting UK Capital Markets', New Financial, March 2023, https://newfinancial.org/report-unlocking-the-capital-in-capital-markets/

26 William Wright, 'Rebooting UK Capital Markets', New Financial, March 2023, https://newfinancial.org/report-unlocking-the-capital-in-capital-markets/

27 Will Jones, 'Conservative MPs slam financial regulator's "mission creep" proposal to "stamp out sexism in the city"', Daily Sceptic, 30 September 2023, https://dailysceptic.org/2023/09/30/conservative-mps-slam-financial-regulators-mission-creep-proposal-to-stamp-out-sexism-in-the-city/; Michael Bow, 'How regulators are drowning Britain's most valuable industry in red tape', *Daily Telegraph*, 30 April 2024 https://www.telegraph.co.uk/business/2024/04/30/how-regulator-drown-britain-most-valuable-industry-red-tape/

28 Brian Swint, 'The US is winning listings from the UK. Here's how investors can benefit', Barron's, 3 May 2023, https://www.barrons.com/articles/us-uk-market-listings-investors-stocks-ftse-58e0654d

29 Daniel Kalder, 'DEI is driving big companies to Texas', UnHerd, 8 June 2024, https://unherd.com/newsroom/dei-is-driving-big-companies-to-texas/

30 J. R. Shackleton, 'How to create new jobs', Institute of Economic Affairs, 8 October 2020, https://papers.ssrn.com/sol3/papers.cfm?abstract_id=3850666

31 Professor Len Shackelton, 'Conspiracy against the public? Occupational regulation in the UK economy', Institute for Economic Affairs, 28 December 2017, https://iea.org.uk/publications/conspiracy-against-the-public-occupational-regulation-in-the-uk-economy/

32 Iain Mansfield and Toby Hirst, 'Reforming the Apprenticeship Levy', Policy Exchange, 2023, https://policyexchange.org.uk/wp-content/uploads/Reforming-the-Apprenticeship-Levy.pdf

33 Doug McWilliams, 'Why the Growth Commission proposes a cut in the minimum wage', Reaction, 20 November 2023, https://reaction.life/why-the-growth-commission-proposes-a-cut-in-the-minimum-wage/

34 Richard Tyler, 'National living wage rise "ushering in government-directed deals"', *The Times*, 8 January 2024 https://www.thetimes.co.uk/article/national-living-wage-rise-ushering-in-government-directed-deals-r6vqn9mhf

35 Matthew Lynn, 'Britain is squandering its last remaining competitive advantage', *Daily Telegraph*, 3 April 2024, https://www.telegraph.co.uk/business/2024/04/03/britain-squandering-flexible-labour-market/

36 Dr Gary Sidley, 'The tyranny of "nudge"', Daily Sceptic, 15 December 2023, https://dailysceptic.org/2023/12/15/the-tyranny-of-nudge/

37 Christopher Snowdon, 'Vaping Solutions: An easy Brexit win', Institute for Economic Affairs, November 2017, https://iea.org.uk/wp-content/uploads/2017/11/Vaping-Solutions-F1.pdf

38 Niamh Foley, 'New regulations change childcare ratios in England', House of Commons Library, 3 January 2024, https://commonslibrary.parliament.uk/childcare-ratios-in-england/

39 Audrey Ferrie, 'Hospitality businesses face increasing UK regulation in 2024', Pinsent Masons, 12 January 2024, https://www.pinsentmasons.com/out-law/analysis/hospitality-businesses-face-increasing-uk-regulation-in-2024

40 Christopher Snowdon, 'Closing time: who's killing the British pub?', Institute for Economic Affairs, 10 December 2014, https://iea.org.uk/publications/research/closing-time-whos-killing-the-british-pub

41 Jack Devanney, 'Nothing more to say', Gordian Knot News, 7 May 2024, https://jackdevanney.substack.com/p/nothing-more-to-say

42 John Redwood, 'The government should not lurch right but get it right', John Redwood's Diary, 9 May 2024, https://johnredwoodsdiary.com/

43 Matthew Lesh, 'Bangers and Cash: cutting red tape to put Britain at the centre of the cultivated meat revolution', Institute for Economic Affairs, 19 January 2023, https://iea.org.uk/publications/bangers-and-cash-cutting-red-tape-to-put-britain-at-the-centre-of-the-cultivated-meat-revolution/

44 Peter Foster and Madeleine Speed, 'How UK Regulators are missing a chance to make the best of Brexit', *Financial Times*, 27 February 2024, https://www.ft.com/content/07c98087-3914-4107-a6ee-56cc4086459e?accessToken=zwAGGdMJhFvYkc8HyYCHORRBB9Om7lbMQIZFng.MEQCIBDrbhyY25_cKGzWRSbhhAtJ9rHLPfTmDlLcWGJtlm2uAiBSoRATWLaifiHln1Nq6-iM8nudokoAKewcLNE20fDH-Q&sharetype=gift&token=ee3a93ca-7894-4216-9162-afe29e24ec19

45 Matt Ridley and David Hill, 'The effect of innovation in agriculture on the environment', Institute for Economic Affairs, November 2018, https://iea.org.uk/wp-content/uploads/2018/11/Effect-of-Innovation-in-agriculture_web.pdf

46   Kristian Niemietz, 'Home Win: What if Britian solved its housing crisis?', Institute for Economic Affairs, 11 April 2024, https://iea.org.uk/publications/home-win-what-if-britain-solved-its-housing-crisis/

47   Jacob Rees-Mogg and Radomir Tylecote, 'Raising the Roof, how to solve the United Kingdom's housing crisis', Institute for Economic Affairs, July 2019, https://iea.org.uk/wp-content/uploads/2019/07/CC70_Raising-the-roof_web.pdf

48   Carolyn Wickware, 'Two major drug manufacturers pull out of voluntary repayment arrangements with UK government', Pharmaceutical Journal, 16 January 2023, https://pharmaceutical-journal.com/article/news/two-major-drug-manufacturers-pull-out-of-voluntary-repayment-arrangements-with-uk-government

49   Jamie Smyth and Hannah Kuchler, 'Bayer shifts pharma focus away from "innovation unfriendly" Europe', Financial Times, 16 January 2023, https://www.ft.com/content/f2f7ee6f-0d81-419a-b8e8-da2d3919cf47

50   Diego Zuluaga, 'Taxi and private hire vehicle regulation: a briefing', Institute for Economic Affairs, 8 December 2017, https://iea.org.uk/publications/taxi-and-private-hire-vehicle-regulation-a-briefing/

51   Gareth Corfield, 'In a "shed surrounded by sheep", a British pioneer eyes a slice of a £460bn industry', Daily Telegraph, 9 September 2023, https://www.telegraph.co.uk/business/2023/09/09/simon-thomas-paragraf-semiconductors-us-taiwan-china-uk/

52   'A new hate-crime law in Scotland causes widespread concern', The Economist, 27 March 2024, https://www.economist.com/britain/2024/03/27/a-new-hate-crime-law-in-scotland-causes-widespread-concern

53   'House of Lords: 47 peers rebuked for missing anti-bullying training', BBC News, 18 May 2021, https://www.bbc.co.uk/news/uk-politics-57158866

54   Ross Clark, 'Has the true cost of net zero finally been revealed?', The Spectator, 28 September 2023, https://www.spectator.co.uk/article/has-the-true-cost-of-net-zero-finally-been-revealed/

55   'The bigger picture: life without oil', https://www.grantcountybeat.com/mypdfs/life-without-oil.pdf

56   Heather Stewart, 'Union urges Labour not to ban new North Sea licences without plan for jobs', The Guardian, 17 May 2024, https://www.theguardian.com/business/article/2024/may/17/union-urges-labour-not-to-ban-new-north-sea-licences-without-plan-for-jobs; Kate Andrews, '"We've cut carbon emissions by decimating working-class communities": the leader of the GMB union on the folly of net zero', The Spectator, 16 September 2023, https://www.spectator.co.uk/article/weve-cut-carbon-emissions-by-decimating-working-class-communities-the-leader-of-the-gmb-union-on-the-folly-of-net-zero/

57   Annabel Denham, 'We must end the Net Zero delusion before it's too late', Daily Telegraph, 11 March 2024, https://www.telegraph.co.uk/news/2024/03/11/we-must-end-the-net-zero-delusion-before-its-too-late/

58   Martin Williams, 'Labour's biggest corporate donor Ecotricity accused of "greenwashing"', OpenDemocracy, 3 July 2024, https://www.opendemocracy.net/en/dark-money-investigations/ecotricity-labour-biggest-donor-greenwashing-carbon-credits-dale-vince-keir-starmer-offsetting/; Dale Vince, Facebook, 22 September 2021, https://www.facebook.com/dalevince/posts/weve-just-launched-our-latest-campaign-with-the-daily-express-this-one-is-the-mo/403952541099107/

59   David Turver, 'Budget will increase energy bills by £1.4 billion to subsidise wind power', Daily Sceptic, 7 March 2024, https://dailysceptic.org/2024/03/07/budget-will-increase-energy-bills-by-1-4-billion-to-subsidise-wind-power/

60   James Baggott, 'Car makers must sell 22% EVs in 2024 or face huge fines under tough proposals', Car Dealer, 30 March 2023, https://cardealermagazine.co.uk/publish/car-makers-must-sell-22-evs-in-2024-or-face-huge-fines-under-tough-proposals/282071

61   Matt Oliver, 'Vauxhall owner threatens to close UK car factories', Daily Telegraph, 25 June 2024, https://www.telegraph.co.uk/business/2024/06/25/vauxhall-stellantis-threatens-stop-making-electric-vans-uk/

62   Amy Hawkins, 'Battery power: how China could take charge of the electric vehicle market', The Guardian, 29 July 2023, https www.theguardian.com/environment/2023/jul/29/battery-power-how-china-could-take-charge-of-the-electric-vehicle-market

63   Low Carbon Vehicle Partnership, 'Lifecycle emissions from cars', https://www.zemo.org.uk/assets/workingdocuments/MC-P-11-15a%20Lifecycle%20emissions%20report.pdf

64   Global Energy Monitor, 'Global Coal Plant Tracker', https://globalenergymonitor.org/projects/global-coal-plant-tracker/tracker/; Global Energy Monitor, 'Creative Commons License', https://globalenergymonitor.org/creative-commons-public-license/

65   Flora Champenois, Lauri Myllyvirta, Qi Qin and Xing Zhang, 'China's new coal power spree continues as more provinces jump on the bandwagon', Centre for Research on Energy and Clean Air, 29 August 2023, https://energyandcleanair.org/publication/chinas-new-coal-power-spree-continues-as-more-provinces-jump-on-the-bandwagon/

66   Thomas J. Duesterberg, 'China's flag is red, not green', Wall Street Journal, 7 April 2024, https://www.wsj.com/articles/chinas-flag-is-red-not-green-emissions-water-pollution-coral-reefs-1d9fc481?st=a42w94g0cm37kmn&reflink=article_email_share

67 Flora Champenois, Lauri Myllyvirta, Qi Qin and Xing Zhang, 'China off track on all key climate commitments as coal power approvals continue', Global Energy Monitor, February 2024, https://globalenergymonitor. org/report/china-off-track-on-all-key-climate-commitments-as-coal-power-approvals-continue/

68 Liming Chen, Chunquan Zhu and Carol Zhou, 'How Chinese enterprises are acting on climate by meeting China's dual carbon goals', World Economic Forum, 27 July 2023, https://www.weforum.org/ agenda/2023/07/chinese-enterprises-climate-dual-carbon-goals/

69 Jean Pisani-Ferry, 'The case for Greem realism', Project Syndicate, 27 February 2019, https://www.project-syndicate.org/commentary/green-new-deal-costs-realism-by-jean-pisani-ferry-2019-02

70 Ambrose Evans-Pritchard, 'Milei's Argentina is fast becoming the Texas of Latin America', *Daily Telegraph*, 8 May 2024, https://www.telegraph.co.uk/business/2024/05/08/milei-argentina-shale-fracking-texas-of-latin-america/

71 Jonathan Leake, 'New Zealand to lift oil drilling ban amid blackout fears in blow to Starmer', *Daily Telegraph*, 9 June 2024, https://www.telegraph.co.uk/business/2024/06/09/new-zealand-brings-back-oil-drilling-amid-fears-of-blackout/

72 Szu Ping Chan, 'The transition to net zero has turned into a quasi-religious debate', *Daily Telegraph*, 8 September 2023, https://www.telegraph.co.uk/business/2023/09/08/mervyn-king-net-zero-transition-bank-of-england-inflation/

73 Christopher Jasper, 'Demand for electric cars slows sharply as customers revert to petrol', *Daily Telegraph*, 4 April 2024, https://www.telegraph.co.uk/business/2024/04/04/electric-car-demand-slows-petrol-vehicles/; Matt Ridley, 'Why I'll be buying a brand new petrol car just before the 2030 ban', *Daily Mail*, 10 July 2023, https://www.dailymail.co.uk/debate/article-12276725/Why-Ill-buying-brand-new-petrol-car-just-2030-ban-says-MATT-RIDLEY.html; Mark Duell and Jamie Phillips, 'Our £25,000 heat pumps left us out of pocket – and operating a NASA spaceship would be easier', *Daily Mail*, 14 April 2023, https://www.dailymail.co.uk/news/article-11972635/Britons-complain-problems-heat-pumps-amid-soaring-energy-bills.html

74 Matt Oliver, 'Small manufacturers forced to answer 300 questions on net zero', *Daily Telegraph*, 25 February 2024, https://www.telegraph.co.uk/business/2024/02/25/small-manufacturers-forced-answer-300-questions-net-zero/

75 Rupert Darwall, 'Net Zero's days are numbered', *The Spectator*, 23 February 2024, https://www.spectator.co.uk/article/net-zeros-days-are-numbered/

76 Emma Gatten and Ben Riley-Smith, 'Sunak's new gas plants ease risk of blackouts', *Daily Telegraph*, https://www.telegraph.co.uk/news/2024/03/12/rishi-sunak-new-gas-power-stations-blackout-risk-net-zero/#:~:text=Britain%20will%20build%20new%20gas,an%20article%20for%20The%20Telegraph.

77 Sam Dumitriu, 'How Spain eliminated environmental impact assessments for most renewable projects', 17 February 2024, https://www.samdumitriu.com/p/how-spain-eliminated-environmental

78 Hayley Dixon, 'XR billionaire funds Khan climate network', *Daily Telegraph*, 11 November 2023, https://www.telegraph.co.uk/news/0/xr-billionaire-funds-sadiq-khan-climate-network/

79 C40 Cities Climate Leadership Group, 'The future of urban consumption in a 1.5°C world', C40 Knowledge Hub, 13 June 2019, https://www.c40knowledgehub.org/s/article/The-future-of-urban-consumption-in-a-1-5-C-world?language=en_US

80 C40 Cities, 'Deadline 2020: How cities will get the job done', https://www.c40.org/wp-content/uploads/2021/07/Deadline_2020.pdf

81 'Miliband will bring wholesale deindustrialisation', Net Zero Watch, 19 January 2024, https://www.netzerowatch.com/all-news/miliband-will-bring-wholesale-deindustrialisation

82 Jeremiah Green and John R. M. Hand, 'McKinsey's Diversity Matters/Delivers/Wins Results Revisited', *Econ Journal Watch*, vol. 21, no. 1, March 2024, pp. 5–34, https://econjwatch.org/articles/mckinsey-s-diversity-matters-delivers-wins-results-revisited

83 Sekou Bermiss, Jeremiah Green and John R. M. Hand, 'Does greater diversity in executive race/ethnicity reliably predict better future firm financial performance?', *Journal of Economics, Race and Policy*, vol. 7, no. 1, March 2024, pp. 45–60, https://ideas.repec.org/a/spr/joerap/v7y2024i1d10.1007_s41996-023-00132-0.html

84 'What is diversity, equity, and inclusion?', McKinsey & Company, 17 August 2022, https://www.mckinsey.com/featured-insights/mckinsey-explainers/what-is-diversity-equity-and-inclusion?cid=eml-web

85 Bernard Gouw, 'Impact Topic: Justice, Equity, Diversity & Inclusion (JEDI)', B Lab Global, 21 December 2023, https://www.bcorporation.net/en-us/news/blog/evolving-the-standards-for-bcorp-certification-impact-topic-justice-equity-diversity-inclusion/

86 Thomas Harris, 'The EDI Tax: how equity, diversity and inclusion is hobbling British business', Free Speech Union, March 2024, https://freespeechunion.org/the-edi-tax-how-equity-diversity-and-inclusion-is-hobbling-british-businesses/

87 Georgina Cutler, 'Corporate wokeness: warning British firms pose "dangerous" working environments for employees with different ideologies', GB News, 17 August 2023, https://www.gbnews.com/news/woke-news-british-firms-inclusion-scheme

88 David Craig, 'Blame Tory Ministers for the NHS's Woke-ification', Daily Sceptic, 15 April 2024, https://dailysceptic.org/2024/04/15/blame-tory-ministers-for-the-nhss-woke-ification/

89 Daniel Hannan, 'Labour is plotting a devastating economic blow – and its pensions raid is just the start', *Daily Telegraph*, 10 February 2024, https://www.telegraph.co.uk/news/2024/02/10/labour-plotting-devastating-economic-blow-and-pensions-raid/

90 'Equity, diversity and inclusion in supply chains – private sector and third sector', Shoosmiths, https://www.shoosmiths.com/insights/articles/equity-diversity-and-inclusion-in-supply-chains-private-sector-and-third-sector

91 'What is a B Corp?', B Lab United Kingdom, https://bcorporation.uk/b-corp-certification/what-is-a-b-corp/

92 'The "legal requirement" for a B Corp in the UK – an explanation', https://drive.google.com/file/d/1hoiswtPoGeKW3nJqwketYsXBsFKn4aG5/view?pli=1

93 Chris Pandolfo, 'Scale AI CEO explains why his company will hire for MEI, not DEI: "Merit, excellence and intelligence"', Fox Business, 15 June 2024, https://www.foxbusiness.com/fox-news-tech/scale-ai-ceo-explains-why-his-company-hire-mei-not-dei-merit-excellence-intelligence

94 'Environmental, Social and Governance sourcebook', https://www.handbook.fca.org.uk/handbook/ESG.pdf

95 Wilma Rix, 'Diversity on boards: listed companies to "comply or explain" and publish data', Linklaters, 4 August 2021, https://www.linklaters.com/en/knowledge/publications/alerts-newsletters-and-guides/2021/august/04/diversity-on-boards-listed-companies-to-comply-or-explain-and-publish-data

96 Tilak Doshi, 'Central Banks and ESG investing: a fatal combination of incompetence and overreach', *Forbes*, 29 August 2023, https://www.forbes.com/sites/tilakdoshi/2023/04/29/central-banks-and-esg-investing-a-fatal-combination-of-incompetence-and-overreach/?sh=29571a232a61

97 Douglas McWilliams, 'Eco-fanatics are creating a new housing crisis', *Daily Telegraph*, 25 January 2024, https://www.telegraph.co.uk/business/2024/01/25/eco-fanatics-are-creating-a-new-housing-crisis/

98 'Developer fined £600k for destroying Greenwich bat roost', BBC News, 11 December 2020, https://www.bbc.co.uk/news/uk-england-london-55273516; 'Government must get a grip on the haphazard implementation of environmental regulations', UK Parliament, 21 September 2023, https://committees.parliament.uk/committee/518/built-environment-committee/news/197533/government-must-get-a-grip-on-the-haphazard-implementation-of-environmental-regulations/

99 Alice Hancock and Sylvia Pfeifer, 'How global trade could fragment after the EU's tax on "dirty" imports', *Financial Times*, 9 January 2024, https://www.ft.com/content/ca51ebf5-fbb8-4c88-a93d-ded3d6d3bcdd?accessToken=zwAGEUhmWSJ4kdPKUev1-7hMiNOpPd7T1tO83Q.MEUCIQDdVmJrcMbTww_mjbHPG4jyXC_jYsIz_bRbi43ZDnH8YQIgZTIGTGpnayeElvD58baBA2wXPQYV6SKDNuxs7UE0Hck&sharetype=gift&token=67660e41-b4d2-4650-b8e3-8ada1617eaad

100 Department for Environment, Food & Rural Affairs, 'BNG launch date confirmed', Gov.uk environment blog, https://defraenvironment.blog.gov.uk/2024/01/18/bng-launch-date-confirmed/

101 'Education, health and care plans', Gov.uk, 13 June 2024, https://explore-education-statistics.service.gov.uk/find-statistics/education-health-and-care-plans

102 Mark Lehain, 'Why all schools should be "warm-strict" on behaviour', *TES Magazine*, 6 September 2019, https://www.tes.com/magazine/archive/why-all-schools-should-be-warm-strict-behaviour

103 Matthew Chilcott, 'Phillips v Aneurin Bevan University Local Health Board', Consensus HR, 30 November 2023, https://www.consensushr.com/phillips-v-aneurin-bevan-university-local-health-board-consensus-hr-herts-beds/

104 Adam Carey, 'Tribunal orders London borough to pay £4.6m over dismissal of director', Local Government Lawyer, 21 March 2024, https://www.localgovernmentlawyer.co.uk/employment/395-employment-news/56799-tribunal-orders-london-borough-to-pay-4-6m-over-dismissal-of-director#:~:text=The%20London%20Borough%20of%20Hammersmith%20and%20Fulham%20has,claim%20as%20%22vastly%20excessive%2C%20disputed%20and%20highly%20unprecedented%22.

105 Petar Lekarski, 'Universal credit rule change to put tens of thousands of people at risk of having benefits cut – here's what you need to know', Money Saving Expert, 22 September 2022, https://www.moneysavingexpert.com/news/2022/09/universal-credit-rule-change-job-searching/

106 Daniel Hannan, 'Whether Britain faces an epidemic of bad mental health or of idleness, the solution is the same', *Daily Telegraph*, 16 March 2024, https://www.telegraph.co.uk/news/2024/03/16/britain-faces-epidemic-bad-mental-health-idleness-solution/#:~:text=The%20solution%20is%20often%20the,stay%20at%20home%2C%20feeling%20superfluous.

107 Tom Haynes, 'War on landlords risks billions for economy and thousands of jobs', *Daily Telegraph*, 20 March 2024, https://www.telegraph.co.uk/money/property/buy-to-let/war-landlords-billions-economy-thousands-jobs/

108 Ruby Hinchcliffe and Daniel Martin, 'Landlords to get five years to hit net zero targets', *Daily Telegraph*, 28 March 2023, https://www.telegraph.co.uk/money/property/buy-to-let/landlords-get-five-years-hit-net-zero-targets/

109 'Index of Private Housing Rental Prices, UK: October 2023', Office for National Statistics, 15 November 2023, https://www.ons.gov.uk/economy/inflationandpriceindices/bulletins/indexofprivatehousingrentalprices/october2023

110 Melissa Lawford, 'Michael Gove's crackdown risks killing the holiday let market', *Daily Telegraph*, 14 April 2023, https://www.telegraph.co.uk/business/2023/04/14/is-michael-gove-about-to-kill-the-holiday-let-market/

111 Competition and Markets Authority, 'CMA finds fundamental concerns in housebuilding market', Gov.uk, 26 February 2024, https://www.gov.uk/government/news/cma-finds-fundamental-concerns-in-housebuilding-market

112 Sam Bowman, 'Why has Britain become so poor?', *The Times*, 30 July 2023, https://www.thetimes.co.uk/article/why-has-britain-become-so-poor-lw22lhvkh

113 Duncan McClements and Jason Hausenloy, 'Cooped up: quantifying the cost of housing restrictions', Adam Smith Institute, 5 February 2024, https://www.adamsmith.org/research/cooped-up-quantifying-the-cost-of-housing-restrictions

114 Duncan McClements, 'Cooped up: quantifying the costs of housing restrictions', Adam Smith Institute, 2023, https://static1.squarespace.com/static/56eddde762cd9413e151ac92/t/65c2518698cfe71ca5997107/1707233675548/Cooped+Up+FINAL.pdf

115 Tom Utley, 'From the local deli to Jeremy Clarkson's TV farm, TOM UTLEY asks: Why can't meddling politicians stop stifling business?', *Daily Mail*, 23 March 2023, https://www.dailymail.co.uk/debate/article-11896891/TOM-UTLEY-asks-meddling-politicians-stop-stifling-business.html

116 Ben Wright, 'The creeping criminalisation of business risks Hunt's plans for economic recovery', *Daily Telegraph*, 31 January 2023, https://www.telegraph.co.uk/business/2023/01/31/criminalisation-business-risks-hunts-plans-economic-recovery/

117 Jeff Desjardins, 'Visualizing how the demographics of China and India are diverging', Visual Capitalist, 8 January 2020, https://www.visualcapitalist.com/populations-china-india-diverging-demographics/

118 ICAEW Insights, 'UK fraud makes massive leap to £2.3b', ICAEW, 28 February 2024, https://www.icaew.com/insights/viewpoints-on-the-news/2024/feb-2024/uk-fraud-makes-massive-leap-to-23bn

119 Zoe Wood, 'Patisserie Valerie ex-chair says he was tricked by false picture of company's health', *The Guardian*, 9 June 2019, https://www.theguardian.com/business/2019/jun/09/patisserie-valerie-luke-johnson-says-he-was-tricked

120 James Titcomb and Melissa Lawford, 'British Tech tycoon Mike Lynch cleared in $11bn US fraud trial', *Daily Telegraph*, 7 June 2024, https://www.telegraph.co.uk/business/2024/06/06/mike-lynch-verdict-autonomy-fraud-trial-san-francisco-jury/

121 'The future is here: is your compliance function ready?', Compliance Professionals, https://www.complianceprofessionals.co.uk/building-future-proof-compliance-function/

122 'The total tax contribution of UK financial services in 2020', City of London in association with PWC, https://www.cityoflondon.gov.uk/assets/Business/total-tax-contribution-2020.pdf

123 Simon Duffy, 'NYSE considers 24/7 trading; Goldman Sachs moves senior banker to Paris amid post-Brexit overhaul', The Banker, https://www.thebanker.com/NYSE-considers-24-7-trading-Goldman-Sachs-moves-senior-banker-to-Paris-amid-post-Brexit-overhaul-1713870639

124 Denise Rose, Kate Goodrich and LaRessa Quintana, 'Texas set to launch its first National Stock Exchange', Jackson Walker, 11 June 2024, https://www.jw.com/news/insights-texas-national-stock-exchange/

125 Ben Wright, 'The creeping criminalisation of business risks Hunt's plans for economic recovery', *Daily Telegraph*, 31 January 2023, https://www.telegraph.co.uk/business/2023/01/31/criminalisation-business-risks-hunts-plans-economic-recovery/

126 RFE/RL's Russian Service, 'Wanted former Wirecard executive spied for Russia for years, investigative journalists say', RadioFreeEurope, 1 March 2024, https://www.rferl.org/a/russia-wirecard-marsalek-spy/32844424.html

127 Nikhilesh De, 'FTX's failure is sparking a massive regulatory response', Coin Desk, 14 November 2022, https://www.coindesk.com/policy/2022/11/14/ftxs-failure-is-sparking-a-massive-regulatory-response/; Becky Yerak, Soma Biswas and Andrew Scurria, 'Crypto exchange FTX is the rare financial blowup that will repay victims in full', *Wall Street Journal*, 8 May 2024, https://www.wsj.com/articles/crypto-exchange-ftx-is-the-rare-financial-blowup-that-will-repay-victims-in-full-5ef57ee0?st=938eil6ytevopaq&reflink=article_email_share

128 Kate Beioley, 'UK regulator "didn't understand" effect of loophole on investors being exploited in LCF scandal', *Financial Times*, 25 March 2021, https://www.ft.com/content/5e1f8ba5-fc6b-4c4d-a6ab-a0c0227b2095?accessToken=zwAGGdLPy_Igkc9eH4uI_GtMTdOmq6DAInsglQ_MEYCIQDUeiDWsBXWV_uRaQ13CXahf1mGeF5r4fMwZ5qN4G3wzQIhAPE-KEyHblQaK4vNwFiExkzsxO9dw1DUUPNL52MxXyov&sharetype=gift&token=d8f804c6-447b-4e4e-a204-5b1442728fc3

129 Chris Dorrell, 'Fraudsters stole £1.2bn in 2022 as UK labelled "fraud capital of the world"', CityAM, 11 May 2023, https://www.cityam.com/fraudsters-stole-1-2bn-in-2022-as-uk-labelled-fraud-capital-of-the-world/

130 Lawrence White and Iain Withers, 'Insight: Welcome to Britain, the bank scam capital of the world', Reuters, 14 October 2021, https://www.reuters.com/world/uk/welcome-britain-bank-scam-capital-world-2021-10-14/

131 Home Office news team, 'Reducing Net Migration Factsheet – February 2024', 23 May 2024, https://homeofficemedia.blog.gov.uk/2024/02/01/reducing-net-migration-factsheet-december-2023/

132 Georgina Sturge, 'Migration Statistics', House of Commons Library, https://commonslibrary.parliament.uk/research-briefings/sn06077/

133 'Long-term international migration, provisional: year ending June 2023', Office for National Statistics, 23 November 2023, https://www.ons.gov.uk/peoplepopulationandcommunity/populationandmigration/international migration/bulletins/longterminternationalmigrationprovisional/yearendingjune2023

134 'Do immigrants pay more in taxes than they claim in benefits and services?', Full Fact, 5 November 2013, https://fullfact.org/immigration/do-immigrants-pay-more-taxes-they-claim-benefits-and-services/

135 Economic Consulting Team, 'The fiscal impact of immigration on the UK'. Oxford Economics, 18 September 2018, https://www.oxfordeconomics.com/resource/the-fiscal-impact-of-immigration-on-the-uk/

CONCLUSION

1 Rt Hon Sir Keith Joseph Bt MP, *Monetarism is not enough* (Barry Rose for Centre for Policy Studies, 1976), https://cps.org.uk/wp-content/uploads/2021/07/111028102723-MonetarismisNotEnough1976.pdf; Friedrich A. Hayek, *The Road to Serfdom*, (Institute of Economic Affairs, 1999), https://www.iea.org.uk/sites/default/files/publications/files/upldbook43pdf.pdf

AFTERWORD

1 Thomas Smith, Isabel Atkinson, James Browne, Danae Ellina, Icaro Rebolledo, Rhea Subramanya, Eleni Arzoglou, 'The Economic Case for Reimagining the State', Tony Blair Institute for Global Change, 9 July 2024, https://www.institute.global/insights/economic-prosperity/the-economic-case-for-reimagining-the-state

2 Fraser Nelson, 'Whisper it, Labour may actually be serious about overhauling the NHS', *Daily Telegraph*, 11 July 2024, https://www.telegraph.co.uk/news/2024/07/11/whisper-it-labour-actually-serious-about-overhauling-nhs/

3 Will Jones, 'Miliband Orders Immediate Ban on New North Sea Oil', Daily Sceptic, 11 July 2024, https://dailysceptic.org/2024/07/11/miliband-orders-immediate-ban-on-new-north-sea-oil/

4 'UK Government denies claim Ed Miliband ordered immediate ban on new oil and gas licences', Rayo, 11 July 2024, https://hellorayo.co.uk/northsound/local/news/uk-government-denies-north-sea-drilling-reports/

5 Toby Helm and Robin McKie, 'Labour's "rooftop revolution" to deliver solar power to millions of UK homes', *The Guardian*, 13 July 2024, https://www.theguardian.com/environment/article/2024/jul/13/labours-rooftop-revolution-to-deliver-solar-power-to-millions-of-uk-homes

APPENDIX A

1 'National population projections: 2021-based', Office for National Statistics, 30 January 2024, https://www.ons.gov.uk/peoplepopulationandcommunity/populationandmigration/populationprojections/bulletins/nationalpopulationprojections/2021basedinterim

2 Recent good news from the Falklands seems to imply that ban on oil drilling is not fully being imposed. Jonathan Leake, 'Falkland Islands eyes economic boom in talks to exploit huge oil field', *Daily Telegraph*, 30 June 2024, https://www.telegraph.co.uk/business/2024/06/30/falkland-islands-oil-field-exploit-navitas-uk/

APPENDIX B

1 Robert M. Solow, 'A contribution to the theory of economic growth', *Quarterly Journal of Economics*, vol. 70, no. 1, February 1956, pp. 65–94, https://www.jstor.org/stable/1884513

2 Groningen Growth and Development Centre, 'Penn World Table version 10.01', University of Groningen, https://dataverse.nl/api/access/datafile/354095

3 'Investment and Capital Stock Dataset', International Monetary Fund, https://data.imf.org/?sk=1ce8a55f-cfa7-4bc0-bce2-256ee65ac0e4

4   Groningen Growth and Development Centre, 'Penn World Table version 10.01', University of Groningen, https://www.rug.nl/ggdc/productivity/pwt/?lang=en; 'Economic Freedom', The Fraser Institute, https://www.fraserinstitute.org/economic-freedom/map?geozone=world&page=map&year=2021;   'World Economic Outlook April 2024', International Monetary Fund, https://www.imf.org/external/datamapper/datasets/FPP; 'OECD Data Explorer', OECD, https://data-explorer.oecd.org/

5   Groningen Growth and Development Centre, 'Penn World Table version 10.01', University of Groningen, https://www.rug.nl/ggdc/productivity/pwt/?lang=en; 'Economic Freedom', The Fraser Institute, https://www.fraserinstitute.org/economic-freedom/map?geozone=world&page=map&year=2021;   'World Economic Outlook April 2024', International Monetary Fund, https://www.imf.org/external/datamapper/datasets/FPP; 'OECD Data Explorer', OECD, https://data-explorer.oecd.org/

6   'Principal Projections – UK Population', Office for National Statistics, 30 January 2024, www.ons.gov.uk/peoplepopulationandcommunity/populationandmigration/populationprojections/datasets/tablea21principalprojectionukpopulationinagegroups

7   'Economic and fiscal outlook March 2024', Office for Budget Responsibility, https://obr.uk/efo/economic-and-fiscal-outlook-march-2024/

8   International Monetary Fund, 'World Economic Outlook Database', https://www.imf.org/en/Publications/WEO/weo-database/2024/April\

APPENDIX C

1   Department for Work and Pensions, 'Benefit expenditure and caseload tables 2024', Gov.uk, 19 April 2024 (updated 21 May 2024), https://www.gov.uk/government/publications/benefit-expenditure-and-caseload-tables-2024

APPENDIX D

1   'MBTI World Population and MBTI by country statistics', Typology Triad, https://typologytriad.wordpress.com/mbti-population-by-country/

2   Oliver Wright, 'Rachel Reeves: Labour will be more pro-business than Tony Blair', *The Times*, 24 April 2024, https://www.thetimes.com/uk/politics/article/rachel-reeves-labour-business-tony-blair-9chlj9qog; Joe Mayes, 'Starmer targets difficult-to-reach 2.5% growth rate for Britain', Bloomberg UK, 26 June 2024, https://www.bloomberg.com/news/articles/2024-06-25/uk-labour-to-seek-economic-growth-of-at-least-2-5-starmer-says

ACKNOWLEDGEMENTS

———

In addition to the many authors referenced within this document, I would like to thank in particular the two core members of the team who worked with me in creating this book: Michelle McGhie and Mikhail Traykovskiy. Both have spent over a year helping to pull everything together, page by page, with Michelle keeping the overall shape and structure of the book from spinning out of control and Mikhail providing not just a vast amount of research and data but also a good portion of what original thought leadership and analysis can be found in these pages.

Great thanks also are due to Tom Clougherty, Robert Colville, Andy Cook, Iain Duncan Smith, Matthew Elliott, James Forder, Fred de Fossard, James Fransham, Regan Hall, Tim Healey, David Hooper, Martin Howe KC, Nic Lewis, Charlotte Lynch, Catherine McBride, Chris McGhie, Douglas McWilliams, Sam Miley, Kristian Niemietz, Christopher Nieper, Neil O'Brien, John O'Connell, Barney Reynolds, Fiametta Rocco, Abdel Karim Saddedine, Alex Selby-Boothroyd, Matthew Sinclair, Rachel de Souza, Liam Strong, James and Margaret Thompson, Mathew Thurley and Toby Young for their various and extensive help and direction on the project.

Thanks are also due, of course, to the many economic and political thinkers and writers whose works are referenced in the book and which are listed on the website, which can be accessed for convenience from the QR code provided in this book. For the analysis of the public sector defined-benefit pensions crisis, most of the analysis is taken directly from Neil Record's magisterial and decades-long work on the issue. The review of, and proposals on, education are indebted to multiple discussions over many years with Mark Lehain. The discussion of reform in the university sector borrows gratefully from 'The Value of University', a report from the Centre for Policy Studies.

Throughout the past couple of decades, up until the summer of 2022, the crucial role that economic growth plays in national prosperity and happiness was barely mentioned in UK politics. Liz Truss made economic growth her central mission as Prime Minister. She continued making the case for growth in 2023 through her Growth Commission and it became the central talking point of the 2024 general election campaign, with numerous headlines saying, even if sometimes equivocally, that her focus on growth had been the right one. Rachel Reeves, the new Chancellor of the Exchequer, spoke about it being her party's 'mission' to make the UK the fastest-growing economy in the G7, and in the final week of the general election campaign, Keir Starmer targeted the 'difficult to reach' growth rate of 2.5 per cent for Britain.[2] It is entirely reasonable to say that without that focus from Liz Truss, the issue would not be achieving this prominence. I believe that history will treat her premiership more kindly than present commentators do, and that wider recognition will be given to her championing growth as the key economic objective for our country. I thank her for her leadership in this area.

Economic models and data for the book were validated by

CEBR. I owe William Lithgow's 1640 quotation at the front of the book to the compendious knowledge of the great Patrick O'Brian.

I would also, of course, like to thank the wonderful team at Biteback, who have nurtured the birth of this book over the last year, helping in so many different ways: James Stephens, Olivia Beattie and my editor, Catriona Allon.

I apologise to any of the numerous people who have given me invaluable advice over the years, whose assistance I have now unpardonably failed to mention here. Any mistakes, errors, misunderstandings, misrepresentations or outright falsehoods are of course, and regardless of any help to my understanding that I may have received from others, entirely my own fault.

Lastly, and above all, I thank my dear helpmate and wife Patricia for her selfless and buoyant support throughout the long and torturous process that led up to the publication of this book.

Jon Moynihan
London
August 2024

INDEX

———